COMMUNICATION IN SMALL GROUPS

THEORY, PROCESS, SKILLS

Fifth Edition

COMMUNICATION IN SMALL GROUPS
THEORY, PROCESS, SKILLS

Fifth Edition

John F. Cragan
Illinois State University

David W. Wright
Illinois State University

Wadsworth Publishing Company

I⟨T⟩P® An International Thomson Publishing Company

Belmont, CA ■ Albany, NY ■ Boston ■ Cincinnati ■ Johannesburg ■ London ■ Madrid ■ Melbourne
Mexico City ■ New York ■ Pacific Grove, CA ■ Scottsdale, AZ ■ Singapore ■ Tokyo ■ Toronto

Publisher: *Karen Allanson*
Executive Editor: *Deirdre Cavanaugh*
Assistant Editors: *Ryan E. Vesely and Megan Gilbert*
Editorial Assistant: *Matthew Lamm*
Marketing Manager: *Mike Dew*
Marketing Assistant: *Shannon Ryan*
Advertising Project Manager: *Tami Strang*
Project Editor: *Cathy Linberg*

Print Buyer: *Barbara Britton*
Permissions Editor: *Yanna Walters*
Production: *Anne Draus, Scratchgravel Publishing Services*
Copy Editor: *Catherine Cambron*
Cover Design: *Margarite Reynolds*
Cover Photograph: *Ann Dowie*
Compositor: *Scratchgravel Publishing Services*
Printer: *Malloy Lithographing*

Printed in the United States of America
    3 4 5 6 7 8 9 10

For more information, contact Wadsworth Publishing Company, 10 Davis Drive, Belmont, CA 94002,
or electronically at http://www.wadsworth.com

International Thomson Publishing Europe
Berkshire House
168-173 High Holborn
London WC1V 7AA, United Kingdom

Nelson ITP, Australia
102 Dodds Street
South Melbourne
Victoria 3205 Australia

Nelson Canada
1120 Birchmount Road
Scarborough, Ontario
Canada M1K 5G4

International Thomson Publishing Southern Africa
Building 18, Constantia Square
138 Sixteenth Road, P.O. Box 2459
Halfway House, 1685 South Africa

International Thomson Editores
Seneca 53
Colonia Polanco
11560 México D. F. México

International Thomson Publishing Asia
60 Albert Street
#15-01 Albert Complex
Singapore 189969

International Thomson Publishing Japan
Hirakawa-cho Kyowa Building, 3F
2-2-1 Hirakawa-cho, Chiyoda-ku
Tokyo 102 Japan

Library of Congress Cataloging-in-Publication Data
Cragan, John F.
    Communication in small groups : theory, process, skills / John F.
Cragan, David W. Wright. — 5th ed.
        p.   cm.
    Includes bibliographical references and index.
    ISBN 0-534-54549-1
    1. Communication in small groups.   I. Title.
HM133.C73   1999
302.3′4—dc21   98-16391

*This book is printed on
acid-free recycled paper.*

This edition is dedicated to our grandchildren:
Connor Cragan Frederick, Kyle Robert Frederick,
Brooklyn Elizabeth Wegner, and Jacob Christian Wegner

CONTENTS

CHAPTER FOUR

Structuring Problem-Solving Groups   73

CHAPTER FIVE

Preparing for Group Problem Solving   108

CHAPTER SIX

Building Interpersonal Trust in Small Groups   132

PREFACE

In the thirty years we have been teaching small group communication classes, we have endeavored to evolve a course that teaches practical communication skills that can be used in everyday work groups. Understandably, small group communication research serves as the primary database for the book; however, research findings from other social sciences are also used. As with the previous four editions, we have made a concerted effort to include the latest research findings on small group communication—regardless of the discipline from which they have been derived.

The fifth edition features not only change but a return to appropriate metaphors from earlier editions that students and teachers alike indicated were very helpful in their study of small groups. Conceptually, the changes we made in the previous edition have been extended and strengthened. We continue to believe that there is nothing more practical than a good theory. Pedagogically, we constantly identify those communication skills that must be performed (or avoided!) in order to be effective in small work groups.

Highlights of the fifth edition include the following:

- *Returning the Group Concept Recipe to the introductory chapter.* This flows nicely out of our extensive definition of a small group and lets the student see very early how group process relates to group outcomes.
- *Separating the second chapter of the previous edition into two distinct chapters.* The former 40-page chapter represented information overload for many students who read it. Students told us to separate the theory and process nature of small groups into one chapter and the skills and outcomes into another. We have tried to listen and believe the text is better for this major organizational change.
- *Moving the Problem-Solving Road Map to earlier in the text.* One of the major pedagogical metaphors we created for the third edition was the Problem-Solving Road Map. We have found it is most helpful in understanding the practical nature of group talk and group outputs. Thus, we have moved the Road Map to the new skills and outcomes chapter.
- *Emphasizing general communication theories and specific small group communication theories.* Not only do we integrate small group communication theories in Chapter 2, but we more fully explain their context in relation to general communication theories—especially in the final chapter of the book.
- *Providing new information for leaders of small groups.* Over the past century, social scientists have frequently examined the phenomena of leadership behavior in small groups. We try to furnish new knowledge in this area, particularly in terms of leading and managing teams.
- *Integrating helpful small group inventories into the text.* In the section on focus groups, we provide measures to evaluate the effective facilitation of this form of a one-time meeting group. In the leadership chapter we provide some trait, skill, and situational self-report instruments to help assess one's leadership potential in a small group.

Although the above changes will be very apparent to users of previous editions of the text, new adopters should find them equally attractive for students of small group communication. Our experience has led us to conclude that a "learning by doing" or practical approach is the best way for students to learn basic small group skills. Case studies that depict classroom and real-life groups were selected because they amplify the important aspects of small group communication. The case studies afford one the opportunity to critique work groups on the basis of the principles introduced in the chapters. Numerous examples of groups we have observed firsthand over the years are provided throughout the chapters.

Additional Instructor Resources

There is an *Instructor's Manual* available for this text, which includes a sample course outline, suggested class activities, and a test bank. Also, check in with Wadsworth's *Communications Café*—a state-of-the-art, full-service web site featuring online student and instructional material. Visit us at *http://www.wadsworth.com/communications*. Also available is *Thomson World Class Course*—the easy and effective way to create your own web site. You will be able to post your own course information, office hours, lesson information, assignments, and sample tests. Visit *http://www.worldclasslearning.com* for more information. If you choose to bundle *InfoTrac College Edition* with this text, you and your students will get 24-hour access to a fully searchable online database containing complete articles—not simply abstracts—from more than 600 popular and scholarly periodicals.

Acknowledgments

It was not possible to do this book by ourselves. We are indebted to many people. We would like to thank our professors for the training they provided us in small group communication. They are Ernest G. Bormann, University of Minnesota, and Raymond S. Ross, Wayne State University. We have also been influenced by many of our colleagues and are grateful for their insights. A number of small group communication professors have given generously of their time and talent to provide us with helpful critiques in the writing of the various editions of this book. The reviewers for the first edition were Gene Eakins, G. Evans, Hazel Heiman, Raymond Ross, Donald Shields, Jimmie Trent, and Gordan Zimmerman. The reviewers for the second edition were Brenda Burchett, Rebecca Cline, Hazel Heiman, Kathy Kellermann, Jolene Koester, Gail Mason, Joseph Mele, Eileen Berlin Ray, Jo Sprague, and Lyla Tomsheck. The reviewers for the third edition were J. Douglas Gibb, Jack Holland, Charles U. Larson, David Natharius, Gregg Phifer, Shirlee Sloyer, and Roger Smitter. The reviewers for the fourth edition were Carolyn Anderson, Michael Kirch, Gaylord Mance, David Natharius, Ed Pappas, Roger Smitter, and Ed Streb. The reviewers for this edition were Philip M. Backlund, Central Washington University; Judith K. Bowker, Oregon State University; Lawrence J. Chase, California State University at Sacramento; Loren Dickinson, Walla Walla College; Thomas Endres, University of St. Thomas; Herschel L. Mack, Humboldt State University; William Todd Mancillas, California State University at Chico; and Jean Perry, Glendale College.

Our students at Illinois State University are a constant source of stimulation, and they affirm our approach to the teaching of small group communication that this book represents. We thank them for their help. Elizabeth Asprooth Cragan and Barbara Weller Wright have provided supportive criticism and help in the production of the manuscript. We deeply appreciate their assistance.

J. F. C.
D. W. W.

CHAPTER ONE

DEFINING SMALL GROUP COMMUNICATION

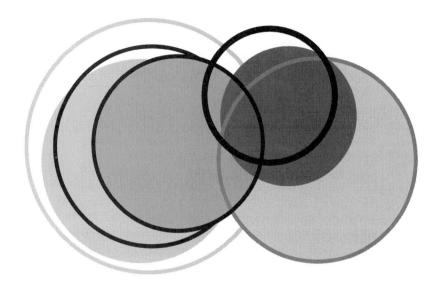

CHAPTER OBJECTIVES

After reading this chapter, you should be able to:

- Explain the rationale for the study of small group communication
- Define the characteristics of a small group
- Apply the group concept recipe
- Know the types of groups that exist in the organizational context

☐ WHY STUDY SMALL GROUP COMMUNICATION?

We study small group communication because it is central to our everyday lives. Most of our working lives we will participate in face-to-face discussions and be expected to work effectively and efficiently toward common group goals. We have all experienced problems with group interaction and know that a relationship between two persons is difficult to maintain. However, a relationship among three or more persons is even more complex; thus, it requires our concerted efforts to study and comprehend the dynamics of small groups.

Living and Working in Groups

The study of small group communication brings with it a natural curiosity to understand small group processes. At the same time, there is a clear expectation that the study of the communication behavior of small groups will lead to pragmatic advice on how we might improve our small group experiences. Our experiences in small groups readily spawn many important questions about small group communication that we attempt to answer. The following hypothetical scenarios are typical of the kinds of situations that raise important questions about communication in our small groups.

The College Scenario Julie signed up for a small group communication class because it was required in her applied computer science major. She doesn't know why the course is required. She likes writing computer programs, but her experiences working in groups have not been great—in fact, they have been horrible. Julie feels she gets ripped off when she works on student projects; she and one or two others do all the work. Julie thinks that a group grade is unfair. Why should her grade suffer because of the irresponsibility of some group members, and worse, why should others get the same grade she does when they didn't do their share of the work?

Julie doesn't think that most people are motivated to do group work. And then there is the group meeting problem. No one is free at the same time as the other group members unless they can meet at midnight. Julie believes that the quality of group work is not worth the time and trouble to produce a group product. Even when the group does get together, there seems to be continual conflict over whose ideas are accepted. Julie finds it especially difficult for her ideas to be heard when one or two persons dominate the discussion, which too often turns to digressions on irrelevant topics. She doesn't think that the group needs to know the personal history of each member to get the job done.

What bothers Julie the most is that although she considers herself a competent communicator, a nice person, and a hard worker, she has a difficult time working in groups. Is the problem with her, or has she just had the bad fortune to be part of some dysfunctional student groups? Are there small group communication theories that would help her understand what happened in past groups and, more important, help her achieve satisfaction working in groups in the future? In addition to knowledge, are there specific group communication skills that would make her a better team player? Julie hopes that her class in small group communication will provide some answers to these questions, and so do we.

The Organizational Scenario Matt's organizational culture went into shock as the profits decreased and the company stock plummeted. The new management team has said that they are going to downsize the organization and flatten the organizational hierarchy. Matt fears that he might be downsized out of the company or flattened out of a management job. He is also worried about two new programs the management team is introducing. One is a high-involvement program and the other is computer-assisted meetings. Matt is sure about one thing: The company is determined to improve the efficiency of meetings and empower the worker to be included in more decision-making groups.

Matt has signed up for an extension class that is taught at night in the hope that he will be ready to succeed in the new organizational culture. He wants to know how to run a computer-assisted business meeting. He wants to learn how to be a good team player when his subordinates are on even footing in high-involvement groups. Matt thinks that most business meetings are a waste of time, so he definitely wants to learn how to run meetings more efficiently. He hopes that the class won't be full of vague theories and silly experiential games. Matt wants the "meat and potatoes" of small group communication. He wants two basic handouts: a list of twenty-five ways to run a more efficient business meeting and a list of twenty-five keys to improving the productivity and quality of small group work.

The Fire Department Scenario Chief Bob Buhs is a progressive leader of a growing fire department. He has signed up for a small group communication short course at a fire conference. He wants to learn how to manage competing work groups. A firefighter's professional existence consists almost entirely of group participation. Engine companies and rescue squads are highly efficient small groups that not only work together but in many cities also live together. A firehouse may contain three work groups: a rescue squad, a pumper truck team, and a ladder truck group. There usually is one captain per shift in charge of the firehouse, with a lieutenant in charge of each company. Now, as any firefighter will tell you, rivalries can develop among the three work groups in the firehouse and the three shifts.

Chief Buhs needs to know why fire groups appear to become so cohesive that they don't readily accept new members and why there is constant conflict among the three shifts. In the past, he has solved his organizational problems by transferring personnel to other work groups and other shifts. However, the chief is concerned about reducing the productivity of emergency teams when he breaks them up. He also wants to know how to keep groups from becoming overly cohesive. Is the conflict that occurs in the firehouse caused by personality clashes, or does the building of group pride naturally foster competition among work teams? Basically, he is looking for some small group communication theories that will help him explain and predict group behavior in the fire department.

Over the years, we have analyzed many scenarios like those just cited, and we believe that the theories and skills presented in this book can help you and people like Julie, Matt, and Chief Buhs become more competent small group communicators. But we do not want to mislead you. We do not mean to overstate the usefulness of small group communication research. Social scientific research requires measured, conservative conclusions based squarely on compiled data, whereas real-life problems often demand instantaneous leaps into the unknown if solutions are to be found. Academic research always falls short of the expectations real life places on it. A wealth of useful advice, however, can be provided about small group communication, and we have included much of that advice in this book.

A Rationale for the Study of Small Group Communication

Communication as a discipline and small group communication as a teachable subject flourish best within a democratic setting. It is natural that free speech, public discussion, and active participation in political groups are prerequisites for a study of small group communication. In addition, the workhorse of modern organizations is the task group. Employees attend meetings, participate in project groups, and exist professionally as part of long-standing work groups. Further, the twenty-first-century vision of intercultural groups flourishing in multinational corporations and a world made safe for democracy continues to foster a rationale for the building and teaching of small group communication theories and skills.

Cultural Rationale America's democratic tradition has made public discussion of affairs of state a moral obligation. Apathy is discouraged in our culture, which means that we have a great many politically concerned citizens who are actively involved in small groups. Moreover, there is a general belief that these groups should focus on rational, group decision making and avoid emotional, undisciplined group activity.

Our towns and neighborhoods are beehives of small group discussions about such issues as new developments that might endanger our children with increased traffic flow, broken sewer mains, faulty dorm showers, overpriced off-campus housing, pollution, nuclear energy, and other public issues that directly affect our lives. The first American reaction to these sorts of political issues is to call a meeting, and sometimes we forget that in many countries, it is against the law to do so. We not only take public discussion as a right but, after more than two hundred years, have also developed certain expectations and protocols with regard to how these meetings are to be conducted and what kind of communication is considered acceptable and effective.

Our right of free association encourages us to form small group discussions about political affairs; however, our democratic form of government does not fully explain our enthusiasm for social grouping. Our country is made up of an almost infinite number of social groups. We belong to fraternities and sororities, Toastmasters and the Elks, gardening clubs and ski clubs, bowling leagues and bridge groups. It might surprise you to discover how many social groups you have become involved in since you left high school. During high school, you were intensely involved in group activity, both formal and informal. Finally, you belong to a family, which is your primary or lifelong group. However, this group may not have many formal meetings—partly because one member or another is always on the way to one organizational group meeting or another.

The socialization process that takes place in these groups produces a societal norm of team play in which we work for the good of the group—often at the expense of our personal needs. Traditionally, the most popular sports activities have been the team sports of football, baseball, and basketball.

The lessons we learn in social and play groups during high school and college days prepare us for the small group communication demands of our professional careers and underscore the importance of being a competent communicator in a democratic society.

The end of the Cold War in the early 1990s and the breakup of the Soviet Union have produced an increased worldwide need for knowledge about small group communication. The new democracies in Eastern Europe and the former republics of the Soviet Union have looked to the Western democracies, especially the United States, to learn how to conduct open political meetings and engage in public policy decision making. Communication professors have traveled regularly in the 1990s to these new democracies to teach courses in argumentation and small group communication. The new world order of the twenty-first century dramatically points up the importance of small group communication theories and skills to a democratic society.

Corporate Rationale　One of the recurring questions on the evaluation forms of private organizations and government agencies relates to the employee's ability to be a team player. The bureaucracy in which you will probably find yourself when you leave college will want you to do at least two things: communicate effectively and accomplish your task objectives within a work group. Your abilities to organize, lead, and participate in small group discussions will be major determinants of your future professional success.

Since the early 1950s, private industry has expended a lot of time and energy on the training of its employees in group communication skills. In fact, in the 1980s, this training in group skills received renewed interest with the development of Theory Z management and the adoption of quality circles (QCs) by thousands of American organizations. Theory Z management places a great deal of emphasis on group decision making, and QCs are special types of problem-solving groups that focus on problems of quality and productivity in the workplace. Some of the most popular books read by Americans in the 1980s examine new ways of leading and managing work groups within an organizational setting (Ouchi 1981; Peters and Waterman 1982).

In the 1990s, two new trends have emerged that further emphasize the need to become a competent small group communicator: (1) the empowerment of primary work groups in organizational decision making caused by the downsizing and flattening of the organizational hierarchy, and (2) the rapid development of computer-assisted meetings accelerated by the miniaturization of the computer, the integration of the computer with other telecommunication technologies, and the downward spiral in the cost of these technologies (Bostrom, Watson, and Kinney 1992; Jessup and Valacich 1993; Naisbett and Aburdene 1990).

As you are beginning your career in the twenty-first century, you will find a work environment built around team performance. This book focuses on the small group communication theories, group processes, and communication skills you need to be a successful member of an organizational work group.

Academic Rationale The academic rationale for the study of small group communication grows out of the cultural and corporate rationales. We need to develop communication theories that explain group process and predict group outcomes, and we need to identify and practice the communication skills needed by participants in problem-solving work groups in private and public discussions. Over the past fifty years, the emphasis of academic research has moved from discussion and leadership skills of primarily public discussion groups to the theory of task groups and group communication skills relating to work groups in the private sector.

Whereas the communication research of the 1950s and 1960s focused on discussion problem-solving methods and leadership skills, communication scholars in the 1970s turned their attention to identifying the group processes of work groups and isolating the communication variables that positively affected group outcomes. The group outcomes of productivity, quality, consensus, and membership satisfaction were examined in terms of what communication behaviors affected them. Another research strategy in the 1970s was to identify communication interaction and process that occurred over time from the beginning of a group's analysis of a problem to its solution. Key communication patterns were discovered, such as the development of group roles and the stages a group goes through in reaching agreement and understanding about a solution (Cragan and Wright 1980).

In the 1980s, three communication theories about small groups were developed: functional theory, structurational theory, and symbolic convergence theory. Functional theory identifies communication variables that need to be competently performed for a group to do quality work. Structurational theory explains the communication patterns and rules that groups create and re-create in their decision making. Symbolic convergence theory shows how small groups create their own symbolic identity through inventing and sharing group fantasies (Cragan and Wright 1990, 1993).

In the 1990s, communication scholars seek to integrate theory and research about group process, communication behavior and group outcomes, and the communication skills needed in the modern organization. New research is focusing on the work group in the organizational setting (Putnam and Stohl 1990), the computer-assisted problem-solving group (Poole and Jackson 1993) and the application of small group communication theory to business problems (Cragan and Shields 1992).

We take the research in small group communication and related social sciences from the past fifty years and construct a teachable model that integrates theory, process, skills, and group outcomes. This model is presented in Chapter 2.

☐ A SMALL GROUP DEFINED

Central to an understanding of small group communication is the knowledge of what constitutes a small group. We define a small group as *a few people engaged in communication interaction over time, usually in face-to-face settings, who have common goals and norms and have developed a communication pattern for meeting their goals in an interdependent manner.* This definition is based on research done by scholars in many disciplines. To understand how we arrived at this definition, it is necessary to take each of the key concepts and examine why it is a necessary part of a definition of a small group. Our definition reveals that there are nine characteristics of a small group. If you walked down the street in the presence of other people, there would be four immediate indications that would help you decide whether a small group was present. They are communication, space, time, and size. Moreover, if you observed a small collection of people systematically you would discover that there were five more characteristics that would tell you that a small group is present: interdependence, norms, structured communication patterns, group goals, and perception.

Directly Observable Characteristics of a Small Group

1. *Communication.* Verbal and nonverbal communication are such fundamental behaviors of a small group that we often overlook them (Fisher 1974). Yet talking and gesturing among a collection of people cue us to the presence of a group. However, the sight of several people talking at a bus stop would not alert us to the existence of a small group. Hewes (1986) developed an egocentric theory of small group communication that argues that for real group communication to occur, there must be more than mere turn-taking, such as "The bus is late again," "Yeah, it's raining," or "I forgot my umbrella." This sort of "group" conversation often occurs, and we realize that each comment is only loosely related to what was said before. Piaget has shown us that children engage in parallel play and talk that is really pseudocommunication. A conversation among three four-year-olds sitting in a circle playing with toys might go as follows: "I like my yellow truck." "My doll's name is Ken." "I just wet my pants." These children appear to be having a conversation, but it is really egocentric communication or, at best, light social banter.

True group communication is not random, but purposeful communication interaction. There are four types of purposeful group talk: problem solving, role playing, team building, and trust building. They are described in Chapter 3.

Purposeful group communication interaction is hard to recognize. It could be just one person asking, "What is the purpose of this meeting?" Or it could take the form of a stimulus and response between two group members, as in this exchange: "What is the agenda today?" "What do you mean what is the agenda? Didn't you read your mail?" And perhaps we should include the statement: "Why are you picking on David? None of us got the memo!" As you see, it is difficult to assess the beginning and end of communication interaction. We could call this an example of communication exchange conflict. Or, if we added loud, boisterous laughter to the dialogue, we could call it tension releasing. But what really happened was that David was only joking about an incident that occurred several weeks ago, and so we would call this a group fantasy. In Chapters 2, 3, and 4, we describe and label the communication interaction patterns of both prescriptive and natural discussion groups.

The communication act of asking a question was one of the first interactions we discovered and labeled as being important to the progress of discussion. In fact, the frequency of questions has become the sign of a successful group, and if most of the questions were asked by one person, he or she was probably the task leader of the discussion. With each discovery we tended to look at the *frequency* of the communication interaction, the *distribution* of the communication interaction among participants, and the *content,* or overall group meaning, of the communication interaction. This purposeful communication interaction is central to a definition of a small group.

2. *Space.* The fact that some people are standing in proximity to one another is probably the first visual impulse we receive that points to the presence of a group. The idea that face-to-face communication must occur for a collection of people to become a small group is common to almost all definitions of small groups. Robert Bales (1950, 33), a famous small group theorist, defined a small group in part as "any number of persons engaged in interaction with one another in a single face-to-face meeting or several of such meetings."

The emergence of new technologies has changed this definition; teleconferencing regularly occurs in business life and group members are face-to-face in *different* places. In fact, Phillips and Santoro (1989) have conducted small group communication classes in which group communication was computer-mediated through the use of such non–face-to-face channels as e-mail and electronic bulletin boards. Integrated communication systems will continue to modify our understanding of face-to-face communication.

3. *Time.* It seems that a collection of people have to communicate with one another for some period before they become a group. For how long, we do not know, but the relation between time and small group development is a major part of many small group theories.

Emergency situations can compress the time it takes for a group to develop. If your professor has a heart attack while lecturing, an effective work team may form rather quickly. A person trained in cardiopulmonary resuscitation (CPR) might immediately step forward as a task leader of a small group of students who would attempt to resuscitate the professor and secure medical help. It might take less than a minute for this group to form and function as a team.

In contrast, the student work group you are assigned to in class may have to meet several times before it starts to become cohesive. New technology is affecting the concept of group time in interesting ways. Computer-assisted work groups can share and store electronic files so that group members can work on the same problem at *different* times. Thus, through the use of interactive computers, people who work on different shifts in a company could become an effective problem-solving group without ever meeting face-to-face or working on the problem at the same time.

4. *Size.* A definition of a small group must contain the characteristic of size. Small group scholars, however, have not been able to agree on the exact parameters. Some believe that two is the minimum number of people (Shaw 1981), whereas others argue that three is the smallest unit (Bormann 1990). Scholars also differ on the point at which a small group is no longer small; Shaw (1981) says twenty is the upper limit, whereas Bormann (1990) indicates thirteen. The interaction patterns of triads appear to be fundamentally different from those of dyads. The communication behavior of three persons talking to one another is different from that of two persons talking to each other. The old adage that two's company, three's a crowd is probably true. We think that the upper limit of a small group is thirteen, in that when a group becomes much larger, it tends to subdivide and form cliques. The tendency for human work groups to fragment into smaller groups may even occur with as few as nine members. Whereas three is minimum and thirteen is maximum, the optimum size of a small task group is five to seven members. This seems to be true regardless of the type of work that is done.

There are two reasons why five to seven is the ideal size for a work group: (1) there is a series of roles that need to be played for a group to do good work, and (2) you need to have a number of people in your group to ensure that there is enough diversity of opinion and knowledge of the task.

Our study of natural groups has led speech communication scholars to conclude that people in groups share roles and that there seems to be a cluster of roles that are essential to a group's success. Although scholars disagree about a minimum list, at least five roles are required for a good discussion to take place. They are the roles of task leader, social-emotional leader (or lieutenant), tension releaser, information provider, and central negative. Roles are so important that we devote Chapters 7 and 8 to a full treatment of them.

If your group consists of only three persons, you'll discover that three heads are better than one—but not better than six! Assuming reasonable competency among all members, six persons are going to generate more ideas and, typically, better ideas than three persons. Also, the discussion is going to be more lively among six persons. It is easier for two persons to browbeat or coerce a third person to go along with an idea than for four members of a seven-person team to pressure three dissenters into agreeing with them. As a consequence, the group must argue and debate alternative plans, and decision-making theory clearly indicates that this communication process produces higher-quality decisions (Gouran and Hirokawa 1986).

Indirectly Observable Characteristics of Small Group Communication

1. *Interdependence.* Kurt Lewin (1951), pioneer in small group research, isolated interdependence as a key characteristic of small groups. From primitive hunting parties to NBA basketball teams, the element of interdependence seems to be present. How collections of people come to recognize their common need for one another is not clear, but the fact that interdependence must be present for small groups to exist is widely accepted by scholars.

It's not easy to develop interdependence in a small group. For one thing, the task must be complex and of such a nature that the group cannot divide it into separate parallel projects. As a member of a student work group, you have probably had this experience with many of your class assignments. Your group instinctively tries to find a way to divide the project into equal parts, with each of you working separately on a part. Most student work groups have minimal interdependency; many in fact are groups in name only. There is a difference between a team and a task group. Teams may exist in which members work in parallel, often for the attainment of separate goals. On the contrary, achievement of a common goal through interdependency is necessary for a task group to exist. H&R Block, for example, may have a four-member team that works on 1040 short forms. Their goal may be to complete 100 forms a day, but they can achieve this goal by working separately with little or no interaction between team members. An emergency rescue crew, however, that is trying to extract and resuscitate an injured truck driver from his cab is a highly interdependent task group that must practice coordinating its various work activities if it is to succeed. Although you are not likely to be a member of an emergency work group, you probably will be part of many decision-making groups that share an intellectual interdependency. It is easy to see the physical dependency of a heart transplant unit, but it takes careful study of the communication patterns of a decision-making group to see the intellectual dependency that takes place in the solution of problems. Interdependency is the key characteristic that distinguishes a group that is a team in name only from a team that is a true task group.

2. *Norms.* Group norms are shared values, beliefs, behaviors, and procedures regarding the group's purpose that usually are agreed to subconsciously by the group. The more the group's norms are manifestly obvious to people outside the group, the more likely it is that the group is cohesive. If groups agree to wear clothing unique to the group, then they are publicly declaring that they are a cohesive group. Although the development of a dress code is one of the most obvious norming behaviors, it is not the most important aspect of group norming.

Norming occurs in three areas of group life: *social*, *procedural*, and *task*. When a group is first formed, the members bring with them the behaviors, beliefs, and values acquired from their participation in other groups. These past experiences create expectations of the way a discussion should take place. Table 1.1 lists the typical dos and don'ts of a discussion group's first meeting in an American culture.

A quick examination of the table indicates that no group in the United States would ever explicitly develop this set of group norms. And yet most Americans, when they first form a discussion group, stay fairly close to this prescribed list. When a meeting is called, we expect to have refreshments, be on a first-name basis with other members, and engage in light social conversation. We do not expect a lot of profanity or crude jokes that might offend somebody. We expect that the meeting will establish a purpose and an agenda and that we will talk about the agenda in a face-to-face context for about an hour. We do not expect people to leave the meeting abruptly, monopolize the conversation, or refuse to speak. We expect a free-flowing exchange of ideas with a lot of questioning and sharing of the work load on the group's behalf. We don't expect to be verbally assailed for the ideas we express, nor do we expect others to support ideas solely on the basis of who said them.

Table 1.1 represents our *expectations* for group norms. This protocol list never survives the first meeting intact, nor should it. Once the group has established a history—after two or three meetings—the real norms will begin to emerge. For example, the group may maintain rules against sexist, racist, or ethnic jokes, but if all the members are of the same religion, they may tell religious jokes. There are many

TABLE 1.1   Expected Norms for a Decision-Making Group's First Meeting

Social	Procedural	Task
Do	Do	Do
—serve refreshments	—introduce people	—criticize ideas, not people
—dress casually	—plan to participate	—support the best idea
—use first names	—establish goals	—commit yourself to group
—discuss uncontroversial	—build an agenda	solutions
subjects	—hold a routine meeting one	—share in the workload
—tell humorous jokes	hour in length	—speak up if you disagree
—tell political jokes	—have someone in charge	—ask questions about group
(they will be tolerated)	—sit face to face	ideas
—tell trend or one-line jokes		
—tell cultural truisms		
Don't	Don't	Don't
—smoke (perhaps)	—leave the meeting without	—push your idea on the group
—swear	cause	—support ideas just because of
—arrive late	—monopolize conversation	people who presented them
—be absent without apology	—stand up and speak in the	—be verbally violent if you
—tell sexist, racist, ethnic, ageist,	meeting (generally)	disagree with ideas
or religious jokes	—demand to lead	—consider your ideas as the only
	—refuse to speak when	ones of merit
	addressed	

stories circulating within the Catholic Church that indicate that the best jokes about the pope are told by cardinals, in Latin. Likewise, the best rabbi jokes are told on the steps of a synagogue. Whereas strangers politely disagree about ideas, highly cohesive groups rant and rave about their differences. Whereas formal, prescriptive group meetings mandate an agenda procedure, a task group whose members have worked together a long time develops its unique way of covering agenda. There is an important distinction between what is at first expected and the eventual acceptance of group norms. The journey from expected to accepted often is a stormy and dangerous period in the group's life. For example, if one group member is a chain smoker and another group member is bothered by tobacco smoke, there may be a protracted struggle as the group tries to establish the social norm of smoking or non-smoking. The norming behavior that finally occurs with respect to the task dimension of the group is more important. The group eventually must develop the custom of openly criticizing ideas without offending group members. In fact, most groups develop a unique pattern or strategy for solving problems. Poole and Roth (1989a) have discovered that almost 80 percent of decision-making groups develop patterns of communication interaction that seem unique to each group.

   3. Structural patterns. After many years of observing everyday problem-solving groups in organizations, we are convinced that four distinct types of group talk fuse together in a rather complex but understandable way. At a practical level, these four types of talk constitute all the essential communication that you need to comprehend to be an effective small group member. The first type of group talk is *problem-solving talk.* In Chapter 3, we explain the four stages of problem-solving talk that a group must go through to solve a problem. Although you will find problem-solving talk easy to spot, it will take more work to discover the second type of group talk, *role talk*. There are two stages of role talk, and in a mature group, five major roles are played. The reason role talk is hard to hear is because it occurs concurrently with problem-solving talk. By this we mean that all problem-solving talk has two meanings: There is the manifest content of the problem being discussed, but there are also roles being played to discuss the problem effectively. For example, a group member may ask a question about a proposed solution that the group is discussing. The question would clearly be problem-solving talk, but by listening to the question in context, we might conclude that the person asking the question was playing the role of central negative and that the question was directed at a person playing the task leader.

Consciousness-raising (CR) is the third type of group talk. This talk is essentially group motivational talk. It produces group identification and pride. Work groups take several breaks from their problem-solving talk and engage in CR talk. In the next chapter, we explain that CR talk, in its pure form, is a special type of group process that has four stages. You will need to know CR in its complete form, so that you can better understand CR moments as they occur in problem-solving talk in ordinary groups. *Encounter talk* is the fourth form of group talk that occurs when small groups solve problems. Encounter talk is interpersonal talk. It deals with personal disclosures of group members that allow the members to develop trust and empathy toward one another. Like CR, there are numerous encounter break moments when the group stops talking about the problem and the members start talking about themselves. Also, like CR talk, encounter talk, in its pure form, constitutes a special group process that comprises three stages. By studying it in its pure form, it is easier to understand how encounter break moments function in a problem-solving group. Most small group theorists contend that groups go through predictable patterns of communication as they seek to achieve their goals.

4. *Goals.* A similarity between interdependence and goals exists, but the concepts are not isomorphic. For example, five men could have the goal of fathering a child but not be interdependent. Yet the same five men could have the common goal of a five-dollar raise and, if they were members of a bargaining team for their union, would have interdependence. Small groups are held together by their need to cooperate in the achievement of a group goal. If the goal can be achieved independently of group action or only through competition among the group members, then the small group "glue" called cohesion may lose its adhesive power.

Cohesiveness focuses on commitment to work collectively toward group goals. Cohesion increases as communication interaction facilitates role taking and as the group stabilizes its norms; moreover, it continues to increase as the quality of the group's productivity increases and the group reaches more and more consensual decisions.

It is easier to give an example of a cohesive group than to say exactly what it is. So far, we have only been able to approach an understanding of it metaphorically. For example, if group members were particles and the group were a magnetic field, cohesion would be the magnetic force that held the particles together, and that force would be in constant flux.

Hall (1953), in his study of aircraft commanders and bomber crews, defined cohesion as "the average resultant force to remain in the group." In other words, there must be more forces, on the average, to persuade the members to remain in the group than forces to persuade them to leave or disband it. In essence, a small group must have cohesion to have "groupness." Individual differences may abound in a particular small group, and yet members must desire to work together to the extent that the common goals of the group are served. One can see that the elements of small group communication of togetherness and willingness to belong are crucial to the very existence of a small group. When individual goals are in conflict with group goals, cohesion dissipates, and productivity and member satisfaction decrease. A college basketball team that is striving to win a national championship may exhibit cohesiveness in pursuing a common goal. Individual team members downplay their personal goals, such as points per game, to achieve a group goal. Conversely, a basketball team at a summer camp whose members are trying to impress scouts may exhibit little cohesion as they try to showcase their individual talents. The players and the scouts may not care much about the common goal of winning the game. Put more directly, a group will not become a group unless it has a common goal that is sufficiently attractive to the membership that they will set aside their personal aims for the sake of group goal achievement.

5. *Perception.* The last way to tell a small group from a collection of people is to see whether there is a perceived boundary line that separates the insiders from the outsiders. In short, do the people think of themselves as members of the group, and do they perceive other people as not being members of the group? If people perceive themselves as members of a group, then they probably are.

This point may seem obvious, but it is important. A symbolic transformation must occur for an effective work group to exist. An individual must come to believe that he or she is a member of a new identity or the individual's productivity and membership satisfaction will suffer. Indeed, if this we-ness does not occur for most members, the group will not exist. In an organization, the task group would be a group in name only, and we would predict that the members would not work well together or be productive.

A communication process by which a small group gains its unique identity is called consciousness-raising (CR). We explain this type of group talk in detail in the next chapter. The communication theory that explains CR is symbolic convergence theory. This theory states, in part, that a new small group will have a memorable CR experience that centers around a group fantasy (Bormann 1990). For example, in the film *Dead Poets' Society*, the student group achieved great cohesion by continually celebrating the central fantasy of the group, which was "seize the day!" When a group names itself, it spontaneously produces one or more fantasies that help it create its we-ness, and the members begin to see themselves as a unique symbolic reality.

☐ Group Concept Recipe

In Chapter 2 we outline the major small group theories that are used to explain human behavior in small work groups. Unfortunately, we do not have one general theory that can explain the communication behaviors that occur in all human groups. However, there are a number of key concepts that come from different theories that, when mixed together, produce a rather rough and unscientific explanation of human groups, in particular the task group. In fact, this book is an elaboration of the nine key concepts that blend together to form a practical description of work groups. The metaphor of concocting a cooking recipe will be used in the framing of the nine key group concepts.

A good work group of five to seven persons contains the following four ingredients:

- Generous amounts of *communication interaction* focusing on team building, trust building, and problem solving.
- At least one helping *role* per person assuring that the five major roles are played
- Several proportions of *ideational conflict* and *norming* behavior

Mix and stir until sufficiently *cohesive*. Apply four taste tests to the batter:

- Is the group *productive*?
- Are group decisions frequently *consensual*?
- Are group members *satisfied*?
- Is the group's work of high *quality*?

The culinary art of preparing a cohesive discussion group that is productive, does quality work, consensual in its decision-making procedures, and happy in its work starts in a well-lighted, comfortable room. At a round table sit five to seven reasonably prepared persons of sufficiently diverse backgrounds who discuss the task at hand. Allow enough patterns to develop. Reinforce positive role taking on the part of group members. At first be cautious about adding large doses of conflict, but if the group norms too quickly, use generous amounts of conflict to thin the batter. When the separate group members begin to think collectively and make continual references to "us, we, they," and "the group," the mixture is becoming cohesive. Soon after signs of cohesion occur, taste testing can begin. Has the group reached consensus on some issues? Is some of the work getting done? Is the work being done efficiently? Are the members reasonably satisfied with one another and do they regularly attend each discussion meeting? Cooking up a successful work group is more of an art form than a science. Experienced group members continually taste the batter in order to help ensure successful group outcomes. (See Figure 1.1.)

☐ TYPES OF WORK GROUPS

The major goal of this book is to turn you into a competent small group communicator. You will be a competent communicator in small groups when you know the necessary theories and skills that produce effective and appropriate communication by you and the other group members. What is effective and appropriate communication varies somewhat by the type of work group you are in and the type of organization in which your group works (Spitzberg 1992; Spitzberg and Cupach 1984).

In Chapter 10, we discuss the impact that the organizational context has on small work groups. In this chapter, we discuss five major types of work groups. They are

FIGURE 1.1   Group Concept Recipe

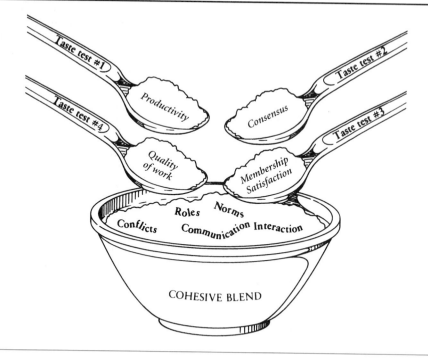

the long-standing work group, project group, loosely formed "prefab" group, quality circle, and cyborg decision-making group. After graduation, you will probably be part of at least one of these groups.

Long-Standing Work Groups

Every successful organization has a number of famous, long-standing work groups that over the years have performed at such high levels of productivity that their group tradition and pride transcend the passage of time and numerous changes in personnel. These groups seem to develop a life of their own such that new members feel compelled to act out the traditional roles and maintain the legendary high levels of productivity. These long-standing work groups have a rich collection of symbols and slogans that have been handed down over the years from one worker to another. Even the communicative interaction among the group members and between the group and the rest of the organization often becomes stylized and predictable over the years.

Pledge classes of fraternities and sororities create over time, within their respective organizations, expectations that literally dictate the behavior of new inductees. The pledgemaster role is so classic that the role invariably plays the person who is asked to perform it; by that we mean a half-century of fraternity brothers in one chapter on one campus could get together at a reunion and discover that they all had essentially the same pledgemaster. Similarly, the roles and communication patterns at Boys Town have become so well established over the years that boys who lived there in the 1940s describe a communication pattern that still occurs in the 1990s. Army veterans describe their military training similarly; and corporations such as General Motors, Firestone, and IBM have work groups with long-standing traditions that seem to demand that each new member perform in predictable ways.

One of the more visible long-standing work groups in our society is the Supreme Court. Presidents and Congresses have tried to "pack" the Supreme Court to ensure that their version of U.S. justice is maintained. However, again and again, the Court has asserted its tradition of independence. The most dramatic example of modern times was the Court's decision that President Nixon should turn over his Watergate tapes to the special prosecutor. Even though Nixon had recently appointed a number of the justices, the group's tradition of independence from the executive branch was reflected in a unanimous decision, and the president had to capitulate.

The legends and stories of long-standing work groups within organizations portray them as larger than life. New members of organizations soon hear the stories of these groups and are attracted to them. Competition to join famous work groups is always keen, and initiation to them is frequently formidable and sometimes dangerous. However, the status that goes with being a member of a long-standing work group is so enticing that the immortality of the group is assured, so long as the organization continues to live.

Long-standing work groups have many strengths, but they also have obvious weaknesses. It is difficult to introduce change into the group even when it is desperately needed. Changing the communication behavior of such a group is particularly difficult. Group meetings take ritualistic and almost religious forms in some groups. When a change in situation demands a change in group policy, tradition becomes an enemy rather than an ally of the group leader. Scottish units of the British army traditionally walked into battle with bagpipes skirling, but this traditional behavior became almost suicidal in the context of World War II. And the British tradition of wearing red coats into battle in the 1700s provided American squirrel hunters with a decided advantage.

In less dramatic but equally detrimental ways, long-standing work groups within organizations develop communication habits that are counterproductive. Because of its traditions, a work group may meet only once a month when in fact it should meet weekly. Our industrialized nation, in which the organizational clocks have been speeded up, has not correspondingly streamlined its ceremonial traditions. Changes for the sake of efficiency are met with resistance, in part because valuable portions of the group's tradition are dropped in the process. This loss of traditions has produced less colorful groups and has reduced the rich variety of groups that used to exist.

Project Work Groups

The complexity and interdependence of modern society manifests itself in organizations such as the project work group. Suppose a collection of highly trained and specialized people were brought together for a brief period—six days to a year—to complete a specified project. The individuals that formed the group probably would not have much history of working together, and the group itself would have no long-standing tradition dictating its expected level of productivity or an established set of symbols or slogans.

The U.S. space program to put a man on the moon by the end of the 1960s quickly recognized the problem of building a project from newly formed work groups. In the absence of established criteria of what a good space work group was, the National Aeronautics and Space Administration created a comparative standard for judgment. The directors of the space program gave several project groups the same task and had them compete against one another to determine excellence in productivity. Professors in small group communication classes often use the same technique when student groups are formed for short periods. Each group determines its success on a comparative basis. For example, the success of each group can be determined by comparing its presentation of a problem-solving group with the performance of the other groups.

Most project groups do not have parallel project groups to be compared with; therefore, the group must generate for itself levels of cohesion and group morale sufficient to meet the productivity goals that have been set by the organization or by the group itself. The project group must clarify its goals, evolve its roles, and establish an acceptable level of productivity. In terms of CR, pride in the group must be built, symbols and slogans need to be created, and the group must establish a tradition. Finally, from the perspective of encounter groups, the project group must engage in self-disclosure, develop interpersonal trust, and tolerate individual differences.

In contrast to zero-history groups that are formed in classrooms in the university for research purposes, newly formed project groups in business organizations do not have the time to build the social dimension and the interpersonal aspects of the group before productivity demands must be met. A new project group must first set its goals and start generating a successful work record so that the group will raise consciousness on its ability to do work and not its capacity to socialize. This requirement places a great deal of pressure on the project leader. Early meetings of project groups require more advanced planning and outside work on the part of the leader than other kinds of meetings in the business environment. The leader must also maintain a high degree of one-on-one contact with group members to ensure that the early work is completed on time and is of high quality.

Once the project group has established a history of good work, the leader can begin to have the group engage in CR. This process can take place in the early moments of a meeting by celebrating the competency of group members and bragging that the group is made up of the cream of the crop. The group might also develop a symbol or slogan to put at the top of the memos they send to one another. If the group members habitually work late hours, for example, and start referring to themselves as "night owls," the leader might send each of them a stuffed owl to put on his or her desk. It is easier for group members to raise their consciousness if they have some territory they can call their own—ideally, a special room that is reserved for them, where they can keep special materials and that they can decorate with their slogans. When a regular room cannot be acquired, portable paraphernalia that can instantaneously decorate a room is the next best thing. Stylized name plates, a couple of placards, and a stuffed owl may be all that is needed.

As the group develops a history of work success and as the members create a symbolic reality that they can take group pride in, individuals in the group begin to engage in specific self-disclosures. At first, these disclosures are comparative ones, such as "This project work group is the best one in the company," or "The people in this group are nicer than the ones in printing products." The project leader must remember to keep self-disclosure within limits. The project group is a temporary formation, and most of the members will be in and out of these kinds of groups. If self-disclosure is pushed beyond the boundaries of what it takes to get the job completed, individuals in the group may later be resentful (when formed into new groups) if they think that people in the organization know too much about them.

The major advantage of project groups over long-standing groups is that the members are free to create their own group tradition. This is also the project group's leading drawback. The project members know that their group is a temporary thing, and it is difficult to get them to commit sizable amounts of energy to building a group that will break up within the next eight months. Also, project group members tend to have a lot of hidden agendas, which often produce a great deal of special-interest pleading. Many times project group members are also representatives of long-standing work groups within the organization. Thus, it is difficult to establish loyalty and trust within the project group.

The trend in American organizations has been to eliminate layers of middle management and empower project groups to make many more substantive decisions. As an organizational worker in the next century, your success will depend in part on your ability to continuously work effectively in successive and often simultaneous project groups.

Prefab Work Groups

Some modern organizations have abandoned long-standing work groups and find that project groups are inappropriate to the product or service of their organization. The loosely formed work group, or, if you will, the prefabricated group, has entered the mainstream of several U.S. service industries. The job descriptions of this type of work group have been meticulously defined and rigidly structured so that a collection of people with no previous experience of working together can quickly form a work group that will produce a predictable level of productivity. Fast-food chains in the United States are the most obvious examples of industries that use prefab groups. These organizations use a highly fluid work force, yet despite the high turnover, each neighborhood outlet reliably turns out the same product in about the same time. This result has been accomplished by building human groups that resemble assembly lines. For example, a hamburger can be assembled by group interaction in a process similar to the serial construction of an automobile. Many large fire departments have gone to the prefab model for building groups because of the high turnover of firefighters from shift to shift through time swapping and the taking of vacation days. People who have been part of long-standing and prefab groups report that there is more membership satisfaction in the long-standing work group than in the prefab work group. The potential for unusually high productivity is in the long-standing group; members reluctantly admit that the productivity of prefab groups is reliably average, but to achieve average group work takes tremendous corporate effort. McDonald's Corporation has developed a training manual more than 700 pages long that spells out how such things as lettuce, pickles, special sauce, cheese, onions, and all-beef patties go together on a sesame seed bun to produce a Big Mac. Likewise, Walt Disney Productions has an elaborate training program that even scripts what an employee says when taking you on a jungle safari, so that every jungle safari in Disneyland and Disney World is exactly the same, time after time.

The weakness of the prefab group lies in its strength: its predictability. The group will perform the way it has been trained to work, but it seldom creates solutions to problems or adapts to new situations. Thus, a prefab group may work satisfactorily for the production of fast-food items, but it is inappropriate at a management level.

Quality Circles

Two Americans, Edward Deming and Joseph Juran, are credited with starting the QC movement in Japan in the 1950s. The movement has now spread to the United States and throughout the world as a means of participatory decision making. Juran (1976, 15) defines a quality circle (QC) as "a small group of departmental work leaders and line operators who have volunteered to spend time outside of their regular hours to help solve departmental quality problems."

The use of workers as an integral part of management problem-solving teams was probably started in 1890 by Ernst Abbé of Zeiss Company in Germany. He asked master and journey craftsmen to assist in the development of new optical machinery. By the 1920s, Bell Laboratories was using teams of people to assist in quality control, and by the late 1940s, IBM had discovered that better electronic computers could be developed by having the engineers consult with first-line supervisors and workers on the production of the product (Ingle 1982).

After World War II, General Douglas MacArthur invited Deming, a statistician for the U.S. government, to Japan to lecture on quality control methods to Japanese management. In the 1950s, Juran went to Japan and lectured on the need for total quality control. Deming's and Juran's efforts, which launched a national Japanese program to improve the images of Japanese products, produced amazing results. By 1960, the Japanese government declared November to be National Quality Month, replete with "Q" flags, seminars, posters, and weekly television programs. By 1973, six million Japanese workers were participating in more than a half million QCs. In 1977, the International Association of Quality Circles was created. Today, thousands of U.S. companies have adopted QC programs (Baird 1982; Ingle 1982). In 1985, Lawler and Mohrman reported that 44 percent of companies with five hundred or more employees had QC programs and that almost all *Fortune 500* companies have them.

The procedure for setting up a QC program has become standardized throughout the world. It seems to work best in industrial settings and with the participation of experienced, skilled workers. The typical structure contains the following elements: a plant steering committee of about fifteen persons, which oversees the program; a program facilitator, who reports directly to the steering committee and is responsible for coordinating QC programs; circle leaders, who normally are line supervisors in a work area; and circle participants, who are nonmanagement employees who volunteer to participate. The circle contains three to fifteen members but often divides into subcircles to solve specific problems (Baird 1982).

Typically, the first thing a QC does is engage in CR and learn problem-solving techniques. The CR discussions invariably produce the name of the QC and the development of a logo. Illustrative of this process is the experience of a QC group at Sundstrand Hydro-Transmission at LaSalle, Illinois. There the second-shift QC team, comprising maintenance, tool room, and tool grind employees, called themselves "Skilled Crafts" and created a group logo. The QC program at Sundstrand, which was started by Ron Zindner, is called T.E.A.M.—"Together Employees Accomplish More."

Once the group consciousness has been created, the facilitator trains the members in group problem-solving procedures. The problem-solving agenda systems and discussion techniques presented in Chapter 4 constitute most of the training. As a historical footnote, the first problem-solving agenda system used by QCs was introduced by Deming and is now known as the Deming Wheel, a four-part schema: (1) plan, (2) do (collect data), (3) check (analyze), and (4) act (control) (Ingle 1982, 9).

Cyborg Decision-Making Groups

A cyborg decision-making group is part human and part machine. The machine part of the group includes personal computers, interactive group software, audiovisual equipment, and electronic information transfer equipment (e.g., e-mail, fax machines). The development of cyborg groups has been so rapid and the technological miniaturization and integration have been so frequent that no one name can be used for labeling the cyborg group. There currently are more than twenty-five names: for example, group decision support systems (GDSS), computer-supported cooperative work (CSCW), and group process design (GDP) (Bostrom, Watson, and Kinney 1992).

Table 1.2 lists the types of cyborg group environment in terms of a time-place continuum. The table also includes the type of groupware that supports each type of group meeting and the advantage and disadvantage of each meeting configuration. As you can see, the same time–same place meeting has the advantage of simultaneous face-to-face communication with the support of computer software. Of the cyborg-type meetings, this is by far the most popular, but given our busy schedules and the diffusion of group members across time and place, groups cannot always meet face to face. A second type of cyborg meeting is different time–same place. This non–face-to-face group has the advantage of coordinating work issues across shifts of a fire or police department. Its disadvantage is the discipline required by members to go to the work room and work by themselves and the need for a facilitator to coordinate and focus group work without face-to-face interaction of group members. In practice, many cyborg groups meet face to face 80 percent of the time, but the other 20 percent of the time, the group's work is stored in group files to which members have access.

The third type of cyborg meeting is same time–different place, which provides the advantage of simultaneous interaction across distances. The popularity of conference telephone calls has been steadily growing, and the integration of fax machines and conference telephone calls is commonplace. The future, however, probably lies with full-motion videoteleconferencing with integrated computer software to transmit and receive information instantaneously. More than two thousand videoteleconferencing rooms exist in North America, and as the costs decrease, the number of such rooms will increase dramatically (Johansen 1992). The disadvantage of this type of meeting is cost of equipment. The fourth type of cyborg group meeting is different

Table 1.2   **Cyborg Meeting Environments**

Type of Environment	Advantage	Disadvantage	Cyborg Support
Same Time/ Same Place	Face-to-face interaction	Scheduling all members for same time	Cyborg meeting room Group software Portable computer systems LCD projector and PC
Different Time/ Same Place	Coordination across shifts	Working alone from stored group messages	Team room Shared files Shift work stations Group displays
Same Time/ Different Place	Simultaneous interaction across distances	Limited videoteleconferencing rooms due to expense	Conference calls Videoteleconferencing Computer screen sharing
Different Time/ Different Place	Group decisions when simultaneous group interaction is not possible	Absence of common group work space and group interaction	Cellular phones with fax and computer access Computer conferencing E-mail

time–different place. There are a number of national electronic bulletin boards in which groups share information and coordinate activities. Electronic mail and group voice mail also support these groups. The advantage is that a group can be formed and reach consensus without face-to-face interaction; its major disadvantages are the absence of simultaneous group interaction and reliance on stored electronic communication. The cyborg group has become a new generic type of group because the support of equipment fundamentally changes the culture of organizational groups that use it. Project and long-standing work groups become demonstrably different when they become cyborg decision-making groups. To understand these changes, we need to understand a cyborg decision-making group.

A cyborg group has a number of features that cause a change in traditional face-to-face decision-making groups. Figure 1.2 shows a diagram of a typical cyborg meeting room. The decision-making group members each have computer terminal access. A group software program drives the non–face-to-face portions of the meeting. Typically, there is a group facilitator, a group recorder, and a technical support system member. Some software systems attempt to build in other roles, such as a social-emotional leader or a central negative, and integrate small group communication theory into groupware design (Poole and DeSanctis 1992; Poole and Jackson 1993).

One feature that distinguishes a cyborg decision-making group from a traditional group is the anonymity of group member contributions. Members can contribute ideas and criticize ideas anonymously. In traditional groups, rank conflicts can occur; that is, the vice-president's idea could be more important than the floor supervisor's

FIGURE 1.2   **Cyborg Decision-Making Group Meeting Environment**

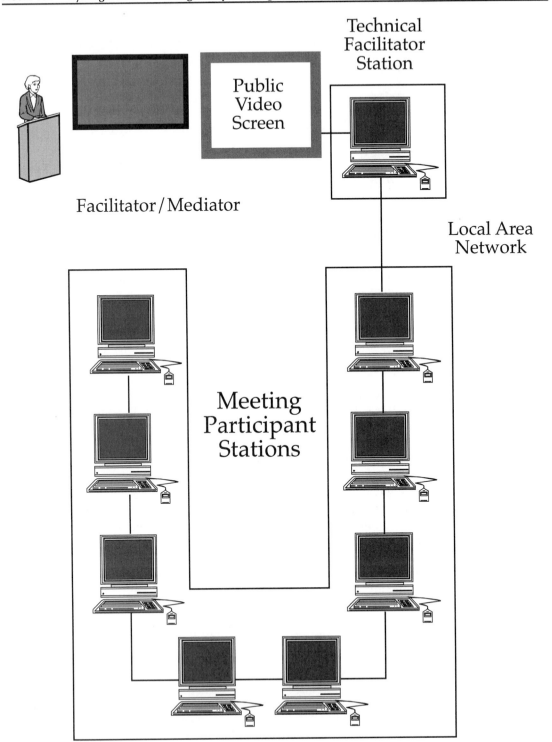

opinion. In a cyborg group, no one knows who said what. Thus, in a cyborg group, the ownership of an idea is transferred from an individual to the group. The next feature, electronic information processing, automates complex tasks such as summarizing group votes and ratings of issues. To see how this works, imagine that your classroom group generates a list of important group skills that are needed for you to be productive. Once you create this list, each member rates each of the items on a scale of 1 to 9, first in terms of importance and then on his or her ability to perform that skill. After much calculation, your group could summarize its rating of each issue in terms of importance and performance. A table could then be created that plots each issue and shows the issues you think are very important but on which your performance is very low. Without the aid of groupware, your group might spend an hour completing this task, whereas a cyborg group could do it in much less time because the cyborg group can simultaneously input their ideas and input the rankings according to importance and performance. The calculations and graph construction are done instantaneously by the computer and displayed on the group's screen. Thus, groupware takes away much of the drudgery and frustration that often bog down work teams.

The third feature is the impact that electronic group memory has on group members. A recurring problem of traditional groups is absenteeism and the changing of group membership. New members are acculturated with greater ease when members can access the group's memory and examine the group's past discussions and decisions. In addition, continuous group members benefit from complete meeting minutes.

One cautionary note needs to be added about cyborg groups. We should not allow the technology part of the group to control the human part. As Poole and Jackson (1993, 287) have pointed out, "an effective group must maintain a balance between independent thinking and structured, coordinated work. Too much independence shatters group cohesion and may encourage members to focus on individual needs. Too much synchronous, structured work is likely to regiment group thinking and stifle novel ideas."

☐ SUMMARY

This introductory chapter highlights several of the important considerations we make in studying small group communication. In part, these considerations are based on cultural setting and certain academic traditions. This book focuses on the small decision-making work group that is found in modern organizations.

A definition of small group is posited, based in large measure on nine directly and indirectly observable characteristics. A small group is a few people engaged in communication interaction over time, usually in face-to-face settings, who have common goals and norms and have developed a communication pattern for meeting their goals in an interdependent manner. The group concept recipe visualizes the important relationship between communication interaction and group outcomes.

The chapter concludes by identifying the five types of groups in an organizational context. They are the long-standing work group, project group, prefab group, quality circle, and cyborg decision-making group.

A College Study Group

CASE BACKGROUND

The communication department has instituted mandatory comprehensive examinations as a requirement for graduation. In the examination, two hours are allotted for each one of five content areas: interpersonal communication, rhetoric/argumentation, small group/organizational communication, public relations, and mass communication. To help students do well on the examination, the department arbitrarily assigned junior and senior communication majors to study groups. The students were not required to stay in the groups, but they were strongly encouraged to attend the first meeting. The following students met in the department conference room for the first time:

- Karen Barnabee, senior, 4.0 honors student with emphasis in organizational communication
- Jarrod Coleman, senior, minor in public relations, basketball player
- Scott Fowler, junior, basketball player
- Shannon Fulton, junior, basketball player
- Colleen King, senior, works part-time in communication office
- Steve Pazmino, senior, member of intercollegiate debate team

CASE LOG

Colleen King opened the meeting by suggesting that everyone introduce themselves. Everyone seemed somewhat surprised by the mixture of students assigned to the group. After some awkward moments, Karen spoke up.

KAREN: We may not be the best study group in the department, but I bet we could beat any other group in a pick-up intramural basketball game! (Nervous laughter)

SCOTT: You're probably right, but our coaches wouldn't let us play! But to tell you the truth, I kind of doubt that I'll have the time to even meet with this group. Jarrod and I practice every afternoon and we have about fifteen road games that start in November and run through March.

SHANNON: The women's basketball practice and playing schedule is just as bad. I don't think I can make the meetings either.

STEVE: You're probably not going to believe this, but the debate team travels more than the basketball team, and the season lasts longer. The research for debate takes up as much time as practicing for basketball! Unless there is some need to study together that I haven't heard yet, I'm for making this our last meeting too.

COLLEEN: I don't want to ruffle anybody's feathers, but everybody has busy schedules, not just debaters and athletes. For example, I'm carrying eighteen hours so I can graduate in June, I work fifteen hours of work-study a week, and on weekends I make pizzas at Garcia's. I just think we're using busy schedules as a cop-out for not forming a group.

KAREN: I think Colleen's right. We're all busy and so are all the students in all the other study groups. They seem to be meeting. My roommate is a communication major, and her group's already had a second meeting. If this group isn't going to meet, I think I'll join hers. I don't want to flunk my comprehensives. If I graduate in June, I have a job waiting for me at State Farm.

JARROD: I don't want to make this the jocks versus the eggheads, but it doesn't sound to me like we would be a very good group. If we can't get along with one another, I don't think working together is going to help me pass the test. Besides, the basketball program can get Scotty and me tutors. So why do we need this group? It would probably be just a waste of time.

SCOTT: Jarrod may sound too hard-nosed about this, but let's be practical. Can this group really help us? Most of the ones I've been in are just bull sessions. I don't think they've ever helped me get a better grade.

SHANNON: Let's not divide ourselves into two groups. We're all communication majors! But Jarrod and Scott make a good point, and let's answer their questions: What good is this group in helping us pass our comprehensives?

COLLEEN: I don't know who the crazy professor was that put our group together, but if you look at our backgrounds, it appears that we all have specialties that would help us all to do better. For example, Jarrod has taken most of the public relations courses, while the rest of us haven't, and Steve knows the argumentation stuff. Let's look at dividing up the work load by specialty.

KAREN: That's a good idea, Colleen. If we each only had one-fifth of the material to read, getting together as a group to share would be worthwhile.

SCOTT: I don't want to sound like the bad guy in the group. As a basketball player, I know about teamwork, and frankly this group is not a team. I don't know if I want to depend on someone else in this group for my knowledge on the test. If even one member of the group blows off their work, we all suffer.

JARROD: Yeah, there's always a welfare case in every group.

SHANNON: You're right, Jarrod. Most study groups I've been part of usually have one or two freeloaders, but this group could be different. We're all highly competitive. We have three Division I starters in basketball. Steve is a top debater. Karen is a 4.0 honors student, and Colleen works harder than all of us.

COLLEEN: I don't know about that, but I think we all have a proven track record. Perhaps we could start small and grow big. We can prove to one another, a step at a time, that we are reliable. We have the talent to be the best study group in the department if we just try.

KAREN: That's the spirit, Colleen! We can do it!

STEVE: We still haven't answered Scott's question, which is, how can this group help us on the exam and is it worth our time?

COLLEEN: Like I said, we could divide up the topics according to our expertise. For example, we

have to write two hours on rhetoric and debate and you could be responsible for that material. Jarrod could put together the material for public relations, and so on.

SCOTT: Wait a minute! We haven't even agreed yet on whether we are going to meet again, let alone dividing up the work.

JARROD: I might meet again if it looked like each one of us would pull our own weight. I can see how having Steve pull together the rhetoric and argumentation material might help me.

SCOTT: Yeah, but how do you know you can trust him? Like he says, he's traveling all the time with the debate team. What if he doesn't get it done? And if we get an NCAA bid, we might not get our stuff done either.

SHANNON: Well, what do you say that we try to prove ourselves to one another one step at a time? If people start missing assignments in meetings, then we'll break up.

SCOTT: That's the only way I'll be part of this group. One slip-up and it's over.

COLLEEN: I think we have the basis for one more meeting. What if we each take one area we feel we know the best and prepare a fifteen-minute presentation for the next meeting? After we hear those presentations, we'll know whether we can help one another and become a productive group.

KAREN: I'll vote for that.

SCOTT: OK, but remember, one slip and I'm out of here.

CASE QUESTIONS

1. What predictions can you make for this group? Will everyone show up for the next meeting?
2. Of the nine characteristics of a small group, which are present in this first meeting?
3. What group roles, if any, can you see forming?

The authors thank Roger Smitter for his assistance in the preparation of this case.

CHAPTER TWO

LEARNING SMALL GROUP COMMUNICATION THEORIES

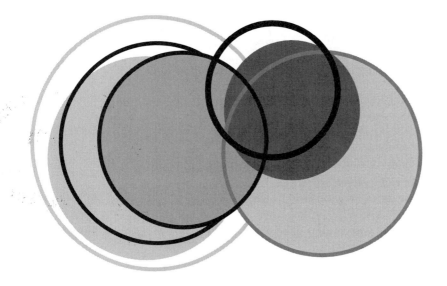

CHAPTER OBJECTIVES

After reading this chapter, you should be able to:

- Describe the model of small group communication
- Recognize the four types of group processes
- Understand the four signposts of a decision-making group

A MODEL OF SMALL GROUP COMMUNICATION

Of the eleven chapters in this book, this one and the next chapter are the most important to understand. In this chapter we explain the relationships among small group communication theories, processes, and signposts. Chapter 3 looks at small group communication skills and outcomes. All the remaining chapters in the book amplify and enrich the basic model laid out in Chapters 2 and 3.

The case study at the end of this chapter provides an example of explaining the bull's-eye model in the classroom. We know that this model may initially be hard to understand, but once you learn the four structured patterns of interaction that occur in a work group, the rest of the book will be easier to comprehend and your ability to participate in groups will improve. Group talk is not random. It is highly structured and predictable. Certain communication forces affect the outcomes of problem-solving work groups. We recognize these forces as team building, trust building, role playing, and problem solving.

We visualize our model as a bull's eye (Figure 2.1). The outer ring contains the theories that explain small group communication that occurs in a work group. The second ring is the process ring, which describes over time the changes in communication interaction that occur when a group achieves its goals. The third ring contains the signposts that tell group members that their group is maturing and doing good work. The fourth ring portrays the communication skills that must be competently

Figure 2.1   **Model of Small Group Communication**

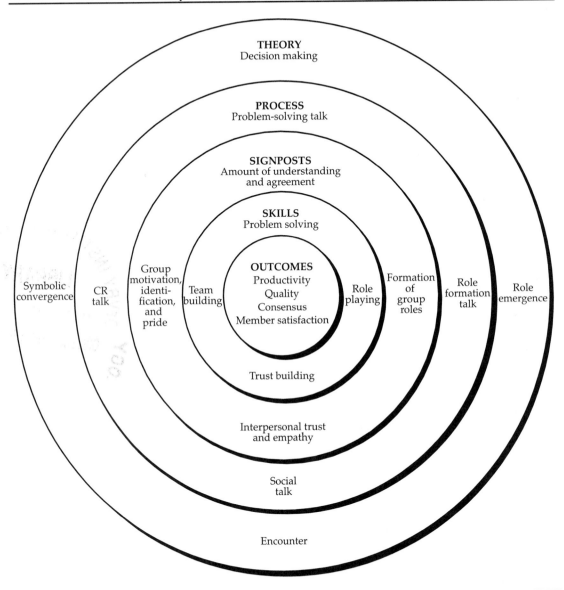

performed if the group outcomes are to be achieved. The center of the bull's-eye shows the four major group outputs of productivity, quality of work, group consensus, and membership satisfaction. Human work groups seldom exist in a vacuum, and the organization affects how the small group is allowed to proceed in solving its problems. Organizational culture partly determines what is regarded as appropriate and effective small group communication.

Furthermore, the bull's-eye is divided into four parts, in that four theoretical approaches (decision making, role emergence, encounter, and symbolic convergence theories) explain four distinct processes that occur in groups (task talk, role talk, social talk, and consciousness-raising [CR] talk). We know these four types of talk are going smoothly when CR talk produces group motivation and pride, social talk has produced group trust, role talk has evolved into the playing of at least five roles, and problem-solving talk has aided understanding and agreement. Decision-making theory indicates the necessary task communication skills that need to be performed; symbolic convergence theory (SCT) dictates the group motivational behavior that is needed; encounter theory forecasts the trust-building skills that must be performed; and role theory explains the type of communication skills that are necessary for each role to be played effectively. Thus, problem-solving skills flow from decision-making theory; trust-building skills, from encounter theory; team-building skills, from SCT; and role-playing skills, from role emergence theory.

In this chapter, we explain in greater detail the relation between small group communication theories, the structured communication patterns that occur in task groups, and the signs of a cohesive group. In Chapter 3, the major communication skills that affect the group outputs of productivity, quality, consensus, and membership satisfaction are discussed. Chapters 4 and 5 focus in greater detail on the relation between decision-making theory and rational communication processes and problem-solving skills. Chapter 6 is devoted to the explanation of small group interpersonal theories that affect group outcomes. Chapter 7 focuses on the role of leader and leadership skills. Chapter 8 details the major and supplementary roles that are played in work groups. Chapter 9 examines conflict as it occurs in all four types of group communication processes. Chapter 10 explains how the organizational context or culture affects problem-solving groups. In the last chapter, we examine the research of small group communication and the generation of small group theories. When you finish reading this book, we hope you return to this model for the purpose of synthesizing and retaining what you've learned in this course.

☐ DECISION-MAKING AND ROLE THEORIES AND PROCESSES

Communication scholars have worked on building communication explanations of group processes since the 1930s. Historically, our discipline has used discussion and pragmatic procedures for reaching group decisions. In the 1960s, the field of speech began to expand its view to include task groups, of which the decision-making group was one. This evolutionary process arose primarily out of a need to provide richer explanations of the communication processes that occur in groups (Bormann 1970a; Cragan and Wright 1980).

Early research in decision-making groups led us to believe that there were only two dimensions of a work group: the *task* dimension and the *social* dimension. We now call these dimensions *problem-solving talk* and *role talk*. At the beginning of this chapter, we introduced you to our general model of small group communication, which integrates what we regard as the four kinds of communication talk that occur in groups: problem-solving talk, role talk, CR talk, and social talk. We want to explain in detail the task and role dimensions of a work group.

In 1939, McBurney and Hance, two scholars working on small group discussion, published one of the first and certainly one of the most influential books in the field. Their approach to the teaching of discussion was constructed directly on John Dewey's theory about human thought processes. In 1910, Dewey published his famous work *How We Think*, in which he explained human thought as a careful, step-by-step consideration of a problem. He labeled this process "reflective thinking." Dewey identified five distinct steps of reflective thought:

1. a felt difficulty
2. its location and definition
3. suggestion and possible solution
4. development by reasoning of the bearings of the suggestion
5. further observation and experiment leading to its acceptance or rejection, that is, the conclusion of belief or disbelief

McBurney and Hance (1939) adapted Dewey's five steps—which describe how a person analyzes a problem—to group discussion. This adaptation to group analysis of problems and solutions is evident in their first steps:

1. definition and delineation of the problem
2. analysis of the problem
3. suggestion of solutions
4. reasoned development of the proposed solutions
5. further verification

McBurney and Hance's adaptation of Dewey's process of reflective thinking is only one example of its use by numerous small group discussion theorists. In Chapter 4, we discuss the many useful patterns and agenda systems that have been developed over the years in a continuing effort to help decision-making groups think and work together.

Kurt Lewin (1951) is regarded as the founder of group dynamics. In the 1930s, scholars from a number of disciplines began to see that small groups had a special identity and that the understanding of them could be an important goal of research. Lewin provided the first coherent explanation of groups in what we have come to call field theory. His notion of a field is essentially the space that individuals share within a group. One of Lewin's basic concepts of field theory is "life-space"—that is, the concept that each individual possesses a life-space within the field or group. In this theoretical explanation of a group, individual group members share some of their life-space with one another; that is, they are interdependent. The notion of a group as a field and the interdependence of the various life-spaces within the group provide a foundation for understanding the group concept of cohesion. Lewin regarded group cohesion as the stuff that holds the group members together in a common life-space.

Robert Bales (1950, 1970) is an influential scholar working on the development of small group communication theories. The work he has done at Harvard University in describing the task and social dimensions of groups, the stages the group goes through in its development, and the major roles that are played by members in small groups forms the basis of most modern attempts to describe how a small group works. Bales's work has been emphasized by communication scholars because he studies communication acts among group members in his efforts to explain the complex interactions of a discussion group.

In 1950, Bales developed an instrument for coding communication acts in a task group that has had a major impact on how small group theorists conceive of task group communication. Bales built a descriptive model of a task group based on the data he compiled with this coding instrument, which he called a system of Interaction Process Analysis. The instrument sorted all human behavior into two major categories: social-emotional and task. Almost all subsequent attempts at describing the pattern of communication in task groups have sorted out these two separate but interacting clusters of communicative behavior.

Further, Bales argued that a group attempts to maintain equilibrium through three stages on the way to solving a problem. The first stage, which he called orientation, is that in which the members arrive at a common definition of the problem. The second stage, evaluation, is the stage in which the group works out a common standard for assessing the problem; and the third stage, control, deals with the members' struggles for status as the group attempts to accomplish its task.

For more than thirty years, Ernest G. Bormann and his graduate students at the University of Minnesota have been systematically studying the communication behavior of small groups, particularly task-oriented groups. This research has spawned two communication theories: role emergence theory and symbolic convergence theory (SCT). Role emergence theory explains the two-stage process that decision-making groups go through in the formation of group roles. SCT explains how individual group members come to create a common group identity through the creation and sharing of group fantasies.

After a number of years of teaching and research using Dewey's approach to group discussion, Bormann became dissatisfied with the rationalistic assumptions that are implicit in the step-by-step thought pattern models that Dewey's reflective thinking procedure inspired. Bormann and his students set up leaderless group discussions (LGDs) and began to study them scientifically to determine how small groups form and make decisions, with special emphasis on the communication behaviors that are associated with each development. Their research efforts produced one of the richest and most widely used explanations of how people communicate in groups in making decisions.

The genesis of Bormann's role emergence theory is Bales's equilibrium theory of groups. Bormann believed that Bales's use of both task and social dimensions and the constant push and pull between them was a useful place to begin, but he also believed that it was important to be able to describe the interplay of these two dimensions over time. After ten years of scientifically observing zero-history, or test-tube, groups discuss and complete tasks, Bormann set forth a role emergence theory of small groups. He found that two kinds of group tension existed: *primary* and *secondary*. Primary tension is the formal uneasiness that every group member feels when a meeting is called. Secondary tension, a more serious kind, occurs later in the discussion and deals primarily with role struggles, especially struggles for leadership. Bormann and his students found that group members try on various group roles and that the group, through a series of rewarding and punishing communication acts, fits people into certain roles. The Minnesota studies also discovered that this role emergence followed noticeable patterns.

The major roles that get established by the end of secondary tension are task leader, social-emotional leader, information provider, tension releaser, and central negative. The task leader facilitates the decision-making process through a number of skills we discuss in Chapters 7 and 8. The social-emotional leader nurtures the group and supports the task leader. The central negative plays devil's advocate and challenges the group ideas and, often, the leader. The information provider is relied on to secure and present to the group objective data needed for decision making. The tension releaser keeps the group loose through the use of humorous stories and the creation of insider jokes for the group. The film *Flatliners* shows how these five roles are played in a task work group.

We have all experienced the phenomenon Bormann has labeled primary tension. When a group of people first come into a room and sit down for a meeting, there is a lot of social tension. There are long periods of silence, people struggle to find light topics to discuss, everyone is careful not to offend anyone else—especially if the group is meeting for the first time. The research at the University of Minnesota indicates that primary tension is broken when somebody finds a common base for humor. This person will many times emerge in the role of tension releaser. Most groups can break primary tension, but secondary tension seems to be a more consistent and serious problem. If primary tension is marked by silence, secondary tension is marked by loudness. Verbal and nonverbal signs of disagreement often can lead to open antagonism and hostility. Bormann's research indicates that there is no set formula groups can use for resolving secondary tension, that each group must develop its own scheme for handling these disagreements and personality conflicts. A good deal of this secondary tension often is caused by a struggle for leadership. The role of leader and other group roles are discussed in Chapters 7 and 8.

Groups develop different tolerance levels for handling social conflicts. Some groups can accomplish work amid a great deal of bickering, whereas other groups must resolve all elements of secondary tension before they can go about their task. Thus, each group establishes a baseline for social conflict such that when it is exceeded, work stops and the group focuses on the elimination of social tension. In their observation of leaderless zero-history groups, Bormann (1975, 176–195) and his students did not find a lockstep or sequential development of a social dimension in work groups. Instead, they observed that groups went through primary tension each time they met and suffered secondary tension at irregular intervals throughout their history. Bormann and his students found that successful groups developed ways of handling this tension and that when the leadership role was resolved, the more severe aspects of secondary social tension disappeared.

In keeping with Bormann's belief that lockstepped rational models such as Dewey's did not reflect ways in which groups made decisions, Fisher (1970) studied both LGD test-tube groups in the laboratory and actual decision-making groups in corporations and churches to see whether there is a natural pattern that groups follow in reaching a decision. By observing the communication patterns of a number of decision-making groups, Fisher determined that groups go through four basic stages in arriving at a decision. He labeled them orientation, conflict, emergence, and reinforcement. Typical communicative behavior during the orientation stage includes showing agreement, being tentative with assertions, and seeking to clarify points of information. During this stage, group members tend to be ambiguous about the proposal. During the conflict phase, members express disagreement, substantiate their beliefs on a given proposal, and align themselves on the favorable or unfavorable side. The third stage, emergence, sees a reduction in the polarization and in the strength of disagreement; in essence, people who opposed the original proposal now become more ambivalent toward it. The final stage, reinforcement, emphasizes consensus by group members on the proposal at hand and in fact produces a tension-releasing phase in which members celebrate their agreement in cheerful verbal interaction (Fisher 1970, 140–145).

In a series of five studies (Poole 1981, 1983a, 1983b; Poole and Roth 1989a, 1989b), Poole rejected Fisher's traditional phasic development of the communication process of decision making and set forth a multiple-sequence model that he believes provides a richer explanation of a task group (1983b, 326). Although some of the groups mirrored the classic pattern, most of them did not. Poole found, as Bormann did before him, that groups solve their problems in recurring and uneven patterns of communication. Poole developed a model that explains more than thirty interactive systems of communication. It is not important for you to understand all the patterns, but it is necessary for you to realize that the various stages of problem-solving talk may be recycled several times. For example, Fisher's orientation stage may have to be repeated numerous times before the group solves its problem.

The easiest way to understand the various decision-making paths is to learn the classic pattern that occurs in about 20 percent of cases. We are now going to walk you through the problem-solving process and the role formation process simultaneously, so that you can see the interaction between problem-solving talk and role talk.

Stage One: Orientation (Task) and Primary Tension (Role)

It seems clear that all human groups in all cultures, when they first get together, experience periods of awkwardness. You certainly can remember times in which you were one of the first people to show up at a meeting and you carried on a rather nervous conversation with a few other people, but the conversation usually was marked by long periods of silence. Even when your task group formally turned attention to the purpose of the meeting, conversation was awkward. Bormann's research indicates that at this point, somebody can release the tension through a humorous comment. The humor that seems to work best relates to the common predicament in which all members find themselves. Once the initial tension is broken, a group tends to devote a lot of energy to orienting group members to the task. At this time, many questions about the purpose of the group, the agenda for the particular meeting, and so forth are asked. In fact, Bales's research suggests that asking a lot of questions to help the group get oriented correctly is important. He found that successful groups asked more questions than groups that weren't successful. Not all groups complete the orientation stage the first time they attempt it. In fact, they may have to return to this stage several times before completing their task. Also, some groups appear to do an inadequate job as a group in part because they did not properly or thoroughly orient themselves to their work.

The use of team-building and trust-building communication helps group members get through primary tension and do a better job of orienting themselves to the task. Some personal disclosures, such as members' names and what experience they have that might help in the task before them, reduce social tension and make people more willing to ask questions. Team-building communication that asks members to share past stories of problem-solving groups they have worked on in the organization helps to build group pride because the group will know that there are lots of capable people on the team. Thus, team-building and trust-building communication helps the group alleviate primary tension and identify where to start on the solution of the problem.

Stage Two: Conflict (Task) and Secondary Tension (Role)

Stage Two of a task group is the most complex and difficult portion of a problem-solving group's existence. At the task level, group members are suggesting ideas about the problem, and these ideas are being accepted or rejected by the group. Simultaneously, there is role talk, which in this case is secondary tension. As the Minnesota research indicates, members are trying out for leadership roles in the group, not by simply saying "I want to lead" but by demonstrating knowledge of the topic, social maturity, and self-confidence in the way they suggest ideas and evaluate the ideas of others. In Chapter 9, we go into much greater detail about the kind of conflict that is occurring in Stage Two, but now it is important to note that the group can become so fearful of Stage Two ideational conflict and Stage Two role conflict that it will break from problem-solving talk. Poole's (1983b, 330) research indicates that these "breakpoints" frequently occur as groups go through a decision-making process. He identified three types of breakpoints: *normal breakpoints*—times when the group stops work (scheduled 9:15 A.M., coffee break) or times when the group switches from one topic to another; *delays*—instances when the group continues to resummarize its analysis of the part of a problem it has already completed, causing a delay in moving to discussion of the next major part of the problem; and *disruptions*—occasions in the process of trying to move on to solutions when the group may abandon its original orientation to the problem and try to create a new structure. Many times these types of breakpoints that Poole describes at the task level may signal that the group is experiencing a secondary tension episode in which the leadership situation is unstable.

In addition to Poole's three breakpoints, two other breakpoints can occur throughout a group's discussion but frequently occur because of the tension of ideational conflict and role formation. One is an *encounter moment,* when a group member starts discussing his or her personal agenda in depth; another is a *CR moment,* when the group members discuss their professional identity in detail. We discuss these later in the chapter. Our point here is that the more ideational conflict a group can tolerate without taking flight, the better the group decision will be.

Stage Three: Emergence (Task) and Recurring Primary and Secondary Tension (Role)

Even though it would seem rational and orderly that group members would discuss the nature and causes of a problem before they would entertain possible solutions to a problem, not all discussion groups proceed in this manner. Sometimes a group member will prepare his or her solution in advance of a group meeting. He or she will introduce and argue for it early in the discussion—long before the group has had a chance to discuss the parameters of the problem. In situations like this, decision-making groups do a lot of bouncing back and forth between Stages Two and Three. They may experience several bouts of secondary tension, and there are delays and disruptions. Hirokawa (1983) discovered that groups that start with the problem (Stage Two) and then proceed to solutions are more successful, on average, than groups that start with possible solutions and work their way back. So it would seem that, when possible, groups should try to get through Stage Two before going to Stage Three.

If a group is meeting only once a week, it will experience recurring primary tension at the beginning of each new meeting, but after several meetings, the tension-releasing role will be played by the same one or two members. Sometimes a group norm will develop around this issue; for example, Gabriel will begin the meeting by telling a story about the problems he has had with e-mail. This strategy for breaking primary tension may become so standard that if Gabriel doesn't say anything at the outset, people will ask, "Gabe, what happened with your e-mail this week?" Recurring bouts of secondary tension are more serious and more difficult to solve than recurring episodes of primary tension. In newly formed groups, if the emergent task leader misses a meeting, somebody else has to assume the leadership group. In addition, when the first leader returns the next week, there may be a protracted struggle for leadership of the group. The dangers of extended periods of recurring secondary tension can best be minimized by the use of team-building and trust-building communication. If the group has spent time building its group identity and pride and group members have made sufficient disclosures about themselves, the group will be better able to handle the shock of a missing task leader, and it will be easier for the group to develop role flexibility whereby people can change roles without experiencing much personal conflict that would destabilize the group.

Stage Four: Reinforcement (Task)

Once a group decision appears to be emerging, there seems to be little social tension. The group compliments itself on the fine solution it settled on and spends some time assessing the impact of its solution. Groups spend a good deal of time working for consensus and group member commitment. Oftentimes a group decision emerges by a bare majority, and then, in Stage Four, the group attempts to convince everybody to get behind the solution and be a good team player in supporting it.

In doing research on the task and role dimensions of work groups, it became apparent to small group scholars that not all group communication could be accounted for by looking at problem-solving talk and role talk. As we indicated in our small group communication model (Figure 2.1), the two additional types of talk are social talk and CR talk. We discovered the importance of social talk in a problem-solving group by first isolating it. Researchers discovered that when a group does not have work to do, it will make itself the work by focusing on members' feelings toward one another. These types of groups are called encounter groups, and in their pure form, they produce personal self-growth. However, the study of encounter groups has helped us to understand how interpersonal talk in a task group helps to build trust and, thus, improve group productivity. To understand how trust-building talk works in a problem-solving group, we must first understand the theory and process of a pure encounter group.

☐ ENCOUNTER THEORY AND PROCESS

In our study of small discussion groups, we have long been aware of the interpersonal dimension and the effects that interpersonal relations have on the productivity of the group. Moreno (1934) was one of the first scholars to explain the interpersonal conflicts that occur in small groups. His attraction-repulsion theory stated simply that we tend to like some group members more than others; in fact, some members tend to be "stars," in that they are liked by most in the group, whereas others became "isolates," in that hardly anyone likes them.

By the 1940s, we began to realize that the interpersonal or social dimension of groups was far more complex. Moreover, there seemed to be a hidden agenda during group discussions that needed to be uncovered and explained. At the National Training Laboratories in Group Development at Bethel, Maine, in the summers of the late 1940s and early 1950s, researchers began to uncover this hidden agenda, at first quite by accident. They discovered that when you took away the task assignment of the discussion group, the group soon developed a new task and started to discuss how the members themselves related to one another. These early training groups, or "t" groups, evolved into sensitivity, therapy, and general encounter groups that dealt exclusively with self-development.

Gerald Phillips (1966), in *Communication and the Small Group*, explained the importance of understanding the hidden agenda of social or interpersonal needs that each person brings to the group if we are to have successful communication and accomplish group goals. William C. Schutz (1966) postulated that there are three basic interpersonal needs that each person expects his or her group to satisfy. These are inclusion, control, and affection. Inclusion deals with the feeling of being "in" or "out" of the group; control deals with "top" or "bottom"—that is, status in the group; and affection deals with "close" or "far"—that is, "cold" or "warm." Schutz believes that people need others to whom they can give and from whom they can receive these three fundamental interpersonal needs. Thus, he calls his theory Fundamental Interpersonal Relations Orientation. We explain this theory in relation to group communication behavior in greater detail in Chapter 6.

By the 1960s, the focus of encounter groups had shifted from learning about people in groups to learning about oneself, with the encounter group as the basic means of self-discovery. Carl Rogers and other clinical psychologists began holding group therapy sessions for "normals." In the 1960s, college students were deeply interested in self-growth, and encounter groups were one of the chief means by which they accomplished their personal goals. By the 1970s, it had also been discovered that encounter groups had the potential to produce not only self-growth but also self-destruction. Lieberman, Yalom, and Miles (1973, 264), in *Encounter Groups: First Facts*, document some of the psychic damage that can occur as the result of encounter group sessions. They point out that several leadership styles in encounter groups lead to substantial harm to group members. The leadership of encounter groups is best left to trained clinical psychologists; the use of this group process as a parlor game can definitely be harmful to some participants.

After studying the communication of encounter groups, we have been able to describe its stages of development and have some understanding of why this group process has such an impact on its participants. A typical encounter group has as its goal the personal growth of its individual members. People join encounter groups to learn about themselves and how they are perceived by others. When an encounter group is formed, it has no formal agenda or structure. We have discovered that when a group of people are put together with no agenda, a rather predictable pattern occurs.

Bennis and Shepherd (1956) described encounter groups in terms of the two major phases of dependence and interdependence, with three subphases in each major phase. The choice of goal and the dependence of the members on their trainer mark the first subphase of an encounter group. As an encounter group moves to the second subphase, the group members are in conflict with one another over the trainer. Bennis and Shepherd found that encounter group members deal first with the problem of authority and then with the problem of intimacy. During this conflict, group members divide into three categories: members who look to the trainer for leadership; members who are dependent on the leader but who solve this problem by attacking him or her; and members who are independent and not threatened by a leaderless group that has no agenda. Task groups and CR groups do not exhibit the three-way conflict behavior that is so typical of encounter groups. Encounter groups move from dependence to independence to interdependence and, in the process, strip away the role facades of group members, thus revealing their increasingly "naked" selves.

The pure CR group focuses on a new sociopolitical identity or a professional identity, with the effect of fusing self with group identities. A pure encounter group has the people themselves as the agenda, and the group process focuses on the individual's feelings and beliefs, with the end product being self-growth. Although these two types of groups do exist in their pure form, most of your experience in groups is probably of the hybrid variety.

Many business retreat seminars and religious retreats, which are held away from familiar sites, form groups that blend these processes of CR and encounter. If a group at one of these retreats focuses on "what it is like to be a manager at Xerox," the communication process will more than likely produce a CR group. However, if the topic a group focuses on is personal values that are stressed in the work environment, the group communication could produce an encounter group. Likewise, at a religious retreat, if the topic is "what it is like to be a Christian," it will be CR; if this kind of group focuses its members' religious values on a topic such as abortion, it would be encounter. The biggest single indication that you are in an encounter group is self-disclosure about you and your values as well as feelings about others in the group. When you moved into a dorm as a freshman or into off-campus housing, you may have found yourself talking all night long with several of your roommates about your personal beliefs. In these discussions, you may have disclosed many things about yourself. Also, as you continued to live together, you may have become more and more open about what habits and values are irksome to you.

Many of the self-help groups that have become popular since the 1960s are hybrid encounter-CR groups (e.g., Parents Without Partners, Alcoholics Anonymous, Weight Watchers). The self-help groups definitely have a we-they syndrome, characteristic of CR, in which the villain is alcohol or fatty foods as well as the people in society who tempt the group members to sin. These groups work hard on creating a new identity of the sober alcoholic or the successful single parent. These groups also have intense encounter moments in which there is clear indication that members will disclose personal feelings and beliefs to the group.

Although you may not participate in a clinical encounter group run by qualified trainers, it is apparent that in the course of working in groups within organizations, you will be involved in spontaneous encounter group sessions. Although these sessions may not go through all the stages of a formal encounter group, which has personal growth as its expressed agenda, does, it is important for you to recognize the communication patterns that are unique to encounter groups. This recognition will help you to better understand *encounter moments* that occur in your everyday work group.

Whereas Bennis and Shepherd sketched out the macrocommunication patterns of encounter groups, Edward Mabry identified microverbal exchanges that characterize stages of an encounter group. He found and labeled three stages of interaction in encounter groups—boundary-seeking, ambivalence, and actualization (Mabry 1975, 305)—after observing the following nine kinds of communication behavior: antagonistic, assertive-supportive, dominant-assertive, aggressive-assertive, assertive, reactive to group laughter, task-determinative, reactive to tension, and supportive (Mabry 1975, 303).

Stage One: Boundary Seeking

The first stage is dominated by antagonism, task-determining activity, and assertiveness, and as Bennis and Shepherd (1956) pointed out, most of this behavior is directed at the trainer or is part of the dialogue about the trainer's role. Mabry labeled this stage boundary-seeking because the group has not yet resolved questions regarding its structure, functions, and overall direction. When twelve persons sit in a circle and look at one another uncomfortably for several minutes, some member soon begins to break the tension with humor. Before long, somebody becomes irritated. He or she is angry because the trained leader (who has been through this process before) refuses to give directions and set an agenda, thereby allowing the emergence of a new leader. When the trainer does not take charge, some of the members form a coalition and attack the trainer for his or her lack of leadership. Another coalition soon forms and defends the trainer's right not to lead. Rebellion reigns supreme until the group members discover that they are free to form their own structure and have their own unique experience.

Stage Two: Ambivalence

Mabry's Stage Two is dominated by types of communication behavior that fit into the categories of aggressive-assertive and supportive. These findings are consistent with the rhetorical descriptions that Bennis and Shepherd (1956) provided of the authority dependence that an encounter group goes through and the brief enchantment that follows when the group's dependence on the trainer has ended. Once the group members realize that they are on their own, they immediately become infatuated with one another and go on a "false honeymoon." They believe that they have now resolved their conflicts and put away their "false faces." They take turns pointing out how phony they were when the group began and how honest and open they are with one another now. The false honeymoon is short-lived.

Stage Three: Actualization

The decline in supportiveness accurately parallels the beginning of verbal conflict that Bennis and Shepherd (1956) found as characteristic of what they described as disenchantment-flight. Mabry's study also found that toward the end of the encounter group, reactions to group laughter increased. The group begins by conducting an intense search for the true identity of each group member. As some members make intimate disclosures and others refuse to be equally open, the group again breaks into two coalitions, in which one side pushes for even more interpersonal disclosure and the other opposes it. This is the period in the life of an encounter group when many people experience self-growth; this is also the period in which emotions are rubbed raw, in some cases producing emotional damage to individuals. During this period, the skills of a trainer are needed, preferably one who is a licensed clinical psychologist or psychiatrist. This emotional intensity finally produces catharsis, and the group finds itself feeling close and interdependent. In fact, this euphoric after-glow produced a significant number of encounter group junkies during the late 1960s and early 1970s. These people went from one group experience to the next, and some of them began to call themselves "trainers" and started their own groups. When properly supervised, the encounter group communication process can produce what Bennis and Shepherd called "valid communication," which can and does lead to personal growth.

Everyday work groups in organizations also have encounter moments. These are times in the group discussion when the conversation breaks from the task at hand and centers on the personal feelings or beliefs of an individual member or the group as a whole. Small group researchers have identified this phenomenon as the hidden agenda that periodically surfaces when group members discuss personal issues. The management of this agenda is so important that a group role called the social-emotional leader exists in all successful task groups. We discuss this role in detail in Chapter 8. It appears that the amount of personal disclosure, or encounter moments, or indeed full-scale encounter group sessions, appears to vary from occupation to occupation and even from work group to work group.

Army combat teams, firefighting teams, police units, and medical emergency work groups that face danger together and are highly interdependent on one another for their survival need to self-disclose. These groups usually demand high levels of personal disclosure on the part of the membership. The group members argue that they need intimate knowledge of one another so that they can trust one another in emergency situations. It is common for members of these types of groups to report that their work group colleagues know them better than their own families. Joseph Wambaugh's book *The Choirboys* certainly demonstrates this reality for police officers.

Many work groups can find themselves involved in full-blown encounter group sessions that spontaneously occur because of the availability of "down time." *When a work group is kept together but does not have work to do, it will make itself the agenda.* The group will either talk about itself in terms of its professional identity and, thus, generate a CR session; or it will focus on the team members as individuals in terms of their values and feelings, thus becoming an encounter group. Japanese work groups, for example, have a much higher expectation than American work groups that members will play together as well as work together. Japanese workers and families may actually take vacations together, whereas a group in an American company may find involvement at the personal level in cocktail parties, golf outings, or after-work social hours. However, if any collection of five or six persons leave their work environments for a common vacation (i.e., sharing food and housing), encounter group sessions are almost inevitable. Two movies that vividly depict this phenomenon are *Four Seasons* and *The Breakfast Club*; if you have ever taken a group vacation over spring break, you no doubt have experienced the self-disclosure that occurs and the social conflict that tends to arise; these are the expected communication behaviors of encounter group sessions.

The establishment of interpersonal trust in a group is difficult to achieve and measure, although its presence or absence is readily recognized by its group members. Risk taking on the part of individual members is essential if trust is to be built in the group. The dangers of risk taking are greater in a group setting than in a dyad because there is more potential for a person to be taken advantage of by other group members.

The major fears that form a barrier to establishing trust in task groups are the fear of not getting credit for the work we do, the fear that the work load will not be equitably shared, and the fear that individual self-disclosure will be used to the detriment of the individual, both inside and outside the group. Because most organizations reward individuals and not groups, group members always worry initially about their colleagues' motives. If a supervisor or a coworker had developed a reputation for taking credit for other people's work, most people would not trust that person in the group. We also worry that we'll be taken advantage of in terms of the amount of work we do for the group. Until a work group has produced some common effort, group members constantly look for signs that the workload is not equally shared. As a work group engages in more and more face-to-face discussions, group members begin to disclose more personal kinds of communication. Although this information helps the group to understand the individual better, that same information could be used against the individual if someone had malicious motives.

These fears are not unreasonable, and to some degree, they will always be present in a work group. The best we can hope for is to keep these fears at a minimum and hope that as the group develops a history of successful work together, trust will begin to be established. Research has shown that the best way to facilitate group trust is to maintain open lines of communication (Leathers 1970).

Trust is difficult to build in groups, but it is even harder to rebuild. Once group members have been betrayed or taken advantage of, the road back to a working relationship is steep. Therefore, it is crucial that a group protect its trust as a precious commodity. When a member becomes suspicious, he or she should bring his or her fears out into the open for full discussion. Continual dialogue, combined with an honest effort by each group member, is the best way to maintain interpersonal trust in the group.

☐ SYMBOLIC CONVERGENCE THEORY AND CONSCIOUSNESS-RAISING PROCESS

Bales's research at Harvard University and Bormann's research at the University of Minnesota have clearly demonstrated that not all important group communication can be explained by problem-solving talk, role talk, or social talk. There exists a fourth kind of group talk that relates to the group members' common symbolic identity (Bales 1970; Bormann 1975). Bales and Bormann have called the communication that tends to generate this group feeling of oneness "group fantasies." Furthermore, Bormann has developed a theory called "symbolic convergence," which explains how both small and large groups create a common identity through the use of shared group fantasies (1985, 1990). Symbolic convergence theory (SCT) explains how small decision-making groups come to create a unique symbolic identity that becomes the source of group pride and motivation. SCT can be seen at work in quality circles. Quality circles begin by naming themselves and developing a group logo. This group task focuses the members' attention on their common work experience, and the group will naturally share fantasies about their unique identity that will be expressed by their name and logo. You may be well advised to ask your student group to name itself and develop a logo so that it can experience fantasy-sharing. Bales (1970, 152) describes the effect of a group fantasy as "stimulating in each of its members a feeling he has entered a new realm of reality—a world of heroes, villains, saints, and enemies—a drama. . . . The culture of a group is a fantasy established in the past, which is acted upon in the present."

To understand trust building in a problem-solving group, we have to examine the encounter group process in its pure form. Likewise, to understand team-building communication that affects group identity, pride, and motivation, we need to understand CR as a distinct form. Once you understand the four phases of a CR group, you will better understand how to use it in everyday work groups.

In the early 1960s, feminist groups discovered a group process that was extremely powerful in galvanizing a group of women together in a sisterhood that had a common symbolic wholeness. The women who attended these group meetings had their consciousness raised about their socialized identity as women. They began to see the American society as male-dominated and oppressive toward women. As women's liberation organizations began to form in the late 1960s, these group CR sessions became central to the internal development of the women's liberation movement (Morgan 1970).

Radical revolutionary groups that formed in the 1960s began to adopt the women's technique of holding CR sessions. They also reported that the CR process was effective, not only in creating new political values and revolutionary commitment, but also in actualizing those value structures in society. By the late 1970s, political and religious groups on both the left and the right had adopted the use of CR sessions as an integral part of producing converts to their political causes.

In the late 1960s, a president's council was formed to study the problem of student unrest. In their report to the president, the council members expressed their concern about the processes that had produced the fanatical commitment to causes that was demonstrated by revolutionary acts committed against the government (Report of the President's Council on Student Unrest). In the 1970s, the United States was again shocked by the fanatical commitment of people to a cause. This time the organizations or groups were religious cults such as the Moonies and the Hare Krishnas. The world was shocked in 1978 when more than nine hundred members of the Reverend Jim Jones's People's Temple committed mass suicide. Jones had made extensive use of CR sessions in the running of his People's Temple, and once again, there was a public cry to understand this process. Renewed interest in the powerful impact of consciousness-raising arose with the mass suicide of members of the Heaven's Gate cult in 1997.

Chesebro, Cragan, and McCullough (1973) defined CR as "a personal, face-to-face interaction which appears to create new psychological orientations for those involved in the process" (136). These communication scholars found that a small group CR session was quite different from a task group or an encounter group. They found that if like people gather together for the purpose of discussing a common social, political, or religious value structure, certain predictable communication patterns occur.

For more than twenty years, communication researchers have been studying CR groups in an attempt to understand the role of CR processes in "ordinary" work groups that exist in business organizations. We are not alone in our interest in CR. In the 1960s, CR was the tool of political revolutionary groups. In the 1970s, CR was used systematically by many religious groups. By the 1980s, major American corporations were using this process as a means for creating, heightening, and sustaining an employee's identity with his or her work group and company. Some of the more visible corporations using CR are Amway, Mary Kay Cosmetics, and Williams Insurance Company. However, the popularity of Japanese management theory (Theory Z) and the success Japanese workers have sustained in the areas of productivity and quality control have caused many more American companies to adopt the use of formal or informal CR to build esprit de corp in work groups. A best-selling book of the 1980s, *In Search of Excellence* (Peters and Waterman 1982), underlines the importance of building effective work teams.

A major way in which team pride is built through the small group communication process of CR. In addition, companies periodically bring small work groups together for companywide "rallies." We describe not only the stages of CR in work groups, but also the techniques that are used at rallies to make participants believe that they are part of a larger "we." Similar patterns hold true whether we're talking about the national Democratic and Republican conventions held every four years in the United States, rallies held by Billy Graham or other religious leaders, or corporate rallies held by Amway or Mary Kay Cosmetics.

For you to better understand the CR moments that occur in everyday task groups, it is necessary for you to first comprehend the four communication stages that take place in a pure CR group. Once you understand the CR process, you will know when a task group is "credentialing," engaging in we-they dialogue, or building its own identity.

Stage One: Self-Realization of a New Identity

For CR to occur, it is necessary for everybody in the group to possess the crucial characteristic that forms the basis for the discussion. A women's group must have only women in the group, and a men's group must have only men in it. Likewise, CR sessions on Christianity must contain only Christians, CR sessions on gay liberation must contain only gays, and so on. This CR process could also begin if a group consisted of students meeting to talk about university life or firefighters discussing their identity as public employees. Thus, the first stage of CR begins with the group members establishing their *credentials*. Credentialing often is done through storytelling. A member will relate a personal story about oppression she has experienced because she is a woman, or because she is gay, or whatever. This story will stimulate other members to tell their stories. The stories heighten the excitement of the group, and there is much laughter and conversation as the members establish that they are all of like mind. The personal stories usually depict the oppressor in a dramatic manner. For women's groups, the oppressor would be a male chauvinist, for gays a homophobic person. For college students in an all-night CR session in a dorm, the oppressor may be the incompetent professor. The stories also portray the group members as distinct minorities dominated by a powerful oppressor, and the group members need to raise their consciousness about this societal evil so that they and their comrades can be liberated.

Organizations that use CR sessions as a formal part of their management strategies train team leaders in the techniques of CR. For example, if an Amway group is meeting, the trainer may encourage each member to tell stories about what he or she plans to do after having successfully sold Amway products. An organization that sells retirement homes in the Sun Belt of the United States might invite a married group of people in their fifties to dinner and after dinner encourage a discussion about the kind of retirement life they envision. If you have ever participated in a religious retreat, you will remember that you were broken up into small groups and your group leader began the discussion by encouraging people to share religious experiences. This technique almost always produces Stage One of CR, in which the group members realize that they have a common group identity.

CR sessions can also start spontaneously without any group member intentionally trying to start one. A group of workers may be having lunch in the company cafeteria when one of the people at the table describes how tense a job performance interview with the supervisor was. This story might spark a half-hour discussion in which group members contribute their experiences with job performance reviews. Members usually find these to be enjoyable discussions that are punctuated with humor and laughter. If a group of college students having lunch together discover that they all received a Catholic education, having been taught by nuns and priests, they may spend the entire lunch hour taking turns telling humorous stories about the "theys": nuns and priests. A group of insurance salespeople attending an insurance convention may find that a lot of their conversation is the telling of stories in which they are the heroes, wrestling with the "theys." Nobody planned these discussions; they just got started. In fact, all professional conventions produce a large number of CR sessions simply because all who attend the convention are part of the same profession (e.g., physicians, professors). Today, in American corporate life, more than two thousand companies have formally instituted management structures that encourage CR sessions. These companies have adopted some form of quality circle program—a topic we discussed earlier in the book. In most American companies, however, CR occurs among workers on a hit-or-miss basis. Most spontaneous CR sessions never get past Stage One or Two (Bolkum 1981). If the CR session gets past Stage One, you will know that quickly because the type of communication of the discussion will change dramatically.

Stage Two: Group Identity Through Polarization

In Stage Two, the laughter and storytelling of Stage One disappear and the group intensely discusses the nature of "the enemy." Rhetorically, this stage of the CR session is characterized by a we-they dichotomy. In a CR session in which gay rights were discussed, the "we" would refer to liberated gays and the "they" to the oppressive, heterosexually dominated society. This stage in a CR session often focuses in great detail on the nature of oppression and the specific identity of the oppressors. Thus, women's groups might discuss the specific behaviors that constitute male chauvinism, and a college student group might discuss the lecturing and grading policies of a professor. As people continue to hold CR sessions, the polarization between the "we" and the "theys" becomes greater.

In work groups within organizations, three types of "theys" can emerge in Stage Two of CR discussions. They are the *upward they*, the *lateral they*, and the *downward they*. The *upward they* is the boss—sometimes an immediate supervisor or sometimes the entire upper management of an organization. Many times when groups are doing a lot of CR, these discussions at Stage Two contain rich, vivid descriptions of the "they." The supervisor might be called the "red pheasant" because of the way red pheasants look walking down the rows of a cornfield. When this label was first created, it may have been the result of workers imitating the pheasantlike walk of the boss, to the amusement of the group. Bales (1970) and Bormann (1990) have identified these moments as group fantasies that help to create a common group identity.

Although initially this label may be a description by the "we" workers of the "they" boss, the supervisor and workers eventually resolve the we-they polarization, and all share in the joke. The boss may even take to wearing a T-shirt that designates himself or herself as the "red pheasant"! If there is a lot of conflict between the work group and the supervisor, the CR sessions may generate vicious descriptions that are kept secret from the boss. In working with groups in business and industry, we have run into descriptions of superiors such as "Attila the Hun," "The Ice Queen," "The Mumbler," and "Rose the Nose." Vicious descriptions can highlight some perceived power misuse on the part of the superior. The work group then has some fun with a person's behavioral mannerism, and the description is born and sustained.

All organizations have acquired nicknames, usually humorous, for the building that houses the upper management of the company. This is especially true if the home office is located in a town and regional offices are located throughout the country. In this type of situation, both workers and first-line supervisors can become a "we" versus the "they" at the top. At our university, the central administration building is called Hovey Hall, but many professors, when evaluating administrators' decision making, refer to it as Hovey Heaven. In part, it is called Hovey Heaven because the rank and file believe that what you do with incompetent professors is to promote them to Hovey Heaven. It is also called Hovey Heaven because central administrators tend to hover around decisions instead of making them. One *Fortune* 500 pharmaceutical company has a central administration building with a reflecting pool in front of it and an escalator that works only when a person walks onto it. When sales personnel get together and become involved in a CR session, they refer to the home office as "the Taj Mahal" and have great fun describing the senior administrators floating around on their magic carpets. Another major American firm refers to its main office as "the Puzzle Palace." Other names for home offices of American corporations that we have heard of are "the Head Shed," "the Square Donut," "Disney World East," "the Glass House," and "the Mindbenders Dungeon." These descriptions have the same commonality that the nicknames for supervisors have. The label weaves together some characteristic of the home office building and some frustrating characteristic of the decision making done by the administrators housed in the building.

When CR groups are engaged in *lateral we-they* polarization discussions, they usually are talking about competing group situations. On campus, the competing group might be those students who live on the floor above you or in the dorm across the quad. A *lateral we-they* discussion also could be one sorority talking about another sorority. Sometimes it's students from one college describing students from a competing college. In the U.S. armed forces, it might be the "jarheads" versus the "swabbies" versus the "wingnuts," or "lifers" versus enlisted. In typical American business organizations, these we-they discussions are about competing work groups, such as sales, accounting, and marketing. These discussions normally revolve around the competency of the other group, the two groups' relative importance to the overall mission of the organization, and whether the group is receiving its fair share of financial rewards and promotions vis-à-vis the other group. As a student on campus, you often are asked, "What is your major?" It soon becomes apparent that there is a stereotype of who belongs to each group, and competing groups have derogatory one-liners about your major. When you are in an organization, the question becomes "What department are you working in?" You will discover, if you haven't already, that this is the same game as "What's your major?" Competing work groups have developed stereotypic descriptions that, in a derogatory way, describe other groups' roles in regard to the organization's mission.

The third type of we-they polarization that occurs in CR sessions is the *downward they*, characterized by a "bite-the-hand-that-feeds-you" dialogue. We often have observed that at the same time students are studying for finals and engaging in heavy CR sessions in which the professor (the *upward they*) is vilified, faculty are sitting in groups and consciousness-raising about students (the *downward they*). The professors' conversations mirror those of the students, in that they are describing ill-trained students who have trouble walking and thinking at the same time. A *downward they* Stage Two conversation usually stops if one professor reminds the others that they are being paid to teach students and that if they are competent profession-als, they should improve the students' performance.

Downward they CR discussions occur in all organizations. Physicians have deroga-tory discussions among themselves about their patients. A surgical nurse once said to us, "If you only knew what we said about your body after you had been anesthe-tized!" Army units or police officers often have CR sessions in which civilians are the object of ridicule. Data processors regularly complain about the stupidity of "end-users." We often feel guilty when we realize that we wouldn't have a work group if it weren't for the *downward theys*. That's why we label this kind of CR talk as "biting the hand that feeds you."

It appears that new work groups and new members in work groups want to spend time on Stages One and Two and enjoy doing so. It also appears that the more consciousness-raising a group does, the wider the symbolic gap between the "we" and the "they" becomes and the more difficult it will be for the "we" and the "they" to work in concert together. Established work groups, which have stable member-ship and have done similar kinds of work for a number of years, spend less time in Stages One and Two. They have developed efficient nicknames for their "theys" and do not need to constantly rehash them. Instead, most of their CR talk occurs in Stages Three and Four (De Vuono 1982).

Stage Three: Establishment of New Values for the Group

We have discovered that Stage Three of a political activist group is dominated by a dialogue that is essentially a constant comparison and contrast of the oppressor's es-tablished value structure with the new values the CR group hopes to promulgate. Gay groups might reject heterosexual society's value structure and argue instead that the quality of the relationship is more important. Women's groups might com-pare their belief in equal pay for equal work with the societal practice in which men receive more money than do women in the same job classification. A CR group often transports itself into the future and vividly describes what the new society would look like if its values were accepted. A Christian CR group might envision a world free of sin and discuss that utopia with great excitement, and an African-American CR group might see a country free of racism.

Work groups, particularly work groups that work under tremendous deadline pressure or that face mutual danger, frequently engage in intense Stage Three talk. These conversations invariably produce consensus on the part of the group members as to the unique abilities that allow their group to be successful. These Stage Three CR sessions produce nicknames and slogans for the group. In an American organiza-tion, what usually follows is the making of T-shirts and bumper stickers that display the group's name, logo, and slogan. Police SWAT units; hospital emergency, surgical, and intensive car units; fire department teams (ladder companies, rescue squads, etc.); television news teams; data-processing system design units; and the sales teams of almost any corporation are likely groups that will engage in heavy CR ses-sions after their crisis-oriented work is completed. CR communication is so dramatic and intense that it is a major feature of novels and movies (e.g., Dolly Parton, Jane Fonda, and Lily Tomlin's movie *Nine to Five*; Joseph Wambaugh's novel *The Choir-boys*; Dennis Smith's novel *Engine Number Six*; Robin Williams's movie *Dead Poets'*

Society; Spike Lee's film *School Daze;* and Goldie Hawn, Diane Keaton, and Bette Midler's movie *First Wives Club*).

It is difficult to predict when a group is formed what attributes are unique to it that will make the "we" better than the "they." Ideally, trained small group discussants should focus on the job-related skills that the individuals possess and on good teamwork, which can account for their high productivity. However, because CR group communication is spontaneous and usually engaged in by people who are not familiar with small group theory, the qualities that the group settles on as being unique may have no relation to their work behavior. The group may decide that it is good because it is all European-American or all African-American, all male or all female, all Italian or all Irish, all Catholic or all Jewish. Problems arise when this kind of group identification occurs in an American work group.

An example of how extreme a group can become occurred in a Midwestern fire department we were studying. The city had a large Swedish-American population, so it was not surprising that by pure chance, an engine company of five firefighters who were assigned to the same firehouse were all of Swedish descent: Johnson, Peterson, Olson, Larson, and Anderson. In Stage One CR discussions, they began to share common stories of being raised in a Swedish-American family. In Stage Two conversation, they talked about competing *lateral-they* fire teams not being as good as they were. By the time they got to Stage Three talk, they became convinced that it was their common Swedish heritage that enabled them to be so good at putting out fires. This led them to name themselves the "Oly Brigade." They made up T-shirts for themselves, they cooked Swedish meals at the firehouse, and their menus were written in Swedish. They even developed a team cheer that was completely in Swedish. Finally, they moved to Stage Four CR and went public. At the next fire, they wore their special T-shirts, had blue and yellow ribbons streaming from the back of the truck, and arrived at the scene of the fire singing their Swedish cheer, much to the chagrin of the other fire teams and the fire chief of the city. The "Oly Brigade" was an excellent fire team. They did good work, but they attributed their work success to the fact that they were Swedish, and their rivalry with other groups had become too competitive. Thus, the group was disbanded by order of the fire chief.

It appears that a continuing problem with CR discussions involving emergency work groups is that they raise their consciousness too high and become elitist. They become increasingly difficult to manage, demanding special privileges because they are known for their good work, and they cause morale problems among work groups who are not as intense. Yet the potential benefits in terms of productivity output that come from CR are such that many American and Japanese organizations have made CR sessions a normal part of the workplace for an even nonemergency and nonsales work groups. Quality circle programs are knowingly, or unknowingly, encouraging CR sessions to occur among their problem-solving groups (quality circles).

Stage Four: Acting Out New Consciousness

Chesebro, Cragan, and McCullough (1973), in their study of radical gay groups, found that the final stage of CR dealt with how gays might relate to other oppressed people who were seeking a cultural revolution. More generally, many times the last stage of a CR session might deal with specific action a group might take to further its own cause. When a professor finds six students knocking on his or her door with specific demands about how a course should be changed, chances are the students participated in a CR session the night before that led them to confront the professor. Much of the zealot behavior we see flowing from organized groups of people may be traced directly to their participation in CR sessions that have helped to build their new social identity.

Some organized groups of people combine CR sessions with complete social isolation and continuous fear of punishment. This combination produces bizarre behavior in which people are transported into a sociopolitical identity that is far removed from society's norms and in which they become capable of behavior that the rest of us would not contemplate. The Symbionese Liberation Army's transformation of Patty Hearst into "Tanya," the documented techniques used by the Moonies and Jim Jones, and the mass suicides of the Davidians at Waco, Texas, and members of the Heaven's Gate cult in San Diego, all vividly demonstrate the ability of CR sessions, when used in combination with other techniques, to produce significant changes in the sociopolitical identities of the people who participate in them.

It seems clear from our observation of American corporations that CR communication is a regular and integral part of all work group communication. It directly affects the group member's sense of identification and pride. Stage Four CR talk is easy to spot because it is filled with suggestions on how the group can advance or sustain its identity. Sometimes this conversation becomes a formal planning session for the group, which begins to transform itself into a task group.

In weekly sales meetings, salespeople are clearly in Stage Four CR when they repeat slogans that are directed toward the goal of selling more products. This is the "rah-rah" part of the conversation right before they go out the door to sell. This same type of communication occurs at the end of a high school pep rally (dancing around the bonfire, etc.). National real estate franchises in the United States frequently engage in Stage Four CR at the end of weekly meetings. At Toyota and other Japanese companies, the work groups in their manufacturing plants participate in Stage Four CR each morning before they begin their workday. All organizations periodically bring together the organization's work groups, which have been consciousness-raising on their own, to a company rally for the purpose of reinforcing that they are all part of the large "we" of an organization. Bringing together all the organization's groups has the effect of reducing all three types of we-they conflict: upward, lateral, and downward. When the small group CR sessions are synchronized with the large group rally, dramatic short-term effects can be created in terms of raising the consciousness of all organizational members. Thus, it is important to know how the communication process of a rally works in coordination with the small group process of CR. This rally process is described in Chapter 10.

Although there are many examples of the misuse of CR by leaders who are intentionally trying to control and manipulate naive individuals, you need to remember that CR is a naturally occurring small group process that must take place if a work group is to develop a group identity. There are right and wrong ways to build group identification. In the skills section of this chapter, we outline five team-building skills that will help you build group identity that is safe for group members to participate in and that helps foster group productivity.

☐ Signposts for Assessing the Quality of Small Group Communication

The perfect group is easier to describe than to create. When a person is participating in a real group, it is difficult to observe the development of various communication stages in the group. There are, however, some rough signposts to help determine what is going on at any given time. These signposts are designed to help you assess the four types of talk that occur in groups and help you determine whether the correct amounts of each are occurring in your various work groups.

Signpost One: Amount of Understanding and Agreement

Both Bales (1970) and Fisher (1974) have found the first stage of a task group to center on orientation. The communication during this stage should contain a lot of questions so that the group will understand the nature of the task. There also should be tacit agreement that everybody accepts the general goals of the group. If a group does not have genuine agreement initially, disagreement and conflict over goals will arise in later discussion and the group will have to return to its orientation stage. What this means is that the group experienced a "pseudo-orientation" phase. Many of the members probably held back their feelings at the beginning of the discussion because they felt socially awkward. The difficulty with interpreting the second stage of a task group—labeled ideational conflict by Fisher and evaluation by Bales—is determining whether the misunderstandings and disagreements are really about the task or whether they are the manifestation of the role struggle for leadership that Bormann called secondary tension (1990). Bales provided some suggested ratios between positive and negative actions and between the task and social dimensions. Therefore, if group members constantly agree to everything, the group will experience a "pseudo-orientation" phase; ideational disagreements need to occur if the group is ever to get into the second stage of its development. Also, without idea conflict, group roles will not form.

Task group communication is complex. Problem-solving talk and role formation talk are occurring simultaneously, whereas CR talk and social talk tend to stand out from the task-related discussion. In fact, we have argued that work groups have natural breakpoints in their discussion: sometimes encounter moments, at other times CR moments, and at still other times group flight. For example, a group could be deeply involved in the conflict stage of problem-solving talk when the rash of ideas becomes so intense that the group spontaneously breaks from the task discussion. One of the group members begins a CR moment by ventilating about the supervisor who had given them this task. For the next few moments, the group is in Stage Two polarization as its members vilify their supervisor in a classic upward-they moment. After this ventilation, the group may then return to the ideational conflict with renewed zest to fight it through. So secondary tension in the social dimension and conflict in the task dimension can often produce CR moments. But it is also possible that the stress of problem solving can produce an encounter moment—such as a situation in which a group member discloses how frustrated his or her spouse is about the amount of time being devoted to this research project. Such a disclosure might cause the group to break from their task to spend time in interpersonal discussion about themselves. Finally, the pressure of group problem-solving work may cause a group to take flight to a topic that has nothing to do with any one of the four dimensions of group talk: not encounter, CR, role, or problem-solving communication, but instead procrastinating chit-chat about such general topics as weather or sports, allowing the group to take a break in place.

Sometimes groups are so afraid of interpersonal conflict, either because they are afraid of losing their jobs or because they can't stand to see people argue, that they will agree to almost any suggestion. Time eventually runs out on this group in that their productivity is poor. Thus, although understanding and agreement are the necessary objectives of a task group, if agreement is overwhelming, something is probably wrong. For any task group to produce a worthwhile product, a certain amount of disagreement or ideational conflict must occur, especially in newly formed work groups.

Signpost Two: Formation of Group Roles

As we just pointed out in discussing group understanding and agreement, disagreements about how to solve the group's task occur almost simultaneously with role struggles in the development of a group. Bormann (1990) stated that there are a number of ways in which role formation may take place in the development of a task group but that central to all group scenarios is the notion that people compete for roles and that our society has attached more status to some roles than to others. It stands to reason, then, that the most coveted role—that of leader—is the one we compete for the most. In fact, some companies give monetary and promotional rewards to the person who emerges as leader, heightening this competition.

There is much that can be done to reduce the tension that accompanies role formation. Mature, experienced small group discussants recognize that the best group product will be produced if each group member attempts to determine what is the best role for him or her to play in terms of the group's needs rather than his or her own needs. We all need to recognize that our social-cultural blinders produce certain stereotypes of certain group roles. We also know that if we act on the basis of these stereotypes, we will have problems. For example, we may give nonverbal cues to a woman in the group to take notes and make an athlete the task leader and a jolly, overweight man the tension releaser. To get by these problems, one must listen carefully and attentively to each group member to determine what members should play what roles for the group's success. As a rule, the more culturally and racially pluralistic the group membership, the greater the struggle in role formation. Once the pluralistic group solves its role problems, it will be above average in its productivity. If one does not perceive that the group members are playing various roles, the chances are great that competition for role formation has not yet occurred; if it has not, the group in fact will not have become a group and group productivity will be low.

Signpost Three: Level of Interpersonal Trust and Empathy

A work group must, by definition, divide up the work load, some of which often gets done outside the group's scheduled meeting time. Interpersonal mistrust often sets in when some members think that they are doing more work than others and are being used by the "lazy" members of the group. Brief interpersonal conflicts may occur at meetings; for example: "Did you get your bibliography done?" "No, I didn't get to the library yet." When this kind of interpersonal conflict occurs in a group, sometimes a mini-encounter session will take place at lunch or in the evening at a member's home. Group members will accuse one another of wearing false faces, and unimportant behaviors that occurred weeks ago during a regular meeting are brought up as clear communication signposts to show that the member does not care about the group. When a group struggles through this phase and reaches a resolution, members usually develop a great deal of empathy for one another's situations, and the group renews its energy and improves its effectiveness.

A work group occasionally performs well in its day-to-day group functioning; its productivity is high and the role struggles have been resolved. Then, in a moment of jubilation, the task leader of the group suggests that the work group socialize together for a weekend. The group members suddenly discover that although they can work together, they can't play together. Interpersonal conflicts that were controlled in task situations become unmanageable in a social setting, and the ensuing encounter session results in the conclusion that the group cannot work together anymore as a work group. The level of self-disclosure that it takes for a work group to perform its task is not nearly as high as the self-disclosure that occurs in an encounter group session. Therefore, work groups must carefully consider whether they should meet at irregular times, particularly in social settings. All work and no play might be just what's called for.

Signpost Four: Degree of Group Identification and Group Pride

Just as people learn to take pride in their accomplishments, so do groups. Work groups that are full of pride are easy to identify because the members exhibit symbols and other behaviors that let everyone know their group exists. As a group competes with other groups, it finds itself holding mini-CR sessions. The reinforcement stage of a task group contains many CR moments. However, CR sessions, like encounter groups, usually occur outside the work schedule.

After work, group members may sit around in social setting and begin to discuss how much better they are than the other work groups and what qualities of their group make them superior. Or they may decide that they are oppressed by another arrogant work group. In either case, the group produces a polarization between "we" and "they," the oppressed group also moving through the traditional CR stages that can lead to confrontation between it and other work groups in the company. There is a perceptible level of group pride present in most groups that is continually changing; yet long-standing work groups may develop a somewhat stable, even traditional, level of group pride so that each new member has his or her pride raised until he or she strongly identifies with the group.

CR sessions are not always beneficial for work groups. Some work groups keep pumping up their level of pride to the point where they become uncontrollable by any outside force. When this happens, the organization usually disbands the group. Some of the specialized police and fire units in large cities experienced the negative effects of too much CR, and their supervisors were forced to disband them.

Another situation in which CR sessions are harmful to a group is when one faction of a work group engages in CR in which the other members of the group are the "they" or "the enemy" of Stage Two. This factionalization can occur when a scheduled meeting is held and only part of the group shows up or when one segment of the work group regularly socializes together. So CR sessions are a mixed blessing for work groups. CR is a powerful means for raising group pride and increasing a member's sense of group identity. Nonetheless, not only can CR sessions make a group so arrogant that no other groups will work with or alongside it, but CR sessions can also intensify the polarization between factions within the group itself.

When a group has sufficient understanding and agreement, role formation, interpersonal trust and empathy, and group identification and pride, we have a cohesive work group that has high levels of productivity, membership satisfaction, and consensus. When problem-solving talk is processed effectively, the amount of understanding and agreement in the group increases, directly affecting the group outputs. And when group roles are developed and properly played, group outputs are also positively affected. It is also necessary for personal disclosures to occur to increase empathy and trust among group members. Although levels of trust and empathy vary from group to group, when appropriate levels are established, productivity, consensus, membership satisfaction, and quality of work are increased. Finally, CR talk affects the degree of group identification and pride, which in turn affects group outcomes.

☐ SUMMARY

This chapter opens with a representation of our model of small group communication, which depicts the relations among communication theory, small group process, communication skills, and group outcomes. The rest of the chapter is devoted to explaining the first three rings of this bull's-eye model.

The major purpose of a task group is to do work. The two fundamental dimensions of a work group are the *task* dimension (problem-solving talk) and the *social* dimension (role talk). Although it's true that each task group develops its own way or pattern for reaching group decisions, research in small group communication does allow us to describe a likely process by which the task and social dimensions of a group occur during the decision-making process. These stages include (1) orientation (task), primary tension (role); (2) conflict (task), secondary tension (role); (3) emergence (task), recurring primary and secondary tension (social); and (4) reinforcement (task). Decision-making and role emergence theories explain these processes.

Encounter group processes provide individuals and groups with an opportunity to look at themselves and allow for self-growth. Task groups can find themselves having "encounter moments" or becoming an encounter group for a period of time. Encounter group process stages include boundary seeking, ambivalence, and actualization. Another major group process one sees develop in work groups is CR. Team pride and group identity are fostered through the CR process. The stages of CR are as follows: (1) self-realization of a new identity, (2) group identity through polarization, (3) establishment of new values for the group, and (4) acting out new consciousness. Encounter and symbolic convergence theories explain these processes. The four signposts for assessing the quality of small group communication (amount of understanding and agreement, formation of group roles, level of interpersonal trust and empathy, and degree of group identification and group pride) aid in determining the maturity and effectiveness of the group.

A Classroom Learning Group

CASE BACKGROUND

For Chapter 2, the professor has asked students to prepare a one- or two-page report identifying the theory or group process that they have the most difficulty comprehending. The students also have to identify how they would explain the bull's-eye model. Discussion begins the next class period, with each student's report in hand. The professor divides the class into five-person groups. Each group's task is to identify the three most difficult parts of the chapter and the group's preferred way of explaining the small group communication model. The group is allowed a three-minute presentation on their findings and recommendations.

CASE LOG

After discussing their individual positions in the group, the five persons reached a consensus on the major problems of the chapter and the preferred method to describe the bull's-eye model. The group selected a spokesperson, and the following is an excerpt of their report. The group outlined their three problems as follows: (1) the difference between CR groups and encounter groups, (2) determining the best way to break primary tension, and (3) the sequencing of the four steps of problem-solving talk.

This group had difficulty identifying an encounter group because none of the members had ever been in one. Only two members had seen the *Breakfast Club* movie. They knew that the encounter group had a lot of self-disclosure about private feelings, but they did not know how these groups produced self-growth in their members. The group wondered whether Weight Watchers, Teens Encounter Christ, or Alcoholics Anonymous were encounter groups or CR groups. Two of the members were in a sorority and could identify stages of consciousness-raising while they were pledges, but other members had difficulty recalling other similar life experiences.

The second problem the group had was determining the best way to break primary tension.

They were confused because breaking primary tension occurred by using both social talk and consciousness-raising. They didn't know whether primary tension could be broken by using both types of talk, or social talk alone, or just CR talk. Further, the group wondered whether primary tension could be broken just be waiting it out or by turning to the task as a means of breaking the silence.

The third problem that the group identified was the sequencing of the four steps of problem-solving talk. Does the chronology of the stages of problem-solving talk hold true for all groups? All the members of the group had been in task groups in which the sequence did not follow the pattern. In their experience they found that groups had to go back to previous stages if the group members met multiple times. Also, everyone had been in groups in which members would suggest solutions almost immediately. In general, the members found decision-making to be "messier" than portrayed in the chapter. They questioned whether this messiness came about because group members were not trained or whether the model was not complete enough to portray differences in problem solving.

This group's preferred approach was to wait for the end of the next chapter, in which they would learn about skills and outcomes; in short, they did not feel they knew enough to explain the model. However, they did feel there were three potential ways they could explain the model. One would be to move from outside in: from theory, to process, to signposts, to skills, to outcomes. The second way would be to move from the inside out, by starting with the four outcomes, then moving to the core skills, then the four signposts, then the four processes, and finally the four theories that explain these processes. The third suggestion was to divide the bull's-eye into four pie slices by explaining the effect of problem-solving talk on group outcomes, role talk on group outcomes, social talk on group outcomes, and CR talk on group outcomes. But the group preferred to withhold judgment on which way was best until they had read the next chapter.

CASE QUESTIONS

1. Do you agree with this group's selection of the three main problems? If not, what would you say are the major problems?

2. What would you say to this group to help them solve the three problems they identified?

3. Which of the three ways would you select to explain the bull's-eye? Or do you think there is a better way to explain small group interaction and its impact on group outcomes?

CHAPTER THREE

PERFORMING CORE COMMUNICATION SKILLS

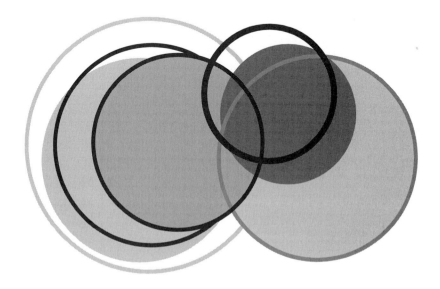

CHAPTER OBJECTIVES

After reading this chapter, you should be able to:

- Recognize the twenty core communication skills for problem-solving groups
- Describe the four major group outcomes
- Understand the group problem-solving road map

This chapter completes the inner two rings of the bull's-eye model. The chapter focuses on the twenty core communication skills and their impact on the four group outcomes. The last section of the chapter explains the relationships among communication skills, processes, and outcomes by means of a road map model.

☐ TWENTY CORE COMMUNICATION SKILLS FOR PROBLEM-SOLVING GROUPS

Table 3.1 presents twenty core communication skills for problem-solving groups that flow from decision-making theory, role emergence theory, encounter theory, and symbolic convergence theory. These core skills actuate the four communication processes of a problem-solving group. When these four sets of skills are performed competently, the four signposts are observable. These twenty skills lead directly to the attainment of the four group outcomes of productivity, quality of work, consensus, and membership satisfaction. It is best to view these core skills as the bare minimum necessary for a problem-solving group to function. By the time you finish this book, we will have introduced you to eighty additional communication skills.

Problem-Solving Skills

■ *Contribute to group orientation.* Everyone feels awkward or withdrawn during the first moments of a meeting, especially if it is the first meeting of a newly formed work group. It is easy for us to hold back and let someone else break the ice. It is also easy to avoid asking clarification questions, although just about everyone is anxious to know the purpose of the meeting. Experienced small group discussants resist these feelings of inhibition and assert themselves at the outset of the discussion, not only by asking questions but also by suggesting and evaluating ideas. These kinds of communication (questions, idea suggestions, and idea evaluations) are risk-taking behaviors. Nobody likes to appear foolish or ignorant, especially in the early stages of group formation; however, successful problem-solving discussions occur more frequently

TABLE **3.1**   **Twenty Core Communication Skills for Problem-Solving Groups**

Problem-Solving Skills	Role-Playing Skills	Trust-Building Skills	Team-Building Skills
Contribute to group orientation	Help in role formation	Risk self-disclosure	Build group pride
Seek information and opinions	Be role-flexible	Avoid stereotyped judgments	Create symbols and slogans
Maximize ideational conflict	Help ease primary tension	Be an emphatic listener	Establish group traditions
Separate people, ideas, and criticism	Ensure that the central negative role is played	Recognize individual differences	Tell sacred stories
Examine advantages and disadvantages of solutions	Support the task leader	Provide emotional security for all members	Initiate group fantasies

when the group members are willing to take communication risks. Communication research has shown the importance of orientation behavior in small groups. It has been established that there is a positive relation between increases in orientation behavior and increases in consensus (Gouran 1969; Kline 1972; Knutson 1972).

■ *Seek information and opinions.* By seeking information and opinions from discussants, one can improve the quality of the dialogue taking place. As a general rule, almost as many questions as statements should be voiced during the evaluation phase of a group. This questioning provides a vehicle for the full exploration of necessary information and opinions regarding the discussion topic at hand. Bales's (1970) research at Harvard University supports the importance of good groups asking lots of questions. When in doubt as to what to do in a group, ask a question. Question asking has been identified as an important behavior in problem-solving groups for more than thirty years (Fisher 1970; Scheidel and Crowell 1964).

■ *Maximize ideational conflict.* If we could reduce this book to one sentence, it might well be this one: Maximize ideational conflict in your work group without adversely affecting role formation, interpersonal relations, or professional respect. Mature, cohesive groups can tolerate a high degree of idea conflict without fear of offending one another personally or professionally and with the central negative role vigorously played. New and fragile groups avoid ideational clashes for fear of offending and, thus, often reach mediocre to bad decisions. Thus, the test of the maturity of a problem-solving group is how much ideational conflict can be tolerated without the group's losing its cohesion.

■ *Separate people, ideas, and criticism.* In new problem-solving groups, it is difficult for members to assert themselves by suggesting ideas to the group. When we don't know other group members very well, we don't want to appear stupid; if our ideas immediately receive negative criticism, we might be unwilling to risk further ideas to more criticism. In Chapter 4, we present two formal group procedures for separating people, ideas, and idea criticism. They are nominal group and brainstorming techniques. If a group does not use a formal technique, the separation of people and ideas can be done informally. The task leader can say, "Let's all suggest ideas and then put them on the table to evaluate." This simple skill tends to give group owner-ship rather than individual ownership to ideas. Simply by allowing time to elapse between the suggestion of an idea and its criticism does much to reduce the fear of personal criticism on the part of group members. This communication skill is so im-portant that virtually all the companies that develop software used in same time–same place cyborg meetings advertise as one of the strengths of their programs that people can contribute ideas from their terminals without fear of criticism. Remem-ber, it takes team building and trust building before a lot of ideational criticism can take place. New groups need to be careful that they do not hurt one another's feel-ings through rapid-fire criticism of members' ideas.

■ *Examine advantages and disadvantages of solutions.* The functional decision-making theory explains that there are key task communication behaviors that must be per-formed well for a group to reach a high-quality decision (Gouran and Hirokawa 1983). Two of these functions are examining the advantages and disadvantages of each proposed solution. The reason these two communication skills must be done competently is to ensure that the group does not bring premature closure to the dis-cussion by quickly agreeing to the first good solution they hear. If the group does not carefully examine the advantages and disadvantages of each solution, it may experi-ence what we label a "false pregnancy." An old cat that comes around the communi-cation building every spring has false pregnancies. She drags a pencil or small stuffed animal around and treats it like her kitten. She shows off her "kitten" to us, and we praise her for being a good mother cat. Then she goes away happy. Some-times new groups act like Thumbelina. They seize prematurely on a possible solu-tion to their problem. They act as though it is the greatest discovery of the twenty-first century and congratulate themselves on the birth of their idea. In truth, what they have is a below-average solution. The group could have had a better solution if the members had been willing to examine the advantages and disadvantages of vari-ous alternatives. Therefore, it should be normative behavior for all task groups to look at the advantages and disadvantages of several solutions to their problems.

Role-Playing Skills

■ *Help in role formation.* Shepherd (1964, 122–123) stated: "A successful group is one in which each member's role is clear and known to himself [or herself] and to others in the group." Although role clarification is a well-understood goal in the development of a group, the means to that end are less clear. Newly formed work groups and long-standing groups that have had changes in membership must engage in a lot of experi-mentation to determine what roles a member can best play. Group development is re-tarded when experimentation is discouraged. Members should be encouraged to try different roles. For example, one member might become comfortable in the role of in-formation provider, but the group might suspect that the person is better suited for a leadership role. It is also important to recognize that role formation is a dynamic, not a static, phenomenon in group development. Even established groups manifest some changes in role playing. So it is important to clarify in your mind continually what roles are being played by what members for the benefit of the group.

■ *Be role-flexible.* Research has shown that people play different roles in differ-ent groups because the tasks are different and the people forming the groups are different. We also know that members change roles within a group when there is new membership. Thus, if you find yourself continually playing the same role in different groups, you are probably in a "role rut."

People get into role ruts not because the other members constantly force the same role on them, but because they campaign hard for a certain role. The easiest ruts to see are those in which the same people continually wind up being the task leader, the tension releaser, and the recorder in group discussions. If you find yourself continually emerging as leader of a work group, try out for another role in a group you join. You may discover that in some groups, you are better able to relieve tension than be the task leader. If you are always the first one to speak when the group grows silent and if you constantly try to make people laugh when they are uncomfortable with one another, you might try resisting your temptation to speak and wait to see whether someone else can play the role. Ideally, groups try to fit the right people into each role. If you push too hard for a given role, it may reduce the optimum efficiency of the group at best and cause unnecessary social conflict at worst.

■ *Help ease primary tension.* If somebody is trying to break the primary tension of the group with humor, that person should be encouraged through positive feedback and not socially ignored with looks of disinterest. We must remember that we all feel socially insecure in the first moments of a small group meeting, and it is only through helping one another that we can get through primary tension. It is also important to remember to use humor that is funny to everyone in the group; thus, sexual, racial, and ethnic humor are dangerous. Lighthearted humor directed at the "theys" who gave the group its problem-solving assignment can provide safe corporate chuckles.

■ *Ensure that the central negative role is played.* High levels of ideational conflict are essential for good group decisions. It is important that group members feel comfortable when playing the role of central negative. Janis (1983, 267) believes that the central negative role is so important in the avoidance of groupthink that he would have groups formally assign a person to the role. We don't advocate formally assigning someone to a role, but we do recommend that all group members be alert that the central negative role is being played. Sometimes this role is called the devil's advocate. If the same person plays this role all the time, there can be harmful side effects. The group will think that the person is too cynical and not loyal to the group. For that reason, it is good to pass the central negative role around and let a number of people play this role at various times.

■ *Support the task leader.* Secondary tension is the period in the group's life when members are searching for a task leader. When a person begins to emerge as leader, all members should encourage and support that member. The leader tends to do more work in a group and shoulder more responsibility; therefore, it is important that he or she have the full support of the group. This is especially important and difficult for the group if the task leader is not the appointed or designated supervisor of the work group. In Chapter 7, we discuss in depth the distinctions between designated and emergent leaders.

Trust-Building Skills

■ *Risk self-disclosure.* When you feel comfortable with the task the group is performing, you should take the risk of self-disclosure. Groups suffer from underdisclosure, especially if the members believe that they are fundamentally different from one another. Disclosure by one member usually leads to disclosure by other members. If you pick disclosures about yourself that are relevant to the group's task and if they are disclosures you have made to other groups in the past without harmful effects, the risks to you should be minimal, and you will contribute to the growth of the group's overall maturity. These self-disclosures are not necessarily weaknesses or insecurities on your part but may in fact be revelations about your strength or expertise. A group needs to know the personal strengths of its individual members to maximize its productivity.

■ *Avoid stereotyped judgments.* Small group research clearly indicates that the more pluralistic a group is, the more difficult time it will have in forming. This is partly due to our tendency to stereotype people. If we notice only a person's gender, age, or race and cannot even remember his or her name, chances are we are stereotyping that person on the basis of demographic information rather than seeing him or her as a distinct individual. Another indication of the stereotyping that goes on in groups can be observed by listening to a new group trying to recall who the missing member is. A newly formed classroom group might say, "The missing member is that old married woman who is trying to be a college student again." When group members are asked about this kind of stereotyping, they usually respond with a cliché such as, "We're good at remembering faces but poor at remembering names!" What they are really saying is that it is easier to stereotype people on their demographics than it is to understand a distinct personality. So fight the tendency to categorize group members superficially, and listen carefully to what each member has to say. This sort of extra effort will go a long way toward building trust and understanding in your group.

■ *Be an empathetic listener.* The empathetic listening skill that is emphasized here is paraphrasing. Paraphrasing should occur at both the emotional and the ideational level of a group discussion. Group members often disclose common past experiences, but no one listens to anyone else. When one group member is talking about his or her successes as a high school athlete, another member might not be empathetically listening but eagerly waiting to tell his or her athletic story. Paraphrasing a person's interpersonal disclosure is an excellent way to assure him or her that you were listening. If you say, "Oh, so you played three years of high school basketball," the other person will probably elaborate on his or her story and feel more emotionally secure in the group. The payoff is an altogether improved perception of that person by the group.

Paraphrasing is also an important communication strategy for clarifying the ideas that a group is discussing. When a group is on an interesting topic, the members tend to throw in their ideas one after another without anyone attempting to paraphrase the ideas to check whether everyone understands what is being said. The paraphrasing of another member's position not only aids in the clarification of the group's thought process, but also reassures the member that his or her ideas are being listened to and appreciated.

■ *Recognize individual differences.* As Carl Rogers (1970, 137) indicated in his well-known book *Carl Rogers on Encounter Groups,* one of the objectives that the National Training Laboratory suggested as being important to organizations is to build trust among individuals and groups for the health of the organization as well as the welfare and development of the individual. In fact, Rogers (1970, 114) said of himself: "I enjoy life very much more when I am not defensive, not hiding behind a facade, but just trying to be and express the real me." The encounter moments in the life of a work group allow the group to better understand the unique qualities of each member. Some of these individual differences everybody likes and celebrates; however, every member has some personality traits and behaviors that are irritating to other group members. Learning to tolerate and accommodate some of the more unpleasant aspects of a group member is one of the surest ways to help a group develop and mature. People do their best work when they feel that they can be themselves in the group. A group environment that is tolerant of individual differences will work toward the elimination of what Carl Rogers has called a personal facade.

- *Provide emotional security for all members.* If the interpersonal climate of a group is safe enough for the most insecure member, then the group as a whole should be quite healthy. Therefore, you should attempt to determine which group member is most likely to feel excluded from the group, dominated by the group, or disliked by the group. If you make an effort to make that person feel comfortable, wanted, and included during the discussions, then the overall emotional security of the group should be strengthened.

Team-Building Skills

- *Build group pride.* CR sessions have the effect of highlighting the positive characteristics of the group that can be the source of a group's pride. Unfortunately, this process is a comparative one, and the group runs the risk of exaggerating its superiority over other groups. Therefore, it is important that the group build its pride on a solid foundation of measurable productivity. It may be necessary for you to play the devil's advocate when CR is taking place and argue that the competing work groups have redeeming values. You may also want to tone down the vilification of the enemy. The upward we-they polarization between first-line work groups and upper management can become so exaggerated that it may hurt promotions within the work group. Furthermore, downward organizational communication may not be perceived as credible, thus injuring group productivity. Although building the group's sense of pride is important, it can reach a point of diminishing returns, where it is no longer helpful to the group's productivity.
- *Create symbols and slogans.* Bormann and Bormann (1976, 70) observed: "Highly cohesive groups also always work out ways to identify their group; sometimes these are as obvious as insignia, or mascots, or the use of nicknames." After a group has established some ability to do work, the naming of the group can be formally discussed as an agenda item with beneficial results. Thinking of a name or logo for a group helps the group to discover what all the members take pride in.

Many of the discussion groups we have had in class could recall the nicknames of their groups years later. These group names often capture the essence of the group. For example, some of our student groups named themselves "The Fantastics," "The Uncohesives," "The Six-Pack," and "The Best of the Rest." "The Fantastics" were indeed fantastic—they won all the classroom games, they wrote the best exams, and they presented the best classroom discussions. "The Uncohesives" had a difficult time in becoming a group. They finally began to take pride in the fact that they had nothing in common and worked together on that basis. "The Six-Pack" was a tremendous party group—they wrote the worst exams, but they had a great time preparing for them." "The Best of the Rest" was not a better group than the "Fantastics" but better than all the rest.

U.S. corporations that have adopted quality circle programs have rediscovered the importance of work groups' developing names and slogans for themselves, depicting their unique contributions to organizational productivity. Custom-designed T-shirts and caps are commonplace today, not only for college groups but also for corporate work teams. Although members will initially think that it is childish to name their group, develop a logo, and write a slogan, once these tasks have been accomplished, they will have powerful rhetorical labels to help them become a group and maintain their group pride.

■ *Establish group traditions.* Tradition plays an important role in group life. Most of us have a member of our extended family who is the keeper of the family stories. At Thanksgiving or other traditional holidays, the family gathers and soon Uncle John or Aunt Mary begins to recall humorous anecdotes about family members. These stories help to maintain the family's sense of oneness and immortality. Many work groups within organizations behave in the same way. You may join a law firm that is a hundred years old and discover that there is a whole collection of stories about the firm's past accomplishments that compel you to do your best. All work groups should spend some time dwelling on their past accomplishments and retelling old stories as a means of both maintaining the group's maturity and assimilating new members into the group. New groups that are formed for short periods need to create a sense of tradition. Even in environments such as data-processing departments, in which small work groups are constantly formed and re-formed to perform tasks of short duration, it is important to celebrate traditions such as "We always have lunch at Charlie's when we finish writing a program in this department."

■ *Tell sacred stories.* Sometimes ill-advised work groups use the mushroom philosophy in orienting a new employee to his or her work group in the organization. The basis of this philosophy is to keep new members in the dark as much as possible. Enlightened supervisors initiate conversations with new employees and inform them, through the company's stories, about what is considered to be correct behavior with the organization. For example, if padding expenses by the sales staff is a long-standing pet peeve among the organization's managers, then the new employee needs to hear the stories about unfortunate Albert and Alice who were fired because they billed the company for a dinner they didn't eat.

Sacred stories are sacred because they are stories that reveal beliefs with respect to productivity, social behavior, and company policy that long-standing members of the organization understand and normally follow. The basis of any practical joke on a new employee usually revolves around getting the employee to go against the principles embedded in a sacred story. In one organization we have studied, a plush elevator is reserved for top management and is supposed to be used only by them and the people who work on the top two floors of the home office building. The marketing work group in this company enjoys instructing a new employee that he or she is required to ride the executive elevator. About the second time the new employee gets on with a group of executives and stops on the third floor, the new employee is told sternly that he or she should not ride on the executive elevator. The vice-presidents of the company are aware of the marketing division's standing joke and always play their roles to the hilt! Thus, the real sacred story is not that one elevator is reserved for executives, but that the vice-presidents know about marketing's practical joke and enjoy participating in it.

■ *Initiate group fantasies.* An important but frequently overlooked communication skill is a group member's ability to initiate group fantasies. This is an essential communication behavior in building group pride, identification, and motivation. There are four types of group fantasies that need to be created and understood about work groups. They are fantasies about individual group members, fantasies about the group's teamwork, fantasies about the group's personality, and fantasies to neutralize negative fantasies about the group.

Ken "Hawk" Harrelson and Tom "Wimpy" Paciorek, sports broadcasters for the Chicago White Sox, are skilled fantasizers. They have created and dramatized nicknames for star players, and the team members as well as the fans in the stands and home television audience have adopted the nicknames. Frank Thomas, all-star first baseman for the White Sox, was nicknamed "The Big Hurt" because he "hurt" the ball when he hit it and he "hurt" the opposition with his batting ability. This fantasy about Frank is much better than ones that could have been created. He could have been called "Finicky Frank" because he walks more than one hundred times a year. He could have been called "Moose" because he is six feet five inches tall and weighs 260 pounds. "The Big Hurt" is the correct fantasy because it dramatizes Thomas's baseball ability and contribution to the team as compared with "Moose," which refers to his size.

The slogan for the Three Musketeers epitomizes the teamwork fantasy: "All for one and one for all!" You can probably quickly make a list of group fantasy types, such as "United we stand, divided we fall," "The chain is only as strong as its weakest link," and "Improvise, adapt, and overcome." The *Chicago Tribune,* in the fall of 1993, headlined their coverage of President Clinton's national health care program with the fantasy "Seize the day!" The movie *Dead Poets Society* created the fantasy "Seize the day" to characterize the students who made up the Dead Poets Society. President Clinton used this fantasy to tell Congress what it needed to do.

Just as an individual can be fantasized about, so can a group develop fantasies that describe its group personality. A group member may dramatize a group as hardnosed, stressing the group's tenacious, aggressive behavior when attacking a problem. There are also well-worn fantasy types for characterizing group personality, expressed in sayings such as "When the going gets tough, the tough get going" and "When our backs are against the wall is when we stand tall." Sometimes the group personality is projected as being synonymous with their leader's personality, such as "Mary's Marauders," "Roger's Rangers," and "Arnie's Army."

In organizations, groups compete and, as a result, develop vilifying fantasies of competing groups. For example, in the fire service, the people who specialize in handling hazardous materials are known as the "Mop and Glow" team, and the firefighters who specialize in rescuing people from high-rise building fires are known as "Dopes on a Rope." Sometimes physicians refer to dentists as those people who "drill, fill, and bill." And for professors, "If you can't do it, you teach it." The fantasy that is used most often to protect new members from negative fantasies comes from Australia. The Australians say they "cut the tall poppy," which means that when one Australian starts to become too successful (for example, Paul Hogan, Olivia Newton-John, or Mel Gibson), other Australians find fault with them and cut them down.

Thus, new members of a successful work group are told: "The reason other people make up nicknames for us is because we are so successful as a group. They're just jealous of our abilities!"

☐ Major Group Outcomes

Task groups are evaluated by answering four questions: What did the group accomplish? How good a job was it? What decision-making process did the group use? Are the group members satisfied with the work they did? The answers to these questions can be found by assessing the group's productivity, quality of work, consensual behavior, and membership satisfaction.

Productivity

Many times after people have worked hard to form a cohesive task group, particularly a discussion group that can be counted on to formulate clear policies, they become cynical and frustrated with what appears to be a lot of wasted effort. In any organization, you can hear daily ventilations of the problem of getting work done in groups. We continually ask ourselves whether group work is superior to individual work. In periods of depression, we say things like "A camel is a horse that has been built by a committee," or "If you want to kill or delay an idea, appoint a task force to study it." We all believe that we waste a lot of time attending group meetings.

The frustration of participating in group discussions and committee meetings is further compounded by mismanagement. Even when groups are formed for the right reasons, the meetings are not well run. We have all been called to meetings that were not well planned. We have all sat through rambling monologues that extended even beyond the already generous amount of time allotted for the group meeting. Our own past experience tells us that group discussions are overused and misused. However, there is a firm research base to support the contention that in a number of different settings and over a range of different types of problems, groups outperform individuals.

Marvin E. Shaw (1976, 71–81) provided a succinct summary of hypotheses gleaned from the small group research, identifying differences between individual and group productivity. One of the most important hypotheses that Shaw proposed is the following: "Groups usually produce more and better solutions to problems than do individuals working alone." The essence of this hypothesis is twofold. First, groups tend to produce more ideas in general and more discussion solutions in particular. This tendency is especially pronounced when we look at the number of ideas that can be produced in a brainstorming session. We can take five individuals and have them brainstorm individually and collectively; almost without exception, the collective group will produce more ideas. A second aspect of the Shaw hypothesis focuses on the belief that groups produce better solutions to problems than do individual group members working alone. Other things being equal, this is a valid assumption. With a larger number of ideas produced, we hope to be able to include a larger number of proposals of high quality. The tendency to produce high-quality decisions is heightened if the decisions have been processed by individuals working in a group.

Sometimes we use groups to solve problems and make decisions when one superior member of the group might have made a better decision on his or her own. We often opt for a group decision, knowing full well that it will take twice as long to arrive at it than if we made the decision on our own. The reason for doing so is not necessarily that we think the decision will be better but that some decisions *ought* to be group decisions. As Americans, we have strong commitments to democratic ideals. Every organization has a collection of decisions that must be reached through group processes.

At our university, we have a parking problem. We think that it is worse than at most places, but it may be that all colleges and universities have parking problems "worse than anybody else's." We are convinced that either one of the authors or any other professor taken at random could make better decisions about how to handle parking tickets than does our parking committee. We venture to say that every faculty member and student on campus believes that he or she could do the same. We use a parking committee, not because it makes better decisions—and certainly not because it makes faster decisions—but because we are committed to the organizational principle that incidents involving competing interests should be resolved through a group process. Although it is tempting to suspend this ideal in the case of parking, we would become hysterical if the principle were to be suspended regarding the curriculum of the university. We would feel fundamentally disenfranchised if professors and students did not participate in the design of the curriculum, and there we have the nub and rub of it. The college curriculum committee does not necessarily make faster or better decisions, but we are unalterably committed to the principle that this committee's work should reflect a group decision. And so, in all organizations, in varying degrees, we find a collection of policies that must be decided on by a group. So the question is not really whether a group decision is better than an individual decision, but how to get the best group decision.

Quality of Work

The Ford Motor Company spent millions of dollars advertising that "Quality is Job 1" in their company. General Motors spent millions telling the world through television ads that they had won the coveted Deming Prize for the production of their Cadillac. Motorola's public relations department tells all their employees, and anyone else who will listen, that the company is dedicated to Total Quality Management. These *Fortune* 500 companies do not throw millions of dollars around dramatizing trivial ideas. They recognize that quality of work is key to surviving in a competitive global market. You need to take the lead from these companies that quality of work is Job 1 for your task work groups.

The core communication skills of team building, trust building, role playing, and problem solving have a direct impact on the quality of work done by a task group. Small group communication competency and the quality of group work have been linked in a number of experimental studies (Gouran, Hirokawa, McGee, and Miller 1993). These studies have established that the competent performance of several problem-solving skills causes groups to make better decisions. We would argue not only that these studies are correct but that the absence of quality can destroy a group. If a work group is judged to have produced low-quality work, that fact will eat through the fabric of cohesion like battery acid. The group's professional pride will take a nosedive. Group trust will be eroded, and members will start blaming one another for poor work. Role instability will occur, and the group will question its decision-making process. A small work group must produce high-quality work or it will soon disintegrate. Upjohn, an American pharmaceutical company, for a hundred years has had the slogan, "Keep the Quality Up," and so should your group.

The role that management plays in evaluating the quality of group work in an organization is critical. In companies that use quality circle programs, management must still decide whether to accept or reject proposals that come from individual quality circle groups. When a quality circle has several ideas rejected in a row, it becomes disillusioned and cynical. Membership falls off, productivity goes down, and team morale is seriously harmed. In companies where organizations have rejected large numbers of proposals, the entire quality circle program has been destroyed. The lesson to be learned is that groups have to start with projects that have high promise of success so that there is a cushion of confidence to soften the rejection of some of their decisions by management. In turn, management must recognize the fragile nature of new decision-making groups. Once a group has established a tradition of quality work, they will be able to handle changes in group and organizational membership.

Consensus

Consensus, or unanimous agreement on a decision by group members, is a key small group outcome variable. When complete agreement is achieved by a group, the benefits the group receives in terms of increased cohesion and commitment to the agreed-upon course of action make this kind of group outcome superior to compromise or majority vote.

If a group commits itself to a consensual decision, the journey will be longer and harder and the discussion will have more conflict than if a decision by majority vote could prevail. However, the communication patterns that are needed for consensus encourage active participation on the part of all group members and require a fair weighing of the major issues. These communication patterns not only produce a more enthusiastic group, but also increase the possibility of a better decision.

A compromise or majority vote decision is not the same as a consensual decision. It is important for a group to be able to say that they all agreed on one course of action. If the agreement is not consensual, then there were members who were unable to state that they were for the course of action. If the group establishes a history of having the same members in the role of the minority, the group's cohesion and, ultimately, its performance will suffer. If a group decision then requires group collective action, the "no" votes during the discussion may turn to negative behavior in carrying out the group's policy. In the long run, it may be worth the extra time and effort to find a policy that everyone can agree to, so that no member will drag his or her feet.

Because consensual agreement is such a valuable output of group discussion, sometimes inexperienced discussion leaders try to force consensus when it is not there. This apparent consensus can be much worse than compromise or a majority vote decision in that members feel herded and browbeaten into agreement. In this situation, the leader might say, "We are all in agreement on Sally's solution, aren't we?" when in fact the group members may not yet have achieved consensus on all aspects of the problem. If a discussion leader is to err, it should be in the direction of seeking out points of disagreement when in fact none remain.

In the day-to-day work of a decision-making group, time does not allow consensual agreement on all or, in some work environments, even on most group decisions. Time pressure does not mean that a group should not strive for consensus. When a group reaches consensus, the members should celebrate that moment and make it a vivid part of their group history.

Member Satisfaction

Within our work environment, we often are assigned to groups. In our communities, we volunteer to be part of civic and social service groups. In the work environment, we say that we tolerate groups because we have to work in them—although if that were the case, how do we explain the social service groups we eagerly join? The answer is that groups fulfill needs that vary from individual to individual; that is, we enjoy being part of some groups. Thus, membership satisfaction is an important test of a good group.

Membership satisfaction is an important group outcome variable. We know this not only because we like to go to certain group meetings just for the personal satisfaction it brings us but also because we find some status in being associated with a group effort. We would not feel the intensity of this variable of member satisfaction unless we were also satisfied, to some extent, with the group product. Although membership satisfaction is the most interpersonally oriented group outcome, it is also related to group composition factors and productivity.

In the course of your academic career, you will probably be part of some loosely formed study group that has as its purpose the intellectual advancement of its members. Some groups are formed for only one semester for one course, whereas others last for several semesters and range over many areas of intellectual interest. If you stop to analyze what attracts you to this kind of group, you might notice that you enjoy the intellectual stimulation of other students. If your group develops some history, you may discover that you derive member satisfaction from the better grades that have proved to be one of the results of interaction. If your group begins to celebrate its proven track record and develops enough pride to name itself and prescribe some regular rituals, you will soon feel a third kind of member satisfaction that derives from the status of belonging to a known intellectual group on campus. Thus, member satisfaction occurs at three levels: the enjoyment of interaction with fellow members, the quality of product produced, and the pride of group membership.

☐ GROUP PROBLEM-SOLVING ROAD MAP: A PROCESS VIEW

When a new group is assigned a problem to solve, its communication process is not random. In fact, research in communication on groups is sufficiently advanced that we can provide a rich description of what is going to happen to the group. Figure 3.1 maps out what we know about small group communication processes. The road that the group must travel to achieve its goals has two lanes. One lane is *problem-solving*

FIGURE 3.1   **Group Problem-Solving Road Map: A Process View**

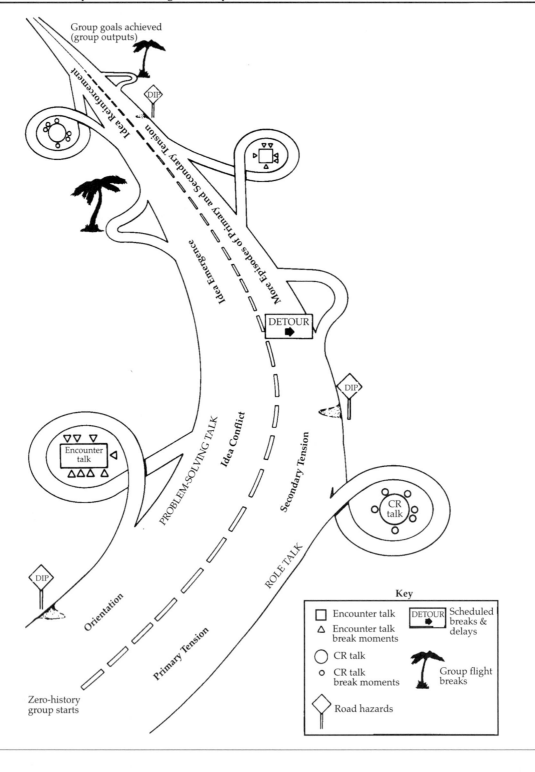

Group goals achieved
(group outputs)

Idea Reinforcement

More Episodes of Primary and Secondary Tension

DETOUR

Idea Emergence

DIP

Encounter
talk

PROBLEM-SOLVING TALK

Idea Conflict

Secondary Tension

CR
talk

ROLE TALK

DIP

Orientation

Primary Tension

ROLE TALK

Zero-history
group starts

Key

☐ Encounter talk

△ Encounter talk
    break moments

◯ CR talk

∘ CR talk
    break moments

◇ Road hazards

DETOUR Scheduled
        breaks &
        delays

Group flight
breaks

talk, which contains the four stages of orientation, idea conflict, idea emergence, and idea reinforcement. The second lane is *role talk*, which developmentally contains two stages: *primary tension* and *secondary tension*, with recurring stages of both. Ideally, a group would stay on this road until it achieves its goals. However, such trips seldom occur. Groups normally take a number of breaks that help to marshal their strength and resolve to solve their problem. For example, sometimes a group may be experiencing a great deal of idea conflict, and some members might become worried that personal feelings are being hurt. At this point, a group may take a break from the discussion and converse about their feelings toward one another. This *encounter talk* may reassure the group members that everyone is OK and they can safely *reenter* the problem-solving discussion. At other times, a group *exits* from problem-solving talk and engages in consciousness-raising (CR), or team-building, talk. The members may spend several minutes taking this *break* while reassuring themselves that they are a good group, possibly reliving some past successes they have had or maybe vilifying competing work groups or the supervisor who assigned them to the task. Again, after this morale-building break, they will reenter problem-solving talk.

In addition to *CR* and *encounter break moments,* groups often have scheduled breaks or unexpected delays that temporarily deter them from their tasks. It is also common for a group to procrastinate by taking *group flight* from its assigned tasks, discussing topics that have nothing to do with the group or its work. Finally, a group encounters *road hazards* on its problem-solving trip. Throughout this book, we illuminate these potential hazards for you. For example, in Chapter 9, we explain a major road hazard called groupthink. In keeping with the road trip metaphor, we are trying to measurably improve your ability to engage in successful group problem-solving trips.

☐ SUMMARY

In the previous chapter you became acquainted with some of the major theories and processes of small group communication. In this chapter we wanted you to begin actualizing these theories and processes through the performance of core communication skills in order to achieve major group outcomes.

Our integrated model of communication shows the interrelated elements that work toward the realization of the major group outcomes of productivity, quality of work, consensus, and member satisfaction. These outcomes are realized, to no small extent, by the competent performance of twenty communication skills in the areas of problem solving, role playing, team building, and trust building. Also, we describe the interactions among the four types of group talk by means of our group problem-solving road map.

A College Classroom Group

CASE BACKGROUND

Harry Gordon, Sue Brodeski, Felicia Jones, Donna Doyle, Bill Baker, Angela Juarez, and Juan DeCardona were members of a sophomore speech communication discussion class. Their professor had arbitrarily assigned them to one discussion group. Their assignment was to present a forty-five-minute panel discussion before the class. They were allowed three weeks to select the topic and prepare for the classroom presentation. They were given four class periods in which to prepare; however, they were urged to meet outside of class as well. Their topic was limited to some relevant campus issue. The professor indicated that they would receive a group grade based on the quality of their panel discussion. This grade would account for 15 percent of their course grade. Each member was to keep a diary of the group interaction and turn it in one period after the panel discussion. There was no grade attached to the diary assignment; however, credit was given for turning it in. The instructor required the group to come up with a name and slogan for itself.

CASE LOG

Meeting One: In Classroom

After the seven members of the group had moved their chairs into a circle, Harry broke what seemed like a long silence with a suggestion that they move around the circle with each person introducing himself or herself, stating his or her major and year in school. Harry indicated that he was a senior business administration major. Sue stated that she was also a senior, majoring in speech communication; Juan was a second-semester freshman who had not yet declared his major, and Bill was a corrections major. After introductions, Harry immediately suggested that the group select the topic.

(Long silence)

FELICIA: Before we go about the task of selecting a topic, perhaps we should just name ourselves.

(Silence)

JUAN: Let's call ourselves the "Chain Gang," since the professor forced us to name ourselves.

(Laughter)

DONNA: That's a good idea! Maybe our group slogan should be "With ball and chain the seven links will be as strong as its weakest link thinks!"

(More laughter)

ANGELA: Yeah, we're chained together in Room 223 for the rest of the semester! The Twilight Zone!

(At this point, Juan jumped up and started walking around the room with an imaginary ball and chain. Group continued to laugh at Juan's miming behavior.)

FELICIA: OK, it's agreed then. We'll be the "Chain Gang"!

HARRY: I don't care what we call ourselves. What's important is our discussion topic and doing a good job with it. With 15 percent of my grade riding on this, I can't afford a "C" in my senior year.

SUE: This group can't be all fun and games with me either. I have to keep my 3.5 average to get my internship spring semester. But since I have my own "ball and chain" that I've been married to for ten years, I can identify with the group name!

(Uneasy group laughter)

ANGELA: We like the name too because Donna, Felicia, and I are roommates in Waterson Towers. But I can't imagine living with them for ten years!

JUAN: Do you have any children, Sue?

SUE: I'm chained to two of them too. I've been a mother and wife for the past ten years but rarely Sue!

(Uneasy silence after Sue's remarks. Felicia finally suggested that they exchange names, phone numbers, and schedules. To their dismay, the group found that the only available time to meet was in the evening.)

Meeting Two: In Classroom

Sue was absent for this meeting.

JUAN: Our chain gang has a missing link.

ANGELA: Maybe one of her kids is sick. It must be difficult coming back to college in your thirties.

HARRY: Well, are we ready to select a topic for our discussion?

BILL: What about the new basketball arena? I think everyone would be interested in that.

JUAN: Well, you're interested in that because you're on the basketball team.

BILL: I thought it was a good idea because I have information on this topic. But you can do what you want.

FELICIA: That's a good one, Bill. Why doesn't everyone else contribute an idea for a topic?

HARRY: I transferred in from a community college and there is no organization to help J.C. transfers. We should have a discussion on that.

ANGELA: I'd like us to discuss the process for bringing entertainment to campus. It seems directed more toward the "townies." What students want to see Tony Bennett or Andy Williams?!

(Laughter)

JUAN: Or what about the townies' attitudes toward college students' drinking?

BILL: Yeah, we're the only university that doesn't allow tailgating parties.

(The next ten to fifteen minutes of the meeting are spent discussing townspeople's attitudes toward college students.)

FELICIA: We've gotten off the topic, I think. Perhaps we should have our next meeting outside of class. Where, my dorm room?

(Everyone agreed to meet at 7:00 that night.)

Meeting Three: In Dorm Room

By 7:30 P.M., Bill, Harry, and Juan had not arrived.

SUE: Here are the women waiting for the men again! Men haven't changed. They were threatened by female leadership fifteen years ago and they still can't handle it.

(Laughter)

DONNA: Maybe Bill didn't show up because Juan trashed his idea about the basketball arena.

FELICIA: Speak of the devil, here comes Bill now.

BILL: Sorry I'm late, but coach kept us late at practice. Where are we?

FELICIA: We're still trying to select a topic. Has anyone got any suggestions?

(After lengthy discussion, the five group members who were present tentatively agreed on "Town-Gown Relations.")

Meeting Four: In Classroom

Sue was the only group member not present for this meeting. The group stumbled through long periods of silence, with Juan making several futile attempts to get the group to laugh. Finally, Felicia bluntly asked why Harry and Juan missed the last meeting. Juan said that he had simply lost the phone number and dorm room; and Harry said that an old friend from high school unexpectedly dropped in. There was a long silence, but the three female roommates indicated nonverbally that they didn't believe either excuse. Harry broke the silence by asking where Sue was. Felicia responded that Sue had come to the meeting in the dorm room and that she had agreed the discussion should be town-gown problems.

HARRY: I wish I had had an opportunity to object to the topic. I commute to town, and this topic is not of interest to me.

ANGELA: We'd have been more than willing to listen to your ideas at the last meeting, but I don't think we have time to go back and pick a topic. Let's go back and make this one work.

FELICIA: I agree. Let's spend this class period working out the major issues of the town-gown topic. First, why don't we each list three major problem areas we see between the town and the university. That should get us started.

(The group spent the rest of the period boiling down their problem lists to five main issues, with everyone but Harry agreeing to research one of the five topics. Harry agreed to interview some townspeople for their side of the story.)

Meetings Five and Six: In Classroom

These two meetings were productive for the group. They effectively sorted out everyone's responsibilities, and everyone came with his or her library research done. The only problem was that the missing link continued to be missing. Felicia assured the group that there must be some good reason for Sue's continued absence. The group agreed to hold one marathon work session the night before the presentation, and Felicia said she would call Sue to make sure she was there.

Meeting Seven: In Dorm Room

Everyone but Sue arrived on time for the meeting. As time passed, the discussion began to focus more and more on Sue's absence.

FELICIA: I've called Sue's house several times but no one answers. I don't know what to think. She seemed so reliable when she came into the group.

HARRY: Let's just write her out of the discussion, and she can get an "F" for the project.

BILL: Maybe part of our assignment is to try to solve this kind of problem. Let's call the professor and see what he wants us to do about Sue.

JUAN: We could just dress up a doll, sit it in a chair, and call it "Sue."

(Laughter)

FELICIA: We agreed that she would be the moderator. I'll try to get hold of her from now until the presentation time. If I can't reach her, I'll do her job too.

DONNA: That's a good idea, Felicia. Who knows what might have happened with a husband and two kids to worry about. Let's give her the benefit of the doubt.

HARRY: Just as long as it doesn't affect my grade, I can live with it.

(The rest of the meeting was spent finalizing the discussion.)

Formal Presentation

Sue met Felicia, Donna, and Angela in the hallway before class. She explained in an emotional voice that she had left her husband and that the last two weeks she had been out of town with her children at her mother's house. Felicia accepted her excuse. The group frantically explained to Sue her role as moderator. The professor and the rest of the class agreed that the "Chain Gang" had presented a thoughtful and stimulating discussion. The professor gave the group a grade of "A" for their panel discussion.

CASE QUESTIONS

1. Can you identify moments in the group's history when members engaged in CR talk? Social talk? Role talk? Problem-solving talk?
2. Can you identify major group roles in the discussion meetings and who predominantly played them?
3. Should Sue receive the same grade as the other group members?
4. How did CR talk and social talk affect the productivity of the group?
5. What trust-building skills would have helped this group?

CHAPTER FOUR

STRUCTURING PROBLEM-SOLVING GROUPS

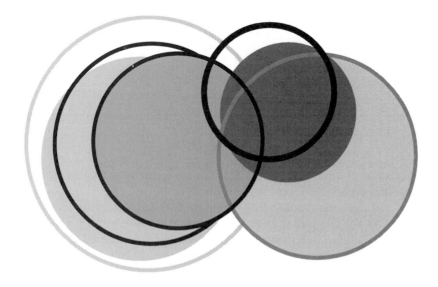

CHAPTER OBJECTIVES

After reading this chapter, you should be able to:

- Explain the major objectives of the various discussion formats
- Perform the steps and unique features of specific decision-making techniques
- Recognize the steps and the unique features of each of the problem-solving agenda systems

DISCUSSION FORMATS
 Roundtable Discussion
 Symposium
 Panel Discussion
 Forum Types
 Colloquy
 Parliamentary Procedure

SPECIFIC DECISION-MAKING TECHNIQUES
 Nominal Group Discussion
 Delphi Technique
 Brainstorming
 Buzz Groups
 Single-Question Form
 Ideal-Solution Form

 Program Evaluation and Review Technique
 Focus Group Interview

PROBLEM-SOLVING AGENDA SYSTEMS
 Dewey's Reflective Thinking: McBurney and
  Hance
 Ross Four-Step Agenda
 Wright Ten-Step Agenda
 Brilhart-Jochem Ideation Criteria
 Functional Approach to Problem Solving
 Cyborg Problem-Solving Systems

SUMMARY

CASE STUDY: THE PARKING COMMITTEE

Frequently, work groups in organizations do not have the luxury of evolving from a zero-history group into an effective problem-solving team. Time constraints, management structure, and the uniqueness of a problem may force a group to use prescriptive group patterns that dictate to the members how and when they ought to communicate with one another. In the past fifty years, we have developed a number of useful methods that have a proven track record (see Table 4.1). In this chapter, we introduce you to a variety of discussion formats, problem-solving agenda systems, and one-time meeting techniques that you will need to know to be an effective problem-solving discussant.

Many systematic procedures have been recommended as ways for groups to accomplish their ends. One way to classify discussion is by its format. The most common formats are roundtable discussion, symposium, panel discussion, forum types, colloquy, and parliamentary procedure. The roundtable discussion format is the most common because its face-to-face interaction pattern facilitates problem solving. A symposium serves an informational function in that it consists of a series of short speeches on a controversial topic in which pro and con positions on various aspects of the topic are presented; or both types of speeches may be included. A panel discussion is a format in which group members interact in a face-to-face context both among themselves and with an audience on a controversial discussion question. Forum types include such subformats as debate forums and lecture forums, in which audiences are given an opportunity to ask the discussion participants questions at the end of the formal presentations. Colloquies usually take the form of an intentional provocation of panel participants by one or more members of an audience. Parliamentary procedure is a formal meeting technique that is used to help meetings run smoothly and in an orderly manner.

Specific decision-making techniques include nominal group discussion, the Delphi technique, brainstorming, buzz groups, single-question form, ideal-solution form, PERT (Program Evaluation and Review Technique), and focus groups.

TABLE **4.1**   **Prescriptive Problem-Solving Group Patterns**

Specific Decision-Making Discussion Formats	Techniques	Problem-Solving Agenda Systems
Roundtable discussions	Nominal group discussion	Dewey's reflective thinking: McBurney & Hance
Symposium	Delphi technique	Ross four-step agenda
Panel discussion	Brainstorming	Wright ten-step agenda
Forum types	Buzz groups	Brilhart-Jochem ideation criteria
Colloquy	Single question Ideal solution	Functional approach
Parliamentary procedure	PERT (Program Evaluation and Review Technique) Focus groups	Cyborg problem-solving system

Buzz groups occur when larger groups are broken into small groups to facilitate participation and idea exchange. Brainstorming is a widely used ideational technique for generating new and fresh ideas. The nominal group discussion procedure emphasizes an equalness of participation and eventually determining priorities for areas of importance to a group. The Delphi technique is similar in a number of ways to the nominal group discussion procedure, but it varies in that members of the group are not located in the same place, and a written mode of group member participation has to be used to gather the data. Ideal-solution form and single-question form are similar in that they emphasize one specific thing that must be accomplished in the group. For example, what is the ideal solution to the problem of an impending strike? Or, what is the single question we are trying to answer to achieve our group's goal? PERT is a detailed planning strategy that is used by certain groups. A focus group interview is a systematic information-gathering technique that is widely used by market researchers.

Problem-solving agenda systems are important tools for group decision making. Agenda systems that are used routinely include the following: Dewey's reflective thinking pattern, the Ross four-step agenda system, the Wright ten-step agenda system, the Brilhart-Jochem ideation-criteria schema, functional approach, and the cyborg agenda system. Dewey's reflective thinking pattern is composed of five steps, and although it is the most widely known, it is not necessarily the best discussion group pattern. The Ross four-step agenda is an adaptation for discussion based on John Dewey's steps of reflective thinking. The Wright ten-step agenda system facilitates a sense of process order and the implementation of a variety of group thought patterns into group discussion. The Brilhart-Jochem ideation-criteria schema emphasizes the importance of the establishment and arrangement of criteria in a basic agenda system. The functional approach stresses the competent performance of four key problem-solving functions without regard to their sequencing. The problem-solving agenda systems that are receiving the most attention in the 1990s are group decision support systems.

These six formats, eight specific techniques, and six problem-solving agenda systems do not constitute an exclusive list of prescriptive group procedures; however, they are certainly representative and are important procedures that any small group communicator should know and use. The remainder of the chapter is devoted to a detailed explanation of these basic problem-solving tools.

☐ DISCUSSION FORMATS

Discussion formats often are passed over as trivial detail in the larger analysis of small group communication. We believe, however, that decisions about the format in which a discussion will take place are major ones. The seating arrangement of a discussion, the sequencing of who speaks when, and the regulation of how long people speak will evolve out of an ongoing group that holds frequent meetings. People will develop a sense of possession over "their seat." Also, the group will develop an unstated time regulation on how long a member can talk. And some people will be allowed to speak longer than others. The six formats presented in this chapter formalize seating arrangements, the sequencing of who talks when, and the regulation of time that members are allowed to speak. These formats evolved out of speech communication literature because they were found to be useful in orchestrating the exchanges of busy people in face-to-face meetings (see Figure 4.1 and Table 4.2)

TABLE 4.2	Major Objectives of Discussion Formats
Format	Objective
Roundtable	To promote equality of participation and spontaneous conversation
Symposium	To present different viewpoints using a series of short preplanned speeches of equal length
Panel discussion	To facilitate semistructured communication interaction among participants on a single topic for the benefit of an audience
Forum types	To stimulate audience participation on an important issue through the use of questions and answers combined with one or more of the other discussion formats
Colloquy	To elicit unprepared responses from discussion participants through the means of prepared questions for the enlightenment of an audience
Parliamentary procedure	To regulate participation in a large discussion body strictly through an organized set of rules to facilitate orderly decision making that reflects the will of the majority

FIGURE 4.1   Discussion Formats

Roundtable

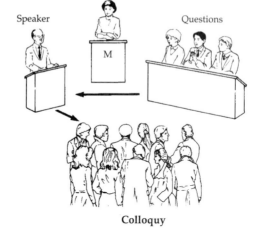

Colloquy

Symposium

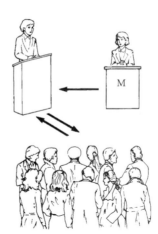

Forum Type (lecture)

Panel Discussion

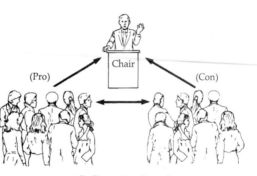

Parliamentary Procedure

Roundtable Discussion

Roundtable discussion has become the most customary way for private discussions to take place. This format is the least prescriptive of the six formats. The seating arrangement is designed to maximize the flow of communication among the members and to produce a sense of equality among them. Yet variations of the roundtable seating format exist that drastically change the open communication and sense of equality. For example, if a rectangular table is used and the designated leader sits at the end by himself or herself, the communication tends to flow between the participant and the designated leader and back to the participant. The rectangular table often is used when a designated leader has a prescribed agenda because it facilitates control by the designated leader. In fact, if a designated leader used a roundtable setting and a rigid agenda system, he or she might be resented for trying to make it appear that an open, free-flowing discussion will take place when in fact it will not. You may have experienced this phenomenon when you have had an autocratic professor who put the class in a circle to appear more democratic. If the professor had left the class in straight rows, you would not have felt badly. It was the mixing of a democratic format with an autocratic style that caused the problem. So it is with discussion formats. The format signals the participants to expect a certain type of discussion; that is, it tells you where you sit, when you talk, and how long you talk.

In most roundtable discussions, there is an expectation that anyone can talk when they have something to say. The minute you make the table a rectangle, there is a tendency to seek the approval of the designated leader before speaking. Therefore, a college discussion group would feel more comfortable sitting around a round table, whereas a Monday-morning forty-five-minute briefing by a supervisor might be more appropriate around a rectangle. If the study group finds itself around a rectangular or square table, it tends to disregard the table's shape and form a circle with chairs around the table. Participants in a formal business meeting that is taking place around a round table usually arrange themselves in a rectangle by leaving a space on each side of the designated leader. In fact, research on these seating arrangements has demonstrated that roundtable seating arrangements facilitate more democratic and spontaneous participation patterns and rectangular seating arrangements promote more autocratic and stilted participation patterns (Shaw 1976).

Finally, a roundtable format implies unregulated and unrestrained discussion. If you were a designated leader calling a group together to discuss a topic and you had forty minutes to reach a decision, you probably would not want to seat the members around a round table unless they had had a great deal of experience working together. In our culture, it is not acceptable behavior to have everyone occupy equal space around a round table with one person tightly regulating the speaking time of each. At a rectangular table, on the other hand, we expect some regulation from the designated leader.

If one wanted to get mystical about shapes, in the world of small group discussion, the circle or the round table would connote timelessness and equality of participation. When we leave the format of the circle and form any other shape, we are signaling that time is our enemy and that we must structure our interaction to reach group goals.

Thus, the rectangular table implies—as the remaining five formats prescribe in a formalized manner—where people sit, when they talk, and how long they talk.

Symposium

A symposium is a series of short speeches that present various aspects of a topic, or the pro and con positions on a controversial issue, within a prescribed discussion format. These speaking assignments are prearranged with the symposium participants and expected to be of the same length. In essence, each speaker covers parts of a whole topic, usually to provide helpful information for the members of an audience to use in their future decision making.

You have probably been a member of an audience at a number of symposiums without realizing it. If you saw a sign posted on campus that stated there would be a symposium on the question of abortion, you might not know whether you were going to hear a series of speeches supporting abortion or opposing it. However, if the symposium announcement stated that the pros and cons of abortion would be addressed, you would expect that both sides would be adequately covered. If you were the person in charge of the symposium, you might plan to have six speakers, three for and three against. Furthermore, you might expect to have two physicians, for and against, to talk about the medical ramifications; two lawyers, for and against, to deal with the legal aspects of the issue; and two members of the clergy to represent religious concerns. You would also prescribe the maximum amount of time the speakers would be allowed to speak, and the audience and other symposium participants would expect you to enforce it.

When you entered the university, your orientation probably included a series of symposiums that provided exposure to various aspects of campus life. Perhaps you went to a session that focused on social activities, and as you sat anonymously in crowd, several speakers were paraded before you. Each speaker seemed enthusiastic about his or her topic and told you just enough to interest you, but not enough to answer your questions. By the end of the day, you were experiencing extreme mental fatigue and frustration. We don't mean to say that all college orientation symposiums are poorly done or that the symposium format inherently produces information overload. We do suggest that, more frequently than not, the symposium format is misused or abused.

Sometimes people who are in charge of orientation symposiums string together a series of speakers who are important in the organization more with an eye to protocol of who should be invited to speak than with an eye to what the audience needs to know. Any time the number of speakers exceeds six you have too many.

Designated leaders of symposium often fail because they do not do enough to ensure that the speeches will be closely tied together so that, when taken as a whole, they will constitute a coherent picture for the audience. Simply bringing together for one hour, on one stage, six persons whose job functions relate to the social activities on campus will not ensure a good symposium. The designated leader should diplomatically explain to the speakers that their talks should be prepared in such a way that a common thread runs through them.

The protocol of the symposium format extends beyond the contextual dimension; there are also various expectations. The audience expects all members of the symposium to be on a platform facing them and that the moderator will rise and formally introduce each speaker. Culturally, we expect symposium speakers to give their speeches standing up at a podium, whereas we expect panel discussants to debate sitting down.

Panel Discussion

A panel discussion is a specialized format in which group members interact among themselves and with an audience on a controversial question. The interaction may be face to face, through a mediator, or through a combination of face-of-face and mediated communication. Traditionally, the seating arrangement of a panel discussion had the discussants sitting on one side of a rectangular table facing the audience, with the moderator seated either among the discussants or at one end of the rectangle.

As television became a widely used medium, a second format was developed in which the discussants sat at either end of the rectangle and the moderator sat in the center of one of the sides with the camera opposite him or her. The use of satellites to facilitate the transmission of information instantaneously around the world has also led to the development of new panel discussion formats. The network news programs regularly beam minipanel discussions into our homes. The panel discussants may physically be in three countries, but working from a planned agenda and with an anchor person as discussion leader, they are able to discuss controversial topics before millions of people. The award-winning *News Hour with Jim Lehrer,* which has been aired weeknights for years on public television (for many years as *The MacNeil-Lehrer Report*), pioneered a new seating arrangement for panel discussion. In this program, the panel discussants are in two places and the discussion is chaired. Lehrer keeps tight control by using a planned agenda known to him but seldom to the participants. Through the use of rear-screen projectors, the television audience can see on their screen two discussants in face-to-face interchange with Lehrer; at the same time, two other participants on a rear-screen projection also interact with Lehrer. Thus, the format allows the television audience to see the spontaneous nonverbal reaction to everyone's comments and to hear the unplanned verbal interaction among participants. This format also allows tight facial close-ups of a panel discussant when he or she presents a prepared monologue that was stimulated by a prepared question. Thus, the *News Hour* has all the classic elements of a live panel discussion. At the same time, use of modern media technology has enabled Lehrer to produce a format that is well suited to television discussion and vastly superior to the format of talking heads sitting in a line before a fixed camera that was common in the 1960s and 1970s. The traditional seating arrangement for panel discussions with live audiences has been adapted to fit both television and the faster pace of our lives. However, the fundamental factors that make a panel discussion what it is remain constant.

Extemporaneous speeches and panel discussions have one thing in common: they appear to be spontaneous while in fact a lot of planning and preparation have gone into both outlines. The panel discussion leader, or moderator, is responsible for keeping the discussants to the planned agenda. A more difficult skill for the moderator lies in planning how much prediscussion interaction is needed by the discussants. If the discussion is rehearsed, it usually fails, and the audience feels that it has been manipulated. If no advance work is done with the discussants, a discussion may appear shallow and random. A good discussion is marked by a diversity of viewpoints interacting within a cooperative mode. If the discussion moderator works too closely in preparing the discussants, the panel participants may feel manipulated and fail to perform to the expectations of the moderator or the audience. Even when the moderator has done appropriate amounts of advance planning and has worked out a reasonable agenda, it is difficult to balance the time allowed for each item on the agenda against the time allotted each discussant. Most people need years of practice to become truly skilled in the role of discussion moderator. One principle should govern the development of a moderator: Truth can emerge only in a permissive and reflective atmosphere. In short, a sense of fair play is all important. The moderator should not rig the discussion to suit his or her bias, nor should he or she allow undue time to be spent on one item of the agenda or on one discussant of the panel.

There is no prescribed period that is the "right amount of time" for each discussant. A general rule of thumb is that the discussant should never speak more than one minute at a time. In a televised panel discussion, the allotted time would be less than that. As a discussant, you should resist the urge to respond with your opinion on every issue but be prepared to speak cogently on the issues that the panel and the audience expect you to speak on. The panel discussion, then, is a *coacting* situation. The discussants not only carry on a semispontaneous dialogue with one another but also interact with a live radio or television audience. This instantaneous dual interaction forms the basis of a panel discussion. One final note about the panel discussion is its relation to the roundtable discussion. Often before the lights are lit for a panel discussion, the discussants have been involved in a backstage roundtable discussion. This advance planning will appear manipulative only if the net result of the panel discussion is a slick, biased view of the topic under discussion.

Forum Types

The best-known example of the forum in the United States is the New England town meeting. The freedom for all members of the audience to question ideas in a public place is a basic right of our governmental system, and the format of the forum aids this democratic practice of evaluating and questioning policies. As defined here, a forum is a question-and-answer period that arises out of another type of public discussion format, for example, a symposium. Whatever the stimulus-response nature of the forum, there is one key ingredient: The audience must have the opportunity and capacity to ask questions and respond to statements. What distinguishes different types of forums from one another is that each type arises from a different communication event. The specific public discussion types include the lecture forum, debate forum, dialogue forum, panel forum, and symposium forum.

The lecture forum is a discussion format established mainly to facilitate the purpose of information sharing. Lectures can be presented on television to various classrooms; this is not a public discussion format because audience members usually do not have the opportunity to ask the television lecturer questions about the material he or she has presented. The debate forum, in contrast, is designed primarily to present the pros and cons of a controversial proposition and, it is hoped, to provoke the audience to ask questions.

The dialogue forum has some rather interesting features. The modes of advocacy and inquiry are uniquely blended into a dyadic or triadic structure to create the dialogue forum. The very fact that an interview is being conducted as public discussion makes its format that of the dialogue forum. Geraldo Rivera's syndicated television program is one example. In it, Rivera weaves together his own questions, questions from the live audience, and phoned-in questions from the television audience to produce an entertaining and informative public discussion. Radio and television programs have used variations of this format for decades as a means of stimulating public discussion of current issues.

The panel and symposium formats become forums when they add questions from the audience. Otherwise, they remain as described above. Where people sit, when they talk, and how long they talk are controlled by the type of forum used. The lecture normally is a twenty- to thirty-minute speech. The debate gives equal time to both affirmative and negative sides—usually fifteen minutes divided between two speakers on a side. The dialogue forum normally begins with a brief statement by the major participant, followed by stimulus questions by the interviewer and audience.

Colloquy

A colloquy is a specialized discussion format that provides an opportunity for representatives from an audience to ask prepared questions of one or more experts on a topic. The colloquy is somewhat formal, and the discussion is closely regulated by a moderator. The television programs *Meet the Press* and *Wall Street Week* are examples of a colloquy. In *Meet the Press*, three reporters ask the questions the larger television audience would ask if given the opportunity. Protocol for a colloquy usually requires that the moderator allow each questioner to ask one question at a time in a serial manner. The expert is allowed only to answer questions, not to ask them.

The colloquy is also a favorite discussion format for politicians on the campaign trail. At college campuses, the political colloquy presents one or two politicians on a stage with three or four student representatives who ask rather blunt, prepared questions in the presence of a large live audience. The nationally televised "debates" between Bill Clinton and Bob Dole in the 1996 presidential campaign were really much more in the format of a colloquy than of a debate. Most of the format was dominated by carefully prepared questions from journalists, followed by the responses of the candidates. These interactions were carefully regulated by a moderator, and little head-on debate occurred between the candidates. One student told us after watching the so-called debates on television that she voted for the reporters. She thought that they had asked better questions than the candidates gave answers. She preferred the colloquies in which members of the audience asked the questions.

Parliamentary Procedure

Parliamentary procedure is almost as old as English culture. It dates back to those romanticized times of armed knights and lords, who were early members of Parliament. One of the rules that evolved from their meetings was that a sergeant at arms should be appointed to disarm the members, so that when arguments broke out, they could not take out their swords and kill one another. The sergeant at arms was also needed to eject forcibly members of the group who did not engage in verbal argument in a civilized manner. Not only did each meeting have its police force, but it also had its "supreme court" in the person of the parliamentarian, who interpreted the rules and regulations and their uses.

There are more than three hundred rules of parliamentary procedure. However, when they are simplified, they are found to be designed to accomplish just a few basic objectives (see Table 4.3). The first is to impose the will of the majority nonviolently and even to suppress the voices of the minority if the majority swells to two-thirds of the assembly. With a two-thirds vote, one can stop discussion on a topic and demand a vote or even adjourn the meeting. The second objective of parliamentary procedure is to force the group rigidly to discuss one, and only one, problem at a time. This problem is called the main motion on the floor. The chair strictly regulates who will talk by formally recognizing a speaker and, if necessary, by ruling a member out of order if his or her comments are not germane to the main motion. This formal regulation of communication is one of the elements that distinguishes parliamentary procedure from other forms of deliberation. No other group format has a formal system for determining whether a member's contribution is germane to the discussion.

The third objective in the use of parliamentary rules of order is to ensure that members have equal opportunity to participate. This objective also ensures that arguments for and against the main motion will be given. When rules of parliamentary procedure are strictly enforced, they produce a discussion pattern that specifies who can talk for how long and how often. They also ensure that there is a major and

---

TABLE 4.3   Minimum Guidelines for Using Parliamentary Procedure

How to Run Meetings
1. Call meeting to order
2. Read minutes of last meeting
3. Report of treasurer and other officers
4. Process committee reports
5. Consider old business
6. Entertain new business
7. Introduce program for meeting
8. Adjourn the meeting

How to Make Decisions
1. Chair entertains new business in the form of main motion
2. Member of assembly seconds main motion
3. Main motion is debated with chair controlling discussion
4. Chair calls for the vote
5. Motion passes or is defeated

How to Protect Individual Rights
1. Have a knowledgeable, objective parliamentarian to protect the rules
2. Rise to a point of information if you do not understand the discussion at hand
3. Rise to a point of parliamentary inquiry to ask the parliamentarian about correct procedures
4. Rise to a point of personal privilege regarding your creature comforts
5. Call for a division of the house if the voice vote was not clear
6. Appeal the decision of chair and ask house members to vote on whether chair is right
7. Rise to a point of order if you believe that parliamentary procedure is not being followed

minor speaker for and against the main motion, that each speech is limited to ten minutes, and that after they are done, members of the group are allowed to speak only twice for a limited time of two minutes each. A final objective is to ensure that the rights of the minority are protected. There are a number of important rules that are designed to guarantee that each person's rights will be protected, regardless of the stance he or she takes in the debate. You will undoubtedly find yourself at some point in an organization that uses parliamentary procedure, and it is important for you to acquire a working knowledge of it at some time during your formal education. Table 4.3 contains twenty minimum guidelines you need to know in a meeting run by parliamentary procedure. There are eight rules used for conducting business, five basic rules needed for a group to make a decision, and seven rules designed to protect a person's rights.

☐ SPECIFIC DECISION-MAKING TECHNIQUES

Over the years, communication professors have become more and more involved as consultants for private industry and government organizations. We are brought in to handle some specialized discussion problems or, in some cases, to do an overall evaluation of the groups that exist within the organization. In doing this field consultation work, a number of specialized discussion techniques have evolved that are used by most consultants and a number of group leaders in organizations. In this section, eight of the most popular techniques are presented; however, communication consultants who work daily with organizations usually develop their own variations. In fact, in the case study for this chapter, we present our version of some of these specific discussion techniques.

These eight discussion techniques are highly prescriptive, and the rules contained in each procedure must be adhered to if one is to benefit from them. For example, brainstorming is a valuable prescriptive procedure only if the rules are religiously followed. Most people who are not trained in discussion methods will tell a group to brainstorm for ten minutes without giving them direction and later conclude that the procedure is worthless. You may have been in a group that was told to brainstorm on some topic and found itself involved first in a random discussion of the topic and then in telling humorous anecdotes, all the time moving away from the task of the group. Your conclusion could well have been that brainstorming was a useless technique. So let us repeat: These procedures work only if you follow their rules. All eight of these techniques are designed to increase a group's productivity dramatically (see Table 4.4).

Nominal Group Discussion

We have all been part of a social group that could be said to be a group in name only. By that we mean the group had little interaction, did not work as a unit, and had little rapport among its members. In short, there was no group cohesion. Thus, to say that a collection of people is nominally a group could be a derogatory statement. However, nominal group discussion (NGD) should not have any of these negative connotations attached to it. It is simply a specialized discussion technique designed

TABLE **4.4**   **Unique Features of Decision-Making Techniques**

Technique	Unique Feature
Nominal group	Four-step process that separates idea generation from idea evaluation, with emphasis on guaranteeing equal participation among all group members
Delphi	At least a four-step process that allows a large collection of people to reach group decisions without face-to-face meetings
Brainstorming	Four-step process containing four specific rules that separates idea generation from idea evaluation, with emphasis on spontaneous group creativity
Buzz groups	Three-step procedure that allows large assemblies of people to generate ideas on a topic quickly
Single question	Five-step process that produces an in-depth answer to a specific question
Ideal solution	Four-step analysis of a solution in which the group has previously agreed on the nature of the problem
PERT	Eight-step process for implementing group decisions that requires complex coordination and careful planning on the part of different groups in attempting to meet a common goal
Focus group interview	Five-step process for systematically gathering information from a group

to ensure equal contributions and participation by all the members to achieve some common goal.

The procedure evolved from two rationales. First, research at universities repeatedly found that people produced more and better ideas working in the presence of others than if they worked separately on the same task. Thus, if we put six persons in a face-to-face setting and have them silently work on the same problem, we will get more and better work from them than if they worked on the same problem in the privacy of their offices. The second rationale that produced the widespread use of the NGD procedure involved the uneven participation patterns that usually occur in roundtable discussions and some brainstorming sessions. There was a need to find a way to ensure that each member of the group would contribute his or her best ideas in a relatively short period of time.

Delbecq, Van de Ven, and Gustafson, in *Group Techniques for Program Planning: A Guide to Nominal Group and Delphi Processes* (1975), provided the most comprehensive treatment of the nominal group technique. Huseman (1977), a communication scholar, presented an abridged, much more concise treatment of the NGD procedure for use in group discussions. Although the NGD procedure could contain as many as six steps, the four most commonly used steps are as follows (Delbecq, Van de Ven, and Gustafson 1975, 71):

1. silent generation of ideas
2. round-robin recording
3. serial discussion
4. preliminary vote

Imagine that you are the chairperson for the committee in charge of identifying events for Black History Week on campus. Your committee has met several times and kicked around some notions about which speakers and musical groups should be included in the program. However, you are a busy group and have to determine at the next two-hour meeting the events that will occur during Black History Week. One of the things you might do to meet your goal is to use a modified form of the NGD. You could seat the members of the group in a semicircle and seat yourself facing them with a large flip chart on a easel standing next to your chair. You should tell the group that you are going to use a procedure to help in the decision making that will require you to be autocratic and rigid in your regulation of the meeting. You should also say that you intend to suspend debate and evaluation of ideas to get everyone's viewpoint. You should now be ready to begin the first step of our four-step NGD procedure. The key to NGD is that it provides democracy of ideas through tyranny of procedure.

Step 1. *Silent listing of ideas.* Group members sit quietly in a face-to-face setting and spend twenty minutes writing down every good idea they have. In this case, participants would be asked to make two lists: one of possible speakers and another of musical groups that could be included on the program for Black History Week. It is important that you provide a model of the behavior you want to take place; therefore, you should work to produce the best list that you can in twenty minutes. Use polite but firm verbal and nonverbal cues that eliminate humorous exchanges of conversation among the members.

Step 2. *Creation of master idea list.* When the twenty minutes are up, or it is clear that everyone has exhausted his or her repertoire of ideas, you should begin the round-robin process of putting each idea on the master flip chart next to you. You ask the first person to state one, and only one, idea, and you record it on the flip chart. Do not allow discussion about the merits of the idea. Move clockwise to the next member and retrieve one suggestion from his or her list. Continue to move from member to member, remembering to include yourself, until everyone's list is exhausted. Sometimes it is helpful to record how often each idea comes up.

Step 3. *Clarification of ideas.* This step allows the group a controlled opportunity to clarify the meaning of phrases that appear on the master list. Sometimes there are only a few ideas that are not clear to all group members; sometimes there are a lot. If you are leading the nominal group, it is important that you limit the discussion to clarification of ideas and leave evaluation until later. Delbecq, Van de Ven, and Gustafson (1975) recommend that you move in a serial manner to each member and achieve clarification of his or her idea in this way. Many times this procedure is too elaborate, and you need only seek clarification of a few phrases.

Step 4. *Straw vote for testing acceptance of ideas.* A secret vote asks each member to rank each idea on the chart in terms of its acceptability. You should hand out standard-looking pieces of paper on which each member records his or her vote. Collect the votes, randomize the ballots for anonymity, and then record the votes on the master list. This should give you some idea of consensus. For instance, I. Reed, an author, may have emerged as the top-ranked speaker, and "the artist formerly known as Prince" may be the landslide choice for the Saturday night dance. On the other hand, there might be a diversity of opinion as to who should be brought to campus, but at least you will now have those differences on the table and should be in a good position to proceed in a roundtable discussion to reach consensus on a decision.

Delphi Technique

The Delphi technique is a method for generating group interaction on a discussion topic with the potential for reaching a decision without the group ever meeting face to face. This procedure is not frequently used, but when it is, it requires that the group members be highly motivated and adept at writing out their comments and have sufficient time to participate in this rather lengthy process. One way to conceptualize the Delphi technique is to think of it as an NGD that is carried on by way of the mails and that allows a large number of people to participate.

The name *Delphi technique* stems from the story of the oracles at Delphi who foretold the future for the Greeks. The Delphi model, designed by Dalkey (1967) and his colleagues, forecasts technological innovations for the Rand Corporation. The technique consists of a series of probes, the first of which is a questionnaire that asks the participants, much as the first step in the NGD procedure does, to list all the issues that might fall under a broad discussion question. After responses to the first probe have been classified into major headings, subsequent probes requesting the same participants to rank or rate the ideas are used until the discussion group starts to arrive at agreement, sufficient information has been gathered, or a satisfactory combination of agreement and information gathering has occurred.

Delbecq, Van de Ven, and Gustafson (1975) described a full-blown Delphi technique that comprises ten major steps and takes at least a month and a half to complete. An abbreviated version of the technique involves four steps. They include the following:

1. collection of participants' ideas
2. synthesis of list of ideas by each participant
3. integration of synthesized lists by one person
4. ranking in order or rating of the ideas on the integrated list by the participants; Step 4 is repeated until agreement occurs

Many professional organizations—for example, the American Medical Association—have memberships spread around the world whose job commitments allow them to get together only once a year at a convention. The leadership of such professional organizations often finds itself in need of participatory discussion and consent on broad policy issues. Time and distance prohibit frequent meetings. The advent of inexpensive fax (facsimile) machines and the internet, which are rapidly becoming as indispensable as the phone, may make Delphi a popular procedure because responses can be cost-effectively made in a day. The four steps of the Delphi procedure are as follows.

Step 1. *Participants' ideas are collected.* A questionnaire is mailed, and each participant is asked to respond to two or three broad discussion questions. For example, if a mailing went out to college student-government leaders, they might be asked to identify their major responsibilities and forecast the major concerns of college students for the next five years. They would be asked to type out their responses and return them in one or two days to a central location.

Step 2. *A List of ideas is synthesized.* The people running the probe produce a master list of all the ideas they have received in the mail and send them out again to all the participants, requesting that the participants classify the ideas in terms of their importance. Participants could also be encouraged to make brief comments on an item that seemed especially important to them.

Step 3. *An integrated master list is prepared.* This step requires a lot of work from the designated leader of the Delphi. If you were the student-government leader responsible for this probe, you would probably have several hundred thick, completed questionnaires on your desk that expressed each participant's opinion about which ideas are important and which are unimportant. It would now be your task to order all these opinions into some manageable questionnaire. The student leaders around the country must trust that you will leave in the major and controversial issues, throwing out only the tangential ones, and that you will not bias the questionnaire in the direction of your favored conclusions.

Step 4. *Participants vote on the issues.* Each participant "votes" on the acceptability of each idea contained in the streamlined questionnaire. The voting usually is done in the form of some rating or ranking procedure. For example, if one of the forecasted problems is that within the next five years, there will be a demand for quiet study-hour periods in the dorms, the participant might be asked to rank that problem among a list of twenty-five in order of importance, or to rate it on a scale of 1 to 7. Once all the questionnaires are returned, the results can be quantified, summarized, and mailed back to the participants. In addition, the results might be published in a student-government magazine or presented in a talk at a national meeting of student-government associations.

Sometimes the Delphi technique is used in combination with other group procedures to determine group consensus. For example, the leadership of an organization might engage in nominal grouping about a broad discussion topic and afterward use a modified Delphi technique as a means of validating or quantifying the results of the initial NGD session. The Delphi technique can also be used as a preconvention method for large organizations, the membership being probed by way of Delphi to determine not only consensus but also disagreement so that the convention programs can focus on similarities and differences at the conference itself. Further, researchers have concluded that although computerized and face-to-face discussions produce equally good decisions, computerized groups are less likely to reach consensus (Hiltz, Johnson, and Turoff 1986).

Brainstorming

Alex Osborn (1959) popularized the brainstorming technique in his now-famous book *Applied Imagination.* As a co-owner of an advertising agency, he was intensely interested in creative answers to the problems of marketing his clients' products. Over the years of conducting group sessions with his coworkers in attempts to come up with new ideas or ads, he discovered that the spontaneous group creativity that created some of the famous television commercials can be systematically and predictably produced if four rules are religiously followed. They are (1) evaluation and criticism of ideas are forbidden; (2) wild and crazy ideas are encouraged; (3) quantity, not quality, of ideas is the goal; (4) and new combinations of ideas are sought. We recommend that the following four-step procedure be used in addition to Osborn's four rules when a group is brainstorming some aspect of a discussion question.

1. Conduct a warm-up session
2. Use Osborn's brainstorming procedure
3. Eliminate duplication of ideas
4. Clarify, order, and evaluate ideas

A social chairperson of an organization is constantly beset with the need to come up with themes for annual events. A fraternity's spring formal is a perpetual problem for the fraternity's social chairman. If you were assigned the task of generating potential ideas for a theme for the annual formal dance, you might do well to bring together some members of the fraternity into a discussion group and follow the four steps of brainstorming.

Step 1. *Conduct a warm-up session.* Even though most people are familiar with the technique of brainstorming, they often forget the importance of following Osborn's rules. It is especially important to remind the group not to evaluate an idea prematurely. A brief warm-up session, practicing on some nonsense issue, often helps to get the group into the wild, freewheeling mood that is needed if spontaneous group creativity is to occur. For example, you might ask members to shout out the uses of a ballpoint pen or a concave navel. Answers such as that the pen could be used as an earplug while skin diving or that your navel could be used to hold salt while eating radishes in bed would not be groaned at or disallowed. It is this sort of silliness that will suddenly spring a truly creative idea that will solve the group's problem.

Step 2. *Brainstorming.* The actual brainstorming session should not last for more than thirty minutes. It often helps if a person from outside the group records the ideas on a large flip chart as they spring forth in rapid succession. Sometimes it helps to have the designated leader write the ideas on the flip chart while a disinterested person takes more copious notes on the side. It is important that the leader encourage "hitchhiking" on ideas; one idea may spring two or three more. He or she should also be enthusiastic, to keep the group excited about their task. Finally, the leader should jump in with the rest of the group to generate as many ideas as possible in a thirty-minute period.

Step 3. *Eliminate duplicate ideas.* Once the brainstorming session is completed, the leader takes the group through the flip chart and eliminates all duplications. The group still does not evaluate the quality of ideas but simply condenses the number of words used to describe them.

Step 4. *Clarify, order, and evaluate.* In this final step, the group categorizes the large volume of ideas into some sensible outline. In the process, most of the vague ideas will be clarified or discarded. Once the ideas are on a flip chart in front of the group in clear outline form, evaluation can begin. How the evaluation of ideas is handled depends on group processes other than brainstorming. The brainstorming technique does not provide for a specific method for differentiating good ideas from bad ones. It was Osborn's belief that the group would consensually recognize the good ideas as they emerged, and in fact, many times this is the case. Brainstorming works best when all members freely contribute ideas. In fact, research done by Jablin and others indicates that levels of communication apprehension that might exist among group members negatively affects the productivity of a brainstorming session (Jablin 1981; Jablin, Seibold, and Sorenson 1977).

Buzz Groups

J. Donald Phillips (1948) created a prescriptive group technique called "Phillips 66," or "Buzz." The procedure is designed to maximize the input of all the members of a large assembled group by breaking them down into groups of six and having them "buzz" for about six minutes on some specific issue, such as "What topics should we be concerned with at our next meeting?" An appointed leader of each buzz group reports his or her findings to the large group. If the questions that the buzz groups deal with are well thought out, then a master list can be made by combining the useful ideas of each group. If the Phillips 66 buzz group technique is well managed, it increases group effectiveness.

The two keys to the buzz group are careful management and structuring. For these requirements to be met, the following steps should be adhered to whenever possible.

Step 1. *Identify the question.* For this technique to work, the question asked of the assembly must be a meaningful one that requires the participation of everybody. If the question is ambiguous or trite, the various buzz groups will treat it flippantly, and in terms of the answers to the question and the general morale of the assembly, the entire effort will be wasted.

Step 2. *Assign duties of designated leaders.* In advance of the meeting, it is important that the buzz group leaders be assigned and that they be properly located throughout the hall with the necessary materials. Each one will need a table for six or sometimes for as many as nine, a flip chart, writing materials, and instructions on how to run the meeting. The instructions to the designated leader should inform him or her of the following: (a) he or she should adapt the "telling" style, which we describe in Chapter 7; (b) the leader should be responsible for compiling the list of suggestions; and (c) he or she should prepare the buzz group's list in written form for presentation to the assembly. Sometimes the designated leaders are requested to make an oral presentation in the form of a short report to the assembly.

Step 3. *Actualize the assembly's ideas.* After the designated leaders have made their reports and a composite list has been compiled, it is important that the program chairperson take some action based on the collective opinions and suggestions of the group.

An example of how the results of a buzz group discussion can be used is in combination with a keynote speaker at a convention. An organization frequently will invite a national figure to keynote their convention and to speak about the issues central to the interests of the membership. In this situation, the chairperson will ask the keynote speaker in advance to make a twenty-minute opening presentation, after which the buzz technique is used to solicit specific questions that the audience wants answered. The Phillips 66 method will facilitate the identification of the five most important questions that were generated in the buzz groups. The speaker, sensitive to the group's needs and interests, spends about five minutes answering each of the five questions. This technique has provided a valuable feedback vehicle for the speaker and has generated interaction among the assembly's participants.

Single-Question Form

Carl E. Larson (1969) reported this discussion technique in a research study that he conducted on forms of analysis and their effectiveness in small group problem solving. A major feature of this discussion technique is that it is especially appropriate for use in one-time meeting groups in educational settings. Larson advocates the following steps in the single-question form:

1. What is the single question, the answer to which is all the group needs to know to accomplish its purpose?
2. What subquestions must be answered before we can answer the single question we have formulated?
3. Do we have sufficient information to confidently answer the subquestions? If yes, answer them. If no, continue below.
4. What are the most reasonable answers to the subquestions?
5. Assuming that our answers to the subquestions are correct, what is the best solution to the problem? (Larson 1969, 453)

This technique is a useful procedure in a one-time meeting when a tentative decision is needed to meet some pressing deadline. For example, assume that you are the chair of the Student Entertainment Committee (SEC), and the student-body president suddenly wants to know how many concerts the SEC will sponsor next year. If you have time for only one meeting of the SEC, you might well use the single-question technique, as follows.

Step 1. *What is the single question?* The answer might be, how many groups can we bring in for the $80,000 allocated to the SEC?
Step 2. *What subquestions must be answered?* What groups do we want? How much is the fee for each group? What is the rental on the auditorium? How much money will we make from each concert?
Step 3. *Do we have sufficient information?* The answer is no, so we must proceed to Step 4.
Step 4. *What are the most reasonable answers to the subquestions?* The answer to question one is that we could not agree on what groups to bring in; however, we did agree on three categories of groups we would like: rock, country, and rhythm and blues. We estimate their fees at about $20,000 per group. The rental on the auditorium is about $5,000 per concert. We estimate $10,000 revenue from each concert.
Step 5. *What is the best solution to the problem?* The SEC concludes that the student association can plan on five musical concerts for the next year.

The single-question form has no doubt been used in your classroom and extra-curricular groups.

Ideal-Solution Form

Another discussion technique, the ideal-solution form, was used by Carl Larson in his 1969 study on small group forms of analysis. Larson lists the following essential steps in this discussion pattern.

1. Are we all agreed on the nature of the problem?
2. What would be the ideal solution from the point of view of all duties involved in the problem?
3. What conditions within the problem could be changed so that the ideal solution might be achieved?
4. Of the solutions available to us, which one best approximates the ideal solution? (Larson 1969, 453)

This technique is a good one for determining the best among several alternatives. The ideal-solution form can be used, as is the single-question form, as a technique for a one-time meeting. The ideal-solution technique works well when there are vested interests in the group. For example, in our community, a group made up of city officials, homeowners, and builders sat down to solve a common problem, using the ideal-solution technique.

   Step 1. *What is the problem?* Everyone at the meeting agreed that basements were being flooded by sanitary sewer backups.

   Step 2. *What is the best answer for each party?* The homeowners thought that the builders should pay for the "illegal hookups" of the sanitary sewers. The builders thought that the city was responsible, and the city thought that the homeowners were responsible.

   Step 3. *What change is needed?* Some party has to accept responsibility for the problem.

   Step 4. *What is the best solution, given the circumstances?* The city agreed to accept some responsibility and to approach the Environmental Protection Agency for funds. The city manager agreed to contact the appropriate state agency to begin the solution phase of the problem.

   With the ideal-solution form, the group was able to address solution alternatives in a constructive way, even though each party had strong feelings about each of the alternatives and had met in a less than friendly atmosphere to try to select the best solution.

Program Evaluation and Review Technique

PERT is a systematic technique for implementing group decisions that require complex coordination and careful planning on the part of different groups in attempting to meet a common goal. In 1958, the U.S. Navy developed PERT, a quasi-mathematical procedure, in an attempt to meet their goal of building the Polaris missile system (Phillips 1966, 88–89). Since PERT was first used by the U.S. government, it has been widely adopted both by government and by private organizations.

   PERT is an elaborate planning system usually comprising eight steps that cryptically display each event that must take place for the project to be completed. The steps are as follows:

Step 1. *State the final event or goal of project.* Here the group clearly defines the event that must take place, such as the event of putting a person on the moon.

Step 2. *List events that must happen before the final event can occur.* A group usually brainstorms a list of all these events without regard to their chronology.

Step 3. *Assess the order of the events.* The group takes the brainstormed list and places it in chronological order, noting especially those events that must happen simultaneously.

Step 4. *Make a diagram that connects all events in chronological order.* Sometimes groups develop elaborate wall charts so that they can trace the progress of their project.

Step 5. *State specific activities that occur between events.* The group often identifies strategies and action plans to move to and through events. If the goal were to build a car, the group would list the activities that would have to occur between completed drawings and completed die castings of each part.

Step 6. *Specify time needed.* The group needs to develop a time line for the whole project and estimate the time for completing each event in the PERT chart.

Step 7. *Are the deadlines feasible?* After the project has been estimated in terms of time, the group must compare its expected deadlines with the actual time allocations. If you were working on such a project and had allowed yourself more time to complete the project than your superiors had allowed, you would need to rethink the project and find a quicker way to do it.

Step 8. *Determine critical path.* In the PERT chart, some events will be more crucial and more difficult to accomplish than others. In this step, the group determines what those steps are and makes certain that enough resources have been allocated for their accomplishment (Phillips 1966, 89–104).

Figure 4.2 contains a PERT diagram for the installation of a milling machine in a small tool and die company. It is oversimplified, but it contains the basic elements of PERT. The final event is a functioning milling machine. Six events must happen before the machine is operational. They are listed and diagrammed in Figure 4.2 with the specific time needed for each activity stated. The critical path (CP) is ADF, which means that it will take twelve days to do the job. If this job had to be reduced to ten days, it could occur only if the ADF path were shortened. It wouldn't help to speed up the delivery of the machine (B), or dig the hole faster (C), or pour the concrete quicker (E). If we want to speed up the job, we have to shorten the CP. This could be done by speeding up the ordering of the steel (A), preparing the steel faster (D), or wiring the machine faster (F). As we've said, this is a simple example. If a PERT chart is built for assessing and sequencing the events needed to produce a new automobile, the chart would be so complicated that a computer program would be needed to determine the CP.

Most decision-making groups do not need PERT to implement their decisions; however, most groups are guilty of not following through with the implementations of decisions *as a group.* Too often the follow-up is left to one or two persons in the group who soon begin to feel overworked. At the same time, the group loses control as the members who do all the work put into effect the group's decisions according to their own, rather than the group's, interpretation. PERT, or a modified version of it, forces the group to plan, systematically and in a participatory manner, the necessary follow-through that is needed to accomplish the decisions of the group.

Figure 4.2   PERT Diagram

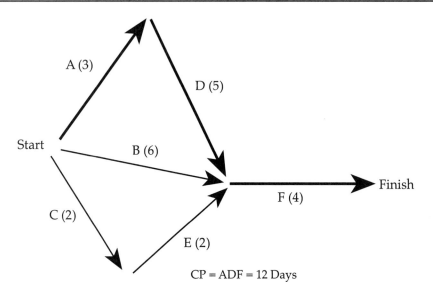

CP = ADF = 12 Days

A. Specifications and ordering steel (3 days)
B. Specifications and delivery time of machine (6 days)
C. Digging foundation hole (2 days)
D. Preparing steel: tapping, threading, etc. (5 days)
E. Pouring concrete (2 days)
F. Wiring machine and testing (4 days)

Focus Group Interview

Focus group interviews have long been used by market researchers as a means for gathering qualitative data about products (Greenbaum 1988; Krueger 1988; Lederman 1990). Shields (1981) introduced focus group interviews to the communication discipline when he argued that small group communication theories could be used as the underpinning for teaching students how to conduct focus group interviews. Subsequent research suggests that a dramatistic-based focus group interview may be superior to a rationalistic-based group interview (Haag 1988).

Focus group interviewing is a systematic process for gathering information. If a company is going to introduce a new product like a hair spray, it is not uncommon that the company would go to the market and ask groups of consumers to discuss their feelings about current hair sprays. In a focus group interview, the discussion would be structured, and the group moderator would have spent a great deal of time constructing an interview outline that would be used to focus the group on the pertinent questions the manufacturer wanted answers to on the general topic of hair sprays. Likewise, organizations often want information about their policies and use focus group interviews as a one-time-meeting technique for asking their employees about their policies. For example, the parking department on your campus could gather together four or five groups of students or faculty and conduct a group interview that focused on parking and how it could be improved. This group process is probably the most popular means for gathering information of a qualitative, in-depth nature.

As we've indicated above, a focus group interview requires a great deal of preparation and a good working knowledge of small group communication to be productive. Five basic steps need to be followed.

Step 1. *Determine participants.* The ideal size of a focus group is eight to ten members. When a group gets much larger than twelve, it becomes difficult to keep the group focused on one conversation at the same time. Likewise, when the group is smaller than five, group interaction can be lost, and it becomes a collection of personal interviews. The demographics of the focus group are also important. If a study is being done of newspaper readership, we would want to qualify our participants to make sure that they all read the newspaper. We would probably also want the demographics of age, race, gender, and income of our focus groups to be representative of our larger readership. Sometimes the focus group is intentionally skewed toward one demographic characteristic because of the kind of product we are focusing on. For example, if we were conducting a study on sexual harassment, we would want to focus on women; or if we were concerned with retirement housing, we might want our subjects to be sixty-five or older. The general rule is that we want to make certain all ideas that are pertinent to our topic are represented.

Step 2. *Arrange the meeting room.* Focus group interviews are such a central part of market research that most of the urban-based market research companies have their own permanent meeting room that they use for focus group interviews. These rooms usually have the following characteristics in common: There is a waiting room outside the meeting room so that the group will be brought as one body to the meeting room; there is a large round or oval table that allows for face-to-face interaction; permanently installed tape-recording equipment is used to record the meeting; and one wall contains a one-way mirror that allows for visual observation of the group. Focus groups frequently are conducted without the luxury of a formal room. Restaurants are good alternatives. It is not uncommon for a group to be served dinner in a private dining room and a focus group conducted at the end of the dinner. Regardless of where the group meeting is held, the group needs privacy—freedom from disturbing noises and with acoustics appropriate for recording the meeting.

Step 3. *Build the focus group outline.* An outline long enough to guide a discussion for about ninety minutes is needed. A rough rule of thumb is to generate twelve subtopics that are likely to produce six to eight minutes of discussion. Some subtopics will fall flat with little or no interest, whereas other issues will so excite the group that ten minutes is not enough time for the group to discuss them. For example, if the registrar is conducting a focus group on ways to improve the registration process, an issue that dealt with obtaining class overloads might not require much discussion, whereas topics like closing required courses without notice might produce a great deal of discussion. A general rule on building focus group outlines is to prepare more questions than you need. Groups often are willing to talk for two hours if the discussion is interesting, but the group and the sponsor of the research will feel cheated if the meeting only lasted forty minutes. If you are using a dramatistic outline, in addition to the rational questions you will need many scenarios to kick-start the group as you introduce each topic. Some groups need more kick-starting than others. In a group meeting focusing on parking, the topic of metered parking spaces might be introduced with the following scenario: "I've had a number of students abruptly run out of my class to 'feed the meter,' only to return enraged that they were too late! They would say things like, 'Why do we have only sixty-minute meters when we have one-hour-and-fifteen-minute lectures! It's a plot!' "

With any luck, this scenario would kick-start the group into a discussion of metered parking on campus. Sometimes dramatistic scenarios are not needed because there are one or two persons in the group who spontaneously dramatize at the mere mention of the topic. The important point to remember is that most good focus group interviews are good because the moderator spent a great deal of time preparing a detailed outline.

Step 4. *Conduct the group interview.* After preparation of a focus group outline, the next important factor in determining a successful discussion is the communication skills of the moderator. First, the moderator must be an empathetic listener. The group interviewer has to be genuinely interested in the opinion of the group members. The group will educate the moderator only if he or she is truly interested in learning. Second, the moderator must keep the group focused on its topic. If the group is supposed to be talking about hair spray and the group wanders into a discussion of new cars, the moderator must get the group back on track. The moderator must regulate participation. Regulating participation usually means controlling dominant members and drawing out quiet ones. However, an autocratic style usually is not advisable. The group conversation should flow smoothly with periods of intense discussion punctuated with humor. A moderator does not want to be a "Smokey the Bear" who stomps out an idea before it has a chance to spread throughout the group. Third, as just noted, a moderator needs to kick-start the group on many issues through the use of dramatistic scenarios. In essence, a good moderator is a pyromaniac of group discussion. He or she keeps throwing out scenarios like lit matches, watching to see which ones light fires. Finally, a good moderator needs to ask questions that were not in the planned outline spontaneously. Good discussion breeds good questions. The moderator needs to know when to depart from the outline and when to allow the group to depart from the outline if the subtopic is germane. Focus group members will always thank their moderator when a good interview is conducted because they feel that they learned so much by being present.

Step 5. *Analyze the data.* It is dangerous to draw conclusions on the basis of one focus group interview. The benchmark for most studies is five groups, with three being a minimum and twelve a maximum. There are three touchstones that a researcher looks for when analyzing a focus group interview: *redundancy, intensity,* and *creativity.* In our parking example, did all five of our student groups trash the metered parking on campus? In other words, after the third meeting, did the moderator know that when the parking meter issue came up, almost everyone in the meeting would be upset? The second touchstone for analyzing a focus group is intensity. How strongly held are the views that the group has expressed? How emotional are group members? Are they polarized on a given subtopic, with strong feelings running both ways? In a mail survey, it often is difficult to gauge how strongly someone feels on a issue when the person has checked 8 on a scale of 1 to 9. But when you see the person face to face, you have a much better indication of the intensity of his or her beliefs. The last touchstone is creativity. Group discussion often produces synergy. Out of the collective mind come new ideas that did not exist before the discussion. Market researchers who conduct focus group interviews often report that focus groups with a politician's constituents surfaced new unmet needs that the politician then addressed by way of legislation. Likewise, enlightened administrators adopt new ideas that surface in focus group interviews.

The focus group interview is a one-time-meeting technique that can be put to many uses. In addition to qualitative market research, focus groups can be used to build quantitative instruments like questionnaires. They help the researcher determine what questions to ask and the right ways to ask them. Focus groups are also widely used as parts of organizational audits and political campaigns. A person who is skilled in small group communication is in a position to do a better job of moderating a group interview than one who is not. It may be helpful for your small group communication class to conduct a mock focus group interview so that your class can observe this group process.

☐ PROBLEM-SOLVING AGENDA SYSTEMS

In Chapter 2, we indicated that two communication scholars had used Dewey's discussion of how a rational mind works as a springboard for devising a rational group thought pattern for problem-solving discussions. Just as the parliamentary procedure format forces a group to discuss one idea at a time, so problem-solving agenda systems dictate the manner in which we can resolve a problem and recommend a course of action. The six problem-solving agenda systems described in this section are not only recommended as procedures for groups to solve problems, but are also used successfully as outlines for conducting panel discussions. Dewey was probably right to say that moving from a "felt difficulty" in a step-by-step sequence to the verification of the solution is an aesthetic way to bring the mind the resolution of a problem. However, as we will discover, the problem-solving agenda of the everyday, ongoing group described in this section does not follow Dewey's prescriptive procedures (see Table 4.5).

Dewey's Reflective Thinking: McBurney and Hance

In Chapter 2, we indicated that McBurney and Hance created the first prescriptive agenda system for a problem-solving group to be derived from John Dewey's five-step reflective-thinking process. The McBurney-Hance five-step problem-solving agenda system comprises the following:

1. Definition and delineation of the problem
2. Analysis of the problem
3. Suggestion of solutions
4. Reasoned development of the proposed solutions
5. Further verification (McBurney and Hance 1939, 11–13)

McBurney and Hance broke the group thought process into two parts: consideration of the problem and evaluation of the possible solutions. We still see this dichotomy

Table 4.5   Unique Features of Problem-Solving Agenda Systems

Agenda System	Unique Feature
Dewey: McBurney & Hance	Five-part system: two parts on problem and three parts on solution, with emphasis on testing alternative solutions
Ross	Four-part system: two parts on problem and two parts on solution, with emphasis on criteria step for evaluating solutions
Wright	Ten-part system: three parts on problem and seven parts on solution, with emphasis on an exhaustive examination of solutions
Brilhart-Jochem	Five-part system: one part on problem and four parts on solution, with emphasis on brainstorming possible solutions before developing criteria
Functional	Four-part system: one part on problem and three parts on solution, with emphasis on competent performance
Cyborg	Automated system: agenda options determined by group, which facilitates anonymous, simultaneous, and rapid generation and evaluation of ideas

today in the field of rhetoric. In the late 1960s and early 1970s, it was fashionable to say that a person was either part of the problem or part of the solution. McBurney and Hance, like Dewey, devoted two steps to an analysis of the problem and three steps to the solution. The two problem steps allow the group to focus on the causes of the problem in the belief that (a) once causes are explicitly stated, solutions will be manifestly obvious; and (b) through the testing of various solutions, the group will arrive at the best solution.

This five-step procedure makes a fairly good outline for a panel discussion. However, communication scholars observe that everyday groups that are not aware of the McBurney and Hance agenda system do not follow the five-step process sequentially when presented with a problem. Yet practical experience with this agenda system and others similar to it indicates that groups of people who have only limited work experience with one another and who can meet only a few times work quite well if they follow the five-step agenda system. As long as the discussion leader does not zealously force the group through the steps but allows for needed digressions and regressions, the system works adequately as a problem-solving agenda system.

Ross Four-Step Agenda

As communication scholars taught the McBurney and Hance problem-solving agenda system to discussion students, adaptations of it began to appear. One of the more important ones was developed by Raymond Ross (1974b, 323). His agenda system comprises four major steps as follows:

1. *Definition and limitation:* a concise but qualified statement of the felt difficulty, problem, or goal
2. *Analysis:* the determination of the type or nature of the problem and its causes
    a. Puzzles—questions of fact
    b. Probabilities—reasonable predictions—chance
    c. Values—beliefs, attitudes
3. *Establishment of criteria:* a group consensus on the standards to be used in judging solutions
    a. Minimum or maximum limits, or both
    b. A rating of hierarchical importance
4. *Solutions*
    a. Suggested solutions
    b. Evaluation in terms of the criteria
    c. Decision and suggested implementation or action

As one can see, Ross's agenda system concentrates two steps each on the problem and solution phases. His system differs from that of McBurney and Hance in two significant ways. First, the Ross agenda presents a much more systematic examination of the nature of the problem. Ross recommends that the three substeps included under the analysis stage should be taught sequentially; he argues that one should look objectively at the facts of a situation before making a value judgment about it. For example, if a group were discussing the topic of legalized abortions. Ross would recommend that the group determine how many abortions were occurring before judging whether it was a detriment to society.

The second addition that Ross makes to a problem-solving agenda system is the introduction of the criteria step. Ross (1974b, 328) explains this step as follows: "*A criterion is a standard or yardstick by which we may measure or evaluate something.* In the case of group discussion, it refers to an *agreed-upon* standard." In other words, criteria are the standards by which a group evaluates its solution. Ross additionally suggests the concept of *weighting*—that is, rating criteria according to their hierarchical importance: "Weighting may be profitably considered by a group if some of the criteria are close together in importance." The solution step in the Ross four-step agenda depends on the criteria step being satisfied.

The utility of the Ross system is that it seeks consensus on criteria for judging potential solutions. If a problem-solving group can achieve this goal, its chances of reaching agreement on a course of action are greatly enhanced. Our observation of groups using this system is that discussion groups do not clearly establish criteria and then judge solutions against it, but that an interaction occurs between suggested solutions and the establishment of criteria to judge them by. However, the fact that the group is directed to develop criteria makes for better problem-solving discussion and probably enhances the quality of the decision reached by the group.

Wright Ten-Step Agenda

The Wright ten-step agenda system is, to some extent, an accumulation of group thought patterns and agenda systems that were developed in the past by various speech and small group scholars. The Wright agenda system is unique in many respects, in that it adds several new dimensions that permit a high degree of flexibility and utility for various kinds of groups. The steps of the Wright agenda system are as follows:

1. *Ventilation:* period of primary tension for the group
2. *Clarification of problem and establishment of group goals:* definitions and limitations clarified
3. *Analysis of the problem:* according to the facts, probabilities, and values
4. *Establishment of general criteria:* minimum standards necessary for considering general solutions (e.g., feasibility and utility)
5. *Suggestion of general solutions:* one typical strategy is to brainstorm for solutions
6. *Evaluation of solutions according to Steps 3 and 4:* disregarding for the remainder of the discussion those proposed solutions that do not meet general criteria
7. *Development of situational criteria:* group standards and norms appropriate to this specific problem area
8. *Evaluation of solutions according to Step 7 criteria:* narrowing of solutions to select the best solution for this particular problem area
9. *Selection of the solution:* the best solution for this specific problem area
10. *Implementation of the solution:* how will the solution best be adapted and actually put into practice? (Wright 1975, 34)

This agenda system is much more solution-oriented than the two previously mentioned agenda systems in that seven of the ten steps (Steps 4 through 10) deal with the solution in some way. The first step, ventilation, is appropriate for problem-solving groups, especially if the group has not met before. The second and third steps, which are problem-oriented, are similar to the first two steps of the Ross four-step agenda system. And although Steps 4, 5, and 6 appear fairly traditional, their relation to the two unique steps that immediately follow them offers a satisfactory way for groups to suggest and evaluate solutions. These steps are especially appropriate for ongoing groups.

Perhaps a detailed example would be helpful in outlining and emphasizing the solution steps of the Wright agenda system. Imagine that a town council were to consider designating jogging routes throughout the city. Some general criteria (Step 4) might already be established: Streets must be wide enough to accommodate joggers and so on. Several jogging routes are suggested (Step 5). The town council then evaluates the solutions—the proposed jogging routes—according to the general criteria. For example, Vernon Avenue is wide enough for joggers, but it also happens to be one of the most heavily traveled streets in the city. In other words, the solution might meet the general criteria, but it will not solve the specific problem—that is, the fact that Vernon Avenue has a great deal of automobile traffic. The town council now moves to Step 7 and develops situational criteria that are most appropriate for the specific problem area. In our jogging route example, council members suggest the following situational criteria:

1. Jogging routes should offer scenic beauty with trees and greenery
2. Routes should favor pleasure-oriented users over business users
3. Trails should not be too hilly so that families may run and jog together

The council members then evaluate solutions according to the Step 7 criteria and come to the conclusion that Vernon Avenue definitely should not be used as a jogging route. At Step 9, in which solutions are selected, the emphasis is placed on solving the specific problem in the best way. It is important that the advantages and disadvantages be examined. Finally, Broadway Avenue is selected as the best place in the city to locate jogging routes. This location meets both general and specific criteria.

The Wright agenda system is a highly functional one for both one-time-meeting and ongoing discussion groups. For one-time-meeting groups, the ten steps provide the necessary structure for the achievement of a meaningful solution to a problem. Ongoing groups are able to adapt their group thinking patterns with the aid of the Wright ten-step agenda. This adaptability is the advantage of this problem-solving agenda system over a number of others—the advantage being that a group could use three to ten of the steps, depending on the complexity of the problem the group is considering. Two other points of the Wright agenda system need to be emphasized. One is Step 7, which allows the group to alter the criteria in light of the initial solutions that the group suggests. Second, the Wright agenda includes Step 10, implementation, which often is the most difficult and neglected step of decision making.

Brilhart-Jochem Ideation Criteria

In 1964, two speech communication scholars, John Brilhart and Lurene Jochem, reported the results of their research on the utility of a problem-solving agenda system. Their research demonstrated that if members of a group brainstormed their possible solutions to a problem and then determined the criteria for evaluating their solutions, they would generate more and better ideas than groups that used traditional procedures, such as the Ross and Wright agenda systems, which propose evaluative criteria before suggesting solutions (Brilhart and Jochem 1964).

As a result of this research, Brilhart (1974, 110–11) recommended the following five-step creative problem-solving sequence:

1. What is the nature of the problem facing us—present state, obstacles, goals?
2. What might be done to solve the problem or the first subproblem?
3. By what specific criteria shall we judge among our possible solutions?
4. What are the relative merits of our possible solutions?
5. How will we put our decision into effect?

Brilhart made two contributions to the development process of agenda systems. The first one, mentioned above, says that the group should consider possible solutions before developing criteria to evaluate them. The second contribution is closely tied to the first. Brilhart and Jochem (1964) introduced the idea of using the discussion technique of brainstorming at a new place in the problem-solving agenda system. In fact, Brilhart (1974, 111) recommended that in Step 2, one should "list *all* ideas which group members suggest without evaluation." One of Brilhart's contributions to problem-solving discussions is his demonstration of the utility of integrating specific discussion techniques into problem-solving agenda systems. In the case study for this chapter we present a group that does not use an agenda system and look at the problems this causes.

In the 1990s, brainstorming and NGD are routinely used in problem-solving agenda systems. The groupware for computer-assisted problem-solving meetings invariably include brainstorming and NGD as options in their agenda systems (Jessup and Valacich 1993).

Functional Approach to Problem Solving

In the 1980s, a functional theory of small group decision making was developed (Gouran and Hirokawa 1983; Gouran, Hirokawa, McGee, and Miller 1993; Hirokawa 1985, 1988; Hirokawa and Pace 1983). By comparing various discussion agenda systems in terms of effectiveness to produce high-quality decisions, Hirokawa was able to isolate four key communication functions that could explain the high-quality decision better than any other given agenda system (1985, 1988). The functions he found important to quality decision making are as follows:

1. Understanding the problem
2. Marshaling a range of alternatives
3. Assessing positive consequences of each alternative
4. Assessing negative consequences of each alternative

The important conclusion that communication scholars make about the functional approach is that the competent performance of the four functions is more important in terms of getting a good decision than the sequencing of the functions. For more than fifty years, small group decision-making scholars have believed that the key to successful agenda systems was the sequencing of the steps. For example, in the Ross four-step agenda, it would be important to define and limit the problem before analyzing it. However, functional theorists argue that competent performance is more important than sequencing, and one agenda system may be as good as another if used competently. Hirokawa (1983) added one caution to the functional approach. He maintained that if a group radically departs from its agenda (such as discussing proposed solutions before analyzing the problem), the quality of the group decision may suffer.

Cragan and Wright's (1993) research suggests that the four functions may not be of equal importance in solving every problem. Putnam and Stohl (1990) and Billingsley (1993) added a further cautionary note that the functional approach to decision making may need to be refined when dealing with real-world groups because role talk, consciousness-raising talk, and encounter talk also affect the quality of a group's decision. This caution applies to all agenda systems, however, in that they deal almost exclusively with problem-solving talk.

Cyborg Problem-Solving Systems

In the 1990s, adaptive structuration theory was developed and tested to explain and predict the problem-solving efforts of cyborg groups (De Sanctis, Dickson, Jackson, and Poole 1991; Poole and De Sanctis, 1992; Poole and Jackson 1993). Researchers at the University of Minnesota developed a communication-based theory (adaptive structuration theory) to explain the interaction process between humans and group decision support systems (GDSS). They found that different groups use the options available in groupware differently and that the quality of the group work varied (De Sanctis et al., 1991). Our point in presenting these research findings is to emphasize that the use of computer-assisted meeting (CAM) rooms and computerized agenda systems does not predict success or failure for the group. One of the keys to success is how well the group can adapt and integrate technology into its problem-solving process.

Cyborg groups have literally hundreds of groupware packages available to them. Each package allows the cyborg group to create its own problem-solving agenda system, and the packages automate and incorporate many of the one-time-meeting techniques into the groupware. Commercially available groupware can be evaluated by answering the following questions:

1. What features does the program have for the group to create its own agenda?
2. Does the groupware have anonymous idea generation features?
3. What options does the program have for organizing group ideas?
4. What decision aids does the program have for evaluating ideas?
5. How much role flexibility does the GDSS allow?
6. Does the program have automated team-building or trust-building options?
7. In what ways does the program summarize and display group work and allow for different-time or different-place work?

Your university or place of business may not have a CAM room, but growth in the use of these rooms is so rapid you may soon have one. Figure 1.2 in Chapter 1 shows how a CAM room is laid out. Most CAM rooms seat between six and fifteen persons around a U-shaped table. Each member has a private computer terminal, and at the front of the room, there is a public viewing screen, which is akin to an electronic flip chart, that displays the group work (i.e., idea generation and voting). Most groupware allows the members simultaneously and anonymously to enter agenda items, which then can be displayed on the public screen. This software option is essentially an electronic nominal group procedure that allows the group to create a list of agenda items and, through anonymous voting, to reduce the list to the items the group wants to cover. The unique advantages that a cyborg group has over a completely human problem-solving group are speed (everyone can talk at once) and anonymity (the computer program allows people to suggest and criticize ideas without identifying themselves). Thus, there is more group ownership of ideas than individual ownership. GDSS packages retain the advantages of brainstorming and nominal group processes, which are the separation of ideas from people and the separation of idea generation from idea criticism. Most groupware systems allow group participants quickly and anonymously to evaluate a list of ideas that have been generated in four ways: assigning weights, rating, ranking, and voting.

If a student group has the responsibility to spend $100,000 on five bands to come to campus and play a concert that would be free for students, they might use groupware to generate a list of twenty-five bands. The group could then anonymously assign weights in terms of how badly they wanted a given band, but they have only 100 points to use. They could use 100 points on one band, 50 points on two bands, 25 points on four bands, and so on. The computer program would take the anonymous entries and display them instantaneously in rank order. This process might reduce the total number of bands to those that got some points and indicate which bands were most popular. The second process of rating would allow group members anonymously to rate all twenty-five bands from 1 to 10. The computer program would then point out the mean scores for each band, thus helping the group to evaluate which bands it wanted. The third way to evaluate the list of twenty-five bands is by rank ordering them from 1 to 25. The value of the GDSS package is that the individual rank orders are individually rank ordered and displayed. The fourth common aid is voting. The group could simply vote yes or no for each of the groups, or they could vote for five of the twenty-five.

These evaluation procedures can quickly produce a group decision on which five bands are preferred by the group. However, this quick process may not produce the best decision. Most groupware programs have additional decision-making aids to allow a group to produce a more sophisticated analysis when trying to reach a decision. The two most popular ones are shareholder's analysis and an allocate model. The shareholder's analysis allows the group to probe into the question of who has a stake in the outcome of the decision. In the case of our band analysis, we might determine that if one of the five bands is a blues band, the students that it attracts might be quite different from those that a hard rock or gospel group might attract. The analysis might allow the group to realize that they cannot just pick five bands on the basis of popularity. They may reach the conclusion that the student body is diverse in terms of its musical tastes. Therefore, to be fair to everyone, they might want to have five bands that run the spectrum of the tastes of the various stakeholders (students) on campus.

Assume that our hypothetical student group has decided to have five different bands that represent five different stakeholders on campus. The group has to decide how to spend the $100,000. The allocate model helps groups to solve this problem. Each member of the student group can anonymously enter in his or her distribution of the $100,000. A member could use all of it to get the greatest blues band in the country or choose to allocate $20,000 to each of the five bands. Again, the group can view the scores and reconcile the difference.

Most software systems provide many useful options in the decision-making process of a group, but most computer-assisted agenda systems restrict the role process, encounter process, and consciousness-raising process of problem-solving groups. Role-playing, team-building, and trust-building talk are not accounted for in the other problem-solving agenda systems that have been discussed; however, some progress is being made with GDSS software. Two software packages, SAMM and Group Systems V, have a "mood meter" that allows members to record, on a scale of 1 to 5, how they think the meeting is progressing. Also, SAMM allows for any member of the group to become the task leader and run the task processes from her or his terminal. Group software has improved the ability of members to play the information provider role, central negative role, and task leader role. Little software is available to assist the group roles of social-emotional leader and tension-releaser. Our own experience as facilitators for business decision-making groups tells us that trust-building and team-building processes are important. We usually include activities that facilitate these processes when we run meetings.

☐ SUMMARY

This chapter focuses attention on group patterns that can be applied to discussion situations in both ongoing and one-time-meeting groups. Twenty patterns are described, and the time and place at which each would be useful are explained.

The problem-solving group patterns are classified according to the following major headings: *discussion formats, problem-solving agenda systems,* and *specific decision-*

making techniques. The section on discussion formats addresses such issues as the seating arrangement of a discussion and the participation patterns of various types of discussion. Six major discussion formats are examined: roundtable discussion, symposium, panel discussion, forum types, colloquy, and parliamentary procedure. The roundtable discussion is developed as a private discussion format, whereas the remaining five are designed to serve as formats for public discussion. Whatever the type and nature of each format, each of them is concerned to varying degrees with *where you sit, when you talk,* and *how long you talk.*

Specific decision-making techniques are the second major type of problem-solving patterns covered in the chapter. The following eight specific techniques are identified and explained: NGD, Delphi technique, brainstorming, buzz groups, single-question form, ideal-solution form, PERT, and focus group interviews. The majority of these are described in terms of their utility in one-time-meeting groups. In addition, some of the techniques—for example, brainstorming—are discussed in light of the ways in which they could be used within problem-solving agenda systems. The extent to which the discussion techniques and problem-solving agenda systems work effectively in group discussions is largely determined by the kind of group that uses them. A knowledge of the three major classes of discussion patterns presented in this chapter is vital to our understanding of what makes good groups work.

Problem-solving agenda systems constitute the third set of problem-solving group patterns. The agenda systems discussed in this chapter include the five-step agenda system based on Dewey's steps of reflective thinking, the Ross four-step agenda, the Wright ten-step agenda, the Brilhart-Jochem ideation-criteria schema, the functional approach, and the group's own agenda. An illustration of the use of each of these methods is given. Some agenda systems are viewed as being more problem-oriented and other more solution-oriented. The discussion of each of these highlights the analysis, criteria, and solution phases of the problem-solving sequences.

When you have mastered the use of these twenty group problem-solving patterns, you can add them to the twenty core communication skills identified in Chapter 3. If you are keeping score with us—and we hope you are—we have now identified forty communication behaviors that have the potential to improve group outcomes.

CASE STUDY

The Parking Committee

CASE BACKGROUND

A blue-ribbon committee was appointed by the president of the university to explore the perennial problems of parking on campus. There were nine members on the committee:

- Charles Borris, vice-president of administration service, chairperson of committee
- Paul Ruzzo, president of the Civil Service Council
- Arlene Turner, assistant to the university engineer
- Bill Robertson, professor and chairperson of political science
- Roberta Jones, assistant professor of special education
- Barbe Johnson, graduate student and teaching assistant in the Department of Communication
- Melinda Hubbert, student-government representative
- Mike Winchell, vice-president of student-government association

This committee has had three meetings. During these meetings, a great deal of ventilation has taken place in that everyone got an opportunity to describe vividly their best examples of the parking problem. The problem seemed to extend beyond parking regulations into the operations of the parking department itself. Faculty and students depicted the parking department as a place populated by insensitive administrators who enforced parking regulations like "fanatical fascists." In an equally stereotypic manner, the administrators and staff on the committee described faculty and students as "lawbreakers who constantly try to circumvent campus regulations."

At the close of the most recent meeting, Charles Borris had strongly urged members to bury the hatchet and come to the next meeting with positive suggestions on how to solve the parking problem.

CASE LOG

Charles Borris opened the meeting by reminding committee members that they were to come prepared to present reasonable solutions. Arlene handed out a typed sheet of paper that contained her four suggestions. The rest of the group seemed surprised by this behavior, and Mike and Melinda were openly upset.

MELINDA: We were not told to write out our suggestions to be handed out. I think it's unfair! This committee is stacked against the students!

MIKE: I agree! Why are you doing this, Dr. Borris? You're acting just like the parking department—making regulations without consulting the constituents.

CHARLES: I have no intention of co-opting any committee member's right to make suggestions, nor have I closed my mind to any suggestions. I happen to think that Arlene has some good ideas here. Let's provide her with an opportunity to at least present her ideas.

ROBERTA: Frankly, Arlene, if our committee were to recommend this idea to the president, the student newspaper would crucify us. I can just see the headlines: "Committee duped by Borris: Fines Increased from $15 to $25."

MELINDA: I can just see the cartoon that goes with that caption—it'll show us as committee members all peeking out of Dr. Borris's pocket. (laughter)

MIKE: Yeah, we'll have a pretty "blue ribbon" tied around our collective necks with the ribbon being held by Borris's hand. (more laughter)

(While the group is in a state of laughter, Bill Robertson got up from the table and calmly wrote each person's name on the top of the chalkboard.)

PAUL: Hey, Bill, are you planning on giving a lecture on the "Fall of Greek Democracies"?

BILL: Well, Paul, as a matter of fact, in a way I am. It's clear that this committee is going to fail unless we begin to pull together. We were all in favor of forming this committee, and we all volunteered to serve on it. I believe we all truly want to find a solution to our parking problem, so let's get to work. What I propose we do is the following:

1. Go around the room and have each person list his or her best solution to the parking problem.
2. Give an explanation of why it would work.
3. After all the solutions have been presented let's take a vote by secret ballot and see what solutions emerge that we have in fact agreed to.

Barbe, why don't we start with you. What is your favorite suggestion?

BARBE: The most important suggestion I have is pay-by-the-day lots for computer students. Currently, you have to either pay by the hour or buy a sticker for the year. Many students commute only two or three days a week, and it would be more economical to pay only two dollars a day.

BILL: Fine, Barbe. What's your idea, Paul?

PAUL: I feel that an employee of the university should not have to pay for a place to park. However, if we must charge a fee, it should be based on one's ability to pay. The civil service personnel receive only half the average salary of faculty members, and yet we still have to pay the same amount. That's just not fair!

BILL: Charles, why don't you give us your best suggestion.

CHARLES: I don't care to make a suggestion at this time.

BILL: Come on, Chuck, give me one.

CHARLES: I really think that this is a waste of time writing ideas on the board like this. What we should be doing is to write our ideas down, like Arlene did, and bring them to the next meeting.

MELINDA: With all due respect, Dr. Borris, I think we are doing the right thing. We need to discuss openly our ideas even if there is conflict.

MIKE: Yeah. Besides, we already came prepared to this meeting. We don't need to go home and think about our ideas all over again.

CHARLES: I think we should adjourn the meeting until all of the people have written down their suggestions.

ARLENE: I can go along with the way we are doing it now Charles. Bill, write down my idea about raising the parking fine to twenty-five dollars.

BILL: Now wait a minute, Chuck. You and I have served on a lot of university committees together and we've never gotten this formal before. Where does it say in the university handbook that people must write out their ideas before submitting them for discussion?

CHARLES: I am just trying to provide some order and direction for this committee. I thought that was my job when the president appointed me chairperson of this committee. This meeting is getting out of control like the previous meetings have.

ROBERTA: Dr. Borris, I believe you put your finger on it. For you the meeting is "out of control" when ideas are introduced that you do not agree with. You seem unwilling to let this committee reach conclusions that run counter to your current positions.

CHARLES: Sounds like you no longer want me to serve as chairperson of this committee. You can go to the president tomorrow and ask him to remove me as chair of this committee!

PAUL: Nobody wants you to resign as chair, Charles. We just want a little more freedom to discuss our ideas.

BILL: Maybe Chuck's got a point. What do you say that we all type up our three top ideas and the rationale behind them and have a free-flowing exchange of ideas at the next meeting.

ARLENE: I can support that.

CHARLES: Fine. Our next meeting will be at four o'clock on Wednesday. Please bring your *written* suggestions to the meeting, with copies for everyone.

CASE QUESTIONS

1. In polarized groups, what is the best way to ensure equal participation in presenting suggestions?
2. Was Bill Robertson's suggestion for solving the group's conflict a good one?
3. Is it normal for a committee to create ground rules as they go, or should Dr. Borris have introduced his ideas of meeting procedure earlier?
4. How can you allow ideational conflict without the discussion turning to procedural and interpersonal conflict?

CHAPTER FIVE

PREPARING FOR GROUP PROBLEM SOLVING

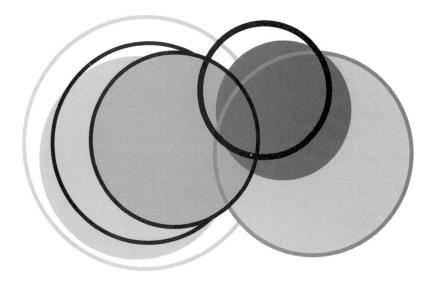

CHAPTER OBJECTIVES

After reading this chapter, you should be able to:

- Know the commitments of an ethical participant
- Use the research and organizational strategies for good decision making
- Test evidence and construct arguments in problem solving
- Prepare a discussion outline

In our complex society, small groups have short periods of time in which to meet for face-to-face discussion. In corporations, a decision-making team of four or five persons may manage only one hour a week, and volunteer groups working on community issues may be able to schedule only one meeting a month. Given the complexity of group structure and the brief time that groups have for discussion, it is amazing that any work gets done. Groups that have successful discussions are groups that have done their homework. Each member has done extensive preparation on the topic for discussion so that those precious sixty minutes when the group is in face-to-face discussion will be productive.

In this chapter, we detail the essential preparation skills you need to be an effective discussant. In addition to behaving ethically in a discussion, you need to know how to research and organize the material to converse intelligently on a complex topic. Also, you need to be able to analyze evidence and construct and analyze arguments that occur during the discussion.

☐ GROUP ETHICAL STANDARDS

Work groups in general and decision-making groups in particular have, over time, established certain unstated ethical standards that most people assume will be operative when they interact with other people in a small group. The communication discipline has a long tradition of teaching these ethical behaviors as part of its teaching of discussion courses. The expected ethical behavior in a problem-solving group includes ten commitments to your fellow discussants:

1. To doing your best
2. To the group good

3. To rationality
4. To fair play
5. To good listening
6. To preparation
7. To ideational conflict
8. To objectivity
9. To tolerance
10. To social maturity

Commitment to Doing Your Best

Each group member brings a unique personality, set of social experiences, and knowledge of the job, the discussion topic, or both to the group. Implicitly, the group expects each member to make available his or her special talents for the group's benefit. When it appears that a member is holding back some talent or knowledge, conflict usually ensues. The person who is "sandbagging" usually thinks that he or she has the right not to contribute. But the group will believe that an ethic has been violated. Sometimes these conflicts develop over role selection. A person may possess vast experience at handling interpersonal conflict but refuse to play the role of the social-emotional leader.

At other times, a person may avoid the responsibilities of task leadership because he or she does not want the extra work. But again, if the group believes that this person is best suited for task leader, they will be offended if he or she does not assume the role of leadership. In fact, some people may go through life constantly asking the question, "Why me?" It seems as though every group they join demands that they play roles they do not want to assume.

People who possess expert knowledge or skills that are in high demand often find themselves in a "role rut," in that each group they work in "forces" them to play a role that draws on their expertise. In discussions, that role often is information-provider, if the person has exceptional research and synthesis skills. On basketball teams, it often is the person who is forced to play the rebounder, when he or she would prefer to be a top scorer.

People who have had a lot of experience working in groups and who are constantly forced to play roles they do not like often hide their talents from the group. This then becomes an ethical issue: Does a person have a right to withhold knowledge and expertise from the group? The ethical standards that have emerged from group discussions say no, that a person must do his or her best.

Commitment to the Group Good

Of the ten most frequently played roles in group discussion that are presented in Chapter 8, the one negative role is the self-centered follower. The communication behavior that frequently is exhibited by this role is special-interest pleading. When people work in groups, there is an assumption that they are working for a common good. When a group member appears to be using the group for his or her individual ends, conflict ensues in which the self-centered follower is accused of unethical behavior.

A violation of this ethic in team sports is easy to spot. The self-centered follower is the player who sacrifices team victory to achieve individual honors. In group discussions, the self-centered follower is not always so apparent. Sometimes it is a person who has personality conflicts with the leader and works against the group's goals as a means of attacking the leader. Occasionally a person will use the group for his or her own professional advancement. This often happens in corporate settings when people must produce a group product but are rewarded and promoted on an individual basis.

The ethical issue is whether a person must sacrifice his or her individual goals for the group's goals when the two are not in concert. Many small group theorists would argue that a person has an ethical responsibility to put the group good ahead of his or her own good.

Commitment to Rationality

Group decisions pose threats to individual convictions. The process of reasoning out a conclusion that several people can accept requires a commitment to rational thinking. It means that each member must be willing to abandon his or her previous beliefs on an issue if sufficient arguments are marshaled in the discussion to justify a change in opinion. Later in this chapter, we sketch out the kinds of rational argument that normally are accepted as the means to establish a conclusion that the group can accept. You will discover that most of the rational thinking that occurs in groups has already become normative behavior. What you may have difficulty with, if you have had little experience in group discussion, is the tact that is required to persuade somebody in the group to change his or her opinion while maintaining his or her active cooperation in the group.

Ideally, groups should reach only conclusions that have been rationally accepted by the group's members. However, in day-to-day discussion groups, this ideal seldom is achieved. Groups will develop procedures for handling beliefs that are intensely and emotionally held by the group members. Each person in the group may have the unwritten right to have the group agree with him or her, not because the member has demonstrated rational argument but because it is an important emotional issue for that member. Sometimes we call these issues pet peeves. One member of a group may dramatically assert that their weekly meetings must break immediately at noon so that they have a full lunch hour. Another member may become totally irrational about the thought of a weekend meeting, whereas another member will meet any place but at one certain spot. Most groups will attempt to accommodate one or two pet peeves per member if their acquiescence does not jeopardize the major work of the group.

Finally, a commitment to rationality has its justification rooted in our intellectual search for truth. Certainly one of the most time-honored ethics of discussion is the belief that well-meaning people who have been trained in group methods can reason together and that the product of their discussion is our best facsimile of intellectual truth.

Commitment to Fair Play

In a court of law, the prosecuting attorney presents only those arguments that prove the guilt of a defendant with the expectation that the defense attorney will present those arguments that suggest the defendant's innocence. The judge and jury then objectively sort out the truth of the matter. The fair play of the courtroom is not fair play in a group discussion. Group members must objectively search out all evidence and arguments that support their individual viewpoints; however, during a discussion, they should not conceal arguments or evidence that might help the group.

Group discussants should not attempt to manipulate or entrap one another in their common search for truth. In a court of law, lawyers may use clever strategies that unnerve witnesses or infuriate their opposition. But in a discussion, there is no opponent; everyone should be working cooperatively for the common good. Therefore, a good discussant does not compete against the other group members.

In small groups that are composed of more than seven members, there is a tendency for cliques to form. Power struggles ensue between rival factions. These struggles often can subvert the group good. Members can get so intense about their internal structure that no work gets done. A commitment to fair play requires that power plays within the group should not jeopardize the group's goals.

Commitment to Good Listening

An ethical standard that all discussants should endorse is a commitment to good listening. Listening goes beyond just hearing fellow group members talk. For us to be able to play the role of an active listener in a discussion, we must listen attentively to what fellow group members are saying. How often we respond to member contributions shows whether we have been listening or not. Heightening our awareness of good listening and using favorable listening habits can only help us in achieving the other previously mentioned ethical standards that discussants should continually try to attain.

Commitment to Preparation

Occasionally discussion groups spontaneously create an idea that is truly remarkable. But most of the time, productive results of group work stem from a lot of hard work by the individual members, most of which is done *before* the discussion convenes. If you want to have a good discussion, do your homework!

When you observe an experienced roundtable discussion on television, you do not see the hundreds of hours of research that go into its preparation. Few people, even those who are experts on a subject, can glibly recall the necessary evidence and arguments in the heat of a face-to-face discussion without sufficient advance planning. An hour-long discussion requires at least ten hours of preparation by each member and probably even more on the part of the task leader. This ratio of ten to one is a good benchmark to follow in respect to routine business discussion; however, major policy decision-making discussions may require months of work to formulate an effective policy. Group discussions are only a waste of time when time is not taken to prepare for the meeting.

Commitment to Ideational Conflict

In addition to your commitment to do your best to work for the group good, to deliberate rationally, and to be a fair player, you should work on your communication skills so that you can attack a person's ideas without attacking the person. In Chapter 9, we describe several group techniques for minimizing this problem, but in routine day-to-day discussions, each member must work at separating the person from the idea.

Experienced discussion groups have a high tolerance for verbal argument. They interrogate and examine arguments in a vigorous manner and at the same time avoid injuring the people who formulated the arguments. Newly formed groups usually have to verbalize the fact continually that ideas, not people, are under examination. So when you are a member of a new group, it is often helpful to say explicitly that you want to examine the argument with no intended offense against the person. You'll remember from Chapter 4 that nominal group discussion and brainstorming both separate people from their ideas to maximize ideational conflict.

Commitment to Objectivity

Dispassionate objectivity is a highly valued quality of a group member. If a person has a reputation for being objective while reasoning together with other discussants, his or her career usually is significantly enhanced in the company. When you are in a discussion, make a concerted effort to separate the facts from your opinion. In other words, don't color the data to fit a group outcome you might want. Also, your job description within a company may produce a kind of "occupational blinder" that in subtle ways keeps you from viewing the data objectively. For example, if you are in a marketing department, you'll have to work hard to escape the mind-set of market research and try to see the problem as sales or advertising might. So being objective in a discussion is hard work, but it is worth the effort.

Commitment to Tolerance

Most people that you work with in groups will not have had the benefit of the course you are now taking. As a consequence, you may be initially shocked at the ill-mannered group behavior you confront. Try not to be too judgmental about your colleagues. Most of them don't intend to be so uncouth; they just have not had formal training in small group discussion. Many of them may have aggressive communication styles that you find abrasive, but be tolerant. By following your example of good group skills, most problem-solving groups are educable and in time will mature.

Commitment to Social Maturity

For a group to make good decisions, a great deal of ideational conflict must occur. Some evidence will be found to be useless, and many arguments will turn out to be flawed. It is through this collective examination of evidence and reasoning that groups can arrive at solutions that are better than those of an individual acting alone. So don't be defensive when arguments you advance are defeated or evidence you researched is dismissed by the group. In fact, you should willingly participate in the close scrutiny of evidence and arguments you have advanced to ensure their correctness. A clear mark of a mature discussant is the ability to have many of your arguments shot down and not take it personally.

☐ ANALYZING TOPICS FOR PROBLEM SOLVING

Many groups struggle with defining their purpose, especially in identifying the goals that the group hopes to reach. Even within an organization, when a company executive has mandated that a collection of employees form a group, the group's mission usually is so vague that the members must hold several discussions in their attempt to determine what kinds of questions they need to ask to meet the group's goals. In Chapter 4, we list numerous one-time-meeting techniques that are designed to help discussion groups efficiently formulate and organize their task.

Traditionally, groups have clarified their purpose and structured their discussion by breaking down their topic into three general question types: *questions of fact, questions of value,* and *questions of policy.* Table 5.1 shows the major characteristics of these discussion questions.

Questions of Fact

A typical topic for discussion in a city government might be "Should the city contract with a private garbage collector to supplement city efforts?" In a meat-packing company, an executive discussion group might deal with the topic "Should we continue to use nitrates for preserving meat products?" Both of these discussion groups have a question of policy before them; however, before they attempt to answer their respective policy questions, they will seek answers to numerous questions of fact and value.

Both groups will have a natural tendency to ask, "Is there a problem?" This question is not solely a question of fact because there is an implicit value judgment involved. But initially, the groups will treat the question as a question of fact, and the discussants will try to present the facts that will answer the question. The city government group might ask the question, "Is all the garbage collected weekly?" and the meat-packing group might ask, "Are consumers being harmed by ingesting the company's meat products?" Both groups would seek expert testimony in attempting to answer their questions, but what if authorities on the subject came to conflicting

TABLE 5.1   Discussion Questions and Their Characteristics

Type of Discussion Question	Characteristics of Discussion Question
Question of fact	1. Empirically verifiable 2. Usually requires little group discussion if facts are verifiable
Question of value	1. Deals with unquantifiables such as "worth," "good," "benefits" 2. Not empirically verifiable
Question of policy	1. Almost always uses "should" or equivalent word in question 2. Advocates a change from the status quo

conclusions regarding these questions of fact? In other words, what if some council members claimed that garbage was collected in their wards, while others claimed that it was not? What if some experts claimed that nitrate in meat causes cancer, while others asserted the opposite? Caught in the swirl of conflicting testimony, the groups might seek more explicit information to help answer their questions of fact. The members of the meat-packing group might examine the original cancer studies in an effort to determine what they believe are the facts. The city discussion group might conduct its own study to determine whether all the garbage is collected each week. Although these two groups might think it a simple matter to answer their respective questions of fact, they will discover that most facts are hard to verify. Research and reasoning are required on the part of the discussion group, and decision-making groups often move on to questions of value and, ultimately, questions of policy, even though the members differ about what the facts are. As a general rule, the more a group can agree on the facts of a topic, the easier it will be to reach a consensus on their ultimate question of policy.

Questions of Value

Questions of value are even more difficult to answer than questions of fact, partly because it is difficult to frame the question so we can verify the answer, but mostly because of the emotions that are attached to each value. Questions of value produce the biggest breaches in a group's commitment to rationality. It is difficult for us to compromise our values, and yet compromise is required for decisions to be reached.

Many groups attempt to answer their questions of value by establishing criteria that will allow for verifiable evidence to be used. The aborting of a human fetus has been a long-standing emotional controversy in the history of Western culture. A group discussing the legality of abortion might ask the value question, "Is an abortion immoral?" After much discussion, the group might discover that all the members believe in the sacredness of human life and then proceed to reduce their question of value on the morality of abortion to the question of fact: "When does human life occur?" The group members would then be able to seek out expert testimony and examine scientific research reports. They may then find that some people believe that life occurs at conception (the spiritual argument); some believe that life occurs when the baby can sustain its life outside the mother (the clinical argument); and some argue that human life occurs at birth (the legal argument). The group would probably conclude that they had three value structures present in the group that were almost impossible to resolve and that a policy decision would, by definition, violate somebody's value structure. Successful groups manage to reach decisions that explicitly compromise some members' values while at the same time maintaining group unity.

Questions of Policy

Despite the lack of clarity and agreement that exists in the group in regard to questions of fact and value, the group eventually must act. The group must decide what must be done. Answering a question of policy is ultimately a comparative process in which various alternative courses of action are compared. The process usually is quite rational and pragmatic in that the advantages and disadvantages of each proposal are examined. However, the problem in answering a question of policy lies in the difficulty of forecasting the impact of new courses of action.

After various alternatives have been set forth and examined, the group must finally recognize the "right" policy. The right policy seldom is verifiable because of the inherent limitations of assessing what the outcome of our action will be. This difficulty is one of the reasons discussion theorists have clung to the process of group discussion for arriving at truth. In our legal system, we do not defend any given jury's decision as being just, but we defend the legal system's due process as our best chance at achieving justice. Small group theorists have devised numerous systems for dealing with questions of policy.

Research and Organizational Strategies for Problem Solving

In some quarters, group discussions have the bad reputation of being an inefficient use of valuable time. In the business world, you frequently hear people complaining about the low productivity of a meeting they just attended. Some people even calculate the salaries of the seven or eight persons present and estimate the amount lost to the company. This sort of criticism often is justified. Part of the reason groups waste time relates to a lack of time spent in preparation for the meeting. Sometimes we harbor the feeling that the leader is responsible for setting the agenda, and therefore, all we have to do is show up and see what happens. The fact of the matter is that good discussants spend as much time researching the discussion topic as does the leader. When we see a good roundtable discussion on television that appears casual and relaxed, you can be sure that a great deal of time was spent by each panel member researching the subject. On occasion, a television discussant will have a whole research staff to support those few minutes of air time. Whether you are participating in a campus discussion, attending a corporate business meeting, or working in a public group on social policy, there are basic research and organizational strategies you can use to ensure that you are well informed and able to make a positive contribution to the group.

Library Research Strategies

Libraries of the future may be called informational retrieval systems. With computer, laser beam, and microfiche technologies, we can now do a literature search from our home-based terminal. Some corporations have already placed all their data on computers so that all information has to be retrieved at the computer terminal. For most of us, particularly when dealing with a political policy issue, the conventional library is still our major resource for printed material. So it is important to know how to obtain information in college and public libraries that has not yet been computerized. But check to see how much has been computerized. Our own university library has an on-line computer system that allows a person to scan all holdings in the library from a computer terminal. These terminals are located within the library, in academic departments, and in student residence halls. If your library doesn't have such a system, you will have to do it the old-fashioned way!

Four indexes form the basis for gathering materials on a given subject. They are *The New York Times Index, The Monthly Catalog of United States Government Publications, The Reader's Guide to Periodical Literature,* and the library's card catalog of its holdings. Start with the library's card catalog and locate the four most recent books on your subject. Go to these books and look at their footnotes and bibliographies to determine what materials the authors used in writing their books. Find the major works that were most often footnoted on the four books, and examine their bibliographies to see where the authors of those books got their information. This process will soon reveal to you the major works on the subject and the individuals whom most people regard as the experts on the subject.

Observational Research Strategies

The information you receive secondhand can be confusing and contradictory. When this occurs, there is no substitute for direct observation. If you are a member of a parent-teacher association that has received continual complaints about traffic patterns at an intersection near a school, you may determine that the printed material you got from the police department, such as traffic flow studies, and your random phone calls to parents in the school neighborhood leave you unable to decide whether there really is a traffic problem. In this case, you may want to see for yourself.

Systematic observation includes more than just your direct observation. Certainly walking down to the intersection and watching the traffic flow when school lets out is one way to look at things, but there are ways to make your observational patterns more reliable. One way is to develop an operational definition of "traffic flow," which might mean simply counting the number of cars that go through the intersection during a given time period and comparing this information with the number of cars flowing through another intersection that has traffic lights. A second procedure is to develop an observational definition of "dangerous." This task could be accomplished by having several people during specified periods record their subjective evaluation of the "dangerousness" of the intersection on several scales, such as "most dangerous" to "least dangerous." If the observers all tended to evaluate the traffic situation in the same manner, you may have acquired, through your own systematic observation, the data you need to form your opinion.

Interpersonal Research Strategies

Our technological society tends to highlight questions of fact and underemphasize questions of value in regard to many questions of policy. Many times discussants come well prepared to discuss the facts of a problem but have not carefully thought out their positions on the fundamental values of a policy change. We may think that we know our value structure, but in the heat of a discussion, we may find ourselves unable to articulate it, or we may even state positions that in retrospect are not really ours. Therefore, it is important that you carefully consider in advance of a discussion what your values are on the topic. One technique that will help you in this preparation is to make a list of what values are at stake in the discussion and then talk out to yourself the feelings you have about each one. This exercise will help you to refine your thinking so that you can make a better contribution to the group. It also will help you to control any excessive emotionality that may be present when you articulate your value structure on a given topic.

Organizational Strategies

Discussants occasionally have overresearched and underorganized their topics. They bring voluminous materials to a discussion, but they discover that an hour-long face-to-face meeting provides little time to search through books or fumble through notes for needed material. Therefore, experienced discussants condense their information onto note cards and may well make up visual aids that display critical charts and tables for the group to refer to during its deliberations. When public discussions are held on television, vital items of information, particularly statistical tables and charts, are prepared in advance so that they may be called forth on the television screen for the home viewer's benefit. No matter how well researched a discussion topic is, it must be organized to meet the time and situational constraints of the particular discussion situation.

☐ REASONING SKILLS OF THE PARTICIPANT

When a group member goes off to the library to do research on a topic, he or she must determine what information should be gathered so that the group can make a rational decision. Generally speaking, three types of evidence are gathered: facts, statistics, and opinions. If the campus parking problem is being researched, a good fact to gather may well be a written copy of the current parking policy. Because these policies usually are vague, interviews might be conducted with the parking officials to gather their opinions about the parking policy. Statistics on how many tickets are given annually and how much money students pay in fines might also be valuable evidence. Thus, the evidence gathered for discussion can be classified into factual evidence, authority opinion, and statistics.

In the process of gathering evidence, the context in which we find it will later help us to test its acceptableness. As the researcher reads the parking policies over several years and listens as experts sketch in the evolution of the policy over a period of time, he or she begins to put the parking issues into perspective. He or she might learn, for example, that the parking policies have been examined and altered in the midst of great conflict every year. Or that they are etched in stone and are handed down unchanged from year to year. He or she might find that there is systematic data on parking or that there is a dearth of statistics. Although the researcher does not write down the historical backdrop or context in which evidence is found, he or she tends to form a mental picture of what has taken place, which will form a valuable part of the discussion when the group attempts to evaluate the problem.

Tests of Evidence

Finding and testing evidence occur simultaneously during the research process. Presumably, a discussant would present to the group only evidence he or she thought was valid. It often is embarrassing to present evidence in a discussion only to find

TABLE 5.2   **Tests of Evidence**

Evidence Type	Questions to Test Evidence
	Is the evidence:
Factual	directly observable?
	authoritatively reported?
	statistically acceptable?
Opinion	authoritative?
	objective?
	recent?
	consistent?
	sufficient?
Statistical	acceptable operational definition?
	well designed?
	replicable?
	objectively reported?

out that other group members have dismissed the same data because of obvious deficiencies in it. Therefore, it is useful to have some general rules of thumb for assessing the acceptableness of evidence in a discussion (see Table 5.2).

Tests of Factual Evidence A group's eyewitness observation produces what the group calls *directly observable* facts. The written parking policy is a fact that can be directly observed by the group. However, most of the factual evidence a group will deal with depends on *authoritative reporting*. Thus, most work groups must examine the authoritativeness of the source of its facts. This examination requires that the group treat factual statements as though they were opinions. If the evidence passes the opinion-evidence test, the group will then regard the evidence as fact. Likewise, most of the "facts" present in a discussion are derived from statistics. Therefore, most factual evidence in discussion will have to pass the statistical tests.

If a group is dealing with a problem of unemployment in the United States, seeking out unemployed people to prove that they exist would probably not be a wise or feasible expense of the group's time. Yet the group might reasonably examine the authoritativeness of agencies and people who report the number of the unemployed. And the group might examine the statistical acceptableness of their reports in attempting to determine how many people in the United States are unemployed.

Tests of Opinion Evidence In deciding whether we should accept somebody's opinion as acceptable evidence, we first determine whether it is authoritative—that is, whether the person knows what he or she is talking about. If we are dealing with medical opinions, we regard the possession of a medical degree as at least a sign that the person can be believed. We also accept firsthand information as authoritative; for example, you know when you have a headache! However, most discussions generate a large number of authoritative opinions that typically seem to contradict one another. When this occurs, we usually decide whom we are going to believe on the basis of *objectivity, recency, consistency,* and *sufficiency*.

In reading a magazine article or a scientific study or just listening to someone talk, we try to determine whether he or she is objective about the issue in question. If he or she seems unduly biased, we tend to dismiss his or her opinion unless the statements are in contradiction to the known bias of the speaker. In a court of law, such statements are called reluctant testimony. If the director of student parking says that the parking laws are unjust toward the students, we tend to write that statement down. Likewise, if a student receives an "F" in class but still maintains that the course and the professor are outstanding, the testimony is believable because it contradicts an expected bias.

When we have two statements by physicians that list the causes of lung cancer, and one statement is from 1933 and the other from 1995, we might accept the more recent statement, under the general belief that new knowledge has come to light since the first statement was made. If we have two statements from unbiased sources and compare them on the basis of consistency and sufficiency, we will choose the one that is logically consistent, not only with itself but also with other assertions that we have already found to be acceptable. In addition, the statement chosen should contain sufficient information so that the group will feel confident that the source is reliable. Sometimes fragmented opinions indicate the presence of a dishonest source. For example, if a source claimed that the rain yesterday cost a candidate the election, that statement by itself might be regarded as internally inconsistent or, at best, insufficient.

Tests of Statistical Evidence The *objectivity* of a source is important to a group in determining whether or not the members should believe the statistics reported. For example, an organization that is already on record as opposing national medical care might claim to have shown that the average American family has $1,000 for medical care. Yet they might not report that the mode (that is, the amount most frequently found) in this study is $200 per family. So an old adage is still true: "Statistics don't lie, but people lie with statistics."

Even when a discussion group accepts that the source of a statistic is objective, members may still question the findings because of their disagreement with the operational definitions of key concepts used in the study. A study reported in a professional journal might report that 20 percent of people experience stage fright when giving a public speech. The group members' own experience may indicate that they seldom see people who experience stage fright—that is, who are unable to give a speech. A close examination of the study could reveal that the researcher's operational definition of stage fright arose from one item on a questionnaire that asked people if they had ever experienced stage fright when giving a speech. In almost every piece of research, there is room for argument about whether the operational definitions used in the study capture the meaning of what is actually under investigation. So when group discussants read a statistic that 30 percent of the people who live in the United States live in poverty, they should immediately ask themselves, "What is the operational definition of poverty used in the study, and do I agree with it?"

Sometimes work groups, by necessity, get deeply involved with a topic and, as a result, most closely examine a number of statistical studies. The results of these examinations will lead the group into a consideration of the research designs of the major studies to see whether they have been replicated. The controversies that surround birth control pills and their linkage to medical problems such as cancer pro-

duce highly technical public discussions that often center on the design of the research (i.e., how the experiments were set up). Discussants want to know whether
there were good controls; how the sample was taken; what was the size of the dose;
and whether it is possible to generalize from the laboratory animals used in the experiments to humans. They will also ask whether several researchers using the same
procedures came up with the same findings; that is, was there replication? Lay discussion groups are capable of delving into and competently evaluating complex issues if they have been given sufficient time and motivation. However, superficial
treatment of important problems by uninformed sources is not only boring to listen
to, but also dangerous in terms of the conclusions that can be reached.

Types of Argument

In our commitment to rational discussion, the normative behavior for a discussant is
not only to research evidence on a topic thoroughly, but also to marshal that evidence in some manner so that logical arguments are built that will justify the conclusions the group reaches. There are four types of small arguments that are most frequently performed using the facts, statistics, and opinions that we gather. They are
arguments from *authority assertion, sign, example,* and *cause.*

In fifth and sixth grades, most of us learned the important parts of a sentence and
how they relate to one another by going to the blackboard and diagramming sentences. In 1958, Stephen Toulmin developed a system for laying out logical arguments that is very much like diagramming sentences. Toulmin (1958), a British logi-
cian, stated that a rational argument is essentially movement from acceptable data
through a warrant to a claim. This definition of argument was interpreted and developed by two American communication scholars, Douglas Ehninger and Wayne
Brockriede, and has now become a routine way for explaining rational argument to
debaters and group discussants (Brockriede and Ehninger 1960).

Toulmin's system contains six components: three major parts and three minor
parts. The major components are data, warrant, and claim; the minor parts are backing, qualifier, and reservation. So an argument starts with acceptable evidence. From
that evidence, we make an inferential leap (i.e., warrant) to some claim or conclusion. The backing is evidence that supports the warrant and, thus, helps to justify the
acceptableness of an inferential leap. A qualifier expresses the degree of confidence
or probability we attach to our claim. The reservation expresses our doubts about the
acceptableness of the argument. The layout of these six components is as shown in
Figure 5.1.

Argument by Authority Assertion The most common form of rational argument in
discussion probably is argument from authority assertion. Because we live in such a
complex society, we often are forced to form conclusions that are merely restate-
ments of conclusions reached by people we regard as experts. This kind of argument
lays out on the Toulmin system in the following manner.

As you can see in Figure 5.2, the acceptableness of an authority assertion argument
finally boils down to the group's belief in the credibility of Dr. Jones as an authority
and, if that is not sufficient, to an examination of Dr. Jones's reasons for reaching
these conclusions. If Dr. Jones did not rely on another authority for her conclusion,

FIGURE **5.1**   **Argument Layout**

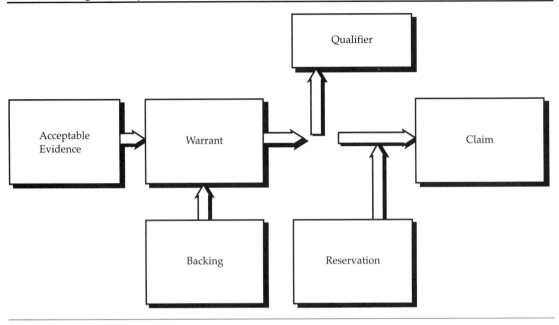

FIGURE **5.2**   **Argument by Authority Assertion**

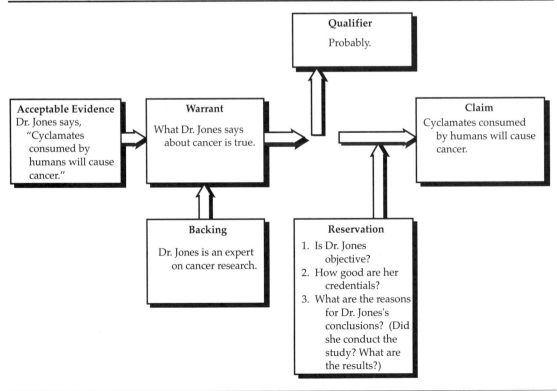

then she probably reached her conclusion on the basis of one or more of the following arguments: sign, example, and cause.

Argument by Sign In our day-to-day lives, we rely on sign argument to survive. Road signs, weather signs, and nonverbal cues from people are used almost instantaneously in drawing conclusions about danger, rain, and emotional mood, respectively. Economists use economic indicators as signs that point to the health of the economy, and physicians use physiologic reasons as indicators of sickness of health.

Finding a reliable set of signs that always point to the same conclusion is difficult for most topics. In the argument in Figure 5.3, we can see the two weaknesses in sign argument. First, the same signs may point to more than one conclusion, and sometimes things occur without the accompanying telltale signs. Thus, group conclusions based solely on sign argument should be quite tentative.

Argument by Example Group discussions are filled with arguments from example. No sooner does somebody state an opinion in a meeting than someone will ask for several examples to support it. Sometimes the examples are short "for instances"; at other times they are statistical summations of hundreds of examples. But in either case, we are making some sort of similar comparisons, thinking that what has been true in past situations will be true in the case that the group is currently discussing.

Figure 5.3   **Argument by Sign**

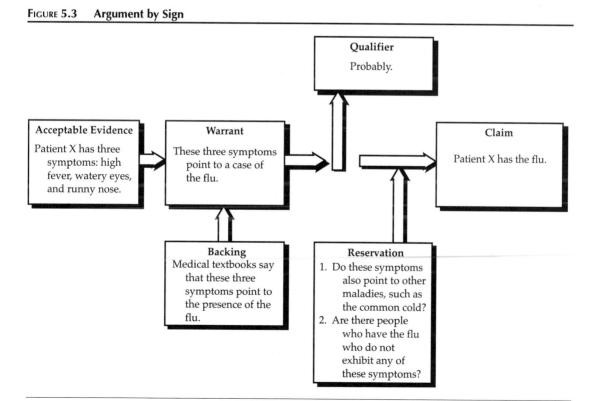

FIGURE 5.4   **Argument by Example**

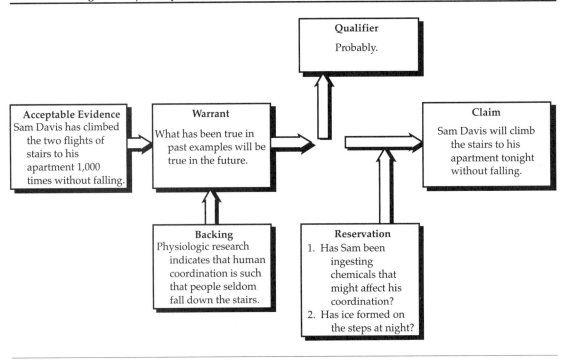

Arguments from example can be broken down in a way that is shown in Figure 5.4. If you look closely enough, you will find that two cases are hardly ever the same. Either the people are different, or the situation is. However, if we get too picky, we become skeptics, and a group will never reach a conclusion. That is why we have developed statistical procedures that allow us to make probability statements such as 95 times out of 100 Sam will climb the stairs successfully. So carefully examine the examples in your data to see whether they are similar to the ones in your claim, but don't get fanatical about it.

Argument by Cause Groups ultimately hope to understand the causal forces involved in a given issue because this understanding tends to produce the best-founded conclusions. Before we knew the causes of such diseases as polio or the Black Death, well-meaning groups drew all sorts of outrageous conclusions based only on arguments by authority assertion, sign, and example. Yet even when our evidence allows us to form causal arguments, there is still much room for disagreement in a discussion group. Cigarette smoking and its cause-and-effect relation to cancer is a good example of a controversy that started out with the argument dependent only on authority, sign, or example and has lasted for decades. As more and more research was done, however, the argument began to center on the issue of causality. Sustaining a causal argument is difficult—first, because most things we call effects have multiple causes. Thus, groups spend a great deal of time listing the various causes of effects and trying to determine the major causes. Another problem we have

FIGURE 5.5   **Argument by Cause**

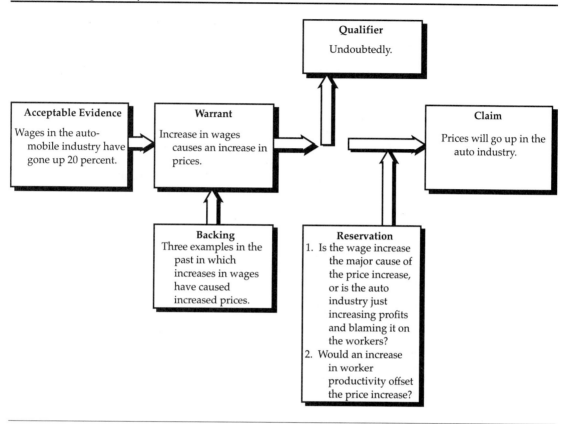

with causal arguments is that intervening factors may offset the normal cause-and-effect relation (see Figure 5.5). Nonetheless, discussion groups should work hard to establish as many causal relationships as their evidence will allow.

☐ PREPARING DISCUSSION OUTLINES

The best way we know how to help you prepare a discussion outline is by providing you with a sample outline developed by Illinois State University students and used by work groups in our classes. The assignment for the students was to prepare and present a forty-five- to sixty-minute panel discussion on a question of policy using Ross's four-step agenda system. The students used brainstorming techniques to help determine their topics. All the discussants spent several hours in the library gathering evidence and developing their arguments. The outlines were developed in advance of the discussion, but the actual panel discussions featured spontaneous interaction before a live audience. In preparing your discussion outlines, you may want to refer to the material in Chapter 4 on formats, agenda systems, and specific discussion techniques, and you may want to be able to test evidence and evaluate arguments.

SAMPLE DISCUSSION OUTLINE

<u>PANEL DISCUSSION AGENDA</u>

Topic: Robots in Industry

Discussion question: To what degree should robots be integrated into industry?

I. Definitions

    A. Robot: "A reprogrammable, multifunctional manipulator (links and joints capable of movement) designed to move material, parts, tools, or specialized devices through variable programmed motions for the performance of a variety of tasks," according to the Robot Institute of America.

    B. Industry: A collection of firms engaged in the manufacturing and/or production-related process.

II. Limitations

    A. Robots

        1. Immobile
        2. Limited to a fixed path

    B. Industry

        1. Large, labor employment
        2. Production processes

III. Analysis

    A. Facts

        1. Basic information

            (a) Description
            (b) Application

        2. Economics

            (a) Robots in industry
            (b) Labor market
            (c) Industrial use

        3. Social, psychological, unions

            (a) Displacement of workers
            (b) Workers most affected

                (1) Unskilled
                (2) Women
                (3) Old
                (4) Young

            (c) Problems of adjustment

   (d) Creation of new jobs

   (e) Job satisfaction

   (f) Inside the United Automobile Workers (UAW), Local 974

     (1) Fears of robot implementation

     (2) Requests of UAW

     (3) Advantages of robot use

     (4) No choice position

  4. Safety

   (a) Occupational Safety and Health Administration regulations

   (b) Worker protection

   (c) Repetitious jobs

  5. International competition

   (a) United States falling behind

   (b) Improvement

 B. Probabilities

  1. Economics

   (a) Robots in industry

   (b) Worker displacement

   (c) Production capabilities

  2. Social, psychological, unions

   (a) Takeover by robots

   (b) Displacement of workers

  3. International competition

   (a) Numbers of robots

   (b) World leaders

 C. Social values

  1. Economics

   (a) Robots in industry

   (b) Labor market

   (c) Industrial use

  2. Social, psychological, unions

   (a) Jobs

     (1) More rewarding

   (b) Technology

     (1) Easier work

     (2) Better work

     (3) Less fear

(c) Education

(1) Appeals for greater funding
(2) More technological training
(3) More courses offered

3. International competition

(a) Aiding other countries

IV. Solution Criteria

A. Cost benefits

1. Less waste
2. Increased production
3. Less total wages paid out
4. Reduced employee-benefit cost
5. Greater world competition

B. Health and safety

1. Better working environment
2. Eliminating tedious jobs
3. Fewer on-site injuries

C. Quality control

1. Reduced human errors
2. Greater accuracy
3. Repeatability
4. Improved inspection techniques

D. Human factors

1. Greater job satisfaction
2. Increase in new technological jobs
3. Retrained displaced workers

V. Possible Solutions

A. Implemented to fullest extent

1. Remain internationally competitive
2. No regard to social costs

B. Robots should be used

1. Given technology is available
2. Protection from hazardous jobs
3. Cost-effective
4. Improved quality
5. Retrain workers

C. Should not be implemented

    1. Too expensive
    2. High social costs

□ SUMMARY

In this chapter, we present ten new communication skills you need to learn and practice. A discussant's ethical standards include the following ten commitments to fellow members: to doing your best, to the group good, to rationality, to fair play, to good listening, to preparation, to ideational conflict, to objectivity, to tolerance, and to social maturity.

Another group expectation for participating in discussion is organizing your information for a meeting so that you are prepared to discuss the topic. To meet this expectation, various research and organizational strategies for discussion are presented.

The reasoning skills of the participants are also found to be crucial to good participation. These include applying the tests of evidence both before the discussion in the research process and during the discussion as you work with material you have gathered. Evidence based on facts, opinions, and statistics should all be appropriately tested. In a commitment to rational problem solving, the normative behavior for a discussant also includes the facility to use logical arguments in reaching group conclusions. Four types of arguments are analyzed; these include arguments from authority assertion, sign, example, and cause.

⚇ CASE STUDY

A City Council Meeting

CASE BACKGROUND

City Council

- Jesse Harmon, mayor, retired business executive
- Emily Lamps, self-employed insurance agent
- Ichiro Kamata, biology professor
- Paul Segobiano, electrician
- Steve Simms, public relations director of a local manufacturing company
- Sally Wong, homemaker

The newly seated council is having its second working meeting since the election. Newly elected members include Emily Lamps, Steve Simms, and Sally Wong. The major campaign issues were the ward versus a council at large form of city government, town-gown relations, and the perceived uncontrolled growth of the city.

On the Friday evening preceding the Monday meeting, a police officer delivered an agenda and numerous background materials to each councilperson.

CASE LOG

Mayor Jesse Harmon opens the meeting with some routine announcements, and the minutes of the last meeting are approved as distributed. The first item on the agenda is consideration of a noise ordinance. Emily speaks first on this issue.

EMILY: As you know, I was elected because of one issue, and that's noise. The excessive noise that permanent residents of my neighborhood have to endure each spring and fall must be controlled. The police, whom I call repeatedly, tell me we need a strong noise ordinance if we are going to be able to shut down the large stereos that the students have blaring out their windows late into the night.

STEVE: I went through all our material for this meeting and didn't find any studies on other towns that have a similar noise problem. Before I take a position on this resolution, I would like to have the facts.

EMILY: I can get you the facts. Just come to my house after the meeting and listen to all rock music blaring through the house. That's all the facts I need, and all the facts you should need to do something about the problem. And another fact is a lot of people agree with me that there is a serious noise problem. It's the will of the voter!

STEVE: If the will of the voter is the issue, then I suppose the city council should agree with me because I got more votes than Emily. But I'm also concerned about the students—they have rights too in this community. Just because they don't vote in large numbers doesn't mean we should take advantage of them.

SALLY: I don't live near the university like Emily does, but I can empathize with her problem. I'm always having to tell my teenagers to turn down their stereos. I can imagine what a whole apartment building full of them must sound like.

PAUL: We're all aware of the problem of periodic noise complaints about students playing their stereos too loudly. What we need is an enforceable city ordinance that's fair to both students and their neighbors. Currently, we don't have a definition of "loud noise" that the police can act on. The fact of the matter is we've never conducted it. With all due respect to Emily, I recommend that we table the motion until we have better information to make a judgment on this issue.

JESSE: Paul's suggestion is a good one! We should table the noise ordinance proposal until we get additional information. The next item on the agenda is a discussion item dealing with the ward system.

STEVE: It's time for our town to elect by wards. Almost all the towns in our state with a population of over fifty thousand have the ward system. It's especially important for our town because the university students have special needs and they have no representation on the city council.

ICHIRO: It would appear that you think we already have a ward system and you represent the student ward. I object to your assertion that students have no representation. All of us on the council represent them.

JESSE: That's right, Ichiro. We don't care if every town in the country has a ward system. We believe we are a unique community and we take special pride in the fact that everybody on the city council represents the whole city and we're not voices of special interest groups.

SALLY: It's not just students who feel unrepresented. People living in the new subdivisions also believe that their voices are not heard.

STEVE: I know we could spend all night on this issue, but I would like to have a clear vote by the council at the next meeting. I'll put in writing my reasons for moving to a ward system.

JESSE: Fine, Steve. The final item on the agenda is to approve the Zoning Commission's recommendation to rezone the property on Business 55 for commercial usage by the new mall. Let me begin the discussion by lending my support to this proposal. We have been a growth-oriented city and this mall is one more accomplishment for city government.

PAUL: I agree with Jesse. The new mall does two important things. It creates new jobs and adds to the tax base.

SALLY: This mall will add more congestion to Business 55, and people trying to get to work from my subdivision are snarled in traffic as it is. Lots of people have told me that they are not in favor of another mall.

ICHIRO: As you know, my area of research in biology includes water conservation. I have already gone on record as saying that our water supply is finite, and we stand a real risk of outgrowing it. We need to be selective about the type of growth we allow. One more strip mall is not worth the strain on our city services.

JESSE: The water problem is short term because of the drought. Historically, we have ample water. Therefore, I don't see water as an issue. As to the congestion, that, too, is temporary. We are adding an extra lane in both directions so the road can handle the additional traffic. So I still stand for growth, jobs, and an expanded tax base.

STEVE: With all due respect, mayor, I think you stand to make a lot of money. It's not a well-kept secret that you own half the land that the mall will be built on and that your wife's brother is a real estate agent. So this mall has more to do with family growth than with city growth! And I don't think it's fair that you should be pushing this issue.

PAUL: I think that's uncalled for, Steve. The mayor has always worked for the good of the city, and someone is going to buy the mayor's land—if not the mall, it will be something else.

JESSE: I've donated thousands of hours of public service to this city. My family's lived here for three generations, and this is the first time anyone has accused me of selfish motives. It's outrageous!

EMILY: Although Steve is not the most tactful person, his point is a reasonable one. Because you own the land the mall will be built on, there certainly is the appearance of impropriety. Maybe you should sit out voting on the zoning issues that deal with the mall.

PAUL: Let's all give ourselves time to cool off over this issue. I move that we postpone this item until the next meeting.

JESSE: That's a good idea, Paul. Meeting adjourned.

CASE QUESTIONS

1. For her to be prepared for the next meeting, what kinds of evidence will Emily need to pass a noise ordinance?

2. What arguments would best be made to get the ward form of government resolution passed?

3. Was Ichiro fair in accusing Steve of representing the students?

4. Is it ethical for the mayor to be advocating a new mall when chances are he will personally profit from it?

CHAPTER SIX

BUILDING INTERPERSONAL TRUST IN SMALL GROUPS

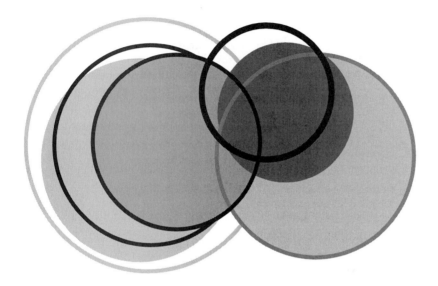

CHAPTER OBJECTIVES

After reading this chapter, you should be able to:

- Know the interpersonal relationships in small groups
- Understand the major personality descriptors of small groups
- Avoid the twelve deviant personality behaviors
- Recognize the perceived individual differences in group members
- Discern the verbal and nonverbal concepts of a small group
- Perform the ten skills for building trust in small groups

CHAPTER OUTLINE

Social acceptance in a group is an important issue for all of us. During the adolescent years, it seems almost all-important. That's why transferring from one high school to another seems so difficult. You are probably apprehensive about how you will fit in with college groups. Of course, you're probably concerned about how accepted you will be in your small group communication class. We are all somewhat fearful about joining new groups, but some are more apprehensive than others. McCroskey (1970, 1977) developed a scale for measuring communication apprehension in groups. It appears that one or two out of ten persons have a real problem with communicating in groups or meetings. These people tend to be quiet, tense, and nervous. They do not speak as often or with as much confidence as other group members. If you are one of these people, take heart. This class in small group communication will help you (Comadena, 1984). One of the best ways to reduce communication apprehension is through skill acquisition. This book contains scores of suggestions on how you can communicate more effectively in groups. The knowledge in this book combined with your class experience will significantly reduce your communication anxiety.

After communication apprehension, communication competency is the next most important variable that affects interpersonal relations among group members. As

indicated in Chapter 1, the competent small group communicator is highly motivated, knowledgeable, and skilled in everyday personal interaction, particularly in
small group communication (Spitzberg 1992; Spitzberg and Cupach 1984). We identify 100 small group communication skills in the first eight chapters of this book. Fifteen of these skills specifically deal with group trust building. The five core skills are
described in Chapter 3, and at the end of this chapter, we present ten more. Your
knowledge of small groups will be enhanced by the presentation of two theories that
explain interpersonal relations in groups.

Schutz (1966) argues that there are three key interpersonal relationships—inclusion, control, and affection—that seem to affect a group's overall ability to work together. Bales and Cohen (1979) explain that three major pairs of personality descriptors—dominant versus submissive, friendly versus unfriendly, and instrumentally
controlled versus emotionally expressive—help to explain why certain people gravi-
tate toward certain group roles. There are also a number of individual variables,
such as race, economic status, age, and gender, that are socially and culturally dependent and that make it harder for heterogeneous groups to work together. Finally,
the meaning that is carried by way of our verbal and nonverbal language system is
fraught with ambiguity and many times another source of interpersonal conflict in
the group. An appreciation of these interpersonal variables helps us to understand
how small groups, particularly those engaged in problem solving, must struggle in-
cessantly for sufficient cohesion to achieve group goals. Your group communication
apprehension will go down and your communication competency will improve once
you understand and practice the knowledge and skills in this chapter.

☐ KEY INTERPERSONAL RELATIONSHIPS IN SMALL GROUPS

In 1966, William C. Schutz reported that his work on the development of a new
theory of interpersonal behavior would explain the interpersonal underworld of a
small group. He called his theory FIRO, which stands for fundamental interpersonal
relations orientation. This theory is based on the belief that when individuals join a
group, there are three interpersonal needs that they seek to satisfy. There is the need
for *inclusion*, which deals with a person's problem of being in or out of the group;
there is the need for *control*, which deals with structuring people in some pecking order; and there is the need for *affection*, which relates emotionally to how close or dis-
tant people feel from the group. Schutz further classified each of the three interpersonal needs as deficient, excessive, or ideal (Schutz 1966).

Inclusion

When we first join a group, we usually are anxious about how we will fit in. We
worry about being ignored; we worry about how committed we should be to the
group; and we size up the other group members in terms of how much social interaction we should engage in. On the one hand, we want to be included in the activity,
but on the other hand, we don't want to get deeply involved with a group of people
we don't know very well. In this situation, many of us overreact or underreact. We

may dominate the conversation with stories about ourselves and fill every lull with any joke or cliché that comes to mind. When we underreact to social inclusion in a group, we usually withdraw from the conversation, fidget with our coffee cups, or doodle on our notepads. We hesitate to submit any information about ourselves for group scrutiny. Thus, in any group encounter, we can plot ourselves on a continuum from undersocial (i.e., deficient) through social (i.e., ideal) to oversocial (i.e., excessive). Once we are established members of a group, most of us seem to move along the continuum and learn to maintain the appropriate amount of social involvement.

Inclusion Continuum

Undersocial	Social	Oversocial
(Deficient)	(Ideal)	(Excessive)

Control

The division of labor that must take place for any task group to be productive gives rise to the need for control. Some people seem very competitive, assertive, and confident in structuring the various individual tasks. Schutz calls a person who has this tendency to dominate an *autocrat*; this person has a strong desire to create a power hierarchy with himself or herself at the top. At the other end of the continuum is the *abdicrat*. This person abdicates all power and responsibility in his or her interpersonal behavior, goes along with the group, and submits to being placed in a subordinate position. In the middle is the *democrat,* who is comfortable with his or her own competency, is capable of assuming or not assuming group responsibilities, and seeks group decisions with regard to critical action of the group.

Control Continuum

Abdicrat	Democrat	Autocrat
(Deficient)	(Ideal)	(Excessive)

Affection

The need for affection is the emotional dimension of the group. How well liked are we by other group members? How intimate and affectionate should we be toward other group members? Are there cliques within our group? Do some people pair off and not share their intimate conversations with us in the group? These are the sorts of questions we ask in trying to satisfy our needs for affection in the small group. Schutz states that some people are *underpersonal*. These people keep everyone at a distance and seem to reject or not need personal contact to get work done. At the other extreme are those who are *overpersonal* and can't seem to get anything done unless there is a strong love bond connecting them to other group members. They have to feel very close to others before they can work with them. And, of course, we all strive to establish the proper distance between us and other group members that allows us to do our work productively.

Affection Continuum

Underpersonal	Personal	Overpersonal
(Deficient)	(Ideal)	(Excessive)

There are other interpersonal needs that are satisfied by group participation besides the three that Schutz identifies. Three additional needs that are worth mentioning because they occasionally surface as a major reason for a person to become a group member are *prestige, safety,* and the *need to do work.* Some people join a group simply because it is a high-status group in the community and they want to say that they are members. In a business setting, an employee might "hang out" with a certain clique for job security reasons because he or she believes that being part of that group will make his or her position safer. Finally, a person may have to join a group to fill certain work needs. For example, a cardiologist cannot perform open-heart surgery by himself or herself; a team is required to do the job. Even these six needs do not explain everyone's reasons for joining a group, but they are certainly the important ones. Inclusion, control, and affection are interpersonal needs that can be monitored and managed for the good of the group.

FIRO-B

William Schutz developed a measuring instrument that contained six scales of nine-item questions that he called FIRO-B (B = behavior). He developed this instrument to measure how a person relates to other group members in terms of how he or she expresses his or her needs for inclusion, control, and affection and how the person wants others to express their needs for inclusion, control, and affection toward him or her. For example, if a person's need is for affection, he or she might say, "I want to be friendly toward people" (expressed behavior) and "I want other people to be friendly toward me" (wanted behavior). Another person might say, "I like to control people" (expressed behavior), "but I don't want people to control me" (wanted behavior). Yet another person might express the need to include other people in his or her social activities but not want other people to initiate the invitation for him or her to join them.

Schutz's objective was to use the FIRO-B instrument to determine the interpersonal compatibility of group members, in the belief that the more compatible a group is, the better are its chances of achieving its task goal (Schutz 1966, 105). Schutz believed this to be true because a compatible group would not have to spend a great deal of its energy resolving its squabbles and, thus, could devote more time and energy to its task.

Figure 6.1 shows a schema of Schutz's interpersonal theory. By obtaining the scores for each group member in terms of his or her interpersonal needs for inclusion, control, and affection with regard to both expressed and wanted behaviors, Schutz could compile compatibility indexes for the group members and finally assess the compatibleness of one group versus another. The three compatibility indexes are originator, reciprocal, and interchange. Of the three, Schutz (1966, 10) believes that interchange compatibility has the most direct application to groups: "*Interchange* refers to the mutual expression of the 'commodity' of a given need area." For example, in terms of Figure 6.1, if everybody in a group circled 5 on inclusion, 4 on control, and 6 on affection for both expressed and wanted behavior, then the "interpersonal atmosphere" of the group should be very compatible. All the members want and receive agreement on deciding things democratically, and they would all want to see that everyone was involved with the group's activity.

FIGURE 6.1   Schema of Schutz's Interpersonal Theory

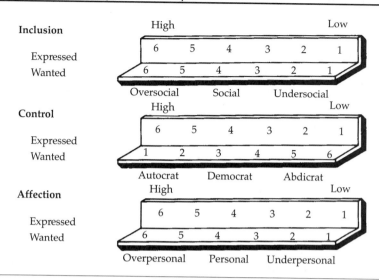

SOURCE: Adapted from William C. Schutz, *The Interpersonal Underworld* (Palo Alto, Calif.: Science and Behavior Books, 1966). TABLE 4–2, p. 60. Reprinted by permission of the author and the publisher from William C. Schutz, *The Interpersonal Underworld.* Palo Alto, Calif.: Science and Behavior Books, 1960.

Application of FIRO-B to Group Problem Solving Although we have serious reservations about the ability of Schutz's theory to predict quantitatively which groups will be most productive (Rosenfeld and Jessen 1972), there is value in using Schutz's FIRO-B to explain qualitatively a work group's interchange compatibility in terms of inclusion, control, and affection—and for that matter any other interpersonal need a group would want to examine, such as status or economic security. It is valuable for a group to assess their interpersonal compatibility systematically, but not empirically. It would be valuable to know whether or not most people like a high degree of group structure, or whether most group members like to restrict their emotional affections to people outside the work group.

Figure 6.2 depicts an imaginary work group in terms of its interpersonal needs for inclusion, control, and affection as measured by Schutz's FIRO-B. As the group is formed, we would expect Ann and Tom to be somewhat withdrawn and disinterested, whereas Mary and Toni would relieve their nervousness by incessant chatter. We might expect that eventually Ann would clash with Jeff or Mary on issues relating to the structuring of the task. However, if we push this analysis too far, we can become fatalistic about group development. After all, what we learn about group communication skills is designed to overcome obstacles such as the interpersonal makeup of the group membership. Schutz's interpersonal group theory explains how interpersonal trust among group members will increase as their fundamental interpersonal relations of inclusion, affection, and control are met.

FIGURE 6.2   **Hypothetical Group in Terms of Schutz's FIRO-B**

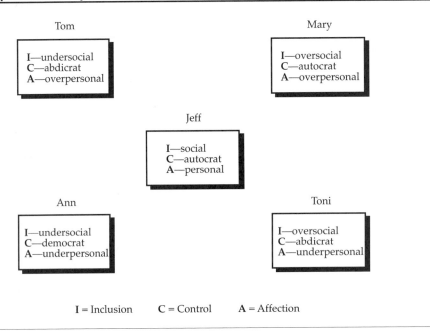

Tom

I—undersocial
C—abdicrat
A—overpersonal

Mary

I—oversocial
C—autocrat
A—overpersonal

Jeff

I—social
C—autocrat
A—personal

Ann

I—undersocial
C—democrat
A—underpersonal

Toni

I—oversocial
C—abdicrat
A—underpersonal

I = Inclusion   C = Control   A = Affection

MAJOR PERSONALITY DESCRIPTORS IN SMALL GROUPS

In 1979, Robert Bales and his associates at Harvard reported their work on the development of a new field theory of personalities in small groups. At the same time, they developed a set of instruments for describing the different personalities and representing them graphically in group life-space. The name they gave to their theory and instrumentation is SYMLOG: systematic, multiple-level observation of groups (Bales and Cohen 1979; Polley, Hare, and Stone 1988). After years of working with their theory, they refined three dimensions of the interpersonal life of group members that are psychologically bipolar (i.e., if you like behavior at one end of the pole, you will reject behavior at the other end of the pole). The three psychological dimensions are dominant versus submissive, friendly versus unfriendly, and instrumentally controlled (accepts authority) versus emotionally expressive (rejects authority). Bales and his students developed a three-dimensional cube with these three pairs of behaviors, thus creating twenty-six possible behavior types, which often collapse into sixteen more broadly described personalities of group members (Polley et al. 1988, 81–84). It is readily apparent that, at times, Bales's SYMLOG shadows Schutz's FIRO, but Bales's picture of personalities is different enough that we need to look at the interpersonal dimension of groups with it.

Dominant Versus Submissive

If a group member is on the high end of the dominant-submissive scale, he or she will act overtly to other members in the group (i.e., initiate conversations and often speak rapidly and loudly with few pauses) and try to dominate the speaking time of a group. From a nonverbal perspective, the high dominant takes up a high degree of group space, the eyes are alert, the shoulders squared, and, for the most part, the arms and legs are in an open position. Furthermore, the dominant person values prominence and personal power (Bales and Cohen 1979, 355; Polley et al. 1988, 349–350). At the extreme end of the pole, the submissive person is introverted, often speaking only when asked a direct question and giving a brief answer to the question. This type of person would also score high on communication apprehension in group settings. Nonverbally, high submissive group members take up little group space; often their eyes are cast down and their arms and legs are folded across the body. They appear passive, powerless, and uncommunicative. They appear willing to give up their personal preferences easily, or at least to suppress their personal needs and desires (Bales and Cohen 1979, 385–386; Polley et al. 1988, 347–350).

Friendly Versus Unfriendly

Group members who are perceived as being friendly strike a balance between talking and listening. They are easy to talk with and appear to seek equality between their ideas and those of other group members. They don't seem competitive and are humanistic and flexible. Nonverbally, their behavior is marked by good listening skills. They look at the person they are talking to and they appear comfortable while they're listening. On the other hand, they seldom give nonverbal cues that they want to interrupt another speaker. High friendlies value democratic decision making and equality (Bales and Cohen 1979, 366–367; Polley et al. 1988, 349–350). Highly unfriendly people in a group are very negative. They disagree a lot. They often appear as though they do not want to be members of a group. They seem unapproachable and indifferent, even to friendly communication. An important nonverbal cue that marks a high unfriendly is that he or she literally does not make eye contact with the person who is speaking. These people might even pick up reading material and glance at it with total indifference to the group conversation. If they make eye contact with a group member, they will often do it with their eyebrows raised, making them appear skeptical. They seem to prize their own self-sufficiency and are concerned only with their own self-interest. They feel a continuing need to dissent from group opinions (Bales and Cohen 1979, 371; Polley et al. 1988, 345–350).

Instrumentally Controlled Versus Emotionally Expressive

Group members who are neither friendly nor unfriendly but score high on being instrumentally controlled (i.e., accepting authority) are viewed as emotionally neutral, straight-arrow types who are analytical and task-oriented and are sticklers for following group rules and norms. They have a strong work ethic. Nonverbally, this type of group member is impersonal in expression and keeps his or her eyes on the task, the body clearly projecting that he or she is at the group meeting to get work done (Bales and Cohen 1979, 368–369; Polley et al. 1988, 349–350). Group members who score high on the emotionally expressive end of the continuum often "march to the beat of a different drummer" (i.e., they reject authority). They are viewed as creative, playful, and dramatistic. They reject group conventions and quickly show their feelings and emotions on a given topic. They often hold unconventional beliefs and search out new ways to solve group problems. In terms of nonverbal cues, emotionally expressive group members show sudden shifts from preoccupation with the feelings of group members to the group task. They might actually stand up and act out a creative group idea, whereas at other times, they may appear detached with a blank look on their faces (Bales and Cohen 1979, 373–374; Polley et al. 1988, 346–350).

☐ APPLICATION OF SYMLOG TO GROUP TRUST BUILDING

SYMLOG is a user-friendly way for a work group to engage in group self-analysis. If your group has the time and the interest, you could classify each one of your members as one of the twenty-six personality types by using Bales's personality rating instruments (Bales and Cohen 1979, 504; Polley et al. 1988, 345–350). If you have less time, Bales provides a minimal rating form in which you just rate each person in the group on the three bipolar personality traits: dominant-submissive, friendly-unfriendly, analytical-emotional (Bales and Cohen 1979, 458). Average the ratings of each member and determine his or her personality type. The Bales system helps to structure the casual observations that group members have made of one another and allows each member to clearly see how other group members view him or her as a participant.

Small group researchers have always been interested in the relation between personality type and the propensity for certain personality types to play given group roles. Figure 6.3 suggests a possible optimum fit between the five major group roles and five of the twenty-six group personality types identified by Bales. The task leader is democratic, rational, and task-oriented. The social-emotional leader is nurturing, warm, and supportive. The tension releaser is funny, dramatic, and creative. The central negative is critical, aggressive, and unconventional. The information provider is respective, patient, and humble. However, it is possible that a group could be formed in which the leader is authoritative and unfriendly, and the other roles could be played by personality types that are not well suited to group roles. So the question arises, can the five major roles be played well only by certain personality types? There is currently no research to answer this question. It would appear that people are adaptable and educable, and part of training in small group communication involves maturation. In other words, a naive person, untrained in small group communication, could enter a group as a submissive, unfriendly, emotionally expressive person and, after training, learn to become a friendly, assertive, task-oriented group member. Our point is quite simple: Bales's twenty-six personality types are not cast in stone—you can change how you are perceived as a group member through training. SYMLOG profiles the group members as perceived by the other group members. It is a form of systematic group self-disclosure. It allows the group to build interpersonal trust by adapting their group personalities.

FIGURE 6.3   **Adapting SYMLOG to Group Roles**

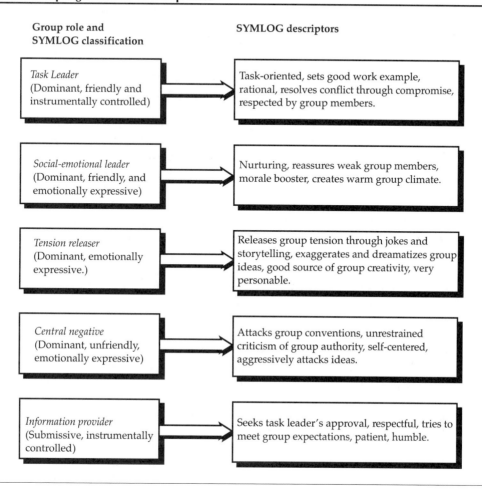

Group role and
SYMLOG classification

SYMLOG descriptors

Task Leader
(Dominant, friendly and
instrumentally controlled)

Task-oriented, sets good work example,
rational, resolves conflict through compromise,
respected by group members.

Social-emotional leader
(Dominant, friendly, and
emotionally expressive)

Nurturing, reassures weak group members,
morale booster, creates warm group climate.

Tension releaser
(Dominant, emotionally
expressive.)

Releases group tension through jokes and
storytelling, exaggerates and dramatizes group
ideas, good source of group creativity, very
personable.

Central negative
(Dominant, unfriendly,
emotionally expressive)

Attacks group conventions, unrestrained
criticism of group authority, self-centered,
aggressively attacks ideas.

Information provider
(Submissive, instrumentally
controlled)

Seeks task leader's approval, respectful, tries to
meet group expectations, patient, humble.

☐ DEVIANT PERSONALITY BEHAVIORS THAT HARM GROUP TRUST

After teaching classes in small group communication each semester for the past twenty-five years and reading thousands of student diaries, we have evolved what we call our "dirty dozen" list. These twelve stereotyped group personality behaviors inhibit and disrupt interpersonal trust among group members. The ideal group member is task-competent, socially mature, self-assured, assertive, and communicatively competent (McGrath and Altman, 1966). The "dirty dozen" behaviors deviate from the ideal description cited above. These twelve behaviors need to be avoided if interpersonal trust is to be built in the group.

Aggressing An aggressor is an abrasive and overly dominant person in the group. People with this personality type put themselves up and put others' ideas down. They overreact to criticism and attack others personally for disagreeing with the aggressor's ideas. Aggressors are outspoken and bold to the point of recklessness. When a decision is made, they feel like they beat others out, and others feel humiliated and angry. Being assertive and dominant can be good qualities in a group member, but in this case, too much of a good thing is detrimental to the group.

Doormatting These people are too submissive for both their and the group's own good. In the words of Harris's *I'm OK, You're OK* (1967), the doormat definitely thinks that he or she is not OK. These members constantly irritate the group because they are always kicking themselves before the group has a chance to do it. The minute others challenge their ideas, doormats give in and proceed to describe how inadequate they are. Other group members have no respect for these people because they do not seem to respect themselves. The doormat is literally the doormat of the organization; everyone walks over him or her. Doormats always complain that life is falling in around them and that they are not in control of decisions (Harris 1967). Consequently, the other group members are frustrated because the doormat will not take responsibility for group decisions. Furthermore, the group does not like the doormat to act as if he or she can't affect group outcomes.

Eggheading Although task competency is an important group personality variable, a person who portrays himself or herself as or flaunts the fact that he or she is much more knowledgeable than other group members can become a royal pain in the group's psyche. Eggheads parade their intelligence before the group and demand that deference be paid. The egghead selects a vocabulary that is beyond many group members. This negative personality type is an intellectual snob who quickly becomes insufferable in group decision making. Sometimes group members wait cautiously for hours for an opportunity to pounce on any error the egghead might make in his or her thinking process. If defeating the intellectual becomes the center of group activity, the best possible solution can often be lost. On the other hand, domination of a group by an egghead can often eliminate the potential synergetic nature of group decision making.

Airheading The airhead goes under a variety of group names: dunce, dummy, Neanderthal, and group idiot. The airhead projects a group personality that would earn a low double-digit I.Q. score. This person backs away from all ideational conflict with the claim "I just don't understand what's happening." When group members chide the airhead with comments like "How could you have graduated from college?" the airhead seems to be mystified by that fact also. Group members always suspect the airhead of faking it—nobody can be that dumb. Airheads avoid doing a lot of the hard work for the group because they don't appear to be intellectually fit. As a consequence, other group members become angry and sometimes complain that they don't have any excuses for not working, compared with the airhead. The airhead has been personified in many movies as being the "dumb blond"; however, it has been our experience in studying groups that airheads are randomly distributed across gender and hair-color types.

Whining Crybabies, or whiners, exhibit extreme social immaturity. You ask them to come to a meeting and they whine. You ask them to do work in the group and they whine. You criticize them and they cry. Whiners avoid doing their fair share of the work simply because it's so irritating to hear them whine when they are assigned a task. Ironically, whiners seem to complain that they are given too much work to do when in fact they are doing less than the average. Whiners complain about minor things in group procedure, even down to the size of the meeting room, the comfort of the chairs, and the room temperature. Group members may have legitimate complaints, or they may have some individual idiosyncrasy that would require group adaptation. For example, a group member might be a diabetic and need to take frequent snack breaks during long work sessions, or a member might be allergic to smoke or animal hair. Most groups adapt to these individual needs; however, for the whiner, it is not possible for the group to make adequate compensation. No matter what the group does, the whiner still whines.

Self-Confessing Sometimes a group member will show up for a task-group meeting and decide to turn the meeting into an encounter-group session—in effect, asking the group for its emotional support of his or her feelings. When these feelings are not related to the group and the interpersonal disclosures seem to be unnecessarily intimate, we say the group member is engaging in a negative communication behavior, inasmuch as the behavior causes the group to turn its attention away from the group goals. Once in a while a work group's productivity will go way down even though its cohesion and member satisfaction remain quite high. When this happens, a task discussion group has unknowingly transformed itself into a therapy group. Most experienced small discussion groups restrict self-confessing behavior to either before or after the meeting.

Help Seeking Whereas self-confessing behavior seeks help from the group at the interpersonal level on subjects not related to the group's task, help-seeking behavior usually is a request on the part of the group member that the group testify to that particular member's value to the group. Sometimes this communication is in the form of sulking; at other times, it takes the form of acts of self-mortification. All group members need "stroking," but if this behavior occurs too frequently in discussions, little work will be done because the group members will be too busy reassuring one another that they are capable of doing good work.

Recognition Seeking This behavior calls attention to itself by boasting. Kindergarten classes attempt to stop recognition seeking from interfering with daily work by restricting it to a given day. This day is called "show and tell." In some adult groups, this activity is called "bring and brag." At reunions, it is called "stand and shout." In the course of a group's history, all group members will seek recognition; in fact, good groups often formalize these occasions. But in the context of routine meetings, recognition seeking is a negative communication behavior.

Special-Interest Pleading A group member is quickly labeled a self-centered follower if the member is engaged in special-interest pleading. One of the basic assumptions of a discussion group is that the members will come to the meeting with a permissive and reflective attitude and prepare to be persuaded by argument and evidence. When a member speaks on behalf of some outside group and not as a member of the group that is currently working together, the group thinks that the member is making a special-interest plea. If a discussion group contains five teachers and one student, there may be occasions when the student engages in special-interest pleading on behalf of students. If several members begin to engage in this behavior, it becomes extremely difficult for the group to reach consensus about its conclusions.

Playing the Clown   Although the tension releaser uses humor for positive effects in the elimination of primary tension and the lessening of group conflict, horseplay at inappropriate times by the tension releaser or by other group members is a form of negative communication behavior. Groups can easily be tempted to digress from their work, and clowning around is one of the favorite ways. Sometimes, particularly after a hard work session, the whole group will get silly, and everything will seem hilarious, but most of the time, excessive goofing off will hurt group productivity.

Blocking   This foot-dragging behavior normally is used to stop decisions from taking place. Delaying tactics are used by various group members in the course of a discussion. The repertoire of blocking behaviors is quite large. It includes absenteeism, emotional tirades, filibustering, and incessant procedural objections. People who become blockers of group decision making seem to adopt an attitude that things should be "my way, or no way." If they can't get the group to agree with them, then they punish the group by not allowing it to reach a decision. A person playing the central negative role also engages in blocking behavior, but out of a concern to improve the group product and not out of selfish motivation. Thus, it is hard to distinguish between ill-motivated or well-motivated blocking, except that the central negative will challenge the group decision intellectually on its merits, whereas the blocker will use emotional tirades and tactical procedures.

Foddering   After observing more than 300 hours of quality-circle group meetings in American corporations, Stohl and Schell (1991) identified a deviant group behavior they call *farrago*, which means mixed fodder for cattle. Foddering is so devastating that it can make an otherwise good group dysfunctional. Farragos are competent group members who epitomize a group's value structure for work, but they are pyromaniacs of interpersonal relations. They commit excessive amounts of time in overinvolving themselves in group life. They use hallway gossip, half-truths, and innuendo to create constant group crises. They set interpersonal fires to focus attention on their perceived heroism. Everything they do is all-important, and what other group members do is trivial. The irony of foddering behavior is that, according to Stohl and Schell, it flourishes in organizations that allow for a great deal of participatory decision making by work groups.

PERCEIVED INDIVIDUAL DIFFERENCES IN SMALL GROUP COMMUNICATION

What you see is often what you get in group member behavior. Societal stereotypes based on gender, age, race, education, socioeconomic background, and so on are a very real part of the early information stages of a small group. In fact, self-disclosure by group members is necessary if stereotypes are to be broken down so that the group can function.

The research based on these demographic and personality variables and how they affect group formation, productivity, and membership satisfaction is unreliable and incomplete. For example, Marvin E. Shaw (1976, 187), an eminent psychologist, suggested the following hypothesis: "There is a tendency for the group leader to be older than the other group members." However, McGrath and Altman (1966, 62), in their thorough review of the leadership literature, reported quite the reverse; that is, "education, but not age or other biographical characteristics," is required for leadership. And even when researchers agree on their conclusions, the exceptions are so numerous that the findings are not very helpful in making judgments about group behavior.

Sometimes research findings that attempt to sort out differences in human behavior based on demographic or personality differences produce great social controversy, because such research attempts to prove causal links between, for example, the gender of a person and some predictable social behavior. We suspect that Shaw's (1976, 188) hypotheses dealing with the differences between men and women in groups are controversial for you; they certainly are for us. Shaw's hypotheses are that "women are less self-assertive and less competitive in groups than are men; women use eye contact as a form of communication more frequently than men"; and that "females conform to majority opinion more than males." The indictment frequently given to Shaw's hypotheses is that the studies he reports are from the 1930s and 1940s and may not accurately depict the behavior of women as they participate in small groups today. However, we all know that the sexual composition of a group matters. If sexism exists in society, a natural expectation would be to see this manifestation in groups. The same would be true of racism and ageism. Ironically, many of the studies that have attempted to sort out the demographic influences on a group have in turn fueled the controversies surrounding the stereotyping that initially spawned the studies. Therefore, most of the advice that we provide in this section is based on our own observation of student groups in classrooms, work groups in business, and communication studies conducted from the 1970s up to the present.

Gender

Groups with both men and women appear to have different problems in the formation of group roles than do groups made up of one gender. The biggest problem centers on who will be the task leader. The problem with female leadership is a cultural and unfortunate one. In the recent past—and we hope that this will be less true in the future—it seemed that the American woman was forced to choose between being popular and being intellectual and between being athletic and being sexually attractive. Furthermore, even now, she is provided with few role models of female leadership of male-female groups and is given little opportunity to play the role of task leader in her formative years. Few television programs, movies, or novels provide dramatic examples of a woman successfully leading male-female groups. In addition, segregated sports programs in high school do not provide opportunities for a young woman to try out the leadership role of a male-female group. Conversely, the American man is conditioned to compete for the task-leader role and made to believe that "losing" to a woman is twice as bad as losing to a man. The culture is also inundated with examples of male leadership and male-dominated occupations. So we can expect that gender will be an issue in most coed groups and that this struggle will be particularly intense if the group has a tradition of being all-male. Thus, such incidents as the accession of a community's first female fire chief, first female sheriff, or first female naval admiral are news events.

Bormann, Pratt, and Putnam (1978, 150–153) simulated a corporate structure made up of small work groups at the University of Minnesota and tape-recorded the discussions of all the groups. This particular case study produced female dominance of the organization, a dominance that many men deeply resented. One group of men, the largest, withdrew from participation and became silent observers. Some men competed vigorously for leadership roles and felt "castrated" when they lost. The smallest group of men remained active in supportive roles in their work groups. In essence, most men in this simulation had difficulty adapting to female leadership and power in the organization. In addition, Bradley (1980) discovered that women who demonstrated task competence in male-dominated problem-solving groups were treated more positively by the men than were women who did not demonstrate this competence; but Bradley also found that women who displayed this competency were not as well liked by group members. Yerby (1975) found that male group members experienced attitude difficulties with female leadership. On the other hand, Alderton and Jurma (1980) found that group members were equally satisfied with male and female leaders when performing similar task-oriented behavior (also see Hirokawa, Mickey, and Miura 1991 for similar results). Bunyi and Andrews's (1985) research indicated that gender was important in leadership emergence but that task competency was more important than gender.

Spillman, Spillman, and Reinking (1981) reported that both biological sex and psychological androgyny affect leadership emergence in the early stages of group interaction, but their influence dissipates over time. Owen (1986), after examining the personal journals of female leaders, found that most female leaders believe that they became a leader by default and were reluctant to be called "leader." Andrews (1992), after reviewing nearly half a century of gender-leadership research, lamented that as long as workers report a preference for male managers, women shy away from leadership, and language is perceived differently depending on the gender of the speaker, we must continue to consider gender an issue in the study of small groups.

The least disruptive roles that women play in groups appear to be the social-emotional leader, because of the stereotype that women are more nurturing than men, and the recorder role, because that is the traditional role women played in male-dominated work environments of the past. Gouran and Fisher (1984, 635) summarized sex role research in small groups by pointing out that men are more likely to emerge as leaders and that women are more likely to engage in self-disclosure and to be more aware of others' feelings in the group. Therefore, both women and men should be aware of the potential for people to be stereotyped into a particular role based on their sex. Also, one should look at conflict within the group to see whether the disturbance is a result of disruptive or debilitating stereotypes.

Culture and Race

Racial discrimination is a worldwide problem. It is particularly embarrassing to Americans because of our open commitment to justice and equality for all people. In racially mixed groups, race is an issue that pervades the group's formation. The first manifestation of race as an issue is majority versus minority. Because most Americans have been raised in a majority environment of their race, nobody is used to being stereotyped as the "minority." The fact that a group might think of itself in minority-majority terms complicates the evolvement of group roles. If a person of one race objects to a person of another race playing the role of task leader, he or she might be accused of being racist when in fact the person has nonracial reasons for objecting. On the other hand, the objections may be racially motivated, either consciously or subconsciously. Because of this ambiguity, motives in racially mixed groups can be difficult to determine.

Real and perceived cultural differences always cause problems in the socialization of a group. Such problems are most clearly manifested in the tension releaser role. For example, if a long-standing work group has been using Polish jokes as a means of tension release, the arrival of one of "those people" will cause the group a great deal of stress until it can find a new basis for group humor. The problem would be intensified if a group has been using racial humor and then becomes racially mixed. If a group is just starting out, members will feel tense until they can find a range of humor they can use to help in socializing the group.

The 1980s film *Gung Ho* humorously explores the conflicts between American workers and Japanese managers in a Japanese-owned auto plant. Many of the problems covered in this movie still occur in multinational corporations. When American workers consciousness-raise themselves, an American versus Japanese fantasy often chains out. American workers refer to the secretive Japanese who hold midnight meetings. They talk about the "rice paper ceiling." At an intercultural training program for Japanese and American workers, a frustrated American stated that the rice paper ceiling is worse than the glass ceiling. She meant that a glass ceiling is a barrier that American women complain about (i.e., they can see upper management, but they just can't get there), but the rice paper ceiling is worse because they can't even see through it (i.e., they never know what upper management is planning).

Research in the 1990s has demonstrated that training in small group communication can significantly reduce cross-cultural and racial conflicts in groups. Hammer and Martin (1992) successfully used training in trust building and team building to induce cooperation between American workers and Japanese managers. Kirchmeyer and Cohen (1992) significantly increased the contributions of ethnic minorities in work groups through the constructive use of interpersonal conflict. Bantz (1993) further evidenced our ability to build cross-cultural work groups successfully. What is clear from this research is that special efforts must be taken if culturally diverse groups are to become effective.

Age

The return of older women to college campuses has produced classroom discussion groups that point up some of the problems that can occur when there are large differences in age among group members. The diaries from students in our small group communication classes indicate that a woman in her late thirties working with six others in their late teens will initially be perceived as a parent-type person, and not as a social equal. Sometimes the person labeled as a parent type does in fact feel and behave that way. A group will eventually process the perceived difference in ages and resolve it to the point where the parent type is a fully accepted member of the group.

In business and industry, the age difference usually occurs in reverse. A young person joins a group that contains older and established members. In this situation, the young person is treated as a kid and does not receive equal social status in the group. The young person overachieves and constantly seeks recognition for his or her contributions. The issue at stake is one of equality. On the issue of age, sometimes group members have a difficult time understanding the needs of the parent type or kid as they try to interact on an equal level with other members.

Another problem that age difference accentuates is the norming of the social conversation and social activities the group will engage in. A young person who finds that everyone else in the group is talking about purchasing retirement homes and the ins and outs of retirement annuities may feel that he or she is on the outside looking in at the group. Likewise, an older person coexisting with younger group members may feel socially uncomfortable in conversations that deal with the latest dancing trends and night spots in the community. Groups that contain marked age differences must work harder to find social conversations that will serve as a common denominator by which group members can share their experiences.

Education

It is generally assumed that there is a connection between academic achievement and the ability to perform the necessary skills in day-to-day discussions. This assumption is based on the idea that people who go to college are intellectually more capable than those who do not and that the training the former receive in college enhances their ability to solve business and social problems.

In groups where there are marked differences in the educational levels of achievement, there is the expectation that people with more education should assume more responsibility in the discussion process. If the educated people in the group perform poorly or reluctantly, they can easily be held up to ridicule and scorn. If all members of a group have college degrees or at least some college experience, the socialization process is greatly facilitated. Despite gender, race, or age differences, the group can reliably draw on a set of common experiences, even though the members may have gone to different colleges at different times. When people have shared similar experiences in the armed services or have lived in similar kinds of neighborhoods, such experiences can also serve as a common ground for discussion participants.

Occupation

Occupations in our society frequently are ranked in national polls according to their status. Even if they were not, people seem to have a natural inclination to form some kind of "pecking order" based on occupation. When a group contains marked differences in status as determined by occupation, a definite impact can be felt. This impact is particularly strong if some of the members are in the professions (e.g., physicians, lawyers, professors, dentists) and the others are not. The people in the professions may hold unfounded and stereotyped views of blue-collar workers' intellectual abilities. Likewise, the blue-collar members may have some long-standing resentment against physicians and lawyers. These prejudices normally surface in discussion groups that must agree on a common decision.

Role playing in a mixed occupational group can be difficult. The professional people might object to a blue-collar person emerging as task leader because they would feel loss in status, or the blue-collar members might distrust leadership from a person who is a professional. Movies and television dramas often exploit this conflict among occupations by producing surprising turnabouts in crisis situations. The scenario usually calls for a small group of people from mixed occupational backgrounds to be thrown into a common crisis. In the crisis, it is discovered that one of the low-status people has some special expertise that allows him or her to emerge as task leader of the group. However, most group discussions do not take place in a crisis context, nor do most group tasks require a specialized skill or knowledge database that only one member possesses. Thus, most groups have to struggle through their differences in occupational status with no clear way to solve their problem. The tension usually is reduced by finding some basis of equality outside group members' occupations.

Income

Money doesn't make a difference in groups, but a lot of money does! Major differences in the wealth of individual members affect the group, not only in terms of the status that members may attach to wealth but also in terms of their overall lifestyle differences. Even when group members find common topics to discuss, their perception of the same topic can be quite different. For example, if three students in a group are discussing where they are going to go over spring break and two of the students indicate that they are going home to work at part-time jobs to help pay for their education, while the third student indicates that she is flying to the Bahamas to go deep-sea diving, chances are the two working students will at least humorously chide the affluent one. The result of this conversation will have an impact on the affection and inclusion aspects of the group.

When socially concerned citizens form discussion groups to grapple with our country's problems, differences in wealth and, consequently, lifestyles in the group can produce conflict and alienation. If a group of midwestern grain farmers forms a discussion group to deal with low subsidy supports for their products, differences in income may matter. The wealthy farmers in the group may want to take one of their $80,000 tractors, drive it to Washington, D.C., and set it on fire. The small family farmer cannot afford the time or the tractor and may feel left out of the group and frustrated because lack of wealth did not allow for full participation. Conversely, a wealthy group member may be excluded from the group on the ground that he or she has not directly experienced the problems of the group; or the wealthy person may be made to feel guilty for not spending his or her wealth to reduce the problem the group is discussing.

Homogeneity and Heterogeneity

If you are in a homogeneous group, no doubt group member values, abilities, and opinions are very much alike; thus, there should be less conflict in the social dimension of the group. However, task performance might not be as effective as that of a heterogeneous group. Shaw's (1976, 235) synthesis of the research on homogeneity-heterogeneity produced two hypotheses: "Other things being equal, groups composed of members having diverse, relevant abilities perform more effectively than groups composed of members having similar abilities"; and "groups whose members are heterogeneous with respect to personality profiles perform more effectively than groups whose members are homogeneous with respect to personality profiles."

Culturally, Americans are committed to the principle that heterogeneous groups are better than homogeneous groups. Small group research appears to support the American ideal of pluralism. Although groups that contain diverse memberships might encounter a number of problems in becoming a group, the rich and diverse backgrounds of their members make them potentially more capable of solving group problems than are homogeneous groups. In short, it would be naive for you to ignore individual differences in group members, but it would be foolish, given his or her potential contribution, to exclude a person from membership because of demographic or personality differences.

☐ VERBAL LANGUAGE CODE IN SMALL GROUPS

DeVito identifies six principles of verbal communication that form the foundation of good group discussions. They are equality, confirmation, inclusion, balanced talk, honest criticism, and fairness (1992, 171–180). To be an accepted member of a problem-solving group, most people would want you to speak to them as equals, accept them for who they are, include them in the conversation, allow them specific opportunity to express their opinions, be honest in your evaluation, and not use offensive and demeaning language. These are minimum expectations for holding a civilized group discussion. On the other hand, following these six principles does not entirely cover key verbal behavior that is required for effective group decision making. Our verbal code is fraught with ambiguity that must be grappled with if we are to know what each of us is really saying. Verbal communication in small groups is highly redundant. One of the major reasons for this redundancy is our need for clarity. In a dyad, only two persons need to know what is being said. In a group discussion, six or seven persons have to understand the subtleties of the verbal code being used. Therefore, a close examination of language and thought is necessary to improve group decision making.

Differences Between Language and Thought

Two-person conversations often are marked by misunderstandings when the participants cannot express themselves clearly enough. This problem is even more complex in a group discussion. The two basic problems that dyads have with verbal communication codes are the same as those in small groups. The first problem with our verbal code is the relation between symbol and thought; the second is the group context in which it is used. It is a matter of semantics. What do the words we use mean? Ogden and Richards (1923) said that there is no necessary symbol between a word and a referent, whereas another well-known semanticist, S. I. Hayakawa (1964), made the same observation with his statement that "the map is not the territory." The first problem that is central to the verbal language code comes down to the difference between language and thought.

FIGURE 6.4   **Difference Between Language and Thought**

There are many ways in which we can quickly demonstrate to ourselves how inaccurately language symbols represent our thoughts. Even simple words, when uttered to a group of people, can produce various thoughts in the minds of a group. For example, if a group member asked, "What is the block?" we can see in Figure 6.4 the possible resultant lack of common thought processes in the group.

The person asking the question might have believed that the symbol "block" referred to the same object he was thinking about, but obviously it did not. Words often do not say what we mean, or at least they do not say enough of what we mean so that we can be certain that other members of the group understand our thoughts. Group discussants should continually promote more clarity and try to reduce the gap between language and thought. This process can be helped by defining key words.

Many unfortunate and unnecessary conflicts take place in group discussions because the group failed to take the time to carefully define key recurring concepts in their discussions. However, even when group members attempt to define their key concepts, the group can continue to have difficulties because of the many ways a concept can be defined. It is, therefore, useful to examine the eight basic ways a word can be defined.

■ *Definition by origin.* If someone is called chauvinistic, one way to get at the meaning of the term is to look at its etymology, or origin. It turns out that *chauvinism,* from the French word *chauvinisme,* refers to Nicolas Chauvin, who was an officer in Napoleon's army. Chauvin used to get on his soapbox constantly and boast how superior his country was to all others. People used to say, "There goes Chauvin again!" Eventually, when somebody bragged about the superiority of his or her country or group, that person would be labeled chauvinistic. In today's society, this term is mainly used to describe men who are chauvinistic in their attitude toward women. Established groups often create key words, and new members should seek the origin of those words if they are thinking of becoming a member of that group. For example, a new member might be called "Ed, the Motormouth." The etymology of the expression in the group might refer to the last new member of the group whose name was Ed and who talked far too much for a new member. Thus, to be called "Ed, the Motormouth" would be a bad thing and an indication that the newest member should talk less.

■ *Definition by negation.* As strange as it sounds, we often define things in terms of what they are not. When we say that people are not immortal, we are defining human beings for what they are not, not for what they are. When we say that a couple is childless, we are defining that couple in terms of what they do not have, not in terms of what they have. Small groups often develop definitions of what a good member of their group is by developing a list of things that a person does not do. For example, a good discussant is not rude, not dominating, and not ignorant.

■ *Definition by example.* One way of eliminating the ambiguity between a word and the thought it stands for is to provide a specific example of the thought. For example, in explaining what a dog is to a child, we often bring the dog over and show it to the child. In small group communication classes, instructors often play group games or create simulations so that the student can clearly see examples of group communication behaviors that are difficult to comprehend in the abstract. The sixteen leadership communication behaviors can be quickly comprehended through the use of classroom demonstrations that create such behaviors as regulating participation or verbalizing consensus. In group discussions, people often bring in pictures and diagrams of key objects because definition by example is one of the best ways to produce clarity in a discussion.

■ *Definition by description and classification.* We use description so automatically that sometimes we forget how basic this definitional process is to our understanding. If you open an encyclopedia, you might find a picture of an oak tree. Beneath the tree would be a list of characteristics that makes this tree an oak tree. Once described in terms of what is "oaky" about it, the tree is then classified in terms of what it has in common with other trees and how it differs from flowers. In group discussions, incidents often are described and then classified in terms of the group's priority system. In small group communication research, we might describe certain communication behavior and classify that behavior as autocratic leadership behavior. The description and classification system in small group processes frame what otherwise would appear to be a confusing set of events, thus giving the group a sense of procedural clarity and helping it to proceed in an orderly manner.

■ *Definition by analogy.* The clarity that a definition by analogy can provide is based on how closely alike two things are. If they are analogous and the group members have firsthand knowledge of one of them, they will have a simultaneous understanding of the second thing, even if they have not experienced it. There are two kinds of analogies: figurative and literal.

We have all experienced the process by which a hypodermic needle puts fluid into our bodies. Some mass communication theorists have drawn a figurative analogy between this process and the process by which television commercials put ideas into our heads. If we imagine that a television set is a hypodermic needle, a television ad is a fluid, and our intellectual comprehension is the arm into which the needle is plunged, we understand mass communication persuasion by the analogy of the hypodermic needle. The point we are making here is that although figurative analogies have the appearance of making us feel that we understand something that was previously unfamiliar to us, when we push for a one-to-one correspondence between the familiar and the unfamiliar, we find that figurative analogies are absurd. However, despite our cautionary note about figurative analogies and their use, complex ideas tend to be best remembered when they are defined by a figurative analogy.

When a group has developed a history of solving problems, literal analogies become an important part of group discussions. If group members can conclude that the current problem is analogous to one they resolved last month, then they will probably proceed to look at the same solutions. Literal analogies are almost examples but not quite; for that reason, one should be cautious in their use, because we tend to treat two analogous cases identically when in fact they are not examples of the same thing.

■ *Definition by function and purpose.* The function of an airplane is to provide transportation. We might also say that the purpose of an airplane is to fly. There is a close relation between function and purpose, but they are not the same. The task leader's primary purpose may be to lead the group to the accomplishment of its group goals; in doing that, the leader and other group members perform various communication leadership behaviors or functions. Purpose implies intent and function implies behavior. To simply define a group in terms of its function would beg the question, to what end or for what purpose? Thus, if a group can define its purpose, it then can define the functions it needs to perform to accomplish group goals.

■ *Definition by operations performed.* In operational definitions, each word is defined in terms of some measurable behavior so that we can look across cases and quantitatively assess the similarity of like cases. However, in most face-to-face discussions, small groups do not have the time or the resources to provide their own operational definitions of key concepts and perform their own experiments. Yet, when on rare occasions groups conduct their own research, they attain an unusually high rate of agreement about the meanings of words for which they have worked out operational definitions.

■ *Definition by context.* Because of the many denotative and connotative meanings that words acquire, we often do not know the meaning of a word until we hear it in context. For example, take the word *pitch*. What is the meaning of this word? In the context of a baseball game, we know what the word *pitch* means; in the context of a singing lesson, *pitch* means something quite different; and in the midst of a sales meeting, *pitch* has another meaning. Written transcriptions of group meetings often are misleading because they do not reveal nonverbal contexts in which the words were used. As we see in the next section, much of this meaning is carried by nonverbal cues.

Language theorists have pointed out that the meaning of a word depends on not only the sentence and paragraph in which it is used, but also the nonverbal behaviors that accompany the verbal communication. Thus, understanding what is being said in a group discussion is a complex affair.

Group-Created Language and Thought

Small groups that work together daily, or even weekly, over time develop their own abbreviated language for discussing their work and for facilitating group decision making. A new member of a long-standing work group or an outsider observing the communication of an established group will be bewildered by an array of idioms and acronyms that have meaning only for group members.

Bormann (1990) demonstrated in his studies at the University of Minnesota that group members will initiate fantasies that chain out and become part of the group culture. Bales (1970) also pointed out in his studies at Harvard University that groups create their own symbolic world through dramatizations about the group. In Chapter 2, we explain how the consciousness-raising process takes place in newly formed groups. The creation of unique group language is a clear sign that symbolic convergence has occurred.

Work groups that are parts of large organizations are notorious for their use of acronyms. We attended a meeting in Washington that was called by the OEO to discuss funding of a project that would be supervised by MCHRD and occur at the ATTAC; but the whole project had to be approved by the OMB, assuming we had no problems with the EEOC. It was some time before these two midwestern university professors could decipher the language code of the federal employees. We later discovered that the meeting had been called by the Office of Economic Opportunity (OEO) to discuss funding of a project that would be supervised by the Mayor's Commission on Human Resources and Development (MCHRD). The meeting would take place at an Area Technical Training and Assistance Center (ATTAC); but the whole project had to be approved by the Office of Management and Budget (OMB), assuming there were no problems with the Equal Employment Opportunity Commission (EEOC). Sometimes we mistakenly think that confusing acronyms are the special communication form of the federal bureaucracy, but as a new student on campus, you may have encountered an array of acronyms without ever going to Washington. As a freshman, it might have been confusing to hear a student say that he or she needed a GPA booster so it would be necessary to take some "GenEds" from the "Real Life Experiences" listings.

All work groups develop acronyms and technical jargon that allow them to talk about their work efficiently. Sometimes it takes several months for a new member to master the group's language. Once he or she has done so, the member will feel a sense of inclusion in the group and may even enjoy watching another new member become bewildered on confronting the group's "language" for the first time. Sometimes group members mistakenly think that everybody speaks their language and proceed to release public communiqués that contain the group's ideas encased in the group's technical jargon. The public often ridicules federal publications and university research because the group's language appears to be—and may in fact be—a "foreign language" to them.

Long-standing groups often provide a unique group label for certain behaviors that they want to praise or blame quickly. For example, in an American culture, if somebody were accused of being "a Benedict Arnold," most Americans would know that the person was being labeled a traitor. Small groups develop similar labels, but because the group's history is not published, a new member would not know what the label referred to. So if a new member were told to not be "a Greenwood," he or she might be bewildered. However, the established members of the group would know that Jack Greenwood was a former member of the group who always used to come late to meetings. They would know that whenever a member arrived late for a meeting, he or she was immediately labeled "a Greenwood" and called such for the remainder of the meeting. Over time, groups develop an elaborate array of idioms that are based on the past history of the group. It may take a new member several months to uncover the important incidents in the group's past that give meaning to the verbal expressions that punctuate the group's daily discussions.

In sum, the language we use is not the same as our thoughts—just the best representation we have of them. Group language, then, is only a rough representation of the individual and group thinking that have taken place in a discussion. Furthermore, the unique language developed by the group will have meaning only for its members.

☐ NONVERBAL LANGUAGE CODE IN SMALL GROUPS

Numerous colleges and universities have adopted courses in nonverbal communication. Many of you have been introduced to the nonverbal area in your introductory speech course or in a course on interpersonal communication. The purpose of this section is to stress the importance of certain nonverbal variables in small groups. For convenience, we discuss nonverbal communication in small groups according to two major dimensions: environmental and personal.

Environmental Dimensions

The nonverbal environmental variables that affect communication in the small group are proxemics, objectics, and chronemics. The descriptions that follow are intended to enhance our understanding of how these variables influence group discussions.

Proxemics The major concern of proxemics is the study of space. We are concerned not only with the personal bubble, or personal space, that we carry around with us, but also with the territory, or fixed space, in which we find ourselves. Each person brings to the group his or her personal bubble or life-space. In a group in which a person is influential, he or she might occupy more of the group's life-space than other, less influential members. Conversely, a person who occupies a large amount of personal space may not give the time of day to other group members; such behavior could lead to a bad discussion situation.

One should be able to recognize that personal space is dynamic, whereas territorial space is not. Territory, as a basic proxemic variable, is fixed space. When we consider territory, we often think of a protected area. Many of us protect fixed spaces that belong to us—in our home, work, and play environments. Many of us have seen how an infant has little fixed space that he or she can call his or her own; however, it is amazing how quickly the child starts to stake his or her claim to new territory in a room and then in a whole house! The difference between personal space and territory can be described as follows: if you claim a room as being yours—for example, an office—that is territory; however, if you alter the amount of space you take up in a room when, for example, other employees come into your office, then you have changed the dynamic variable we identify as personal space.

The way in which personal space and territory relate to group discussions is the subject of study of small group ecology. By and large, small group ecology is concerned with such things as seating arrangement, who sits next to whom, and the shape of meeting tables. Knapp (1978, 131–140) identified numerous variables that are concerned with seating behavior and spatial arrangements in groups: leadership dominance, task, gender, acquaintance, motivation, and introversion-extroversion. These are all relevant topics for the study of small group ecology.

In terms of seating arrangements, we typically see the task leader taking a prominent position at the head of the table. If the group is having a panel discussion, the moderator typically sits in the middle. The task leader's lieutenant, or social-emotional leader, usually stakes a territorial claim in which he or she can assert his or her personal space bubble in a discussion group.

In terms of who sits next to whom, a number of factors are involved. First of all, people who are dominant in asserting their personal space can sit anywhere they want and next to whom they please. In many classrooms, we are sure that you have noticed how certain students have asserted themselves in where they will sit and next to whom. Introverted people do not get a great choice in selecting where they will sit or who they will sit next to.

The shape of meeting tables also governs the territory that is available to group members. In Chapter 4, we make no small point about "roundtable" and square table" discussions. In fact, if group members insist on a square or rectangular table, people will begin to see how their personal space bubbles are being minimized or enlarged in this given discussion territory. On the other hand, if the task leader and other group members encourage a roundtable discussion format, the likelihood of providing equal life-space for each member in the group setting is noticeably enhanced.

Objectics Just as the places in which group discussions are held have nonverbal nuances, so do the many artifacts and fixtures that accompany them. Think of the setting when you are called to the boss's conference room for the "big meeting." Name tags indicate the place you should sit at the long oak conference table. Glasses of ice water are set at each place. Pens and company stationary are placed by each discussant's name tag. Dignified landscape paintings line the walls of the conference room. This setting is much different from the informal meetings held around co-workers' desks on a daily basis! one of the basic differences between formal and informal discussion meetings occurs because of the influence of the nonverbal dimension of objectics.

The nonverbal variable of objectics is concerned with objects and artifacts. Objects in group discussions can include paper, pens, chalkboards, flip charts, and the like that are necessary for the group's functioning. Artifacts typically are things that "dress up" the discussion setting. For example, decorative items on conference room walls dress up the formal discussion meeting. A general knowledge of objectics helps discussion planners to assess the impact of various objects and artifacts on the formal-informal dimension of discussions.

Chronemics A third environmental nonverbal variable is chronemics, or the study of time. Time has a tremendous impact on small group communication. First of all, one of the major differences between groups is their history: Is the group a zero-history group, or does it have a definite history? We know that the amount of time group members spend in a given group shapes, to no small extent, the group's historical tradition and acculturation processes.

In addition to what constitutes time in small groups—history or no history—small group practitioners are concerned with the "when" aspects of chronemics. Staff meetings typically are held at the same time each week—"Monday morning meetings," Friday lunch meetings," and so on. Whether or not the designated day and hour of the meeting is best for group members is largely immaterial; the important point for many organizations is to have regular meetings, in part for their own chronemic sense of normalcy.

Group meetings differ culturally in terms of chronemics. For example, Japanese work groups socialize after work, but the socialization is regarded as a continuation of work meetings and members dare not miss them. In fact, a great deal of decision making is accomplished in these social settings.

One further impact of chronemics on groups is *how long* the meeting lasts. Most people start to get uncomfortable if a two-hour meeting lasts longer than its assigned time. Most informal discussion planners must insist that their discussants adhere to time limits. The facets of chronemics (what, when, and how long) represent the importance of considering environmental nonverbal variables in small group discussions.

Personal Dimensions

The nonverbal personal variables that affect communication in the small group are vocalics, kinesics, and eye behavior. Each of these dimensions is related to how we perceive communication interaction and role behaviors in small groups.

Vocalics The sounds a person makes that accompany his or her verbal messages are called vocalics, or paralanguage. Many speech practitioners have devoted their careers to enhancing the voice and the diction skills of students. How sounds come out of a person's mouth influences a listener's perception of the person communicating a verbal message. Contrast a discussant who carefully enunciates each and every syllable and couches these syllables in golden, pearly-shaped tones with a group member who casually states his or her ideas with no such vocalic exaggeration. On the other end of the continuum is the discussant who mutters his or her opinions in a low-pitched, gravelly voice.

In addition to the voice and diction aspects present in paralanguage, group members must be vigilant to identify emotional nuances that might accompany another member's contribution. The member might verbally say, "Yes, yes!" but the sound of his or her voice says, "No, no!" Just as with other elements of the nonverbal code, vocalics must be interpreted in light of both the individual involved and his or her interrelation with the given group situation.

Kinesics In a broad sense, *kinesics* refers to body language. Various categories of body language that are of concern to communication scholars include posture, hand and arm gestures, facial expression, and total body movement. Many times a discussant's interest in the topic at hand is indicated by his or her posture in a chair. A member who is sitting up straight in his or her seat is probably paying attention to the discussion topic. On the other hand, a member who is slouching and overrelaxed reflects a nonchalant attitude.

Hand and arm gestures often represent not only how expressive a person is, but also the enthusiasm he or she feels for a given topic. Some kinds of gesticulation can even indicate the role a person is playing in a group. Reporting results from a scientifically researched study, Baird (1977, 360) concluded that gesticulation of the shoulders and arms contributed significantly to members' perceptions of leadership behavior. In addition, other body actions, such as the crossing of legs, folding of arms, and finger pointing, may indicate, either intentionally or not, some aspect of a member's attitude toward the group. Facial expression, too, can reflect a member's feelings, although it is difficult to be sure what many facial expressions mean in terms of possible emotions conveyed. Nonetheless, a careful analysis of kinesic behavior by group members will help in understanding the general feeling of the group, using another lens of nonverbal communication.

Eye Behavior One of the standard axioms of small group leadership states: If you want to know who the real leader in the group is, closely observe to whom the other participants address their remarks. In most small groups, this method of identifying the leader holds true. Eye behavior of discussion participants can also display a number of personality and social dimensions. If a person does not look directly into the eyes of other group members, is it because he or she fears reprisals from the group? Or by not looking at someone, does he or she express lack of interest in a particular person or the ideas that person tries to present or both?

By considering the personal dimensions just discussed as well as the three environmental variables, one is able to make an assessment of how significant nonverbal communication is in small group discussions. Certainly the impact of particular nonverbal dimensions is more significant in some groups than in others. For example, the personal dimensions of the nonverbal code are typical of one-time-meeting groups; on the other hand, both personal and environmental nonverbal communication variables might combine to suggest subtle changes in the development of an unspoken language code in ongoing groups.

☐ COMMUNICATION SKILLS FOR IMPROVING INTERPERSONAL TRUST IN GROUPS

In Chapter 3, we identified and explained the five core communication skills for building trust in small groups. They are risking disclosure, avoiding stereotyped judgments, being an empathetic listener, recognizing individual differences, and providing emotional security for all members. In this chapter, we present ten more skills for building and maintaining interpersonal group trust.

■ *Managing group chronemics.* In the early life of a work group, interpersonal trust can be destroyed if group time is not properly managed. The scheduling of group meetings is crucial for group trust because everyone jealously guards his or her own time. The meetings need to be at a time when everyone can meet, and they should start and end on time. Absenteeism from group meetings wreaks havoc on interpersonal trust. Missing a meeting shows disrespect to other group members of the group task. Also, group members who are present at the meeting tend to talk ill of the missing member. Likewise, impromptu meetings that intentionally leave members out destroy trust. The excluded member feels hurt and bewildered. Especially in the formative stages of a work group, it is important for all members to be present at group meetings.

■ *Optimizing your group personality.* The research on small group communication paints a picture of the ideal group member. The ideal group member should be friendly, intelligent, socially mature, assertive, self-assured, creative, rational, communicatively competent, empathetic, and tactful. None of us achieves the ideal, but we should strive to optimize our group personalities. We can work on becoming better group members. The ten descriptors above are, for the most part, skill-based. Therefore, you can improve as a group member by working on the skills. For example, we are all friendly—just not all the time or with everybody. If you make an effort to be friendly with your group members, even when you don't feel like it, you will soon have the ability to join a new work group and be regarded as a friendly person.

■ *Promoting an open and supportive climate.* Gibb's classic study (1961) on defensive and supportive group climates demonstrates the need for openness if trust is to be built in a group. Gibb identifies six pair of behavior that either create a supportive climate or produce a defensive climate: evaluative versus descriptive—don't be judgmental; control versus problem orientation—don't be manipulative; strategy versus spontaneity—don't plot against group members; neutrality versus empathy—don't be indifferent to individual needs; superiority versus equality—don't put others down; and certainty versus provisionalism—don't be a know-it-all.

■ *Keeping self-disclosure within limits.* Every group needs a level of self-disclosure such that members know on whom they can depend. Some work groups require more self-disclosure than others. Members of a team of firefighters who must often work cooperatively within a burning building require a great deal of disclosure from one another so that they know they can trust the other members to save their lives. On the other hand, the members of an accounting team that is conducting an audit of a corporation need to know less about one another. A work group can err in either direction; the group can be either underdisclosed or overdisclosed. The goal is to find the level of self-disclosure that is fitting to get the job done.

Self-disclosures by a member are always interesting to a group but often can occur as a means to avoid the work at hand. The basic rule of thumb is that self-disclosure should only occur when personal conflicts have stopped work from taking place.

■ *Heightening awareness of the nonverbal code.* If you could observe your group functioning from behind a one-way mirror but could not hear them, you would soon realize that the nonverbal group code was conveying a great deal of information. You would be able to assess the overall emotional state of the group and the general cohesion of the group as it worked on its task. However, if the nonverbal code were to be taken in context with the verbal code, you would be able to make a much more accurate assessment of the group's structure and potential for group operations and work. We emphasize the importance of nonverbal communication primarily because this dimension of communication has not received adequate attention and application until recent years. In the past, we concentrated on the rational verbal aspects of group discussion. Blending the nonverbal code with the group's verbal language system provides us with a more accurate picture of what is taking place in the group. It would also be an error to overemphasize nonverbal communication and rely on it as a primary means for inference about what is going on in the group.

■ *Ensuring that individual needs are satisfied.* Membership satisfaction is one of the four outputs of task groups. Schutz (1966) identifies three fundamental needs for membership satisfaction: inclusion, affection, and control. You want to strive to be democratic, social, and personal with each member. Determining the right level of interpersonal involvement with each group member is difficult. Our best advice is the trial-and-error approach. Draw out through questions silent members so that they become included more as part of the group. Offer responsibility to members who seem to abdicate control. Ask for personal disclosures from people who seem underpersonal.

■ *Reducing new-member apprehension.* Attempt to reduce a new member's anxieties regarding how he or she will be treated by the group. It is a good idea to spend some time describing the social diversity that exists within the group so that the new member's fears of compatibility will be eased. There is always the question, How will I fit in? Most people have exaggerated fears about how much conformity it will take to be successfully assimilated into a work group. It is also important to tell stories about the group's past successes and failures, especially failures. Stories that point out that existing group members have made "beginner's mistakes" and still been given the chance to improve are particularly useful.

■ *Translating interpersonal trust from word to deed.* Talk is cheap. Judge me by what I do and not by what I say. Actions speak louder than words. These clichés punctuate an important point about group life. Although self-disclosure needs to take place for trust to be built, deed-producing disclosure is far more important than verbal disclosure. Cooperative work behavior cements interpersonal trust in a group. Some of these behaviors are key: attending group meetings, sharing group work, helping group members with outside projects, and keeping group conversation confidential.

■ *Avoiding disruptive interpersonal group behaviors.* Earlier in the chapter, we identified the dirty dozen deviant personality behaviors. Strive to avoid them. At one time or another, we have all committed these group errors, like playing the clown or whining. We gave dramatistic names to the dirty dozen, such as airheading and eggheading, so that they would be easier to remember. By monitoring your group behavior, you will become more sensitized to your weaknesses. Of the dirty dozen, each of us has three or four we are particularly prone to commit. Identify yours and work to avoid them.

■ *Fostering a cooperative climate.* Our educational systems emphasize competitive, not collaborative, learning. Our business organizations preach teamwork but reward and promote individuals. It is little wonder that building interpersonal trust in an interdependent work group is difficult. Competitive climates invite cheating and dishonesty. Cooperative climates promote honesty and harmonious relationships. Interpersonal group trust is impossible in a competitive environment. To foster cooperation, the group needs to be continually reminded that it has a common goal, that group members will share equally in the rewards, and that everyone's contribution is valued. The making of a rational argument in a work group is not for the purpose of winning a debate but should be part of a cooperative effort to find the right answer.

☐ SUMMARY

The interpersonal relationships that people develop and foster in small group communication are the focus of this chapter. These relationships include the dimensions of inclusion, control, and affection, which are measured to no small extent by the amount of disclosure, trust, and empathy that group members have for one another. In addition, one must consider the dominance, friendliness, and rationality of various personality types in the group.

Our perception of individuals as group members often is tempered by deviant personality behaviors. Individual differences considered in the chapter include gender, race, age, education, occupation, and income. How these differences are perceived by members often indicates the heterogeneity or homogeneity of the group's composition.

Crucial to our understanding of individual group members is a basic comprehension of how verbal and nonverbal codes function in groups. Eight ways in which a word can be defined are included to illustrate differences between language and thought. Further, group-created language and thought are discussed in terms of the way the verbal code operates uniquely in a group. On the other hand, the nonverbal language code is determined in part by both environmental and personal dimensions of nonverbal communication. Proxemics, objectics, and chronemics are the environmental nonverbal variables presented in this chapter. The personal nonverbal concepts that are considered are vocalics, kinesics, and eye behavior.

The chapter concludes with ten skills for improving interpersonal trust in small groups.

Diary of George Cramer

CASE BACKGROUND

George Cramer is taking a small group course at Midwestern College. George is a transfer student from a junior college located in the northwestern United States. He transferred to Midwestern College because he heard that the school had a good accounting department and because he is interested in becoming a certified public accountant. George is taking the small group communication class because he feels somewhat uneasy in group settings, and because he would like to move up the managerial ladder, he wanted to learn how to lead work groups. George has felt like an outsider ever since he arrived on campus. He hasn't joined any social organizations, and he feels that his dorm floor is full of freshmen who are into first-year college social activities that do not appeal to him.

George has been assigned to a classroom work group whose task is to examine and report on a major small group communication dimension. The group will be required to give a class presentation for which group members will receive a common grade. Each member must turn in an individually kept diary of the group.

George's group consists of the following members:

- Pat Riley, junior, English literature major, 25, female, white, Catholic, divorced, no children, lives in off-campus apartment, raised in large industrial city
- Dale Dickson, freshman, physical education major, 18, male, white, Protestant, single, lives in dorm, from small, rural southern town
- Marlene Goldstein, junior, mass communication major, 20, female, white, Jewish, engaged, lives in sorority house, raised in a large eastern city
- Aaron Reed, sophomore, premed major, 19, male, black, Protestant, single, lives in off-campus apartment, from a medium-sized midwestern city
- Lusharon McDaniels, senior, criminal justice major, 21, female, black, Protestant, single, lives off campus, from large western city
- George Cramer, junior, accounting major, 20, male, white, Protestant, single, lives in dorm, from small town in the northwestern United States

CASE LOG

Entry, First Meeting

Today was our first meeting. Our group looks very interesting. It doesn't look like we have much in common, but that's what is interesting. The women dominated the meeting, particularly Marlene. She thinks that because she is a mass communication major, she knows all about our topic, which is "group norming." However, Lusharon believes that her background in criminal justice makes her an expert. We didn't get much done and I didn't have much to say.

Entry, Second Meeting

The women were at it again. Talk! Talk! Talk! I don't think "us guys" got three words in edgewise. I hate to stereotype, but Marlene sure is pushy! She keeps trying to organize us, and nobody's appointed her leader. I think Dale objects to Marlene's bossiness, but he doesn't say much either. I don't understand Aaron at all. He seems bright, but he doesn't assert himself and attempt to shut Lusharon up. She's as bad as Marlene! We still have not "normed out" our opinions on what to do on the topic.

Entry, Third Meeting

Hooray for Aaron Reed! Today he tried to take charge of the meeting and give the group some direction. Lusharon sided with Marlene and attacked Aaron's knowledge of group communication because he spends most of his time with his nose in a book or a test tube studying chemistry. I really felt sorry for Aaron and wanted to say something to him, but I didn't. What really surprised me was that Dale seemed to take the women's side while Aaron was being picked on.

It looks like Marlene has firmly established herself as leader of the group, and Lusharon is "the wicked witch from the west" who supports her. I can't understand why Lusharon would not support another black person as group leader. Oh well, we have our assignments for the next meeting. I'm assigned to compile a bibliography of articles from sociology on group norming. That's all right with me; I'll do what I'm told.

Entry, Fourth Meeting

Aaron was absent. I told the group that they had been too rough on him, especially Lusharon. It turned out that it was Get George Cramer Day! Pat Riley seems like the nicest woman of the three; she at least defended me when Lusharon accused me of being a "typical, mousy accounting major who doesn't speak up!" I told the group that they had gone too far on personal attacks on both Aaron and me. Our group didn't need to engage in quasi-psychological analysis of our members to get this job done. I submitted my bibliography and left early. I'm not sure this is a good classroom exercise.

Entry, Fifth Meeting

The night before the meeting Pat Riley called me at the dorm. She said she called to apologize about the last meeting, and that I was right that the group overstepped its bounds. She tried to assure me that the group would stick to the job at hand. With those assurances, I agreed to continue to meet with the group.

The meeting was the best work session we had. I felt that Lusharon was still hostile toward me, but Marlene made several attempts to include me in the discussion, and Aaron and I had a friendly chat at the end of the meeting. The group agreed to meet at Pat's apartment for our last meeting before our presentation.

Entry, Sixth Meeting

Tonight our group became a group. We all felt that we were part of a common effort. The meeting was very friendly, and Pat was a great hostess! Marlene is still a little pushy, but she did a great deal of work on the topic, and if it wasn't for her, we would still be trying to figure out our topic.

After our presentation was all planned out and ready to go, we ended up talking about our feelings toward one another in the group. Dale really surprised me. All along he had been threatened being a member of a group; he said he did not have much ability to make a contribution, given the topic of the group. Dale's statement caused Aaron to confess that his premed studies had prevented him from working for the group as hard as he should have, but he was pleased that Marlene had done so much work and thanked her for it.

I was also surprised that the group had gotten together without my knowing it and presented me with the "Research Award" for all the library work I had done. I was flattered.

I am certain that our presentation will go well tomorrow. I only feel bad that our group will break up just when we were starting to work well together.

CASE QUESTIONS

1. How would you describe George's interpersonal relationship with other group members in terms of affection, inclusion, and control? Did his relationships change over the course of the meetings?

2. What key disclosures occurred in the group that helped in the group's interpersonal development?

3. What kind of stereotyping did George seem to do? In what ways were George's stereotypes wrong?

4. What trust-building behaviors occurred in this group?

CHAPTER SEVEN

LEADING SMALL GROUPS

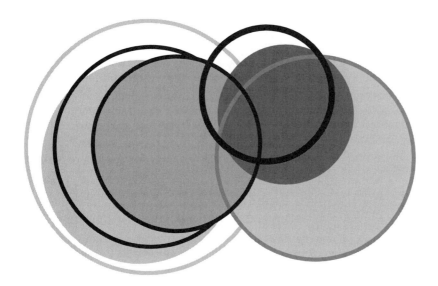

CHAPTER OBJECTIVES

After reading this chapter, you should be able to:

- Know the differences between designated and emergent leadership
- Understand the bases of leadership power
- Distinguish the stylistic approaches of designated leadership
- Identify the motivational styles of designated leadership
- Explain the leadership communication skills

THEORIES FOR LEADING SMALL GROUPS
  Designated Leader Perspective
  Emergent Leader Perspective
  Small Group Leader Model

COMMUNICATION SKILLS FOR LEADING PROBLEM-SOLVING GROUPS
  Leadership Communication Skills in
    the Task Area

Leadership Communication Skills in
    the Procedural Area
Leadership Communication Skills in
    the Interpersonal Area

SUMMARY

CASE STUDY: LEADING A CORPORATE TASK FORCE

You will spend much of your professional life leading small groups. Because we all continually find ourselves in leadership positions, a great deal of research has been devoted to determining the qualities of a leader and the correct leadership skills. In this chapter, we present seven approaches to small group leadership, showing how each approach emphasizes a different aspect of leading a small group. These approaches have been tied together in our definition of leading small group discussions.

The first distinction that needs to be made is the one between leader and leadership. We define small group leadership as *communication that positively influences the group to move in the direction of the group's goals.* A leader of a discussion may be appointed or may emerge from group discussion. Later in the chapter, we discuss the differences between a designated and an emergent leader. Are the terms *leadership* and *leader* synonymous? We think that the answer is no. *Leadership* is a much broader term. It is part of the communication process of a discussion and can be performed by any group member. Therefore, it is possible to have a person appointed as leader of a discussion group who exhibits no leadership. Conversely, a person does not have to be the leader to move the group toward its goals. However, most people who emerge as leaders have previously performed leadership functions for the group.

Although most leadership behaviors can be performed by a number of individuals in the group, we normally assume that a leader possesses certain qualities or abilities to aid him or her in moving the group toward its goals. Certain situations—for example, the kind of organizational structure of which a group is a part—will cause one person to emerge as the appointed or elected leader, in preference to another with similar leadership qualities and communication abilities. Although we can be quite specific about leadership functions in a discussion, it is difficult to define in the abstract who the leader of a discussion is and how that person came to be leader. Several key concepts fit together roughly to form a composite picture of a group discussion leader. When we look for personal qualities in a leader, we think in terms of maturity, fairness, fluency, and so on. We may also think of the person in terms of how authoritative he or she is, or how much power he or she possesses. We also consider whether the person has the ability to motivate group members and whether he or she would have better leadership qualities than others in a given situation. After detailing these seven basic approaches, we present a conceptual model of how these various concepts interact to form a definition of a discussion leader. Finally, we identify necessary communication skills for leading problem-solving groups.

☐ THEORIES FOR LEADING SMALL GROUPS

The seven approaches to discussion leadership are classified according to two research perspectives. The first perspective covers research that compares the formal or designated leader with nonleaders. The second perspective views leaders as emerging from the small discussion group and describes the qualities and functions of leadership. The first research perspective focuses on trait, power, stylistic, and motivational approaches. Our second leadership perspective discusses the situational theory, role-emergence theory, and functional theory.

Designated Leader Perspective

Most small work groups are formed within formal organizational structures. The formal structure spells out designated leader roles that typically are filled through appointment rather than election. When a member of a group is appointed leader, he or she may or may not have received support from other group members. In fact, the designated leader could be brought in or transferred to the group, never having met the members of the work group. Sometimes a person designated discussion leader for a one-time business meeting has his or her first contact with the group when he or she phones the members to call the meeting. Such a situation is particularly likely when a problem-solving group is formed on a companywide basis and people are brought together because of their given areas of specialization. Although many designated leaders may have emerged from their groups to become the designated leaders, many researchers have found it useful to disregard how people become designated leaders and focus instead on distinctions between those who are designated leaders and those who are not.

Trait Approach Small group researchers have long been concerned with determining the differences between leaders and nonleaders with respect to how they *look, talk, think, act,* and *feel.* The differences that exist between leaders and nonleaders often are trivial and almost always difficult to generalize across small group situations. However, certain characteristics have been found repeatedly by social psychologists. Those that are most important to a student of small groups are the personal traits that can be improved on, such as speech fluency, cooperativeness, and knowledge of task. A supervisor would be ill-advised to appoint a person as designated leader of a work group simply because the person possesses the physical, mental, and personality qualities that we report here. However, the possession of certain attributes may influence the supervisor to appoint a person as leader.

Research demonstrates that leaders look different from nonleaders. Physical appearance has proved to be a distinguishing variable. Designated leaders tend to be slightly taller, heavier, and physically more attractive than other group members and seem to possess the athletic ability and stamina necessary for leadership.

Leaders talk better than nonleaders. Researchers from various disciplines have discovered that fluency of speech, confidence in tone, and frequency of communication sort leaders from nonleaders.

The findings of small group researchers also support the idea that leaders think better, in that they score higher on standard I.Q. tests and show more mental agility in performing problem-solving tasks. Although leaders tend to be brighter, they must not be too much brighter than the average members of the group, or they will be rejected. This point of diminishing returns is also true of height; although most leaders are taller, they tend to be only slightly taller than other group members.

In addition to the preceding traits that appear to distinguish leaders from non-leaders, leaders act differently from other group members. Many of these actions are in turn governed by certain personality characteristics that leaders possess. By and large, small group communication research findings seem to suggest that leaders normally are more extroverted, self-assertive, persistent, and responsible than other members of the group. In essence, the favorable personality characteristics cited in the preceding sentence will help their possessor to be a good leader. Leaders tend to be active, not passive, group members, displaying a panorama of personality characteristics that assist in leading small groups (Stogdill 1974).

By contrast, individuals who have high degrees of communication anxiety in groups tend not to emerge as leaders (Hawkins and Powell 1991). On the plus side, training in small group communication tends to reduce communication apprehension (Comadena 1984).

Psychologists have demonstrated that people can be crudely classified into four emotional states that affect the type of designated leader they might become. These states were originally labeled dominance, inducement, submission, and compliance (Marston 1928). If you're a big D (dominance), you tend to be a take-charge, hard-driving, risk-taking leader. If you're a big I (inducement), your approach to leadership is one of persuasion, in that you convince your subordinates to work hard, and you sell the importance of your work group within the organization. If you are a big S (submission), you tend to let the group have its way and you delegate a lot of leadership decisions to the group. If you are a big C (compliance), you manage your work group "by the book"; you are a stickler for rules and regulations. Management consulting companies use numerous paper-and-pencil tests that will profile you in terms of your emotional bases of leadership. One of the most popular instruments was developed by John Geier, a communication scholar.

The trait approach to leadership asks us to look at a composite of desirable qualities that usually distinguish leaders from nonleaders. Our discussion to this point has focused on how leaders look, talk, feel, think, and act differently from other members of the group. (For an excellent report of research findings in support of the trait approach, consult one or more of the following: McGrath and Altman 1966, Shaw 1981, and Stogdill 1974. Other important qualities of a leader, such as gender, race, and communication skills, are discussed in Chapter 6.)

Power Approach Because leadership includes influencing and controlling group members in the direction of the group's goals, scholars have focused on the concept of power as one of the means by which a leader can exert influence on the group. French and Raven (1968), reporting in Cartwright and Zander's volume *Group Dynamics: Research and Theory*, identify five bases of power that a designated leader may have in varying degrees: legitimate, expert, referent, reward, and coercive. Here, information power and group power have been added to the original list.

In formal organizations, legitimate power flows from the job title, and most group members follow reasonable directives simply because the directives come from the formally designated group leader. In group discussions, a designated leader exercises the legitimate power of calling a meeting and setting the initial agenda.

Expert power is attributed to a person for what he or she knows. If a designated leader is knowledgeable about the work the group is doing, expert power and legitimate power combine to exert control over a group's direction. Expert power may also be possessed by a group member who is not the designated leader. In the latter case, a leadership struggle may occur between the designated leader, who has legitimate power, and the group member who has expert power. Khan, Rahim, and Uddin (1994) found both expert and legitimate power to be associated with effectiveness and commitment.

The third basis of leadership is referent power—sometimes called attraction power, or charisma. This power is generated by the desire of the group members to identify and associate with an attractive leader. A sociogram would probably reveal that most members of a group prefer to associate with a leader who has referent power.

The fourth basis of leadership is information power, which is based on information about the organization that does not come primarily through the formal channels of communication. Group members who have a lot of this power know how to get things done because they have contact with organizational members outside the work group.

Reward and coercive bases of power are treated together because we see them as being two sides of the same coin, although many designated leaders may complain that they have too few rewards to hand out to group members and prefer not to use their coercive power. French and Raven (1968) argue that coercive power will be accepted by group members if it comes from a person who also has legitimate power. The person who has the most referent power may also have the most coercive power; if he or she refuses to associate with a given member, the rejection may be quite painful. The designated discussion leader frequently rewards group members by publicly complimenting them for their contributions to the discussion.

One way to analyze the ability of a designated discussion leader in terms of the influence and control that leader has over the group is to examine the distribution of the bases of power among the group members. The more these bases are concentrated in the designated discussion leader, the greater is that person's ability to control and influence a discussion or lead a work group. Conversely, the more these powers are shared equally or occur disproportionately among group members, the less influence and control the designated leader will have (Jurma and Wright 1990).

Power too often is viewed as a competitive force for influencing groups and group outcomes. This book looks primarily at interdependent work groups that have common goals they try to achieve in a cooperative manner. Thus, we conceive of group power as the additive force of all group members who are cooperatively working to achieve a group goal. The designated leader possesses some of this power, but the other group members must share their power if the group is to be effective. Group members who view their team colleagues through a competitive rather than a cooperative lens may resist power pooling.

Effective designated leaders must use leadership power that they don't personally possess but that is present in the group. For example, a designated leader may assign an inexperienced worker to a new task and, on completion of the work, ask the group member with the most expert power regarding the task to evaluate the rookie's job. If the expert gives it high praise, the rookie will feel rewarded, more so than if the appointed leader had praised the task. Thus, the designated leader used power he or she did not have for the group good. In Chapter 9, we discuss power as it is viewed in competitive group situations.

Stylistic Approach Under the first research perspective of comparing leaders with nonleaders, it was only natural that the type or style of leadership performed by the designated leader would be examined. A major study, often referred to in discussions of the stylistic approach, was reported by White and Lippett (1968). They examined the adult designated leader in the following three contexts: autocratic, democratic, and laissez-faire. In essence, the first style of leader was able to set policies, whereas the democratic type of leader facilitated group discussions about policy decisions and the laissez-faire type allowed complete freedom among the group members. This classic study found that autocratic leaders give a lot of orders, have power to approve and praise people and their ideas, and, in general, are somewhat critical. In contrast, the study showed that democratic leaders give a fair number of suggestions, exercise self-discipline, and are noncritical and matter-of-fact in their relations with other group members. White and Lippett (1968) found that laissez-faire leaders exceed the other two styles only in giving information. Two communication researchers, Sargent and Miller (1971), reported much the same kind of results in terms of the behavior of autocratic and democratic leaders, particularly in relation to task-oriented communication. Autocratic leaders rush through the question-and-answer process, whereas democratic leaders encourage much more member participation and discussion. Democratic leaders are perceived to be better performers and superior leaders when compared to autocratic leaders by their subordinates (Luthar 1996).

A tendency in analyzing the styles of leadership approach is to characterize one leader as being more leader-centered and another as being more group-centered. Typically, we think of leader-centered leaders as being more autocratic than group-centered leaders, who follow a more democratic, or even laissez-faire, style of leadership. A designated leader who follows a leader-centered approach in a discussion may do so because of time constraints and the fact that the meeting will run more efficiently if he or she controls member comments and the like. On the other hand, a group-centered leader encourages member participation and interaction. Wischmeier (1955), in one of the more important studies done in the field of communication, points out the paradox of designated discussion leadership styles: Group members perceive the leader-centered leader as doing a more effective job; however, they seem to enjoy greater individual satisfaction and like the group better in general under a group-centered leadership. Not surprisingly, then, when one leadership style is favored over another, there will be pluses and minuses for the task and social dimensions of small groups. One communication researcher, Raymond Ross (1974a), suggested that when you visualize the styles of discussion leadership on a continuum, the person who has been designated leader must learn to play the styles-of-leadership continuum like a violin. Ross further suggested that it takes a virtuoso to play the styles of leadership appropriately across different group situations.

Researchers have also been defining the leadership styles of designated leaders of work groups, paralleling the research done initially on leaders of discussion in the 1940s and 1950s. Douglas McGregor (1960) popularized two views of management or leadership style. He posited that some leaders reflect a Theory X style (the "my way or the highway" approach). This style flows from an assumption that an organization is controlled through the exercise of authority and that subordinates must be carefully watched. McGregor's second style (Theory Y) emphasizes "people skills." This style assumes that workers enjoy work and that they will work hard if they are kept motivated by humanistic leaders. A leader using this style would be sensitive to group member needs and seek input before making decisions. A third style is called Theory Z (a team management approach). William Ouchi (1981) believes that much of Japanese management's success is due in part to the use of Theory Z. A leader using Theory Z would continually invite group members to participate in management decision making. Thus, the line between the designated leader and the other members would be blurred. Today, decision-making groups that focus on quality and productivity and contain both supervisors and subordinates are called quality circles, which we discuss in Chapter 1.

Motivational Approach Researchers who work on the motivational approach to leadership try to explain how a designated leader influences the group to get the job done. Some scholars of group leadership refer to general styles that people use to motivate their work groups. These motivational styles should not be confused with the stylistic approach to leadership discussed in the preceding section, although there are some striking similarities. The motivational styles focus on the social and task dimensions of the group and attempt to explain how much direction and control the leader needs to have to get the work done. The two theories discussed here are Blake and Mouton's "managerial grid" and Hersey and Blanchard's leadership theory.

Robert Blake and Jane Mouton (1964) constructed a two-dimensional matrix for classifying a designated leader's motivational style. One side of the matrix consists of nine cells of concern for people (the social-emotional dimension) whereas the other side consists of nine cells of concern for production (the task dimension). Thus, Blake and Mouton's managerial grid contains eighty-one potential slots in which a given designated leader might fit. Low production but high concern for people would be rated 1/9, or "country club." This kind of leader is extremely concerned with the members' happiness but not too concerned about reaching a decision in the discussion group. On the other hand, a 9/1 rating, or "task master," would be just the opposite kind of leader—having no concern for the feelings of the group members and highly task-oriented in wanting to get the job done at all costs. The ideal leadership style, using the Blake and Mouton approach, is the 9/9, or "team player." This leader is extremely interested both in accomplishing the task and in group member satisfaction. For a number of years, managers in corporations referred to themselves as 5/5's, 2/8's, and so on, although they really hoped that they approached the ideal of a 9/9 rating.

Although most scholars accept the position that a good designated group leader must be concerned with both the task and the social dimensions of the group, many disagree with the notion that people have a fixed number of abilities with which to lead a group. Moreover, some researchers object to the idea that the ideal motivational leadership style is 9/9. Paul Hersey and Kenneth Blanchard (1977) argue that an effective group leader varies his or her motivational leadership style depending on the members' ability, maturity, and willingness to do a given assignment. Hersey

FIGURE 7.1   **Motivational Leadership Styles**

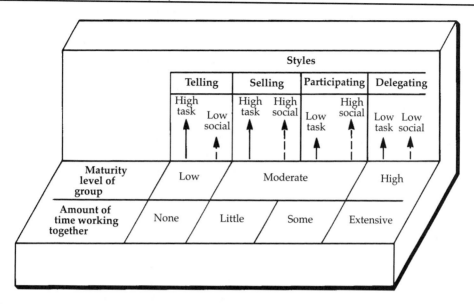

SOURCE: From Paul Hersey and Kenneth H. Blanchard, *Management of Organizational Behavior: Utilizing Human Resources*, 3rd ed., © 1977, p. 170. Adapted by permission of Prentice-Hall, Inc., Englewood Cliffs, New Jersey.

and Blanchard argue that an effective leader needs a repertoire of four motivational leadership styles: *telling, coaching, participating,* and *delegating.* Figure 7.1 shows our conceptualization of Hersey and Blanchard's four motivational leadership styles, which are quite different from one another in terms of the amount of control the leader exerts on the group.

The telling style is used by a task group leader when the group lacks the maturity to know how, when, or where to do a given task. The leader is very directive and walks the group through the work that needs to be done. The fact that this style is low in relationship behavior does not mean that the leader is not friendly or personable, but that his or her energy is focused on how the job should be done. When this type of leadership style is called for, it usually means that a collection of people has just formed a work group and that the designated leader has considerable knowledge and experience with the group's task. Corporations often bring together new employees under the supervision of an experienced worker. If the company is an accounting firm, it may bring together four new accountants and have them report to a veteran certified public accountant. Although the new accountants are well trained and know accounting procedures, they still need a supervisor to tell them how the company does its audit. In fact, most of the initial meetings emphasize the handling of tasks.

The telling style is also used in emergencies. If a person in one of your classes has a heart attack and a student is present who has had emergency medical training, this person usually steps forth to give orders. The specially trained student is so wrapped up in telling everybody how to do his or her job that little time is left for social-emotional stroking. In any case, most of the students who are working on the heart attack victim expect to be reinforced with positive statements by the emergency group leader.

A Monday-morning meeting of a divisional sales force is typical of the situations that call for the coaching style of motivational leadership. The sales manager has probably made up the coming week's sales goals and mapped out the kind of effort it will take to accomplish them. Furthermore, he or she is directly responsible for the results and probably has a mixture of novice and experienced salespeople. In this meeting, the sales manager spends considerable energy convincing the sales force that it can meet the week's goals. The sales manager uses a lot of positive reinforcement, based on past successes and substantial firsthand knowledge of how a sales campaign should go. In fact, any work group that must re-prove its worth on a week-to-week basis probably has a designated leader who uses the coaching motivational leadership style. The coaches of high school and college athletic teams use this style in getting their teams ready for the next game. However, some of the large professional athletic teams have such a mature group that the coach can revert to a delegating style of leadership.

The participating motivational leadership style is typified by numerous small group situations. Volunteer groups and decision-making discussion groups are two excellent examples of situations where this motivational leadership style often is applied. A volunteer organization for the American Cancer Society or American Heart Association usually has a paid designated leader in charge of an all-volunteer work group. In this situation, the success of the group depends on the designated leader's ability to get active participation from various volunteer members. The designated leader has little or no legitimate power and must spend a great deal of time stroking the volunteer work force. Any volunteer work group needs to be constantly told that all the members are nice people and that they are doing a good job! Designated leaders of decision-making groups have much in common with the paid staff leader of volunteer groups. If a group of executives is brought together to make decisions about a company policy, the designated leader for this decision-making group probably wants to adopt a participating style of motivational leadership, sometimes falling back to the coaching style when consensus seems possible.

When a designated leader is placed in charge of a long-standing, effective work group, the leader may adopt a delegating style of motivational leadership because the group is mature, knows its job, and is confident of its ability. Chairpersons of academic departments in colleges often adopt this style of motivational leadership in their day-to-day handling of faculty, the chairperson changing to a coaching style of leadership when conducting monthly staff meetings.

Hersey and Blanchard (1977) stress that a designated leader must adapt to changing situations when selecting his or her appropriate leadership style—for example, when the membership or the task of a group changes. They believe that the designated leader should adopt a leadership style according to the group's maturity level.

Emergent Leader Perspective

Many of the more informal group settings in which we find ourselves take considerably different leadership patterns from those described above. As a matter of fact, certain ongoing groups in organizational structures follow what appears to be a rather low-key, democratic work group approach. In many of these work groups, in which the group has developed a definite history, leaders may be emergent rather than designated. The major approaches to the study of leadership that we consider here are the situational theory, the role-emergence theory, and the functional theory to leadership. Even when there is a designated leader, a natural leader may emerge. In addition, group members can perform certain leadership functions whether there is an assigned leader or not. The emergent leader perspective gives us another lens through which to look at leadership behaviors, regardless of where they originate, and contributes to our study of small group communication leadership in general. The emergent leader perspective has been emphasized by communication researchers for essentially two reasons: our interest in providing communication training for group leaders and our general scholarly interest in describing the communication of work groups to understand their effectiveness.

Situational Theory Fiedler (1967) studied more than eight hundred work groups, from B-29 bomber crews to Boy Scout troops, in a twenty-year search for a theory that would predict leader effectiveness. Fiedler argues that there are four variables that interact in a work situation to determine a leader's effectiveness. They are how much power the leader has, how structured the task is, how well the leader is liked by the group members, and whether the leader is basically a relationship-oriented or task-oriented leader. By studying these variables, Fiedler developed what he called a contingency model that can predict or improve a given leader's performance. His model indicates that task-oriented leaders function best in highly structured and highly unstructured situations—that is, in mechanical or automatic situations and in situations of crisis. Fiedler's findings are consistent with Hersey and Blanchard's recommendation that in either of these situations, the leader should adopt a telling style. According to Fiedler, relationship-oriented leaders perform best in middle-range structured tasks and situations in which formal leadership is not well liked and the leader must depend on developing willing participation of the group members.

Fiedler's Contingency Model hinges on one key test that he administers to leaders. He calls this test the Least Preferred Coworker rating scale. Fiedler asks a subject to think of a person with whom he or she least prefers to work and then asks him or her to rate the person on a sixteen-item scale. Some of the items on the scale are efficient-inefficient, cooperative-uncooperative, friendly-unfriendly, quarrelsome-harmonious. If a leader fills out this scale in a way that describes his or her least preferred coworker in terms of the worker's inability to do the job, then Fiedler classifies the leader as task-oriented. Conversely, if the leader focuses more on the social dimensions, Fiedler describes this person as a relationship-oriented leader.

Fiedler is so convinced by his findings that he would adjust situations before he would try to train leaders (1996). In contrast, we believe that a person can develop a wide range of communication competencies that will serve that person well in a number of different leadership situations. Our belief is supported by Wood (1977), who has studied the situational approach to leading group discussions.

Wood acknowledges Fiedler's attempts to match leader styles with situational requirements; however, she focuses on adaptive behavior and how it calls for some form of adjustment by a leader to the constraints of a situation. Wood's most important finding is that leaders of purposive discussions engage in adaptive behavior. This idea seems to be supported by the fact that the leaders in her study were responsive to failures in previous discussions; that is, the leaders varied their oral behaviors to achieve overtly expressed discussion goals. For example, a certain type of leader—Leader B—was found to adapt his or her leadership behaviors from the first meeting to the second. He or she wanted to arrive at consensus in an expeditious manner in the second meeting and was much less interested in drawing out the ideas of all members than he or she had been in the first meeting. Consequently, Leader B adapted his or her leadership behaviors on the basis of the group situation, with particular emphasis on the members' expressed group goals.

Role-Emergence Theory We have all observed the situation in which a work group in an organization has a designated leader, but the members turn to another person as their "real" or "natural" leader. The formal and natural leader often are one and the same person, but when this is not the case, some accommodation must be worked out. For example, in the army, a second lieutenant may be the formal leader of a rifle platoon, and the "lifer" sergeant is the natural leader of the group. When this situation occurred in Vietnam, the sergeant often would be the decision maker while on patrol in the field; the second lieutenant would function as leader back at the base camp.

As we indicated in Chapter 2, Bormann (1975, 1990) and his graduate students have been interested in how a natural leader emerges in a small discussion group. Their research reveals several communication processes or paths by which a leader emerges. Bormann metaphorically refers to this process as the "method of residues." Members of the group gradually are eliminated from competition until one person remains. He or she is the "residue" or candidate for leader. The Minnesota studies report that although there are many patterns of leader emergence, all the patterns go through two basic stages. The first covers a relatively brief period, usually no longer than one meeting, in which about one-half the group's membership is eliminated from the possibility of being the group leader. How people come to be eliminated from the leadership role is under continual, intense study, but certain communication behaviors seem to be important. The first is the absence of communication; if a member does not take an active part, he or she will probably be eliminated during the first phase of consideration of who will be the leader. In fact, many people intentionally remain quiet because they have no desire to become leader. Among the communicatively active participants, those members who seem irrational, uninformed, or extremely dogmatic also tend to be eliminated during the first phase of Bormann's "method of residues."

Bormann's Minnesota studies describe the second phase as an intense struggle for leadership. Bormann uses four typical scenarios to illustrate how leaders emerge. Scenario I is a pattern of leader emergence, relatively free of conflict, in which, during the second phase, a leader candidate picks up what Bormann calls a "lieutenant." A lieutenant is a group member who reinforces the ideas and suggestions of the leader candidate. He or she also provides much of the emotional stroking of other group members during this emergent process. If only one leader candidate picks up a lieutenant, then that candidate usually emerges as leader, and thus, the discussion group has formed and is ready to go to work.

The second scenario of leadership emergence found by the Minnesota studies is the pattern that boils down to two leader candidates, each of whom has a lieutenant. This scenario produces intense competition and an extended second phase simply because candidates are so well matched that either one could probably lead the group successfully. If the struggle is never resolved, the group never really becomes cohesive. There is a lot of bickering and arguing, and it is uncomfortable to be part of a meeting when this type of struggle is taking place. Because the struggle is not overt—and by that we mean the candidates are not saying "I want to be leader"— the struggle manifests itself in discussions about the problem at hand and how it can best be solved. If one candidate finally emerges, the group's problems are not over, because the second-place candidate usually becomes a central negative. A central negative is an articulate, active group member who forcibly argues against the will of the majority and particularly against suggestions that are championed by the new emergent leader. How the new leader treats the central negative is crucial to the success of the group. Ernest and Nancy Bormann (1988) advise group leaders not to purge their central negatives but to give them important tasks to do because they are capable and respected by other group members.

Scenario III of the Minnesota studies illustrates how a leader is produced as a result of a crisis. Movies and television programs often use this scenario as their basic plot outline. A group of normal people are thrust into an abnormal situation, such as an earthquake, a fire, a flood, or a pestilence, along with assorted malfunctioning of air, sea, and land modes of transportation. In this sort of crisis, a leader quickly emerges who is uniquely suited to deal with it. This Hollywood-genre leader reinforces rather unrealistic, "macho" male characterizations that distort the attributes normally required for a person to emerge as a natural leader of a typical work group in industry and government.

The fourth scenario of leader emergence reported by Bormann is essentially a diary of a group that failed. In this scenario, a leader does not emerge, although there are continual struggles for leadership. The struggle is more diffused than in Scenario II, in that hardly anyone can agree on a likely candidate. The reasons for this complete fragmentation are complex, but studies at Minnesota indicate that some of the problems relate to the racial and sexual composition of the group. Some white members may not accept black leadership or vice versa, and some men may not accept female leadership or vice versa. Bormann, Pratt, and Putnam (1978), in a monograph titled "Power, Authority, and Sex: Male Response to Female Leadership," reported on a rich case history of a simulated corporation, made up of several work groups, that essentially failed. The failure of the entire company revolved around male-female conflicts in the struggle for various leadership roles. The study graphically shows how careful attention must be given to intervening variables such as sex and race as they relate to group formation. Thus, although the studies of leader traits, as compared with nonleader traits, prove to be a scholarly dead end, the way in which traits interplay with communication patterns may provide many useful insights into understanding how leaders emerge.

Functional Theory Since 1960, when Barnlund and Haiman's classic small group textbook, *The Dynamics of Discussion*, entered the market, communication scholars have been concerned with the significant influences that can be used to move the group closer to its goal. These significant influences we identify as leadership functions. As early as 1955, Barnlund had convinced many communication scholars that certain leadership skills can be taught and had illustrated how certain skills—that is, leadership functions—could be taught even to those group members who were not leader types.

The functions of leadership include anything that influences a group, regardless of its source. In other words, a leadership function can be performed by a designated leader or by any group member. The key point is that the function moves the group toward the group goal. It is possible and frequently happens that a leadership function moves the group away from the group goal. For example, if the leader of your discussion asks a member to summarize the main points of the solution and she responds by suggesting that the group adjourn to a local bar, the leadership function performed has been a significant influence that moves the group away from its stated goal. Regardless of who initiated this move, a designated leader or other group member, it influenced the group either positively or negatively.

The many specific leadership functions that can be performed in a group have been classified into two, three, or four major headings. Goal achievement and group maintenance are two general headings for leadership functions. Three-part classification schemas include task, procedural, and social functions; or creative-critical, maintenance, and interpersonal functions. However specific functions are classified, they are significant needs that must be fulfilled or things that must be done to move the group toward its goals. The next major section of this chapter specifies those leadership functions you should know how to perform, whether you are the leader or a participating member in your group discussions.

Small Group Leader Model

The seven leadership theories described above provide valuable insights for the student of group discussion. Figure 7.2 shows our belief that parts of each approach go into the creation of an idealized discussion leader. Scholars who focused on designated formal leaders have demonstrated that certain personal traits, such as extroversion and speech fluency, normally are possessed by a discussion leader. It also seems clear that a leader has certain bases of power that are used to move the group toward its desired goals and that leaders have a repertoire of governing styles and motivational styles from which to select. Fiedler's (1967) research indicates that the leader's traits, power bases, and style interact in ways that determine how effective a leader of a small group will be. Wood's (1977) study suggests that a leader can learn from past mistakes and adapt his or her communication behavior in future group situations. The Minnesota studies explain the communication process that determines who will emerge as the natural work or discussion leader. Barnlund and Haiman's (1960) research identifies the specific leadership functions that must be performed for the group to be effective. The actual or real discussion leader of a group working with a formal organizational structure is potentially a blend of these seven leadership theories.

□ Communication Skills for Leading Problem-Solving Groups

A functional approach to leadership is basically an attempt to specify the communication behaviors that are necessary for the group to work toward its perceived goals. As indicated earlier in this chapter, there is a difference between leader and leadership.

FIGURE 7.2   Discussion Leader Model

FORMAL LEADER PERSPECTIVES

Traits	Power	Styles	Motivation
		Discussion Styles	
Appearance	Group	Autocratic	Telling
	Legitimate	Democratic	
Speaking ability	Expert	Laissez-faire	Coaching (selling)
Thinking	Referent		
		Work Group Styles	
	Information	Theory X	Delegating
Actions	Reward	Theory Y	
Feelings	Coercive	Theory Z	Participating

Idealized leader of real-life group (blend of formal and conceptual leadership perspectives)

CONCEPTUAL LEADER PERSPECTIVES

Role Emergence Theory	Situational Theory	Functional Theory
Emergent task leader with "lieutenant"	Interface of power, structure of task, likability, and constraints in the situation via adaptive leadership behavior	*Task* (seven skills)
Two competitive leader candidates		*Procedural* (seven skills)
"Crisis leader" emerges		
Continual struggle for leadership marked by no clear emergence		*Interpersonal* (six skills)

In this section, we describe three general classes of communication behaviors—task, procedural, and interpersonal—that constitute leadership of a discussion. These leadership behaviors that communication scholars have isolated occur in any good discussion, but the initiator of them is not necessarily the appointed or natural leader of the group. Thus, regardless of what role you may play in a small group, it is important that you understand the minimum communication leadership behaviors necessary to group discussions.

Leadership communication behaviors, when assessed in terms of who performs them, depend on a number of the interacting phenomena that were partially isolated in the preceding discussion of leadership theories. If a designated leader uses an autocratic style, adopts a telling approach in terms of motivation, has considerable legitimate power, and has emerged as the leader according to Bormann's crisis scenario, then we would expect to find that most of the leadership communication performance needed to maintain the group is done by the designated leader. On the other hand, if an appointed leader adopts a laissez-faire style, uses a delegating approach to motivation, has little referent power, and is challenged by several candidates for the emergent leadership of the group, we would expect that leadership communication functions would be dispersed among the group members and that not many of the skills would be in evidence.

It is possible that there could be no connection between a leader's success or failure and his or her communication performance, but once a group has formed and is going about its daily tasks, we can expect that the group members will have developed some unstated agreement as to which members perform certain leadership communication functions. Edwards (1994) found that leaders appeared to be selected on the basis of perceived competence in skills such as organization, goal setting, and generation of new ideas, rather than on the basis of empathetic dimensions such as thoughtfulness and sensitivity. Our examination of student diaries reveals that most classroom groups are quite aware of their particular communication pattern in terms of sharing leadership skills. These group diaries also indicate that when a strong natural leader emerges, the majority of these skills tend to be performed by that leader. It is important to remember that in government and business organizations, many one-time meetings are called in which the specific group members have seldom worked together collectively. In this situation, there is the expectation that the designated leader will perform the necessary communication leadership skills to move expeditiously through the planned agenda. Thus, most formal organizations have the expectation that their administrative personnel will possess the necessary communication skills to adequately run meetings. The following twenty communication skills are the leadership functions needed by groups to service their task, procedural, and interpersonal needs and move them toward the accomplishment of their perceived goals.

Leadership Communication Skills in the Task Area

A number of significant communication skills have to be performed in the task area, regardless of type of group.

Typical task communication skills are questioning, commenting, and attempting answers. It often is necessary for the task leader or active members of the work group to initiate leadership functions in this area to generate enough ideas, evaluation, and description to move the group toward task achievement. The following seven communication skills must be performed in the task area.

■ *Contributing ideas.* Contributing ideas is a fundamental leadership communication skill for groups. This leadership communication skill can be identified as a new or fresh idea presented for the first time in the group. Designated leaders often perform this function when they introduce an item on the planned agenda; however, good groups have active members who contribute their original thoughts on the topic. Sometimes established groups develop a custom of brainstorming a new topic to maximize the number of ideas. One of the advantages that a good group has over an individual is that active groups can outperform even the best individual in the group in terms of the total number of ideas contributed.

■ *Seeking ideas.* Many small groups do not develop formal procedures for generating ideas. Some members are reluctant to contribute their ideas; thus, a recurring leadership function is the seeking of ideas from group members without threatening or embarrassing them. In Chapter 3, we pointed out that asking questions is a core process communication skill. Bales's Harvard studies (1950, 1970) have repeatedly demonstrated that the number of questions asked in a group directly impacts the quality of group decisions. So when in doubt, ask a question!

■ *Evaluating ideas.* One of the most difficult leadership skills to perform, particularly in a public discussion, is the evaluation of ideas. A group will constantly take flight when faced with the reality of having to eliminate from consideration opinions that have been expressed by group members. This is such a sensitive issue that formal procedures (e.g., brainstorming and nominal group discussion) have been developed for separating a group member from his or her ideas. Groups that have a long and successful history usually develop the ability to evaluate ideas openly and freely, but even in the best groups, this evaluation is done with concern for the sensitivity of the person who originated the idea.

■ *Seeking idea evaluation.* Early in a group's history, before group members have developed a sense of group trust, the needed communication skill is that of seeking idea evaluation. The first stage of brainstorming may have produced a flood of ideas, not all of which are good. If the group is to reach a good decision, it must sort the wheat from the chaff. This effort requires the active participation of all group members if each idea is to be competently evaluated. Drawing out people's evaluative opinions is an even more delicate matter than getting their initial ideas. The person who can tactfully perform this leadership function provides a valuable and necessary service for the group.

■ *Visualizing abstract ideas.* Decision-making groups are prone to conversations that become abstract and full of jargon. Sometimes groups communicate only in vague, abstract terms because to equate their ideas with specific, concrete examples would point up obvious differences of opinion among group members regarding the discussion topic. However, not all abstract ambiguity in discussion is flight behavior. Some of it is the natural vagueness that is inherent in symbolic communication. When a group of executives is sitting in a board room discussing the building of a new company facility, the group must discuss their ideas in terms of specific examples. This leadership skill not only clarifies points of disagreement, but also promotes general understanding of what is being discussed.

■ *Generalizing from specific ideas.* The old adage that one cannot see the forest for the trees is an appropriate observation of most discussions. We have all been in group discussions where we have been overwhelmed by trivia. Some groups stone a given idea to death with small pebbles. This problem is at the opposite end of the communication continuum that calls for the performance of the task leadership skill of visualizing abstract ideas. When the problem is too much specificity, the needed leadership communication is to generalize from the series of specific examples to the main idea being discussed. Basically, task leadership skills of visualizing abstract ideas and generalizing from specific ideas work in tandem to keep a balance between too much abstraction and too much specificity in the discussion of ideas.

■ *Processing technology.* In cyborg groups, it is readily apparent that this leadership skill is important. At the University of Minnesota, a groupware system was developed that allows any member of the group to operate the groupware and serve as facilitator. Most groupware, however, can only be run by the facilitator with the help of a technical assistant. More and more groups have increased cyborg characteristics. Certainly the information processing of a group in an organization requires technical assistance and supporting computer databases. In some groups, all members share in this leadership function, whereas in others, this skill is performed primarily by one member.

Leadership Communication Skills in the Procedural Area

By and large, task leadership functions are performed fairly naturally in small groups, whereas communication skills in the procedural area need to be actively fostered and nurtured throughout the course of the discussion. Many times the designated leader will perform the necessary procedural functions, whereas in other situations, a member who is experienced in group operations will emerge to perform them. The seven leadership communication skills that follow must be performed in the procedural area.

■ *Goal setting.* The first expectation that we all have when we are brought together for a one-time meeting is that we will need to decide what the purpose of the meeting is and why we are there. Although it is the clear duty of the designated leader to state the purpose of the meeting, it is also understood in most group settings that the issue of purpose or goal of the group is open for discussion and modification. The leadership function of goal setting is also a recurring communication behavior, in that ideas are continually evaluated in terms of their ability to move the group toward its goal. This evaluation process often reinitiates discussion of what the group's goals are. A sales group may have set its goal as the establishment of sales procedures that will produce a minimum amount of productivity for a given three-month period. However, during the discussion, the group may agree to the idea that a training program is needed. When the idea of a training program is measured against the group's sales goal for the next three months, the salespeople might discover that they like the potential for a long-term training program, and in light of that discovery, they may want to change their three-month sales goal. This continual evaluation of both the short-term and the long-term goals of a group is a procedural communication skill, inasmuch as it regulates the ongoing ideas of the group in terms of its stated purposes. This function is also procedural in the sense that it ought to be the first agenda item of a small group.

■ *Agenda making.* Agenda making is the "map-making" function in small groups that helps the group accomplish its goals in an orderly manner. In Chapter 4, we discussed different kinds of agenda systems in detail. In one-time meetings, one of the clear responsibilities of the designated leader is the advance preparation of the agenda or outline for the group. Some formal organizations even develop written policies regarding the development and distribution of a one-time-meeting agenda in advance as a prerequisite for calling a meeting. In discussions in which there is not a designated leader, the specific agenda will emerge, and the arguments that ensue over what the agenda items should be are manifest signs of a leadership struggle. Once a leader has emerged, arguments over the agenda decrease both in frequency and in intensity, and the new leader, whether or not he or she knows it, will be responsible for agenda-setting. Once the agenda has been settled and agreed to by the group members, it is now incumbent on them to follow it to achieve the group's goals. In essence, the goal-setting function helps the group identify *what* the group's goals are, and the agenda-making function aids the group in *how* it achieves them.

■ *Clarifying.* Group communication is messy! There are always a lot of loose ends, and when people are thinking out loud, it is difficult to know whether everyone is taking in what is being said. The clarification function is a communication skill that produces intentional redundancy in the communication patterns to ensure that all group members understand what is being said. A typical example of clarifying might be the question "What do you mean by that?" or the statement "Let me restate your idea in my own words to see if I understand it." Audiotapes of good group discussions are liberally sprinkled with restatement of ideas. In fact, some researchers have found that redundant group member contributions account for about 50 percent of all oral communication in small groups. This finding supports the idea that successful group discussions require a great deal of clarification of ideas to be effective.

■ *Summarizing.* Good speeches and good discussions have at least one thing in common: They both contain many internal summaries. A novice public speaker often is advised to tell an audience what he or she is going to say, say it, and then tell them what he or she has said. This is also good advice for a designated leader. Each point of the agenda should be introduced, accomplished, and summarized. This adding-up process at each stage of the agenda helps to keep in focus both the ideas under discussion and the logical progression of the discussion. Most face-to-face discussions occur without the group members' taking notes; thus, the leadership function of frequent summaries helps to imprint the topic under discussion in the minds of the group members.

■ *Verbalizing consensus.* One of the four most important outcomes of group discussions is consensus. In most formal organizations, we like to be able to say that a work group has reached unanimous agreement on a course of action. We prefer to talk for another several hours about a problem rather than force a premature vote that might produce a split decision on a policy question, thus hurting the group's cohesion and seriously impairing its ability to function. It is, therefore, important that verbalizing-consensus communication behavior occurs frequently in the discussion. This difficult leadership skill involves finding areas of agreement at different points of the agenda and through various phases of decision making in general. An experienced leader constantly looks for places where he or she can get at least nonverbal agreement on an agenda item. Experienced leaders often follow the summarizing communication skill with the verbalizing-consensus skill. These two skills working in tandem can help produce consensus in decision-making discussions. In fact, communication researchers have demonstrated that a form of verbalizing consensus—orientation behavior—is directly related to the chances of the group's ultimately reaching agreement (Gouran 1969). In other words, you cannot wait until the end of the meeting to seek consensus because it is an incremental process that occurs throughout the discussion.

■ *Establishing work patterns.* All group members should feel a responsibility to work hard to achieve the mutually agreed on goals of the group. If all group members work equally hard, then this leadership skill is distributed across the group and is hard to identify. In contrast, when work patterns are not well established, especially in a new group, the designated leader or some concerned group member may have to model good work behavior and work at making it normative for the group. Two work patterns that are important to establish are that (1) no work is beneath any group member (such as pouring coffee and preparing the overheads) and (2) group members should work outside of group time to compile information that will help in the decision making and overall procedural functioning of the group.

■ *Performing group protocols.* Experienced leaders recognize that their primary function is the handling of procedural issues for the group. This includes several important tasks before the meeting takes place. These tasks are concerned with three types of protocol: environmental, social, and conference. *Social protocol* includes informing the participants of the time, topic, and place of the meeting; estimating how long the meeting will be; and, if possible, providing a published list of meeting attendees and the agenda. *Environmental protocol* deals with the provision of creature comforts to ensure that the discussants will not be distracted from their tasks. There are troublesome but important details that must be taken care of before each meeting, such as seeing that the meeting room is reserved, unlocked, large enough, and comfortable enough for the group in terms of ventilation, temperature, and lighting. The location of rest rooms and the availability of refreshments should also be concerns of the leader. *Conference protocol* is concerned first and foremost with the determination of the agenda and the format of the discussion. In Chapter 4, specific kinds of agendas are listed that can be used or adapted to fit the meeting's purpose. In addition, seating arrangements, name tags, paper and pencils, and multiple copies of supportive information all require advance conference planning.

Leadership Communication Skills in the Interpersonal Area

There are six interpersonal leadership communication behaviors. The first four are oriented toward meeting the social-emotional needs of the group members. The last two skills in this category are more "overriding" in nature; by this we mean that the two conflict skills might deal with ideational as well as interpersonal obstacles.

■ *Regulating participation.* Rules in parliamentary procedure contain many explicit regulations that limit a member's speaking time. Symposium discussions also usually include speaking-time limits for the participants. These rather formalized discussion procedures are discussed in detail in Chapter 4. The everyday discussion that occurs in business and other work environments seldom has formal time limits. Yet there are clear expectations about the need for regulating participation. Nobody likes to attend what is supposed to be a group discussion and discover that it is a monologue. Thus, it is essential that each member be given the opportunity to speak. This leadership communication skill often is performed by the leader, but most trained discussants will impose some self-discipline and regulate their own communication behavior so as neither to monopolize the time or withdraw from the dialogue. Experienced leaders tactfully manage the time allocation of participants. The communication skill that is required to reduce one member's contributions while increasing another's takes a great deal of practice. Nonetheless, this is an interpersonal communication leadership skill that must be performed in all group discussions.

■ *Climate making.* Providing and maintaining a positive group atmosphere in which each member has a sense of psychological safety is the essence of the climate-making function. This communication behavior might manifest itself in the following interchange. The leader might say, "John, you haven't said anything for a while. What are your feelings about this issue?" If the leader's tone makes the member feel secure, John might respond by saying, "Well, Mary, I really agree with what Tom has been saying. What I believe is . . ." Having our ideas and feelings held up for public examination is threatening. If we do not think that the group climate is supportive and open, we withdraw and conceal our opinions. Thus, experienced leaders as well as facilitators of encounter groups project primarily through nonverbal cues that a safe climate exists for the exchange of ideas and feelings. This is not to say that conflict will not occur, but that the conflict will not exceed the safety barriers of good taste and the group's threshold for psychological hurt.

■ *Maintaining mutual respect.* Leadership of a work group should include the deepseated belief that individual group members' opinions should be respected. If you think that you should lead because you know best, you have probably made a mistake either in your assessment of your capabilities or in your need to be a team player. Group success is based on collective wisdom through participation, not on the domination of one bright person. Respect for the feelings of others is a necessary prerequisite for effective group leadership. Most people are thin-skinned; therefore, a leader must constantly be on guard to see that the collective and individual feelings of the group are not harmed. At some time or another, most experienced leaders have said, "It just isn't worth it!" By that they meant that the task goal was not worth achieving, given the interpersonal price that had to be paid. Some professional and collegiate athletic teams seem to set team victory as a goal without regard for the emotional casualties that occur.

■ *Instigating group self-analysis.* Experienced group discussants often initiate a discussion about the discussion when the group becomes hung up on something. This sort of navel-gazing is necessary to maintain the health of the group. Sometimes a group has normed out a level of group productivity that is not sufficiently high to attain the group's goals. When a group member becomes aware of this problem, he or she might jump into the middle of the conversation and initiate the group's self-analysis of its past work performance. Sometimes a group may argue over agenda, and it becomes clear that a leadership struggle needs to be resolved if the group is to progress. In this situation, a group member may put the hidden agenda on the table—that is, the leadership struggle, not the topic under discussion. These typically are emotionally charged moments in group life and should not be entered into flippantly. Some people like to play amateur psychologist and keep the group psyche forever prostrate on the counseling couch. This continual navel-gazing can become dysfunctional and even hazardous to the group's health. Much of the hidden agenda should stay hidden because it eventually will work itself out; when it does not, an experienced group member will perform the leadership skill of instigating group self-analysis.

■ *Resolving conflict.* Groups that have a long history of working together usually have a group member who plays the role of peacemaker and is in fact very good at performing this leadership skill of resolving conflict. Whether the fight is over ideas or personalities, the peacemaker can wade into the middle of the fracas and calm things down. Inexperienced leaders usually overreact to group conflict and sometimes turn a minor skirmish into a brawl. Experienced leaders develop a sense of which conflicts need to be stopped and which ones will work themselves out. There is a fine line between a healthy exchange of ideas and an ugly scene that can mar the group's ability to work together. Until a group has developed its social and task norms—that is, until it has discovered which topics and mannerisms are taboo—members will innocently insult someone else's sacred cow. Language usage is a typical candidate. Profane, sexist, and racist language have the potential for causing the most conflict. Also, the way in which ideas are accepted and rejected in the group will produce conflict until norming occurs. The resolving-conflict function is vital to the group's survival, and the person who can best perform this function in the group is an essential member.

■ *Instigating conflict.* The devil's advocate is a role we all have played on occasion to instigate conflict. The leadership function of instigating conflict usually occurs on the ideational level. The skill needs to be performed when group members are so afraid of offending one another that they sheepishly and often silently accept one another's suggestions. This meek acceptance by members of positions to which they are adverse cannot be resolved until somebody decides to play the devil's advocate. A group member usually will say, "Let me play the devil's advocate for a moment," or he or she might say, "Just for the sake of argument let me say . . ."; whatever verbal expression is used, the implicit meaning is, "Let me separate the idea from the person so that the idea may be challenged." An experienced leader occasionally will react to a lethargic group by intentionally picking a fight with one or more group members. Teachers in a discussion with students over classroom material frequently perform this leadership function. This is often done by stating an obvious falsehood to see if anyone challenges it. The leadership functions of resolving and instigating conflict form a continuum of communication skills that experienced group leaders select from to assist them in managing the interpersonal dimension of small groups.

☐ SUMMARY

Small group leadership is defined as communication that positively influences the group to move in the direction of the group's goals. Seven leadership theories are classified according to two major perspectives: those of the designated leader and those of the emergent leader. The designated leader perspective examines four approaches to leadership. The trait theory focuses on how leaders look, think, talk, feel, and act. The power theory emphasizes seven general bases of power: group, legitimate, expert, referent, informational, reward, and coercive. Autocratic, democratic, and laissez-faire styles of leadership are the major concerns of the discussion of the stylistic approach, and Theories X, Y, and Z are stylistic approaches for work group leadership. The telling, coaching, participating, and delegating styles form the basis of the motivational theory.

In contrast, the emergent leader perspective concentrates on more informed, ongoing group types of leadership. The three theories of leadership treated here are the situational, role-emergence, and functional theories. In the situational theory, various situational constraints come into play and determine not only who is leader, but also some of the adaptive behavior the leader has to exercise. The role-emergence theory presents four basic scenarios; several of them show successful role-emergence patterns and others show unsuccessful ones. The final approach considered is that of identifying leadership functions that have to be performed in the group. It is emphasized that the performance of leadership skills can be done by a designated leader and by any other member of the group. In fact, the last major section of the chapter emphasizes the necessary leadership communication skills that must be performed in the task, procedural, and interpersonal domains of the group.

Leading a Corporate Task Force

CASE BACKGROUND

Mary Schilling is a bright, upwardly mobile executive in a midwestern corporation. She has all the formal training and skills that the company expects of her. For the past five years, she has worked hard and successfully for the company. She has received three promotions and held management responsibilities for two years. Her personnel file contains glowing reports about her abilities.

Last year, one of the senior vice-presidents of the company put her in charge of a special task force that was to reposition an old company product that had leveled off in sales growth. This was the sort of management opportunity Mary wanted. She knew that the clear road to top management always included success with a product through the effective use of a task force.

The senior vice-president gave Mary authority to bring together whatever materials and human resources were necessary to complete the task. Mary gave a lot of thought and planning to the designing of the task force and the calling of the first meeting. She selected a vice-president—Tom—who had been her supervisor when she came to work at the company. She felt sure that he would support her and that his twenty-five years of management experience would be a valuable reservoir of expert knowledge. Mary invited two hotshot marketing experts—Jim and Bill, who were fresh from graduate school—because of their skills in quantitative research. She also included two of the company's best salespeople—Carl and Vince—because they had worked firsthand with the product. Finally, she included an accountant—Sally—who had worked out the original unit cost of production. Mary was pleased that she could include another woman on the task force.

CASE LOG

Mary personally contacted the six group members by phone and secured their enthusiastic support to participate in the task force. Only Tom, the vice-president, seemed somewhat tentative. Mary reserved a meeting room, set a time for the first meeting, consulted everyone's calendar, and sent a printed agenda and a list of the members to all the participants. She checked out the meeting room in advance and was convinced that every premeeting detail had been taken care of. She was truly excited about the prospect of the first weekly meeting.

First Meeting

Mary was elated by the results of the first meeting. It had started with a lot of nervous conversation, and she had envisioned failure. Jim and Bill, the two marketing experts, sat on one side of the table engaged in private conversation; Carl and Vince, the two salespeople, sat huddled on the other side of the table. Sally, the accountant, sat by herself and appeared to be nervous. However, just when things looked grim, Tom came to her rescue. He told one humorous story after another and soon the group was talking and laughing boisterously about their common problems with the company cafeteria and parking. Mary seized this relaxed atmosphere and moved right into the planned agenda.

The group worked smoothly for more than an hour, reaching general agreement on the broad goals for the task force and the yearlong timetable for the completion of their task. They reinforced one another's belief that they had formed a good group and that it would be fun to work together on this enjoyable task. After the meeting, Tom made a special point of complimenting Mary on what a fine job she had done and said that he was glad the company had recognized her leadership potential.

Second Meeting

Mary was not surprised that the second meeting did not run as smoothly as the first. After all, she had built in some real differences of opinion when she brought in two marketing people and two salespeople, but she had not anticipated that the two pairs would polarize so quickly or that there would be so many cheap jokes with hidden meanings traded back and forth about who knew more about the product—the sales force or marketing people. She also thought that Sally would come out of her shell, but she seemed even more withdrawn. Fortunately, Tom was there and he continued to relieve the tense moments with a wealth of jokes. Mary became more aware of her job in terms of resolving the conflicts between Jim and Bill on one side and Carl and Vince on the other.

Third Meeting

This meeting Mary characterized as a disaster! The two salespeople really got into it with the marketing people on why the product was not showing growth in sales. Mary quickly stepped in to resolve the conflict but, to her surprise, was rebuffed by all four of the combative participants. Jim, Bill, Carl, and Vince seemed to challenge her leadership of the group on the ground that she had no expert knowledge of the product. She had not worked out in the field selling the product, nor did she possess technical knowledge about marketing the product. Mary got a bit defensive and quickly listed several of her accomplishments in designing the product while working in Tom's division of the company. At this point, Tom stepped in and put the two young marketing hotshots in their place. The meeting went silent. Mary was pleased that Tom had resolved the bickering but resentful that his action seemed to challenge her leadership of the task force. But Mary was most resentful of stoic Sally. How could she just sit there and not take a position? At least Mary knew where Jim and Bill stood. The agenda that Mary had set for this meeting remained unaccomplished.

Fourth and Fifth Meetings

These meetings were marked by continual conflict between the marketing experts and the salespeople. Sally continued to remain silent. Tom became more and more involved in settling disputes between the sales and marketing people. Mary felt more and more as though she was on the outside looking in. The group simply ignored her for long periods. What troubled Mary the most was why Tom was challenging her leadership of the task force. She was deeply troubled and felt betrayed.

Sixth Meeting

Tom surprised Mary by approaching her right before the meeting and suggesting that he be taken off the task force. Mary gushed that that was the last thing she wanted him to do. She reassured him

that the problems would work out, and he finally agreed to stay in the group. During the meeting, Mary was angry with herself for talking Tom into staying. Tom continued to challenge Mary's leadership and Mary was now firmly convinced that if Tom were not on the task force, she could easily manage the remaining five members, especially if she could get Sally's support. After the meeting, she approached Sally and asked her directly for her open verbal support for the remaining meetings. Sally suggested that they meet for dinner that evening. The results of this dinner meeting were that Sally agreed to support Mary's leadership of the task force actively. Mary then drove to Tom's house, and after a long and friendly chat, they agreed that Tom should leave the group so that Mary would be the undisputed leader.

Seventh and Eighth Meetings

These meetings were even less productive than when Tom was present. Sally was rather obvious in her sudden support of Mary. The four men had clearly closed ranks in opposition to Mary and fought her every suggestion. More and more of the workload, both in and out of the meetings, fell onto Mary's and Sally's shoulders.

Ninth Meeting

This meeting was never held. Mary had great difficulty finding a time when all members could meet. Reluctantly, she went to the senior vice-president who had put her in charge of the task force and calmly explained the problems she had encountered over the past two months. Much to her surprise, the senior vice-president was well aware of the personal and productivity failures of the task force. In fact, he informed Mary that a decision to reposition the old company product would be postponed for a year. Mary was asked to turn in a report of anything that was accomplished, and with Sally's assistance, she prepared a short report of the task force's progress. With the completion of this report, Mary's responsibility for the task force was terminated.

CASE QUESTIONS

1. Was the failure of this group inevitable, or was this the most success that Mary could have hoped for?

2. Was Mary's problem in leading the group the result of latent sexism on the part of the male members?

3. Should Mary have asked Tom to leave the group earlier, or even included him in the group in the first place?

4. If you were writing a diary for other members of the group, what would you say about Mary's leadership in the group?

CHAPTER EIGHT

PARTICIPATING IN SMALL GROUPS

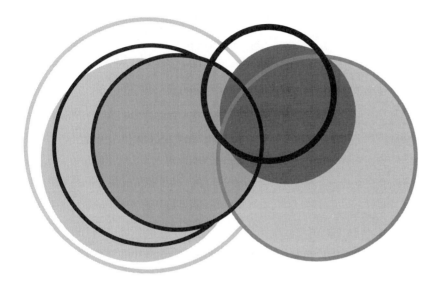

CHAPTER OBJECTIVES

After reading this chapter, you should be able to:

- Describe the most frequently played roles in small groups
- Know the important role communication skills
- Understand the relations among people, roles, and communication skills

In Chapter 7, we defined group leadership as "communication that positively influences the group to move in the direction of the group's goals." Discussion participation is defined as *communication behavior that positively or negatively moves the group in the direction of the group's goals.* Our discussion participation definition includes all the communication leadership skills plus communication that supports or disrupts leadership behavior. These communication behaviors usually are performed by people playing follower-type roles. However, it is not uncommon to find a person in the role of leader who occasionally engages in disruptive communication behavior that moves the group away from its goals. For example, an emergent leader might engage in some blocking behavior in attempts to stop the central negative from playing his or her role. In Chapter 1, we pointed out the importance of separating the basic concepts of people, roles, and communication behaviors. We suggested that people play different roles in different groups and can share roles in the same group. We also explained that in a sense, roles are a concentration of communication behaviors.

☐ FREQUENTLY PLAYED ROLES IN SMALL GROUPS

In the late 1940s and early 1950s, a number of social scientists were interested in identifying different roles people play in small groups. The National Training Laboratory in Group Development came up with a list of roles. Benne and Sheats (1948) reported a similar list of twenty-five roles that people play in group discussion. They used a three-part schema for categorizing group roles: group task roles, group building and maintenance roles, and individual roles. Examples of group task roles are information giver, energizer, and opinion seeker. Encourager, harmonizer, and compromiser are examples of group maintenance roles. Individual roles include blocker, playboy, and dominator.

The labeling of some phenomenon as a role or a communication behavior often is arbitrary, in that a role may be a label for a communication behavior that a person continually uses. The problem with just listing roles and not separating them from communication behavior is that we may label a person as a blocker, for example, when in fact communication may be blocked by various people playing different roles in the group. Thus, it is easier to explain what is going on in a group by limiting the categories of group roles to ten.

Task Leader

Typically, we have come to recognize the task leader in a general sense by who he or she is and what he or she does—or has the potential to do—in the group. The task leader enjoys, for the most part, high group status. He or she is recognized as a mature person who has good problem-solving ability and has had training in leadership skills. In most instances, the task leader is as well educated as any other group member and has a firm grasp of the discussion topic. The task leader's influence usually includes expert power (McGrath and Altman 1966, 62).

Although the task leader has high group status, the person playing that role also feels responsible for the group members and the work the group does. For when the lights are dim and the bands are gone, there is the stark reality of leadership. When a discussion goes silent, all eyes turn to the task leader, whether he or she has been appointed or has emerged from the group. This silence is filled by procedural communication leadership skills initiated by the task leader. As indicated in Chapter 7, the task leader will also perform many of the other leadership skills. In addition to talking more in a group, the task leader typically does more work.

Sometimes, because of the workload that the task leader has and the pressure of that role, he or she might engage in deviant behavior. The task leader might attempt to block critical comment, or even look for sympathy from the group. When this happens in a well-established group, the members of the group—especially the social-emotional leader—will try to reassure the task leader that they understand the difficulty of the leader role and express appreciation for the person's ability to play that role.

Social-Emotional Leader

A social-emotional leader is well liked by the rest of the group members. This leader may not be the most popular in the group, but certainly most members are attracted to him or her. Although a task leader may lead a group and not be personally liked, the social-emotional leader must be well liked. Social-emotional leaders have some experience with handling interpersonal problems and score high on the ability to empathize with other people. The social-emotional leader does not rival or compete with the task leader of the group and may actively support the task leader in a complementary lieutenant role.

Like the task leader, the social-emotional leader is extroverted and speaks frequently in the group. In terms of leadership communication skills, he or she frequently initiates the six leadership communication skills in the interpersonal area. The concentrations of "climate making" and "instigating group self-analysis" are the major functions of the social-emotional leader.

The person who predominantly plays the social-emotional leader is acutely aware of the emotional heartbeat of the group and is constantly on guard for any interpersonal damage that might take place in solving the task. Whereas the task leader is responsible for the group's productivity, the social-emotional leader is responsible for the group's well-being and individual members' satisfaction (Wischmeier 1955, 48). When the discussion is completed, the group members will thank the social-emotional leader for making it an enjoyable experience.

Tension Releaser

The person who plays this role not only has the ability to be funny but also is aware of the sensibilities of the group in given work environments. The ability to tell a joke is not sufficient to play the role of tension releaser. A person may tell humorous jokes in a men's locker room that turn out to be tension-creating, not tension-releasing, in a male-female work group. Tension-releasing humor for a group must be funny to all the group members. Thus, the more heterogeneous the group membership, the harder it is for a person to play this role.

In addition to providing humor to break tension, this person can resolve interpersonal conflict with well-timed humorous barbs. This role mirrors that of the social-emotional leader in that the person must be sensitive to the social demands of the group. What the social-emotional leader accomplishes with empathy, the tension releaser accomplishes through the use of light humor featuring satire or sarcasm.

The tension releaser is always on call to break up debilitating interpersonal tension in the group and to smooth over those awkward moments of first meetings. The more dependent the group members are on one another and on the work the group does, the more important the role of tension releaser is. When a person tries to play this role and fails or plays the role when it is not needed, the group members will accuse that person of engaging in the deviant behavior we label "playing the clown."

Information Provider

The role of information provider is probably one of the most shared roles in small groups; however, when a group has one member play this role, that member has group status for his or her ability to provide accurate and concise data instantly for all major aspects of the discussion topic. The information provider has research skills that exceed the group's norms and sometimes has expert knowledge of the discussion topic. As well as providing a volume of accurate information, the information provider frequently performs the leadership communication skill of contributing ideas and critically evaluates ideas that are not soundly based in the research data.

The job of the information provider is to research and prepare accurate information. When the person playing the role of information provider feels abused by the group, it usually is because the rest of the group members have thrown all the data-gathering responsibilities on him or her. That is why effective groups tend to share the information provider role.

Central Negative

The central negative in a small group usually is not pleased with what is going on. The person tends to have the same abilities as the task leader and in fact continually challenges him or her for the leadership of the group. When the task leader envisions what the criticisms will be on the next proposal, he or she sees the central negative as the one who will voice the criticism. The person who is constantly challenging the leader in the task and procedural areas is said to be the central negative. In fact, if the task leader were to leave the group for some reason, the group members would turn to the central negative for task leadership (Bormann 1975, 260–261).

The three leadership functions that a central negative most frequently attempts to perform are evaluating ideas, making agendas, and instigating conflict. When a central negative is too strong in his or her challenge for leadership, he or she frequently engages in two deviant behaviors: dominating and blocking. When a group member plays the central negative role properly, whether knowingly or unknowingly, the impact is favorable. The central negative forces the group to rethink its position carefully and makes the task leader acutely aware of his or her responsibilities in terms of group productivity. It often is difficult to distinguish between the central negative role, which is mainly positive in scope, and the self-centered follower role, which is a negative one. But the group members usually know their central negative because the criticism that is emitted from this role tends to be strong.

Questioner

As we indicated in Chapter 1, the task leader, the social-emotional leader, the tension releaser, the information provider, and the central negative constitute the five major roles in a discussion group. The questioner is the first of five secondary roles frequently played.

The role of questioner is not played as often as it should be in small groups; only rarely does one person specialize in this role. Yet the role of questioner can significantly increase the quality of the group output. The person playing the role of questioner has the ability to probe the ideas under discussion incisively without threatening or alienating group members and without challenging the task leader. The two task functions that the questioner performs are seeking ideas and seeking idea evaluation. The procedural function that the questioner most often performs is clarification.

Silent Observer

A role in a small group that is not appreciated is that of the silent observer. During jury deliberations, the role of silent observer is an important part of the decision-making process. People who play this role quietly observe and evaluate the discussion being carried on by more active members. However, it is their nonverbal approval or disapproval that ultimately resolves the debate (Forston 1968).

Task groups that exceed five members may have a person who silently observes much of the discussion, but when he or she does make clear—either verbally or nonverbally—what his or her conclusion is, it is decisive. Before the formation of their opinion, people who play the role of silent observer appear pleasant but evasive when asked for their opinion. They listen passively to all arguments and then form an opinion.

Sometimes a person playing the role of silent observer can engage in deviant behavior that Veign (1991) calls "social loafing." The manifestations of this deviance includes sulking, daydreaming, doodling, and exerting less energy than one has.

Active Listener

Predominantly nonverbal and supportive behaviors characterize the role of the active listener in a group. This role frequently is shared and played in good small groups. All members of a group should feel an obligation to listen attentively and encourage other members to explain their positions. A group member occasionally will specialize in the role of active listener by assisting in the performance of two leadership skills: summarizing and verbalizing consensus. The person who plays this role remains argumentatively neutral, while at the same time being actively supportive of any member who attempts to contribute an idea or evaluate an idea under consideration.

Recorder

The role of recorder and the skill of recording are isomorphic in small group discussions. This is the one role in which one communication behavior completely defines the role. At any meeting of importance, a group member is designated as the official recorder of the meeting. Because low status often is attached to this role and a person who continually plays it feels subservient to the rest of the group members, most work groups rotate the role around the group. In formal organizations, a nonmember of the group who has been specially trained in recording is brought in to do the recording. This role has largely been automated in cyborg groups. All the groupware packages allow for the automatic storing and retrieving of group inputs.

Self-Centered Follower

Although the nine roles just listed support the goals of the group, the role of self-centered follower works against the group's best interest. In fact, if this role is played by too many group members, the group will surely fail. The person who plays a self-centered role is using the group for his or her own ends. He or she may engage in special-interest pleading, seeking help, or any of the other ten deviant behaviors. Although all group members engage in some negative behaviors, a person is probably playing the role of a self-centered follower when he or she repeatedly engages in one or more of the deviant behaviors.

Table 8.1 provides you with an opportunity to assess what roles you usually play in a work group. After completing the Group Role Type instrument, you should examine your role flexibility. If you have an 8 or higher on Central Negative, you are

TABLE 8.1   **Group Role Type Indicator**

Instructions: Consider a situation in which you find yourself working with other people for the accomplishment of a task. How do you usually respond to such situations?

Below you will find several pairs of statements describing possible behavioral responses. For each pair, circle the A or B statement that is most characteristic of your own behavior.

In some cases, neither the A nor the B statement may be typical of your response; select the response that you would be more likely to use.

There are no right or wrong answers. Select the statement that is most characteristic of your own behavior.

1. A. Others view me as having similar abilities as the leader.
    B. Others view me as friendly and funny.
2. A. During group discussions, I usually contribute ideas.
    B. During group discussions, I am sensitive to how others are feeling.
3. A. Others view me as having good problem-solving skills.
    B. Others view me as having an ability to be funny.
4. A. Others view me as having an ability to prepare accurate information.
    B. Others view me as friendly and funny.
5. A. I usually try to maintain a happy, friendly atmosphere.
    B. I usually challenge for leadership.
6. A. I usually challenge what is going on in the group.
    B. I usually set the procedures for what is going on in the group.
7. A. I usually evaluate ideas.
    B. I usually contribute ideas.
8. A. I feel a sense of responsibility for the work the group does.
    B. I feel a sense of responsibility for the group's well-being.
9. A. I want personal recognition.
    B. I am willing to make personal sacrifices for the group.
10. A. I am concerned about the work the group does.
    B. I am concerned about having accurate information.
11. A. I try to maintain a friendly atmosphere by being sensitive to how others are feeling.
    B. I try to maintain a friendly atmosphere by telling jokes.
12. A. Others view me as having similar abilities as the leader.
    B. Others view me as having good information-gathering skills.
13. A. Others view me as having an ability to prepare accurate information.
    B. Others view me as having an ability to solve problems.
14. A. I feel responsible for the well-being of the group.
    B. I feel responsible for the work the group does.
15. A. I can use humor to make light of conflict and tension.
    B. I usually challenge what is going on.
16. A. I use humor to keep the group atmosphere light and friendly.
    B. I do more work than others to keep the group moving toward task accomplishment.
17. A. I usually set procedures for task accomplishment.
    B. I usually challenge for leadership of the group.
18. A. I usually tell jokes for the group's benefit.
    B. I usually make sure we have accurate information.
19. A. I feel a sense of responsibility for individual relations in the group.
    B. I feel a sense of responsibility to challenge individuals during group discussions.

(continued on next page)

TABLE 8.1   Group Role Type Indicator (continued)

20. A. I try to maintain a happy friendly atmosphere.
    B. I try to contribute ideas.
21. A. I maintain a happy, friendly atmosphere by telling jokes.
    B. I maintain a happy, friendly atmosphere by being sensitive to how others are feeling.
22. A. I contribute by generating ideas.
    B. I contribute by doing more work than others.
23. A. I usually feel a sense of responsibility for the group's well-being.
    B. I usually evaluate ideas.
24. A. Others view me as friendly and funny.
    B. Others view me as being able to prepare accurate information.
25. A. I feel responsible for the group.
    B. I feel responsible for making light of conflict and tension.
26. A. During discussions, I am usually contributing ideas.
    B. During discussions, I am usually sensitive to the group's well-being.
27. A. I usually challenge group members during discussions.
    B. I am sensitive to how individuals are feeling.
28. A. I feel a sense of responsibility for the work the group does.
    B. I feel a sense of responsibility for the well-being of the group.
29. A. I like to contribute ideas.
    B. I like to evaluate ideas.
30. A. I try to maintain a friendly atmosphere by telling jokes.
    B. I try to maintain a friendly atmosphere by being sensitive to how others are feeling.

Scoring the Group Role Type Indicator

Circle the letters below that you circled on each corresponding item of the questionnaire.

	I.	II.	III.	IV.	V.
1.				A	B
2.		B	A		
3.	A				B
4.			A		B
5.		A		B	
6.	B			A	
7.			B	A	
8.	A	B			
9.	B			A	
10.	A		B		
11.		A			B
12.			B	A	
13.	B		A		
14.	B	A			
15.				B	A
16.	B				A

(continued on next page)

TABLE 8.1   Group Role Type Indicator (continued)

	I.	II.	III.	IV.	V.
17.	A			B	
18.			B		A
19.		A		B	
20.		A	B		
21.		B			A
22.	B		A		
23.		A		B	
24.			B		A
25.	A				B
26.		B	A		
27.				A	B
28.	A	B			
29.			A	B	
30.		B			A

Total number of items circled for each column:

Task Leader	Social- Emotional Leader	Information Provider	Central Negative	Tension Releaser

Developed by Gabriel Vasquez, 1991, at Illinois State University. Used by permission.

probably overplaying this role and run the risk of being viewed as a disloyal and cynical person in the organization. If you score an 8 or higher on Tension Releaser, the company you work for may not take you seriously. The idea here is role flexibility. You should be able to play all five roles. What role you play should be dependent on who the other members of the group are and what the task is; thus, you should expect to play different roles in different groups.

☐ COMMUNICATION SKILLS FOR IMPROVING ROLE-PLAYING IN SMALL GROUPS

Although Benne and Sheats and many other small group communication theorists regard many of the following communication behaviors as small group role types, it is more accurate to say that these behaviors are the utterances people occasionally use when they are playing the established, major roles. As indicated in the preceding section, an established small group role contains more than one type of communication behavior; the only exception to this is the role of recorder. In Chapter 3, we described five key communication behaviors in the formation and maintenance of group roles. These behaviors consist of helping in role formation, being role flexible, helping to ease primary tension, ensuring that the negative role is played, and supporting the task leader. In this chapter, we explain ten additional skills that help ensure that effective role-playing occurs in a decision-making group.

Stressing Group Productivity

We have all been members of work groups that were made up of people whose company we enjoyed, and we know that it makes the work go smoother if everyone likes one another. We've also participated in group work with people we have not been particularly fond of but sometimes have found these unpleasant groups to be more productive than the happy ones. One sign of a worker's professional maturity is that person's ability to work efficiently and effectively with coworkers to whom he or she is not attracted. We seldom can choose who will be on our work teams, and members are never rewarded for how they get along with one another. On the other hand, sometimes they are reprimanded if interpersonal conflicts get in the way of their work. When all is said and done, the most important output is the group's productivity. Member satisfaction and consensus are two group outcomes that enhance productivity, but even if there is little member satisfaction and even if the group seldom reaches consensus, it can still meet its most basic objective—productivity. Unhappy groups manage to be productive when enough of the group members are willing to overlook their individual differences and personality conflicts. Experienced small group participants reduce interpersonal conflict by pointing to the group's goals and the common need all members have for meeting those goals effectively.

Performing the Leadership Role When Needed

There is a tendency to think that only the person playing the role of task leader is responsible for the performance of leadership functions in the group; however, members of mature discussion groups do not hesitate to perform the necessary leadership communication behaviors when needed. For example, most work groups can use an increase in the number of questions asked in the discussion. Seeking ideas and eliciting idea evaluation are leadership communication skills that should be performed by several group members. Similarly, both the summarizing and the verbalizing of consensus that need to be performed after periods of intense dialogue should be done by the group as a whole. Research on group processes suggests that groups produce more ideas and solutions when they draw on all the resources of the group members. It is the obligation of every member of a discussion group to maximize the group's productivity. This is most successfully done when all group members work at ensuring that the crucial leadership functions are performed.

Assisting on Procedure

The efficient running of any group meeting requires meaningful attention to the procedural details of the meeting. Chapter 7 contains advice to the designated leader about the procedural nitty-gritty of running a good meeting. In most group settings, the leader needs help with procedural matters. Sometimes this help involves performing routine tasks such as distributing material or handling refreshments. During discussion, such help may involve giving subtle but important reassurances to the task leader that he or she is following the correct procedure.

Assisting on procedure is an important skill because it shows support for the leader and helps to build solidarity in the group. When several group members spontaneously pitch in on routine procedural matters, the group is demonstrating a sense of esprit de corps and cohesiveness, which are signs of a healthy group.

Energizing

Some small groups seem to have a higher energy level than others, and some discussions crackle with electricity while others sort of drone along. Energizing communication behavior is mostly detected in the nonverbal dimension of the discussion. There is a lilt in discussants' voices, eyes sparkle, and members seem genuinely excited about the topic. In athletics, we talk about members being "up for a game." The social-emotional leader frequently uses this communication behavior in an attempt to raise the level of the group's enthusiasm for its work. All members of discussion groups, while having their emotional ups and downs, should feel some obligation to be enthusiastic and try to excite others about the work at hand.

Compromising

The interdependent nature of a small group requires that some compromises must be reached if group decisions are to be made and group work satisfactorily accomplished. Regardless of what role a group member is playing, one part of that role is the compromising of one's vested interest. If a person appears to be playing the role of compromiser because he or she is forced to settle disputes among other group members, the group is probably not having a good time of it and there is much dissension among the ranks. In mature task groups, members not only compromise some of their own opinions, but also work to find common ground when conflicts occur among them. The social-emotional leader does so at the interpersonal level and the task leader, at the procedural level; all group members engage in compromising behavior at the ideational level.

Encouraging

Within the context of group communication, there are many dyadic exchanges. These person-to-person communication exchanges have a positive effect on the group as a whole. Praising a group member's ideas or showing interest in a member's problems is a necessary part of group discussion. When encouraging communication is performed by a high-status group member, it has an uplifting effect on the whole group. For this reason, experienced task leaders engage in a lot of encouraging communication behavior. Everybody needs to be praised and told that he or she is doing a good job, even the leader.

Observing

As indicated earlier, when a person specializes in the role of silent observer, most of his or her communication behavior consists of the presentation of neutral statements and the affirmation of heated points in the discussion. Most small groups do not have a person who specializes in this kind of communication behavior; but some observing must be performed.

It is important for every group member to sit back occasionally from the heat of an argument and observe the interaction of other group members. These moments of objectivity allow for many important insights. Sometimes these insights relate to adjustments in our own behavior, when, for example, we realize that we have been engaged in domineering and blocking behavior. Sometimes observing allows us to spot unnecessary tangents and put the group back on the right course.

Avoiding the Self-Centered Follower Role

Of the ten group roles, only one has a negative influence on the goals of the group. If a person plays this role in the group, the disruption that occurs is considerable. You should avoid playing the self-centered role, not only because it hurts the group but also because it hurts you. A person who plays the self-centered role never experiences much membership satisfaction and runs the risk of being labeled an organizational deviant who is not a good team player. One of the most important items on a person's work record, in terms of professional advancement, is the perceived ability of that person to work smoothly and effectively within groups.

Even when a discussant is playing a positive group role, he or she should avoid the excesses of that role in terms of deviant behaviors. Task leaders tend to dominate; social-emotional leaders sometimes engage in self-confessing behavior; and tension releasers might err by playing the clown. If you monitor your behavior, you will be able to spot when you are having a negative influence on the group and be able to make the appropriate adjustment.

Maintaining Role Stability

Mature decision-making groups develop clear role expectations after the group has moved successfully through primary and secondary tension. If a member of a group has taken on the role of the primary tension releaser, the group expects that that person will consistently play that role. Likewise, if a person has emerged as task leader, they can't suddenly choose not to be the leader without having a major negative impact on the group. It is important for you to know what role you play in the group because the group consistently expects you to play that role. The longer a group stays together, the higher the expectation for role stability.

Rescuing Roles

Sometimes newly formed groups do not move successfully through primary and secondary tension. There is role instability. Experienced small group participants often can sense what group role is missing and play it. All five major roles occasionally are being played but not with equal effectiveness. For example, the information provider role might be performed by an inexperienced group member who does not have enough task knowledge to do it well. If you see this situation arise, you should help rescue the role by playing the information provider. You could also assist in playing the social-emotional leader or tension releaser if those roles were not being played well. Absenteeism almost always requires that a role be rescued. If the task leader is not present, someone must step forward and play the role.

☐ AN INTEGRATED VIEW OF PEOPLE, ROLES, AND COMMUNICATION SKILLS

As stated in Chapter 1, it is important to distinguish among group members, the roles they play in a group, and the communication skills they perform. Figure 8.1 shows an integrated view of a problem-solving group. A task group contains three to eleven persons, with the ideal number being five to seven. The work group that generates an effective discussion has a potential range of ten roles, with five to six being the ideal number. The minimum number would be three: the task leader and two other roles. In Chapter 7, we described twenty leadership skills, and in this chapter, we presented ten role-playing skills. These thirty communication skills constitute the vast majority of role interactions, and certain clusters of communication behaviors serve to identify a given role, although a small group discussion with eleven persons playing ten roles and performing thirty communication skills probably never occurs. In addition, most small groups perform the twenty processing skills that were described in Chapter 3. A certain amount of discussion time is taken up with the building of group pride and a personal agenda of group members. Figure 8.1 shows fifty communication skills from a total of 100.

A Mature Problem-Solving Group

Good discussions require that key roles be played and that important leadership and role skills be performed. Figure 8.2 shows a hypothetical layout of the proper mixture of people, roles, and communication behaviors needed for a good group. Notice that this well-developed group has formed the five basic roles of task leader, social-emotional leader, information provider, tension releaser, and central negative. In addition, a number of roles are shared by different people. For example, Liz and Maria share the information provider role, while Pam and Maria share the questioner role. In terms of communication skills, Tom, the task leader, engages in most of the procedural and task leadership skills, but not all of them. For example, Kim, playing the roles of silent observer and recorder, still performs summarizing and visualizing abstract ideas. Even Pam, the central negative, performs important leadership skills, such as instigating conflict and contributing ideas. By the same token, Tom and Liz perform many role skills that are important to the group's success, particularly compromising and encouraging.

The people shown in Figure 8.2 are a good group, not only for what they do but also for what they do not do. Few deviant behaviors occur in this group. John, the tension releaser, occasionally overplays his role and makes a fool of himself, and Pam, in her role as central negative, becomes too intense in producing conflict, begins to block the group's progress, and thus focuses attention on herself. Once in a

FIGURE **8.1**   **An Integrated View of People, Roles, and Communication Skills in Small Groups**

People
Minimum is 3;
maximum 11;
ideal size
5–7 persons.

Tom   Liz   Maria   John   Pam   Kim   Juan

Roles
Minimum is 3;
maximum 10;
ideal number
is 5–6 roles.

Task leader	Central negative	Active listener
Social-emotional	Questioner	Self-centered
leader	Silent observer	follower
Tension releaser		Recorder
Information provider		

Communication Skills
Leadership: 20
(from Chapter 7)

Contributing ideas	Goal setting	Regulating participation
Seeking ideas	Agenda making	Climate making
Evaluating ideas	Clarifying	Instigating group
Seeking idea	Summarizing	self-analysis
evaluation	Verbalizing	Resolving conflict
Visualizing abstract	consensus	Instigating conflict
ideas	Performing group	Maintaining
Generalizing from	protocols	mutual respect
specific ideas	Establishing work	
Processing	patterns	
technology		

Role: 10
(from Chapter 8)

Assisting on	Stressing group
procedure	productivity
Observing	Performing leadership
Energizing	roles
Compromising	Avoiding the self-centered
Encouraging	follower role
	Maintaining role stability
	Rescuing roles

Core Process: 20
(from Chapter 3)

Problem-solving
Contributing to group orientation
Seeking information and opinions
Maximizing ideational conflict
Separating people, ideas, and criticism
Examining advantages and disadvantages

Trust-building
Risking self-disclosure
Avoiding stereotyped judgments
Being an empathetic listener
Recognizing individual differences
Providing emotional security for
  all members

Role-playing
Helping in role formation
Being role flexible
Helping to ease primary tension
Ensuring that the central negative
  role is played
Supporting the task leader

Team-building
Building group pride
Creating symbols and slogans
Establishing group traditions
Telling sacred stories
Initiating group fantasies

Deviant Behaviors: 12
(from Chapter 6)

Aggressing	Help-seeking
Doormatting	Recognition-seeking
Eggheading	Special-interest pleading
Airheading	Playing the clown
Whining	Blocking
Self-confessing	Foddering

FIGURE 8.2   Mature Problem-Solving Group, People, Roles, and Communication Skills

People						
	Tom	Liz	Maria	John	Pam	Kim

Roles	Task leader	Social-emotional leader Information provider	Information provider	Tension releaser	Central negative Questioner	Silent observer Recorder

Communication Skills *Leadership:*	Goal setting Agenda making Seeking idea evaluation Regulating participation Summarizing	Climate making Instigating group self-analysis Verbalizing consensus	Contributing ideas Generalizing from specific ideas Seeking ideas	Resolving conflict Climate making	Instigating conflict Clarifying Contributing ideas Evaluating ideas	Visualizing abstract ideas Summarizing

Role Skills and Deviant Behavior:	Listening attentively Compromise	Encouraging Compromising Self-confessing	Seeking help	Energizing Playing the clown	Compromising Blocking Seeking recognition	Listening attentively Assisting on procedure Observing Recording

Team and Trust-Building	"We" identification	Listening empathetically Self-disclosure	"They" vilification	Self-disclosure Group fantasies		Professional stories

while, Liz works too hard at the interpersonal level and engages in self-confessing behavior. But overall, this is a mature work group. Tom makes certain that the procedural functions are performed and does a good job of regulating participation of group members. Liz creates a warm and nonthreatening climate for the group and continually verbalizes the group's consensus. Pam is continually challenging and questioning the majority viewpoint, which helps to refine and clarify the group's efforts. John helps to resolve conflict and keeps group members on their toes with his wit and charm. Maria is continually contributing ideas and important information to form the database for the group's decisions. Kim records the group's proceedings and helps Tom run the meetings, while at the same time aiding the group to reach consensus.

Also, Tom is careful to spend some time in each meeting raising the group's consciousness through the retelling of past success stories. John also helps in consciousness-raising through his vilification of competing work groups. Maria frequently points out that this is the best group she has been in by relating stories about a past work group that she considered to be terrible. In addition to making sure that the group's pride is sufficiently high, the group also is sensitive to one another's personal needs and through this interpersonal talk has learned to empathize with and trust one another. Liz helps in this with her empathy and her willingness to make personal disclosures. The group shown in Figure 8.2 is clearly an experienced group, in that there is clear role formation and the communication skills move the group toward its goals.

An Authoritatively Controlled Problem-Solving Group

Figure 8.3 shows a group that is dominated by the task leader. Members are probably not happy to be part of the group because the group's productivity is almost solely dependent on the abilities and energies of the task leader. Notice that Nancy performs most of the leadership communication skills, but because she does so

FIGURE 8.3   Authoritatively Controlled Problem-Solving Group, People, Roles, and Communication Skills

People	Nancy	Bill	Pete	Sam
Roles	Task Leader Information provider	Self-centered follower	Tension releaser Information provider	Recorder
Communication Skills *Leadership:*	Regulating participation Contributing ideas Agenda making Climate making Goal setting		Climate making Contributing ideas	Clarifying

Role Skills and Deviant Behavior:	Aggressing
	Energizing
		Foddering
		Blocking
		Special-interest
		    pleading
			Seeking recognition	Recording
				Assisting on
				    procedure

Trust and Team-Building		"Upward they" vilification	"Upward they" vilification Group fantasy	

much work, there is a tendency for her to dominate the discussion. Because there is no social-emotional leader in this group, the resolution of conflict is difficult, and Pete has a hard time relieving tension. Bill is playing the negative role of self-centered follower. Nancy's job thus becomes even more difficult, and because Bill is engaging in negative special-interest behavior, he has some personal goals that he is placing above the group goals. Finally, Sam is mostly recording what Nancy does and helping her whenever he can to get through the meeting. It is possible to argue that the group in Figure 8.3 is not really a group because crucial roles are not played and important leadership communication skills are not performed. In fact, when Nancy is not present, Bill and Pete vilify her as an oppressive part of management. The shared group fantasy among Pete, Bill, and Sam is that Nancy is the "Ice Queen." This fantasy relieves tension for the men in the group, but it does not contribute to group cohesion and productivity.

An Uncontrolled Problem-Solving Group

Some decision-making groups are fraught with conflict. Nothing comes easy. The productivity that takes place is always accompanied by a great deal of verbal fisti-cuffs. The group shown in Figure 8.4 fights and kicks its way to every decision it makes. Although the five basic roles are present, two persons are playing negative self-centered follower roles. In addition, many of the leadership communication skills are not being performed, while the discussion is dominated by deviant behaviors.

Lisa and Frank had supported Julie for group leader. When Julie lost out to Tony, Julie, Lisa, and Frank began to engage in blocking communication behavior. It also became clear to the rest of the group that Julie, Lisa, and Frank had their special interests at heart and not the group's. It has become extremely difficult for Greg and Chin to play their roles successfully, given the distrust that exists within the group. It is only Greg's energy, combined with Tony's tenacity in sticking to the agenda, that allows productivity to take place.

In terms of trust building, there is little encounter talk. The group members believe that it is too risky to engage in personal disclosure. In terms of team building, there is a great deal of consciousness-raising talk, but it is mostly negative. Julie, Lisa, and Frank have formed a "we" clique in the group. They often meet outside of group meetings and vilify the "they" (the other group members). Julie has started a fantasy about "Tony the Angel" and portrays him as a company loyalist who is afraid to cross upper management. Tony continually tries to create a common "we" identification. Chin and Jim try to help through the telling of professional stories that indicate that their group is a good group. Yet the group remains symbolically divided into a "we" and a "they"; as a consequence, member satisfaction is low.

The Social Problem-Solving Group

Small work groups tend to socialize too much. An intimate climate is easy to establish, and if there is no role conflict, the group members may prefer to discuss themselves and not their work. Figure 8.5 shows such a group. This group would score high on member satisfaction and consensus but extremely low on group productivity. This group is really more an encounter group than a task group. They all are engaging in self-confessing behavior. Bob is overplaying his role of tension releaser by

FIGURE 8.4   **Uncontrolled Problem-Solving Group, People, Roles, and Communication Skills**

People							
	Tony	Julie	Greg	Lisa	Frank	Chin	Jim
Roles	Task leader	Central negative	Social-emotional leader Information provider	Self-centered follower	Self-centered follower	Active listener Tension releaser	Silent observer Recorder
Communication Skills *Leadership:*	Goal setting Agenda making	Instigating group conflict	Climate making Contributing ideas			Evaluating ideas Climate making	
Role Skills and Deviant Behavior:	Compromising Dominating	Special-interest pleading Blocking	Energizing Encouraging	Special-interest pleading Blocking Seeking recognition	Special-interest pleading Blocking Playing the clown	Observing	Recording Assisting on procedure Compromising
Trust and Team-Building:	"We" identification	"They" vilification		"They" vilification	"They" vilification	Professional stories	Professional stories

clowning around too much, but Michael and Andrea seldom engage in agenda-setting leadership behavior, so Bob's excesses never get corrected. All three group members continually perform climate-making leadership communication, not for the purpose of getting work done, but to ensure that everyone is happy with one another. If this were a social group, the communication patterns would be acceptable, but because it is a task group with work to accomplish, the work output is unacceptably low.

This group is close to being labeled a pure encounter group. Person-to-person talk (personal stories, self-disclosure) takes up most of the group's time. The only team-building talk that occurs relates to the group fantasy that they are the nicest people in the organization and that they enjoy working together. The problem is that they do little work, even though their consensus and member satisfaction are quite high.

FIGURE 8.5   Social Problem-Solving Group, People, Roles, and Communication Skills

People			
	Andrea	Michael	Bob

Roles	Task leader
	Information provider
		Social-emotional
		  leader
		Information
		  provider
			Tension releaser
			Information provider

Communication Skills *Leadership:*	Climate making Instigating group self-analysis Contributing ideas	Climate making Contributing ideas	Climate making Resolving conflict Contributing ideas

Role Skills and Deviant Behavior:	Self-confessing Energizing	Self-confessing Seeking help	Playing the clown Self-confessing

*Trust and
Team-Building:*
	Self-disclosure
	Empathetic
	  listening
	Personal stories
		Self-disclosure
		Personal stories
		Group fantasy
		Empathetic
		  listening
			Self-disclosure
			Personal stories
			Empathetic
			  listening

The mature group shown in Figure 8.2 is productive; the members are satisfied; and the group typically reaches consensus on major decisions. The authoritative group shown in Figure 8.3 is productive; however, there is low membership satisfaction, and "consensus" often is forced. The uncontrolled group shown in Figure 8.4 never reaches consensus on major issues; its members are unhappy—even angry—although it maintains at least a low level of productivity. The social group shown in Figure 8.5 usually reaches consensus; it has extremely high membership satisfaction, but it hardly ever gets anything done. Although we all strive to create mature work groups, sometimes we find ourselves members of the other three types.

☐ Summary

Group participation was defined as positive communication behavior that moves the group toward the group's goals. Communication leadership and role skills typically are performed by people playing certain role types. The ten most frequently played roles in groups include the task leader, social-emotional leader, tension releaser, information provider, central negative, questioner, silent observer, active listener, recorder, and self-centered follower.

In addition to the twenty leadership communication skills presented in Chapter 7, ten role skills are identified. The ten communication skills discussed are assisting on procedure, observing, energizing, compromising, encouraging, stressing group productivity, performing leadership roles, avoiding the self-centered follower role, maintaining role stability, and rescuing roles.

In mature problem-solving groups, we find people who perform numerous leadership and role skills; in fact, certain clusters of these communication behaviors serve to identify given roles that people play in groups. However, most people play more than one role in a group. In this chapter, we present four examples of the relations among people, roles, and communication skills as they might occur in a problem-solving group.

◉◉ CASE STUDY

A Decision-Making Meeting

CASE BACKGROUND

The homecoming committee at State University has been meeting regularly since spring semester of the last academic year. The members of the committee are:

- Tom Carleton, president, Dorm Council
- Diane Wheaton, president, Greek Council
- Carl Greene, president, Black Affairs Union
- Toby Miller, president, Athletic Council
- Maureen McNamara, off-campus representative, elected at large
- Kirk Everitt, fraternity representative, elected at large
- Gail Holmberg, president of student body at State University, ex officio member

Tom Carleton and Diane Wheaton, cochairpersons of the homecoming committee, are pleased with the progress that the committee has made thus far. There seems to be a revived interest in homecoming at State University, and the committee is interested in producing an exciting homecoming weekend. The committee has worked its way down to two decisions: determining the final criteria for building this year's floats and finalizing the sequence of floats.

The purpose of this one-hour meeting of the committee is to produce decisions on the two issues.

CASE LOG

First Forty Minutes of the Meeting

Tom opens the meeting by having Maureen distribute the minutes from the previous meeting. Receiving no corrections to the minutes, he distributes the agenda. The first item on the agenda is a presentation by Diane on the costs of floats last year compared with projected costs this year.

DIANE: As you remember, last year organizations were limited to $300 for float materials, all of it had to be purchased at Goldblatt's and K-Mart, and receipts had to be turned in to the homecoming committee. Cars and float wagons were donated. The receipts from last year show that all but three organizations spent all the allotted money. I called the presidents of all the fraternities and sororities last week, and they all felt that the allowable ceiling should definitely be raised by at least $100. Considering inflation and the increased interest in homecoming, I would recommend to the committee that we raise the ceiling to $400 per float.

KIRK: Why have any limit? Let's take the ceiling off and find out how really great homecoming floats can look. Dartmouth has used that method with their ice sculpturing during their ice festival, and they receive national attention. If we'd throw our energy into homecoming floats, we would make a name for ourselves and this university.

CARL: Let us all bow our heads in reverence to the wealthiest fraternity on campus. (Carl is drowned out by group laughter.)

TOBY: Yeah, if old "moneybags Kilpatrick" hadn't died and left your fraternity all that money, you wouldn't be in favor of eliminating the financial ceiling.

KIRK: I'm serious; why do we always have to put mediocre equality ahead of excellence? It's not that we would spend that much more money than other groups; it's just that people would work harder. With the stuff you buy from Goldblatt's and K-Mart, it's just hard to get enthusiastic.

DIANE: My sorority is capable of spending a lot of money on a homecoming float too, but I think we must have a reasonable ceiling. First, because that is the only way you can have a contest for best float. My sorority has won the Greek "best float" award two out of the past three years, and we take a lot of pride in the work we did to win. If we won because we just spent more money, it wouldn't be meaningful. I like to win when competition is equal. The money ceiling makes it equal. The second reason we need a ceiling is to ensure a large number of floats. If ten wealthy fraternities and sororities build elaborate floats, a lot of other organizations will simply drop out of homecoming. Flaunting wealth is how Greeks got a bad name in the sixties.

MAUREEN: Personally, I don't care if the Greeks want to spend their money on floats. I don't think most students care one way or another.

CARL: I care, and the Black Affairs Union cares. Diane is right. What makes this homecoming parade a universitywide event, and not a Greek orgy, is that we keep a lid on the cost and promote good competition.

TOM: I think all the issues here are out on the table. I appreciate Kirk's concern for excellence, but it seems like there is some consensus to have some kind of cost ceiling on floats. I'm not sure we've arrived at the figure yet, however.

KIRK: I'd like to see a vote on whether we have a ceiling or not before we decide anything else. Better yet, let's not vote on this until our next meeting. It will give me time to poll the fraternities and sororities and see what their attitudes are. The fact that the Greeks spent their limit last year says to me that we should take the lid off and let costs find their own level.

TOM: I don't think we can postpone this decision past today. All organizations need to know the final decision of this committee so they can plan accordingly.

KIRK: I don't think it's fair that this committee should make a decision like this without first checking with the people we represent.

CARL: Now look at who's the champion of equality! (Tense group laughter)

TOBY: Kirk, why are you always throwing a monkey wrench into this committee's decisions? If you really felt that strongly about it, why didn't you bring it up earlier?

KIRK: Hey, look. You don't want to hear my opinion? Fine, I won't give it.

DIANE: Kirk, I understand what you're saying, and it is a reasonable position. In fact, some of the people in my house think the same way you do about homecoming floats. However, when I talked to the presidents of the various houses, they didn't seem to be upset about a ceiling per se but that $300 was too little!

GAIL: I think Diane's right. There is not a lot of sentiment for taking the ceiling off. And Tom is absolutely right—we must get a vote on this issue today. But Kirk does have a point. I like the idea of

getting national publicity on our homecoming floats. I guess I support the idea of keeping things the way they are this year but doing a study to see if we should do away with the ceiling next year. Would you like to head up that study, Kirk?

MAUREEN: I'm for that. Let's do a thorough study and then change the rule next year if we decide to.

TOM: I still need a vote for this year. What if we raise the ceiling to $400, like Diane suggested? All those in favor signify by saying "Aye." (Six ayes.) "Nays." (One nay.)

OK, let's go to the next item on the agenda: the route and sequencing of the parade.

Last Twenty Minutes of the Meeting
Carl Greene distributes a chart showing the order of last year's parade units and a map of the route the parade took.

CARL: Time's about up, so let's make this short and sweet. I move we adopt the same parade route sequence we used last year.

MAUREEN: I second that!

DIANE: Does that mean we draw lots again for what order the floats line up?

CARL: Right.

GAIL: The chancellor expressed an interest to me in riding in a car immediately behind the winning float. Can we make that accommodation?

TOBY: As long as we're passing out favors, we think that the parade route should be extended two more blocks down College Avenue so it would go by the athletic dorm.

KIRK: Now look at who are *really* the privileged ones! Prime rib for dinner every night! (Group laughter)

CARL: Time's running out. OK, we put the chancellor behind the winning float and we extend the parade route by two blocks. Can we all live with that?

DIANE: As I remember, the reason we never go by the athletic dorm is that the parade then has to turn left on Howard Street, and it's a narrow one-way street, especially with parked cars there.

TOBY: The cops can move the cars.

KIRK: I have got to get to class, let me know how the vote comes out.

MAUREEN: I have to go too!

TOM: I think we need more discussion on this issue, but we must have the decision by 8:00 A.M. tomorrow. Let's have a special meeting tonight at 7:30. If anybody has more suggestions or changes, bring them with you this evening.

CASE QUESTIONS

1. How many roles can you identify in this discussion?

2. How many leadership communication skills can you identify?

3. What deviant personality behaviors can you identify?

4. Would you call Kirk a central negative or a self-centered follower? Why?

CHAPTER NINE

MANAGING CONFLICT IN GROUPS

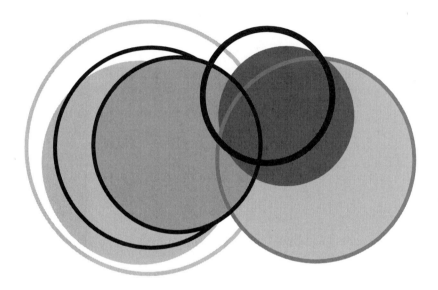

CHAPTER OBJECTIVES

After reading this chapter, you should be able to:

- Avoid groupthink
- Comprehend your individual tendencies in group conflict
- Apply team-building communication skills to reduce conflict

Conflict is pervasive in groups. It is such an important concept that we are devoting this chapter to understanding and managing conflict communication. Most people's initial reaction to the word *conflict* is apprehension, in that there is a certain inherent risk in becoming involved in conflict communication. Right after being fearful of conflict, there is a tendency to avoid it; we search for a way to manage it. We have already indicated in previous chapters that a great deal of conflict in groups is inevitable. In fact, conflict is necessary for groups to be successful. However, there can be too much conflict, thus deterring a group from its goals. Perhaps the best way to understand conflict communication is in terms of its focus (Putnam and Jones 1982).

But before considering specific loci of conflict in groups, it is important that you understand two macro issues of conflict communication, which have been popularly identified as the "risky shift" and the "groupthink" phenomena. The risky shift phenomenon occurs when individuals make riskier decisions in groups than when acting alone, thus enhancing intragroup conflict; the groupthink phenomenon is a dangerous condition in which no conflict communication is occurring.

☐ Conflict Communication: The Risky Shift and Groupthink Phenomena

The book *The Organization Man,* by William H. Whyte (1957), was one of the more popular characterizations of life in organizations in the 1950s. Whyte's description of group decision making was consistent with the academic view of the time—that groups usually made more cautious and conservative decisions than did managers acting alone. In this context, Stoner's (1961) research caused group scholars to reexamine group versus individual decision making. Stoner found that groups made riskier decisions than individuals. Wallach, Kogan, and Bem (1964) quickly replicated Stoner's research design and obtained the same result. These findings took on heightened importance in light of the nuclear confrontation that was occurring at the time between the United States and the Soviet Union. While Wallach and others were finding a risky shift effect in their tightly controlled laboratory studies of groups, Irving Janis (1972, iii) was asking the question, "How could bright, shrewd men like John F. Kennedy and his advisors be taken in by the CIA's stupid patchwork plan (Bay of Pigs)?" Janis (1972, 206) answered his question by proposing what he called the "groupthink" hypothesis: "The greater the threats to the self-esteem of the members of a cohesive decision-making body, the greater will be their inclination to resort to concurrence-seeking at the expense of critical thinking." Janis (1972, 9) called this tendency of some highly cohesive groups to avoid ideational conflict *groupthink,* with the intention of aligning it with George Orwell's novel *1984,* in which Big Brother develops "newspeak," "double think," and "crime think." Thus, groupthink involves the complete conformity of the group at the expense of engaging in conflict communication for the purpose of improving the quality of the group's decision. It's easy to see, in the context of nuclear war, why small group scholars would want to examine the phenomena of risky shift and groupthink carefully. These two macro issues also have importance to you and us as we participate in ordinary problem-solving groups within our own organizations.

Risky Shift

Stoner's (1961) research produced unparalleled excitement, as measured by the number of studies that were conducted, to probe the question whether groups make riskier decisions than individuals. Cartwright (1973, 223) counted 196 studies completed from 1961 through 1971 alone. Early in the decade, numerous scholars replicated Stoner's initial findings, while carefully using the original twelve-item Choice Dilemma Questionnaire (CDQ). Researchers varied age, gender, occupation, and nationality and still got robust findings that supported Stoner's original hypothesis that groups make riskier decisions than individuals (Shaw 1981, 70). As social scientists became convinced that there was a risk-shift effect, they began to concentrate on developing theoretical explanations that account for groups making riskier decisions than individuals.

The initial explanation that was most widely accepted and that had a common-sense basis was the "diffusion of responsibility" hypothesis. The argument explained the results by saying that an individual is more willing to support a risky decision when he or she is part of a group, rather than acting alone, because the responsibility is diffused among the group members. This explanation seemed credible until further research on the risky shift phenomenon started to produce results that showed groups making more cautious decisions than individuals. Researchers found that when they used items for discussion that were different from the original twelve, they often got more cautious results from the group. Furthermore, a close examination of the twelve items in the original CDQ revealed that some of the twelve items produced more cautious reactions by the group than by individuals (Cartwright 1973; McGrath 1984). These new findings shook our confidence in the original findings that groups make riskier decisions than individuals. Clearly, the findings required more elaborate explanations. Three theories were forthcoming: social comparison theory, persuasive argument theory, and cultural value theory.

The cultural value theory suggested that risk is more valued in some cultures than in others. For example, Hong (1978) found that Chinese made more cautious group decisions than Americans, and Americans seemed to make riskier decisions both acting alone and in groups. Thus, it was concluded that Americans place higher value on risk taking and make riskier decisions.

The persuasive argument explanation was clear-cut when all the studies showed groups making riskier decisions than individuals. This explanation merely asserted that the most risk-prone individuals in the group tend to be dominant communicators who influence other group members to their positions. Hamilton (1972) conducted research in an attempt to see whether risk-prone discussants were more interested, verbose, and assertive, but he did not find any difference between low risk-takers and high risk-takers. Furthermore, when research began to show that some groups made more cautious decisions than individuals, both Shaw (1981) and McGrath (1984) concluded that the exchange of information and arguments in a discussion polarized or accentuated previously held positions. Thus, the group discussion itself had a significant and long-lasting impact on the participants' opinions, but one could not predict a direction of the group's decision in terms of risk taking or cautiousness. Some studies suggested findings in which discussion of a topic reinforced initial positions of cautiousness and risk taking (Boster, Fryrear, Mongeau, and Hunter 1982; Boster, Mayer, Hunter, and Hale 1980).

The final explanation is the social comparison theory. This theory argues that we use decisions to compare ourselves with one another and that we will adapt our position in the discussion to our previous self-image of how we compare with the norm. Thus, if we regard ourselves as above-average risk-takers, and everyone in the discussion is conforming to our level of risk taking, we will "up the ante" and suggest even riskier decisions, thus producing the accentuation effect (McGrath 1984). Also involved in this explanation is a sense of conformity; that is, if the majority of the group is in favor of greater risk taking, there is a tendency of deviants to conform. Conversely, if the majority position is cautious, there will be pressure to conform in this direction (Olmsted and Hare 1978). Twenty-five years ago we seriously asked the question, Do groups make riskier decisions than individuals? For a decade or so, we thought they did. As Cartwright (1973, 226) pointed out, "the accumulation of data demonstrates that groups are not invariably riskier than individuals." These hundreds of studies are not without practical value to the average group discussant because they highlight key ideas about risk and conflict in groups.

Organizational culture probably influences risk-taking behavior in groups. Most of the studies done on risky shift have been laboratory studies in which college students have been put together for the first time for a short period to arrive at group decisions; thus, it is difficult to generalize about the ability of these studies to characterize work groups in organizations. However, some of the field studies on the risky shift phenomenon and our own consultation experience in working with organizations lead us to believe that organizations in general and specific work groups within them develop normal behavior with respect to the riskiness of their decisions.

The high-tech organizations that have grown so rapidly in the 1970s and 1980s have developed reputations as high risk-takers. Peters and Waterman (1982), in their book *In Search of Excellence*, celebrate this risk-taking behavior at Hewlett-Packard and other organizations. And numerous articles have been written about Apple

Computer's risk-taking behavior in the development of their computers, especially the Macintosh model. This behavior is in contrast to the stereotyped cautious decision making of public utilities. Our point here is not to categorize corporations on a continuum of being risky or cautious, but rather to emphasize that it is important for you to assess your work group and your organization's risk-taking tendencies, and compare them with your own propensity to take risks.

The research on risky shift seems to say that if you join a work group that has a tradition of high risk taking and you perceive yourself to be a cautious decision-maker, you can anticipate a certain amount of conflict communication that can be attributed to this difference. Conversely, if you are a high risk-taker serving on a committee of other high risk-takers, group communication may intensify your own and other risk-taking tendencies, resulting in a riskier decision than you would have made yourself.

It appears that risk taking is more topic-bound than group-bound. Although some groups may make riskier decisions than other groups and others may make more cautious decisions, it appears that the topics that groups discuss have more bearing on the riskiness of the decision than does the fact of whether group members are high or low risk-takers. For example, one of the twelve situations in the CDQ that produces a risky decision is the problem that relates to an electrical engineer's decision on whether or not to switch jobs. In this problem the group is asked to estimate, on a scale of one to ten, the chances of a new company's surviving; then the group must decide whether the engineer should leave a secure job and take a job with the new company that would provide a better salary and more career opportunities (Hong 1978; Kogan and Wallach 1964; McGrath 1984). Furthermore, when new situations were contrived, other than the original twelve—like gambling problems—groups consistently made more cautious decisions than individuals would have made acting alone. Indeed, our own experience of serving on various university committees lend credence to the topic-bound nature of risky shift. For instance, committees are traditionally more cautious about making personnel decisions than about deciding whether or not to purchase additional equipment: awarding tenure to a faculty member who will be around for twenty-five years is a different kind of decision from purchasing a computer that might be replaced in a relatively short period of time. Here, again, you should examine your group's tendency to treat some topics in a riskier manner than others. Even though you may stereotype yourself as a high risk-taker, you may discover on some topics that you are very cautious. This is also true of groups. In some situations, groups may be high risk-takers; in other situations, they are quite cautious.

Group discussions affect decision making. Although it has long been held in the field of communication that face-to-face discussion affects the opinions of its participants, the research on the risky shift phenomenon, which was primarily conducted by social psychologists, provides new indirect support on the potency of small group discussion. In almost all the studies done in the laboratory and field situations, there was a shift of opinion among the participants as a result of having a discussion. Although it is difficult to predict whether a group or an individual will make a riskier decision on the basis of having a discussion, in almost all cases, the discussions intensify the individual member's tendency to be riskier or more cautious. One explanation for this shift of opinion is that the information and arguments presented in the discussion reduce a person's ignorance on a topic and, thus, allow the group members to move further in one direction or another. Thus, the sharing of information reduces uncertainty. Group members are now willing to make riskier decisions because they have more information, or a group makes a more cautious decision because the group arguments have convinced members to be more cautious. It seems clear that group decision making may produce different decisions from individual decision making. And, as indicated previously, on some topics, groups definitely make better decisions than do individuals (Collins and Guetzkow 1964). Unfortunately, we do not know, after extensive research of the risky shift phenomenon, whether groups make riskier decisions than individuals (Cartwright 1973).

Groupthink

Irving Janis (1983) examined seven decision-making situations for U.S. policy-making groups at the highest level of government, covering the 1940s through the 1970s: Pearl Harbor, the Marshall Plan, North Korea, the Bay of Pigs, the Cuban missile crisis, Vietnam, and Watergate. In five of the seven situations, Janis found the phenomenon of groupthink to be operating. In summing up his analysis of these case studies, Janis generalized his findings as follows: "The more amiability and esprit de corps among the members of a policymaking in-group, the greater is the danger that independent critical thinking will be replaced by groupthink, which is likely to result in irrational and dehumanizing actions directed against out-groups" (1983, 13). Furthermore, Janis discovered that the absence of ideational conflict significantly lowered the quality of the decisions reached. Tetlock and colleagues (1992) reexamined Janis's case studies using Q-sort method and empirically confirmed Janis's findings on groupthink. Courtright (1978) conducted a laboratory experiment to assess the effect of the groupthink phenomenon in a controlled setting. He concluded "that the absence of disagreement is the most important manifestation of the groupthink syndrome" (Courtright 1978, 245). In a more recent study, Cline (1990) replicated Courtright's findings. Although Courtright's study did not show a statistically significant relation between groupthink and poor group decisions, his data tended to suggest that such a relation exists (Courtright 1978, 244). These findings seem to square with our everyday experience with decision-making groups. In fact, the data are consistent with the overall database in small group communication for what makes a good group decision.

Although Janis has articulated eight symptoms that point to the presence of groupthink, he reasons that they start appearing when groups are overly cohesive and try to reach consensus prematurely. For purposes of this textbook, we would call a group having this high-cohesion condition an overly consciousness-raised group. The first symptom is the illusion of invulnerability. As the old adage goes, "pride goes before a fall." Sometimes groups become so full of themselves that they believe they are not capable of mistakes and, thus, are capable of making hasty decisions. Janis's description of the Bay of Pigs fiasco and the decisions of Nixon's committee to Re-elect the President (CREEP) vividly depicts the dangers that face highly consciousness-raised groups. There is indeed the danger that proud, successful groups will skirt the difficult parts of decision making that require conflict because they do not want to cause dissension. After all, the group is too good to be wrong. It is important to remember that just because a group raises its consciousness into be-lieving it is a good decision-making group, this does not mean that it is, or will be, with every decision it makes, especially if it puts satisfaction ahead of productivity.

Two more symptoms of groupthink that Janis found are the group's continuous stereotyping of enemy leaders as evil and stupid and the group's unquestioned be-lief in its own morality. These two symptoms appear when a group engages in too much Stage Two consciousness-raising (CR) talk. If the group places too much em-phasis on the "vilification of the they," it eventually will dehumanize its adversaries, as indicated in Chapter 2. Once this is done, it is easy to morally justify inhuman treatment of the group's enemies. Janis's research of CREEP demonstrated this phe-nomenon when he pointed out descriptions of the people the committee named on the "enemies list." The CREEP group eventually justified to itself the break-in to the Democratic headquarters in the Watergate building, plus a number of other break-ins and other illegal activities, because they were directed against the "enemy." Spe-cialized crime teams, like SWAT and narcotic units, can easily generate these two symptoms because of the nature of their work and, in many cases, the true nature of the criminals they seek to catch. Every year newspapers report instances in which police tactical units, in their overzealous pursuit of the "they" (criminals), have vio-lated the civil rights of Americans. As we said in Chapter 2, it is important not to em-phasize or encourage extended CR sessions that vilify the "they." Your group will stand a better chance of avoiding groupthink if it focuses on its own positive work behaviors and, in the case of decision-making groups, on its ability to engage in ide-ational conflict than if it dwells on the weaknesses of other groups.

Janis depicts three symptoms that move a group toward unrealistic uniformity, which in turn helps to produce the groupthink syndrome. They are (1) a shared group illusion that consensus has been reached on an idea when in fact it has not; (2) the corollary symptom that each member is the only one who thinks that he or she has doubts (self-censorship); and (3) the recurring behavior of the group's attacking any member who dissents as being disloyal. These three symptoms taken collec-tively produce a group culture that is intolerant of ideational conflict. What is miss-ing from a group suffering from groupthink is the role of central negative that we talked about in Chapters 2 and 8. In fact, the group celebrates the absence of conflict as a sign of a healthy group. As indicated before, we think that the sign of a healthy group is an atmosphere in which the members of the group can tolerate large amounts of ideational criticism.

The Iran-contra affair during the Reagan administration highlights the importance of the central negative role. Secretary of Defense Caspar Weinberger and Secretary of State George Schultz shared the role of central negative when they explained to their colleagues on the National Security Council that it was a bad idea to give arms to the Iranians for the release of hostages and take the profits from the sale to finance the contras in Nicaragua. The National Security Council began excluding Weinberger and Schultz from the discussions on the arms deal and proceeded with their plan—a plan that nearly cost Reagan his presidency and jail terms for some of the partici-pants, including Oliver North.

When the groupthink syndrome is present, not only do decision-making teams stifle dissent within the group—a phenomenon we sometimes label "The Smokey the Bear Syndrome," meaning that the group stamps out a deviant idea before it has a chance to spread—but the group also develops insulation to protect itself from any ideas outside the group that threaten the group's consensus. Janis says that there are two symptoms relating to outside ideas. One is the emergence of self-appointed "mindguards," who believe that it is their duty to protect the group from adverse information. During the Nixon years in the White House, these people were commonly called the "Palace Guard." The other symptom is the group's habit of rationalizing its rejection of new information on the basis of its being either inaccurate or irrelevant to a reexamination of the group's policies. The Westmoreland libel trial against CBS, which took place in 1984, brought to the surface information about General Westmoreland's decision-making group that indicates that his team may have been suffering from the groupthink syndrome. Information officers outside Westmoreland's immediate group kept reporting that the size of the enemy force in Vietnam in 1967 was twice as large as General Westmoreland and his group of advisors would accept. The Tet offensive of 1968 indicated that the larger figures of enemy troop strength were more nearly correct. This discrepancy has left many to wonder how Westmoreland could have discounted information from otherwise reliable agents. CBS claimed a conspiracy existed in which Westmoreland's group deliberately lied to President Johnson to make the war appear more winnable. A simpler explanation may be that General Westmoreland's team was suffering from groupthink. The Challenger space shuttle disaster appears to be another example of groupthink (Edelmayer 1987; Hirokawa, Ice, and Cook 1988; Moorhead, Ferrence, and Neck 1991). The NASA decision-making team, as determined by the Rogers Commission, ignored information that clearly indicated the joint decision was flawed (Foley 1986).

The startling conclusion from Janis's and subsequent scholars' research is that consensus-seeking and team-building may work against the quality of group decisions. If a group gets too highly consciousness-raised and pushes prematurely for group consensus, the group is likely to make a poor decision. In fact, in terms of decision outcome quality, good team leaders seem to encourage open inquiry to yield diverse alternatives for solving problems (Chen, Lawson, Gordon, and McIntosh 1996). In addition, Janis (1983) points out that there is a strong association between the eight symptoms of groupthink and six defects in the decision-making process. He argues that the presence of groupthink will cause the following decision-making defects: (1) failure to examine alternative ideas, (2) failure to reexamine the preferred alternatives, (3) selected bias in processing information, (4) no contingency plans, (5) rejection of expert opinions, and (6) failure to reexamine rejected alternatives.

An examination of the groupthink syndrome leads us to make six recommendations to you that will help your groups avoid the debilitating effects of groupthink. They are (1) encourage ideational conflict, (2) assist in the development of the central negative role, (3) guard against leader domination of ideas, (4) keep CR within limits, (5) examine the advantages and disadvantages of a proposal, and (6) use a problem-solving agenda system. An analysis of the jury deliberations in the John DeLorean trial supports the value of these six suggestions in avoiding groupthink (Neck and Moorhead 1992). Table 9.1 lists groupthink symptoms, decision-making defects, and ways to avoid groupthink.

TABLE **9.1**   **Groupthink: Symptoms, Defects, and Cures**

Symptoms	Decision-Making Defects	Cures
■ Group invulnerability ■ Unquestioned morality ■ Rationalization of mistakes ■ Vilification of opposing groups ■ Self-censorship ■ False consensus ■ Forced conformity ■ Blockage of outside information	■ Few alternatives ■ No reexamination of plan ■ No reexamination of rejected plans ■ Rejection of expert opinions ■ Biased treatment of information ■ No contingency plans	■ Maximize ideational conflict ■ Develop central negative role ■ Reduce leader dominance ■ Keep group pride within limits ■ Examine advantages and disadvantages of all proposals ■ Use a problem-solving agenda system

COMMUNICATION CONFLICT INHERENT IN ORGANIZATIONAL WORK GROUPS

Work groups do not exist in isolation from one another but are necessarily parts of a larger organization. The informal and formal structures of an organization largely determine the degree of conflict that occurs within a work group and among the groups that constitute the organization. The reward system that the organization uses for individuals and groups and the procedures to disperse scarce resources are two major touchstones for assessing the degree to which individuals and groups will cooperate with each other. Scholars in a number of academic disciplines have been studying what have come to be called "mixed motive games" to help determine under what conditions individuals will compete and cooperate with one another.

Cooperation and Competition in and among Work Groups

The Prisoner's Dilemma Game has frequently been used by scholars to assess the degree of cooperation or competition that occurs in a group. This game provides a vivid simulation of how conflict can be increased in a group if communication is restricted. Figure 9.1 shows the basic matrix of a Prisoner's Dilemma Game.

The game is called a Prisoner's Dilemma because the matrix simulates the choices two criminals would have if they were caught by police while committing a crime. The police immediately separate the criminals and tell each one that he or she has but two choices: turn state's evidence against the other criminal or remain silent and let the other criminal turn state's evidence. If both remain silent, they both win big (+ $10/ + $10); if one turns state's evidence and the other remains silent, one criminal wins big and the other loses (+ $14/ − $5). When a group forms partnerships and plays this game among its membership, trust is quickly destroyed if no communication is allowed, whereas if full face-to-face communication takes place after each round of a ten-round game, more cooperative behavior occurs (Steinfatt, Seibold, and Frye 1974).

FIGURE 9.1   **Basic Matrix of a Prisoner's Dilemma Game**

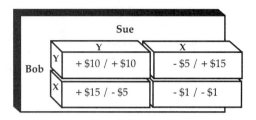

As we can see from Figure 9.1, Y is a cooperative choice and X is a competitive choice. If Bob and Sue both select Y (cooperation), they each win $10; however, if Sue chooses Y and Bob "rips her off" with a competitive X move, then Bob wins $15 and Sue loses $5. If Bob and Sue play several rounds of this game, the simple choice of X and Y can build into a rather involved game to determine if they can trust each other.

It is also quite easy to build a mixed motive game for a group so that there is a high incentive to cooperate or a high incentive to compete. Consider the rather popular game "Win as Much as You Can," shown in Figure 9.2. This game can be played easily by either four or eight persons. When eight persons play the game, there are four partnerships. The game commences with the direction that each partnership decides on either X or Y after no more than two minutes of discussion. This choice is concealed from the other three dyads in the group. At the end of the first round, the dyad choices are revealed. If there are four Xs, all four partnerships lose $1. If there are four Ys, all four partnerships win $1. If three partnerships choose Y and one partnership selects X, the Ys lose $1 each and X wins $3. As you can see, X symbolizes a competitive move and Y indicates a cooperative move. It's apparent that if everybody in the group chooses Y, they can all win money. However, the organization of this game is such that there is an incentive for one partnership to be competitive if they can persuade the other partnerships to be cooperative. Whether people cooperate or compete depends a lot on how the reward system is set up and how much trusting communication is established and maintained among group members. The outcomes of this game also vary considerably if there are three groups of four partnerships each playing the game simultaneously, especially if only one partnership out of the twelve is rewarded for having won the most. In this configuration, there is now a new incentive for cooperation within a group, while increasing competition among groups. These mixed motive games are more than just fun to play. They also simulate reward systems of organizations that either increase or decrease conflict within and among work groups.

Reward Strategies

All organizations have a tendency to structure work in groups but then reward individuals; that is, individuals get promoted, not groups; and salary increases tend to occur in individuals as compared with clusters of individuals being rewarded for group productivity. Organizations run the continuum—from those that reward only

FIGURE 9.2   Win as Much as You Can

Directions: For ten successive rounds you and your partner will choose either an "X" or "Y." The "Payoff" for each round is dependent upon the pattern of choices made in your group.

4 Xs:	Lose $1.00 each

3 Xs:	Win $1.00 each
1 Y :	Lose $3.00

2 Xs:	Win $2.00 each
2 Ys:	Lose $2.00 each

1 X :	Win $3.00
3 Ys:	Lose $1.00 each

4 Ys:	Win $1.00 each

Strategy: You are to confer with your partner on each round and make a *joint decision*. Before rounds 5, 8, and 10 you confer with the other dyads in your group.

Round	Strategy		Choice	$ WON	$ LOST	BALANCE
	Time allowed	Confer with				
1	2 min.	partner				
2	1 min.	partner				
3	1 min.	partner				
4	1 min.	partner				
5	3 min. + 1 min.	group and partner				Bonus round payoff is multiplied by 3.
6	1 min.	partner				
7	1 min.	partner				
8	3 min. + 1 min.	group and partner				Bonus round payoff is multiplied by 5.
9	1 min.	partner				
10	3 min.	group and partner				Bonus round payoff is multiplied by 10.

SOURCE: Adapted from Pfeiffer, J. William, and Jones, John E., *A Handbook of Structural Experiences for Human Relations Training*, Vol. II (La Jolla, Calif.: University Associates, 1974), p. 67.

the individual for performance to those that provide group rewards through profit centers and profit sharing. That is to say, if the product you are working on is a success, there may be bonuses and stock options directly tied to the group effort. Thus, there are a lot of incentives for X or Y in all organizations.

If you are part of a sales team, there might be tremendous incentive to compete with other salespeople if most of the major rewards (like bonuses and vacation trips) are directly tied to your performing better than other salespeople in your group. In fact, you may be reluctant to share your sales "secrets" with other salespeople, even if requested by management. Groups may also become competitive with one another if the reward system of the organization encourages it. For example, if a company has five product centers, we might find that four of the five product centers are producing and profiting 30 percent for every dollar invested, the fifth product center is prospering but getting only a 15 percent return on dollars invested. This situation creates an incentive for the four most profitable groups to request that the fifth group be eliminated and its resources distributed to the four remaining groups so that they may expand. In U.S. universities, this "game" is sometimes played using student majors and credit hours generated as the means for keeping score. Growth in computer science departments in the 1980s and 1990s can justify adding faculty on the basis of increasing student majors, often at the expense of less prosperous departments. In this situation, there are incentives for departments to compete rather than cooperate with others. Consider your own case in a small group communication class. If your class is divided into five discussion groups and the professor tells you that there will be one group that will receive an "A" and one group that will receive an "F," there will be a lot more conflict among the groups than if the instructor allowed the potential for all groups to receive an "A." Likewise, within your discussion group, conflict communication will, in part, depend on the reward system. If everybody receives the same grade, there is a high incentive for cooperation; however, if the professor stipulates that one student will receive an "A," one student will receive an "F," and the remainder of the students will receive "Cs," the group conflict would probably become intolerable if the group were to present a panel discussion on a given topic.

The singling out of an individual in a group or of one group from a number of groups may also become a source of conflict. For example, a basketball team has to work interdependently to accomplish its goal of winning; but if one individual is continually recognized in the sports page for individual achievements, dissension may develop on the basketball team, especially if it appears that the star player is putting individual goals ahead of team goals. Recognition of an individual on a team is always a potential disrupter of group cohesion. In U.S. fire departments, there is a well understood professional norm that an individual firefighter should avoid publicity that characterizes him or her as a hero. Almost all firefighting and rescue work requires members of work teams to work closely with one another in situations in which loss of life is always a possibility. Therefore, it has become important for firefighters to put team goals ahead of individual goals. As a consequence, team recognition in the newspaper is acceptable, but individual recognition is shunned.

Bargaining and Negotiation: A Formal Procedure for Resolving Conflict in Small Groups

Thus far in the book, we have been explaining small group communication as it occurs in a typical problem-solving group or an everyday work group with a common task that can be achieved only through intermember cooperation. There are other types of groups within organizations. One group that is unique is the bargaining or negotiation group. The typical decision-making group in an organization certainly has conflict in reaching agreement on a decision, but we assume that most of that conflict is cognitive, ideational, role, or personal in nature. We assume that the group members share common goals and motives and that they are all seeking to find the best solution. A bargaining or negotiation group has an added dose of conflict that makes the communication process different from that of ordinary decision-making groups in an organization.

Bargaining or negotiation groups tend to have members who are "representative" of other groups. Often the group members come to the negotiation meeting with conflicting proposed outcomes, and the bargaining or negotiation group must somehow reach a compromise on an outcome (McGrath 1984).

We have studied the communication patterns of bargaining and negotiation and have found groups to be quite different from Fisher's explanation of the four-stage development of a task group (1970). It appears that bargaining groups go through three communication stages in the process of reaching an agreement: (1) at the beginning of the bargaining session, the negotiators engage in a lot of information gathering and some rather careful compiling of facts that relate to the case; (2) the second phase is characterized by a great deal of argumentative conflict in which the participants argue strongly for their prediscussion preferred outcomes; (3) if concessions are made and it appears that a compromise can be reached, the bargainers then begin to introduce interpersonal communication with more positive statements about each other (Douglas 1962; Putnam and Jones 1982; Putnam and Roloff 1992). Sometimes groups simply become deadlocked in their negotiations. In 1960, Osgood (1962) developed a model for reducing the communication impasse; he called the model GRIT (gradual, reciprocal, international tension-reduction). Basically, this model calls for one side in the dispute to make a small concession in hopes that the other side will reciprocate. Osgood argues that building on success, the combatants can incrementally move toward settlement through reciprocal concession. If this fails, bargaining and negotiation groups turn to a third party and ask them to intervene in either arbitration or mediation. Federal mediators frequently are asked to solve labor-management disputes. In fact, the very threat of bringing in a third party can instill enough fear in the two sides to make them work toward an agreement.

Social psychologists have been studying the variables that affect the outcome of bargaining and negotiation groups. They found that when the group members regard themselves as formal representatives of some outside group (e.g., a union), these group members are more competitive, make fewer concessions, and are less likely to reach agreement than group members who do not regard themselves as representatives of a formal outside group (McGrath 1984, 99). In addition, bargaining groups have a harder time reaching a settlement if their members were elected by a constituency, if members of an outside group observed them negotiating, if the group member has made prior commitments to his or her group before the decision is reached, and if there has been a history of distrust among the negotiation members from past bargaining sessions (McGrath 1984).

There are entire courses that focus exclusively on communication and negotiation; indeed, you can receive a master's degree in industrial negotiations at some universities. Certainly this book cannot teach you how to conduct yourself professionally as a negotiator, but it does provide much advice on how to resolve and manage conflict that occurs in decision-making groups that ostensibly have a common group goal. Much group conflict can be reduced by following the ethical precepts explained in Chapter 5. Interpersonal conflict can be greatly reduced if group members avoid the deviant personal behaviors explained in Chapter 6. In Chapters 4 and 5, we explained how ideational conflict can be managed by using techniques such as nominal grouping, which separates ideas from people and idea generation from idea criticism. We also explained how to construct and refute the four basic types of argument. However, residue conflict resulting from the competition that organizations create among groups and among group members still remains. Resultant conflict can be caused by continuous disagreement of group members over the goals, problem analysis, and proposed solutions. Therefore, it is necessary for you to possess additional communication skills that will help you manage group conflict and build espirit de corps in your group. The rest of this chapter is directed toward this end.

☐ STRATEGIES FOR REDUCING GROUP CONFLICT

As we indicated earlier, the first eight chapters of this book presented scores of ways to manage group conflict. In this section, we introduce you to three more strategies: using negotiation and bargaining styles, managing professional consciousness states, and conducting team-building organizational rallies.

Using Negotiation and Bargaining Styles

Historically, students were trained in problem-solving discussion to search cooperatively for the best answer. Yet our observations of actual problem-solving groups indicate that all group members do not come to the discussion with the same degree of cooperativeness, nor are all group members as assertive about their opinions. Kilmann and Thomas (1975) developed a categorization of negotiation and bargaining styles based on a person's willingness to cooperate and his or her willingness to assert his or her position. They label these styles as follows: competing (forcing), collaborating (problem solving), compromising (sharing), avoiding (withdrawal), and accommodating (smoothing).

Competing If you use a competing style when you bargain or negotiate, you are assertive about what you want from the group and you are not willing to compromise your basic beliefs to reach a settlement. You view group discussion on a problem as basically a win-loss situation: either your viewpoint wins out or you lose. You marshal evidence and argument to prove the correctness of your view, and you use whatever legitimate or expert power you have to get the group to see things your way. You invariably are involved in a struggle of leadership in the group.

Collaborating Collaborating is the opposite of avoiding. If you use this style, you are approaching a group discussion with the philosophy that everybody can win. You are prepared to immerse yourself in the complexities of the issues or interpersonal conflicts, as the case may be, with an eye toward a solution. You will not hesitate to bring all the issues to the surface and get them out on the table because you have a basic belief in the group's ability to reach an agreement that maximizes the benefits for everyone.

Compromising When using a compromising style, you may be seeking a quick solution to the conflict. Your strategy is to explore what concessions need to be made by all parties to reach agreement. You believe not everyone can get everything they want, especially if consensus is to be reached. If you are using this style, you may find yourself in a leadership struggle, especially if someone else is using a competing style, because you are trying to continually resolve conflict. Collaboration is marked by a creative solution; compromise is marked by an expedient solution (Kilmann and Thomas 1975).

Avoiding If you adopt this negotiation style in a group, you are adopting what firefighters call a "stay low and go" philosophy. Fire officers advise rookies that when they face more fire than they can handle, the only safe place with oxygen is on the floor; so they recommend that the firefighters stay low and get out of there! The avoiding style is unassertive and uncooperative. When you use this style, you gingerly duck or postpone any confrontation. People with little organizational power or without firm beliefs in how the problem should be solved often adopt this approach to conflict situations. This style blends most closely with the silent observer role.

Accommodating If you find yourself frequently using an accommodating style, you tend not to assert your own personal view; in fact, you may avoid taking positions in the discussion that would create controversy. You are willing to set aside your own views on how the problem should best be solved to reduce ideational and interpersonal tensions. You quickly cooperate with people who have a legitimate power and expert knowledge. Using this style, it is easy for you to play the social-emotional leader in the group.

Managing Professional Consciousness States

In Chapter 2, we explained that CR talk is a naturally occurring part of all group discussions and that all groups do a certain amount of Stage Two "we-they" communication. CR talk produces group pride and identity, which can potentially conflict with upward, downward, and lateral "theys." However, not all members are at the same level of group consciousness. In fact, creating a group consciousness for new members and raising the sustaining consciousness of old members are continual sources of conflict. In U.S. organizations, experienced professionals usually refer to five classic states of professional consciousness: burnout, young Turk, "old buffalo," company loyalist, and cynic.

Burnout A burnout has no professional consciousness—it has literally been "burned out" of him or her. In movies and novels, this person sometimes is portrayed as an employee who had fought the good fight at one time but is no longer capable of rallying any professional pride to do the job. He or she is just putting in his or her time until retirement. Certain professional work groups produce a higher percentage of burnouts than others. Police, paramedics, high school teachers, and computer programmers are occupations in which burnout is an occurrence. Also, if a person comes into a job highly consciousness-raised, it is difficult to maintain such professional intensity for a whole career. Thus, anybody in an occupation or any group is potentially susceptible to becoming a burnout. If you have burnouts in your group, you don't expect them to do much work. If they have paid their dues in the past, you tend to protect them.

Young Turk A young Turk is known not by his or her chronological age but by his or her consciousness. We personally know young Turk professors in their sixties and seventies. A young Turk is a highly consciousness-raised group member. If there is no fire in the eyes of a burnout, a young Turk's eyes are blazing. A young Turk is constantly seeking ways to improve the group and raise its status in the organization. Young Turks are quick to act out Stage Four consciousness against the group's "theys," particularly if it means conflict with the "theys." Also, young Turks have a tendency to be impatient and ostracize group members who are not performing at high levels of productivity or at as high a level of exuberance as they do. Thus, young Turks want to ostracize burnouts, and they constantly challenge "old buffaloes" to be more assertive. Young Turks are valuable group members who can raise the level of productivity and pride in the group; but if they are not tempered, they can push the group into burnout or too much conflict with other groups in the organization.

"Old Buffalo" "Old buffaloes" provide stability to the consciousness of the group. An "old buffalo" possesses a level of group pride that is sufficient to do acceptable work in the group for long periods of time. An "old buffalo" puts in a reliable eight hours of work and then leaves his or her professional identity at the work place—as contrasted with a young Turk, who wants to engage in professional talk after work each night as well as intensely at every weekend party. An "old buffalo" tells a young Turk that he or she is too intense and might become a burnout; on the other hand, a young Turk thinks that an "old buffalo" is plodding along at too slow a pace. "Old buffaloes" collect the sacred stories of the group and usually have a good long-range perspective of the group's role in the organization. "Old buffaloes," in addition to providing stability, are excellent at orienting new members to the group and minimizing conflict the work group might have with competing groups in the organization.

Company Loyalist You never hear of a company loyalist actively participating in Stage Two of a CR session. Company loyalists never ventilate about upward "theys" (supervisors), competing "theys" (competing work groups), or downward "theys" (people being served). They embrace an almost static state of group euphoria. Everything about their professional identity is OK every day they work. A company loyalist is the "milk and cookies" person of the organization: he or she has a Pollyanna view of company life. A person who is a company loyalist represents a kind of ideal state of professional contentment in a group. This level of consciousness oftentimes does not seem credible to other group members. People in other consciousness states often try to provoke the company loyalist into saying, in a fit of righteous indignation, something derogatory about the organization or a competing work group. The company loyalist is an important counterweight to the cynic.

Cynic A person who has a cynical state of consciousness in the group has a contemptuous distrust of the company: the group's CR and rally talk are seen as merely one more way to falsely motivate workers. A cynic does not want to be part of a symbolic "we" and would prefer to be independent of all group and organizational influence. As a consequence, a cynic will not only graphically attack the "theys" of a group; he or she will also attack the positive symbolic "we" of the group as hubris.

The cynic can play a valuable role in forming a group's professional consciousness, in that he or she keeps the group humble. However, a cynic left unchecked can demoralize a group's pride and shake the confidence of new members.

Conducting the Team-Building Organizational Rally

You have probably participated in several organizational rallies—a pep rally before an athletic event at your school or a political rally to focus attention on some social issue on your campus. As it turns out, all human rallies appear to contain the same communication elements, whether they are political, religious, or corporate rallies (Cragan and Shields 1981, 189–191). In the 1980s, many U.S. and certainly most large Japanese corporations have placed renewed emphasis on the corporate rally as a means of raising the corporate consciousness and building group organizational pride. We define a corporate rally as *a large group communication process that synchronizes with the stages of small group CR sessions to reinforce the "oneness" of a small group in the corporate culture*. The process, which we are sure you have participated in and observed numerous times, has five steps when done correctly.

Step 1. *Appropriate use of proxemics*. For rallies to have their maximum effect it appears that the participants need to be crowded together in one space—be it a room, an auditorium, an athletic stadium, or a shopping-mall atrium. The room must be small but not too small. This is also important if the event is being televised. People seeing the rally on TV judge its success or failure, in part, on whether the room is crowded or not. People who are responsible for picking the hotel or corporate convention center for rallies have high on their list of priorities the availability of a large space that they can fill with company employees, but not overfill. For example, if the corporation is holding its annual sales meeting and the planners anticipate 2,000 attendees, they do not want to hold their rally in a convention center that holds 8,000 because the presence of thousands of empty seats will have a dampening effect on the company's ability to consciousness-raise. On the other hand, if they select a room that seats only 1,500 and the ventilation is bad, it will also be difficult to "rally" the employees.

Step 2. *Appropriate use of music and banners*. Established organizations have already created over the years, through the process of small group CR and large group rallies, a common identity that is well understood by organizational members (Bormann 1983). Along with the organization tradition, it has been the custom to use music and banners to help reinforce the *we-ness*. Over time, organizations have what they regard as "appropriate" music and banners for their rallies. University graduations contain music, banners, and robes that relate to the pomp and circumstance of long-term learning.

Step 3. *Appropriate use of preliminary speakers*. The political, religious, or corporate rally builds toward the major speaker. In addition to proxemics and music and banners, warm-up speakers are used to "warm up" the audience for the ideas the featured speaker will provide. We call this the John the Baptist role, in that John was loved but not the beloved. He helped to prepare the way for Jesus Christ. In the same way, preliminary speakers must be linked by the audience, but their speech-making powers should not overshadow those of the main speaker. We tend to remember the times when the "baptizing speaker" is better than the main speaker. Each time Paul

Schaffer gets more laughs than David Letterman, Letterman threatens to fire him. At musical concerts if the warm-up group is better than the superstar you came to hear, the audience feels let down when the main group is performing. The same is true of speech making at rallies. National political conventions allow us to see this phenomena at work every four years. The John the Baptist error occurs frequently. In 1972, at the National Democratic Convention, the keynote speech of Barbara Jordan outshone George McGovern's acceptance speech. Other examples include Ted Kennedy's preliminary speech before President Carter's acceptance speech in 1980 and Governor Mario Cuomo's keynote before Mondale's speech in 1984. What these three preliminary speakers did was to portray the consciousness of Democrats vividly, in a more skillful and persuasive way than the superstars who followed them. When corporations are holding their annual sales meeting, it's important that the warm-up speeches only prepare the way for the featured speaker and not take the limelight away for the rally to have its maximum effect.

Step 4. *Appropriate use of the featured speaker.* The major speaker should need no introduction at a rally. Everyone is waiting for the featured speaker. At a religious crusade, Billy Graham would be instantly recognizable. President Reagan's persona would precede him at a Republican gathering. What is true of religious and political rallies is true of a corporate rally. At the Mary Kay Cosmetics annual rally, the rally participants would be eagerly awaiting Mary Kay's speech. The same would be true of a speech given by Ed Rust, Jr. at a State Farm rally.

The mere face-to-face presence of a major superstar has a major CR effect in and of itself. However, for the communication process of the rally to have its maximum impact, the featured speaker's message should contain three elements that draw their persuasive strength from Stages Two, Three, and Four of the small group CR process in which the audience would have participated numerous times preceding this rally. In a Lee Iacocca speech, we would expect references to the Japanese competition, low productivity, and government regulations (Stage Two) that had been standing in the way of Chrysler's growth. He would then go on to describe the new identity of the Chrysler worker (Stage Three) and how he or she had overcome the economic and production barriers. Finally, he might fashion some dramatic statements that might be the theme for this year's new sales program that had previously been discussed in smaller sessions of Chrysler management (e.g., "We're Back!" at Chrysler, or State Farm's "Join the Apple Core"). In a religious crusade, a featured speaker like Billy Graham would focus on sin (Stage Two), the good Christian (Stage Three), and proselytizing (Stage Four) with new Christian behavior.

Step 5. *Appropriate use of collective action.* The last stage of a rally is the same as the last stage of a small group CR session, which is to reinforce the oneness of the consciousness through collective behavior. At a Billy Graham rally, participants are asked literally to get out of their seats and go forth and accept Christ. At a university graduation, students come forth and receive their diplomas. At political rallies and corporate sales rallies, music is played, slogans are shouted, balloons are released, and people march from the hall with the clear purpose of electing their candidate or increasing sales.

Organizations that survive for a long time have developed a balance between small group CR sessions and organizational rallies. If an organization continually holds small group CR sessions and numerous rallies through the year, it will be able to induce a high intensity among its workers. However, there will be a tendency for workers to "burn out" (Bormann 1983). Organizations like Century 21 in real estate, Amway in home products, and Mary Kay in cosmetics create highly motivated sales forces through intense CR sessions and organizational rallies; but they also have high turnover because it is difficult for most people to maintain a highly raised consciousness over a long period. In contrast, corporations like Upjohn, 3M, and State Farm have created identities for their sales forces that are founded on lifelong commitment, with significantly fewer doses of CR sessions and rallies. These organizations seem to have a larger proportion of lifelong sales personnel. The same is true of political and religious organizations. Traditional political organizations, such as the Republican and Democratic national parties, maintain a corps of political operatives as compared with third parties that burn brightly but for a short period. These organizations are indicative of groups that cannot sustain CR over time.

Although many organizations (business, political, and religious) have created formal CR groups and have carefully designed mass rallies to interface with them, most groups spontaneously create CR episodes in their day-to-day group meetings, and organizational rallies may have evolved over time on a "hit-or-miss" basis without much planning on the part of management—they merely adopted practices that worked. We hope that you will be able to recognize when your everyday work group, whether it is a classroom group or a planning group in a company, slips into CR discussion. All people who participate in groups need a sense of group identification and pride, and CR talk is the communication process by which this is achieved.

☐ RESOLVING GROUP CONFLICT THROUGH TEAM-BUILDING COMMUNICATION SKILLS

Through the first eight chapters, we have identified ninety specific communication skills you need to perform competently to be a successful member of a decision-making group. These communication skills fall under the headings of problem solving, role playing, trust building, and team building. In Chapter 3, we explained five core team-building skills: build group pride, create symbols and slogans, establish group traditions, tell sacred stories, and initiate group fantasies. In this chapter, we add ten team-building skills that help to build group pride and manage group conflict.

■ *Move your group away from a mode of advocacy to a spirit of inquiry.* The less a decision-making group resembles a formal negotiation group, the less the potential for harmful conflict. Also, it is possible to produce more ideational conflict in a context of reflective thinking. If your group persists in a mode of advocacy, you need to increase the amount of factual information (Marr 1974) and increase the amount of time the group is in face-to-face interaction (Putnam and Jones 1982). These two efforts will help to reduce unnecessary conflict, especially when a group has taken on a formal negotiation form.

■ *Work toward a compromising or collaborating negotiation style.* Most decision-making groups in organizations do not long tolerate a competing style of leadership unless it happens to involve a powerful appointed leader. On the other hand, groups lose respect for members who constantly exhibit an accommodating or avoiding style. Thus, in most groups, you should try to be assertive and cooperative.

■ *Avoid extreme CR states in a group.* The normative CR state or a work group ideally should be a blend of young Turk, "buffalo," loyalist, and cynic consciousness. If the group is all young Turk, its decisions may be too radical. If it's all old buffalo, the decision may be too incremental. If the group is all loyalist, the group may only restate the status quo. And if the group becomes too cynical or burned out, the group won't arrive at a decision. In addition, a work group should not raise its consciousness so high that it cannot sustain it. Otherwise, the group will experience professional burnout. Too many team rallies can make the group dysfunctional.

■ *Build group pride on work behavior.* A few years ago, we were doing some consulting for Goodyear Tire and Rubber Company in Akron, Ohio. We encountered a proud and productive research team. The team consisted of five men in their late twenties who had all graduated from the University of Illinois. Illini pennants and coffee mugs were displayed everywhere. The group had a tradition of returning to the University of Illinois for homecoming as part of their work group celebration. This group had built its symbolic identity on quicksand. As soon as one of them leaves and the new market analyst turns out to be from Purdue or Ohio State, the group's identity will be in crisis. She or he might be rightfully proud of being a Boilermaker or a Buckeye, and she or he might not like going to Illini football games. This marketing team should have built its identity on work behavior and not college traditions. It's hard to predict what fantasies will chain out to form a group's heroic persona, but discourage ones that celebrate one gender or race or religion or, as in the example above, school. As long as the identity is built on work skills, anybody who can do the job well can be a member. In this way, you will reduce a potential source of group conflict.

■ *Work against premature consensus.* Irving Janis's work on groupthink shows us that proud and productive groups that are effectively led must guard against premature consensus or the quality of their work will suffer. This is especially true when the group deals with complex problems. In addition to ensuring that the central negative role is played, you may want to encourage the use of a formal agenda system that will facilitate an analysis of the problem and a consideration of the advantages and disadvantages of proposed solutions. At the very least, the functional theory of group decision making shows that the quality of the group decision will improve if your communication skills are competently performed: analyze the problem, develop a number of proposals, and carefully assess the pros and cons of each proposal (Gouran, Hirokawa, McGee, and Miller 1993; Hirokawa 1985, 1988). The groupthink syndrome highlights the potential tension between group consensus and the quality of group work. It shows us that effective team-building talk and leadership talk can potentially inhibit problem-solving talk.

■ *Engage in face-saving behavior.* Nobody likes to appear foolish in the presence of colleagues—something often referred to as "losing face." The best way to ensure that group members do not lose face is to develop and use communication strategies that transfer ownership of ideas from individuals to the group. If the group rejects an idea of its own, it's much easier to tolerate than if the group rejects an idea that is intellectually, emotionally, and politically identified with one of its members. In newly formed groups or in groups where there is little trust, nonthreatening small group techniques and agenda systems are the best methods to use to keep a group member from losing face. For example, the nominal group technique would be a nonthreatening procedure because it separates people from their ideas and idea generation from idea criticism. However, even in well-established groups where there is a great deal of trust, you must remember to criticize ideas, not people, and to treat each idea with intellectual respect and curiosity. Finally, one of the clear advantages of cyborg meeting groups is that idea generation and criticism can remain anonymous. Yet even in these types of meetings, it is important for the group to take ownership of the ideas in terms of their acceptance and rejection.

■ *Encourage reciprocal communication.* Despite the best efforts of group members, a work group frequently can fractionalize and polarize around clusters of ideas in attempting to reach a group decision. In formal negotiating teams, this always occurs. One of the best communication skills to use is incremental reciprocity. Putnam and Holmes (1992) suggest that about 40 percent of the time, group discussants will reciprocate in kind; that is, if you compromise a little, others will compromise a little. As the adage goes, one good turn deserves another. Another truism about group work is that all group members must compromise something of themselves for the good of the group. If you show willingness to sacrifice, others will reciprocate.

■ *Signpost ideas.* When a group is reaching a decision, sometimes it is important to identify certain issues as nonnegotiable. If you truly believe that some issues cannot be negotiated, then the earlier in the discussion you identify them, the better (Semlak 1982). You frequently can hear an example of signposting communication by listening to three students negotiating over the particulars of renting an off-campus apartment. One student might quickly indicate that she will not share her bedroom with another roommate, while another student insists that she will not live in a basement apartment, and the third negotiator signposts being within walking distance of the campus. These three students may compromise on such things as price of the apartment, furnishings, and guests after midnight, but they have signposted early in the discussions that a private bedroom, no basement apartment, and walking distance to campus are not negotiable. Although you are expected to sacrifice some for the group good and be a good team player, you should not be expected to compromise on ideas that work against your vital self-interest.

■ *Assess individual risk-taking ability.* To maintain group solidarity and avoid harmful conflict and potentially hazardous group outcomes, a group must assess each member's ability to risk the consequences of the group's activities and decisions. As it is said on the streets, "don't do the crime if you can't do the time," or as it is said on Wall Street, "don't invest money you can't afford to lose." Several years ago, we were members of a faculty group that had to confront the dean on several important issues. The group agreed to drop two untenured professors from the team because if the dean retaliated with extreme prejudice, the untenured professors could be fired, whereas tenured professors could not. On spring break, you might decide, even though you are an inexperienced diver, to join a group of avid scuba divers for a week of coral reef diving in the Caribbean. Your safety and that of other group members may well depend on the group's capacity to assess your risk-taking abilities. Have you ever made a dive over 100 feet? Have you ever swum into an underwater cave? Without making a risk assessment, the group might decide after an evening of CR talk to explore a cave that is 120 feet under water. Too much team-building talk might subject you to a life-threatening dive. It is important for groups to assess the risk-taking abilities of each member.

■ *Conduct identity renewal meetings.* Decision making extracts a toll on a group's professional identity. Some group members will feel unappreciated, others overworked. In addition, organizations generate internal group conflict because they require teamwork but tend to reward individuals. After months of working together, groups can reduce unnecessary conflict by holding identity renewal meetings. These meetings are minirallies in which an outside speaker, preferably an executive from the organization, praises the group's work, pointing out its importance to the overall organizational goals. This meeting is predominantly a CR meeting in which the group focuses on Stage Three issues. It is a good idea to hold renewal meetings away from the regular meeting rooms and, ideally, in a secluded place like a lodge or retreat center.

☐ SUMMARY

This chapter examines the pervasive concept of conflict as it is manifested in small groups. Two macro phenomena, risky shift and groupthink, provide anchors on a general continuum of conflict. There are instances in which groups are more willing to take risks than are individuals. On the other hand, groups can become so agreeable and individuals can all start thinking so much alike that groupthink is the product, at the expense of the ideas-in-conflict process.

Our presentation of the risky-shift phenomenon led us to the following generalizations: (1) it appears that risk taking is more topic-bound than group-bound; (2) group decisions affect decision making; and (3) organizational culture probably influences risk-taking behavior in groups. We made some recommendations to assist your small groups in avoiding the debilitating effects of groupthink: (1) encourage ideational conflict, (2) assist in the development of the central negative role, (3) guard against leader domination of ideas, and (4) keep CR within limits so that outside ideas contrary to the group's ideas will be more easily accepted.

Our discussion of communication conflict inherent in the organizational context focuses on cooperation and competition in and among work groups. Reward strategies and resource distribution procedures are stressed. Bargaining and negotiation are discussed as a formal procedure for resolving conflict in organizations. We also explain organizational rallies as a means of reducing conflict. Finally, we present ten communication skills that reduce group conflict and enhance group pride.

Station House Number Six

CASE BACKGROUND

Captain William Foley has just returned from a meeting called by the battalion commander (BC). At this meeting, station captains were instructed to discuss major personnel and management problems. The captains identified three major problem areas:

1. A conflict between suppression firefighters and those assigned to rescue squads and ambulances. A special point of contention here was the division of labor regarding housekeeping chores.

2. Fire department standards have been changed to accommodate mandatory minority quotas. This has led to what captains think is unusually harsh treatment of probationary firefighters.

3. Excessive transfer of personnel across firehouses and from one shift to another. Many firefighters believe that this has led to a reduction in the effectiveness of the firefighting team on the fireground, at times even endangering lives unnecessarily.

Each captain was instructed to discuss these three problem areas with a select group at his or her respective station. The personnel at Station Number Six who were asked to participate in the discussion were the following:

- Captain William Foley, 56, veteran, high school graduate, thirty years of service in the city fire department, captain of the firehouse
- Lieutenant Martin Vuttera, 35, veteran, high school graduate, graduate of EMT (emergency medical training), thirteen years of service in city fire department
- Firefighter Dennis Arnold, 31, college graduate, EMT-trained, six years of service in the city fire department
- Driver Engineer Jim Quinn, 46, veteran, high school graduate, twenty-two years of service in the city fire department, part-time electrician
- Firefighter Ed O'Bradovitch, 55, veteran, high school graduate, thirty-one years of service in the city fire department
- Firefighter Michael Murphy, 25, high school graduate attending junior college on a part-time ba-

sis, four years of service in the city fire department, son of a retired firefighter
- Probationary Firefighter Zachary Washington, 21, two years' duty in the U.S. Army Reserves, high school graduate, six months of service in the city fire department

CASE LOG

CAPT. FOLEY: The BC has instructed all the captains in his district to get feedback and suggestions from each house on these issues. The first issue is this constant fighting between the rescue squad and the rest of the house. I am tired of all the petty bickering that goes on. As far as I'm concerned, a firefighter is a firefighter is a firefighter, regardless of his or her job function.

QUINN: That's the point, Captain, we're all equal except that the rescue squad keeps asking for special privileges. For decades, it has been the tradition of firefighters to share housekeeping chores equally. Now, suddenly, the rescue squad wants to change these traditions.

ARNOLD: What's wrong with change? Twenty years ago there weren't rescue squads. The record supports our case. We make three times as many runs as you do. We don't have time to be doing dishes. If you're going to be putting an IV into someone's arm, you don't want your hand full of grease three minutes before you do it.

MURPHY: Look, Arnold, the reason you and Vuttera don't have time to do dishes is because you always hang around the hospitals after you make a run trying to make time with the nurses! Sometimes I think you regard yourselves as being on the hospital staff!

LT. VUTTERA: Now wait a minute, Murph! Before you even came into this department I did seven years on the back step of the engine company. So don't you tell me I am not a firefighter! What Arnold and I, and for that matter what the guys running rescue on other shifts, believe is that the amount of work we do in rescue demands a change in the traditional housekeeping rules.

CAPT. FOLEY: Vuttera, I want you and Arnold to present a plan as to what kind of changes you would recommend. We'll discuss your plan the next time we're on shift. Right now, I want to get to this second issue. Evidently the BC has been receiving complaints from probationary firefighters about harassment.

O'BRADOVITCH: Hey, Washington? You been crybabying to the brass?

WASHINGTON: I haven't but I probably should have! You make enough racial slurs in a day to have driven Martin Luther King to violence.

QUINN: We call Murphy "Shanty," and Vuttera "Dago." So if you can't take the heat, get out of the firehouse.

O'BRADOVITCH: You should have been around here when probationary firefighters really got initiated. You wouldn't have lasted a week!

CAPT. FOLEY: Outside of language, do you have any specific complaints, Washington? (Long silence)

WASHINGTON: No, sir.

CAPT. FOLEY: OK, let's get to the last item. The BC is hearing complaints about excessive transfer of personnel. Do you people have any complaints?

O'BRADOVITCH: Bill, you and I have served a lot of years together. I'm telling you, it's just not the same as it used to be. In the old days we used to work with the same people month in and month out, year after year. Everybody knew what everyone else was going to do on the fireground. Remember when I fell through two floors to the basement in that old warehouse on 43rd Street? I knew you would get me out of that fire! These young kids today! They move from one station house to another so fast, I don't even know their names. How can you trust them?!

QUINN: Foley, what are those "clowns" downtown trying to do? You go tell the battalion commander that we want a moratorium on transferring for a year.

MURPHY: I agree with Jim. No more transfers. They can stick those transfers in their bugles!

LT. VUTTERA: Captain, I think the deputy chiefs are not in touch. They don't know what is going on!

They don't know what's going on with rescue and they don't know what's going on when they transfer people.

ARNOLD: They're so dumb that every time we get some of the problems resolved in a house, they up and transfer half of us. What do you say let's start a petition for "no more transfers," and everybody sign it! How about you, Captain? Why don't you draw it up?

CAPT. FOLEY: No petitions! We're not starting any of that stuff in this house! I've got my time in, and I'll retire before I get involved with any of that "radical" stuff!

O'BRADOVITCH: I don't know, Bill. Whose side are you on? Maybe you're buckin' for chief instead of retirement?

CAPT. FOLEY: I'm not afraid to criticize the chief when he deserves it, but there have to be some departmental transfers. A moratorium just won't work.

QUINN: The point is, Captain, nothing ever works. There isn't a solution to this problem.

ARNOLD: I think there are changes that could make the transferring problem clearer. Despite our differences on rescue versus suppression, I think we are really a good work group. Captain, why don't you suggest to the chief that groups that can prove their excellence should be excluded from the policy?

CAPT. FOLEY: That's not a bad idea. Marty, are you keeping notes on what we're deciding?

LT. VUTTERA: Yeah, I've been keeping notes on everything that's been said.

CAPT. FOLEY: Good, then let's have Murphy and Washington draw up criteria for excluding our group from transfers and have it ready for the next meeting.

CASE QUESTIONS

1. Critique Captain Foley's management of this meeting. What did he do well? What could he have done better?
2. What CR states are discernible in this meeting?
3. What was Captain Foley's conflict-resolution style?

CHAPTER TEN

FACILITATING GROUP WORK IN ORGANIZATIONS

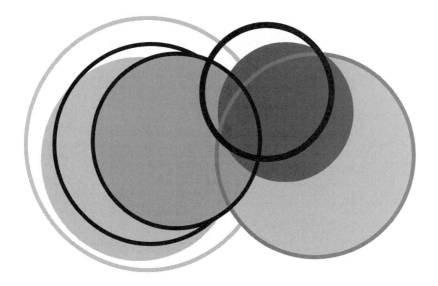

CHAPTER OBJECTIVES

After reading this chapter, you should be able to:

- Know the basic principles used to determine when to call a meeting
- Understand the unique features of each type of routine business meeting
- Understand the principles of intergroup communication
- Recognize the dominant management styles of the organization
- Learn the communication strategies for sustaining groups within the organizational culture

CHAPTER OUTLINE

SMALL GROUP BUSINESS MEETINGS
When and How to Call a Meeting
Types of Business Meetings

PRINCIPLES OF INTERGROUP COMMUNICATION

ASSIMILATION OF GROUPS INTO THE ORGANIZATIONAL CULTURE
Group Loyalty
X, Y, and Z Management Cultures
Intermingling of Groups
Socialization into the Whole
Organization

GUIDELINES FOR EFFECTIVE COMMUNICATION AMONG GROUPS WITHIN THE ORGANIZATION
Role of the Chief Executive Officer
Role of the House Organ
Role of Interpersonal Communication
Channels
Role of Humaneness
Work Groups Are Territorial
Group Goals and Organizational Objectives

SUMMARY

CASE STUDY: THOR DAVIS—UNIT MANAGER

This chapter focuses on the communication among groups in organizations. It is not our purpose to provide a comprehensive treatment of organizational communication but merely to suggest how the theory and practice of small group communication might have application to business and governmental organizations. The first nine chapters of the book present most of what we regard as important in terms of theoretical principles and techniques of small group communication. This chapter takes groups out of the classroom and the research laboratory and places them in the natural settings of business and governmental organizations. Putnam and Stohl (1990) argue that the proper place to study small groups is in an organizational context. They point out that people typically are members of work groups with permeable boundaries that separate them from other competing groups in the intergroup system. Furthermore, they explain the importance of understanding groups within the organizational context because workers typically have divided loyalties across several organizational groups and because the organization influences the decision making of a small group. We expect that at graduation, you will become a member of a small embedded group in an organization; thus, you need to understand intergroup communication.

☐ SMALL GROUP BUSINESS MEETINGS

Decades of consulting with American companies have made it clear that one of the major pet peeves of any employee is the business meeting. Employees think that there are too many of them and that they are poorly run. Mosvick and Nelson (1987) report the findings of a survey that collected managers' complaints about meetings. In David Letterman style, the Top Ten Reasons Why Managers Hate Meetings are as follows:

10. The meetings started late.

9. The meeting was a waste of time.

8. Irrelevant information was presented.

7. No one controlled the meeting.

6. The meeting was disorganized.

5. No conclusions were reached.

4. The leader was inadequately prepared.

3. The meeting was too long.

2. There was no agenda.

1. Some people kept getting off the subject.

In this section, we present five benchmarks you can use when you call a meeting. We also explain the four types of business meetings that any organization will expect you to know.

When and How to Call a Meeting

One of the first decisions you will make as a new supervisor is whether you should call a meeting. The temptation to call one is almost irresistible. Therefore, it is important to consider certain criteria to determine whether a meeting should be called. We recommend enumerating in your own mind the following benchmarks before deciding to call a meeting.

Mastering Time If the almighty dollar governs an organization, then the almighty clock governs the work within it. Time becomes money, and thus, from the organization's perspective, wasting time is a major fault. Moreover, you will find that everyone guards his or her own time jealously. When you call a meeting of a dozen people, you are taking up the time of twelve people who may think that you are wasting their time. So from both a personal and an organizational viewpoint, time is the overriding issue. In calling a meeting, you should be governed by the following seven time constraints.

- *Advance notice of meeting agenda.* Important meeting time can always be saved by sending out agenda and other helpful materials in advance of the meeting. This material should be as brief and succinct as possible and should be proportionate to the importance of the meeting. By that we mean participants should not be asked to read four hours of material to hold a fifty-minute meeting on a minor issue. In preparing for your meeting, think of how much time participants will have to spend in preparing for it, and govern your material accordingly.
- *Create a realistic agenda.* One of the worst things you can do is hand out a meeting agenda that is dead on arrival because you have more items on your agenda than you can reasonably cover in the time allotted. There is a simple way to make certain that the group gets through your agenda in the allotted meeting time. What you do is list each agenda item and classify it as a tell-sell-solve item or a consciousness-raising (CR) item. Then you estimate how much time you think each item will take, knowing that tell items take far less time than solve items. Table 10.1 classifies each agenda item.

TABLE 10.1   **Types of Agenda Items**

	Tell	**Sell**	**Solve**	**CR**
Objective	Leader wants to give information to the group	Leader wants to get acceptance by the group of a proposal	Leader wants to solve a problem by getting help from the group	Leader wants to heighten group members' pride in themselves, the group, and the organization
Group's background	Leader does most of the talking	Leader talks about half the time	Leader talks about 10 to 20% of the time after presenting the problem	Leader either encourages storytelling by group members or brings in guest speakers to brag on group
Group's role	Group listens most of the time	Group listens about half the time	Group does most of the talking	Group ranges from doing all to doing none of talking
Time allotment	Some discussion is necessary to clarify points of information	Discussion is necessary because people tend to believe something is of value or true if they can arrive at that conclusion in an open discussion with their colleagues	Maximum discussion is necessary because the solution to the problem comes from the sharing of knowledge and experience of those with special skills related to the problem	This type of meeting is necessary for building group members' needs to understand how their skills and dedication have played a role in the building of a quality product
Results	Group learns the leader's information	Group accepts the leader's proposal	Group helps to solve the leader's problem	Group feels a heightened sense of pride in their skills, abilities, and accomplishments

■ *Scheduling meetings at the best time.* Routine business meetings are fixed, often on a yearly basis, so that people can schedule around them. If you are setting up a fixed meeting time for a weekly meeting, try not to schedule it an hour before or after lunch on a Friday. If you think about how you schedule your classes at college, you know how meetings are scheduled in business settings. However, if you are putting together an ad hoc meeting, you will want to schedule it when you can get everyone together, and this may cause some inconvenience. The best way to find the right time to hold an ad hoc meeting is to send out a work calendar for the week and have the members check the work periods they have free.

■ *Starting and ending meetings on time.* Some participants of a meeting think that they can arrive a few minutes late, but they expect to come out on time. As an appointed leader of a group discussion, you can delegate everything but control of the clock. People will forgive your interruptions if it appears that you are trying to get them out on time. Also, if you delay the starting of your meetings ten minutes to accommodate the stragglers, you will soon discover that everyone is a straggler and your meetings always start late!

■ *Regulating participation.* As you recall, in Chapter 7, we discussed twenty leadership communication skills of which the regulation of participation was one. In our work with government and business organizations, one of the recurring complaints we hear about meetings is that a few people tend to dominate the meeting and that, consequently, there is not enough time for others to speak. You also recall that in Chapter 4, we recommended the nominal group discussion technique as one means of eliminating this complaint. The leader should do everything in his or her power to see that sufficient time is allotted to all participants in a fair manner.

■ *Getting the job done.* One of the common mistakes made in meetings is to have more on the agenda than there is time to cover. Leaving a meeting with an agenda half done when you had expected that the work would be accomplished is a frustrating experience. Your group goals should be cast in time frames. Don't prepare an agenda that you know you can't finish. As soon as you discover that you can't get through the agenda, set a new goal—such as to accomplish three out of five items.

■ *Meeting follow-up.* Although there are many reasons for a follow-up memo, one of them is to confirm that the members did not waste their time. When group members have worked hard and productively for several hours, they like to know that their efforts were appreciated and that the outcomes were beneficial. Make certain that you cover these two points in a follow-up memo.

Understanding Tradition When you are new to an organization, one of the more important things you need to understand is the tradition of meetings that has evolved and developed in the organization's history. You want to take note of what kind of day-to-day meetings are held, who calls the meetings, what problems get solved through the use of a group, what agendas are used, and what protocol is used for who gets invited to what meetings. A good starting point from which to gather this information is the memo correspondence that was left behind by your predecessor and the calendar of meetings attended during the past year. You may discover that you intentionally violate some of the norms established for group meetings, but you should at least be consciously aware that you are doing so and that you have good reason for making the change.

   If you go to work as a marketing researcher in some large organization, you might discover that you are expected to call a meeting to present the results of your research regarding a new product. The tradition of the company might call for you to begin the meeting with a twenty-minute slide show that concisely and graphically displays your findings. Therefore, if, unaware of the tradition, you sent out a thirty-page report in advance of the meeting and then attempted to lead a roundtable discussion about the product, with the vice-president of marketing as one of the participants, you might discover that nobody had read the report and that the vice-president was mad at you not only for "not doing your homework" but also for trying to usurp power. An examination of the tradition of the marketing division's meeting habits could have told you what is not written down in the company handbook: that a new product's group meeting in this company is an initiation ritual for new researchers. The tradition is that you show off your hard work by means of the twenty-minute slide show and then wait for interrogation by more experienced researchers, with the vice-president standing by.

Every organization has its own tradition of group meetings. We cannot enumerate all their variations in this textbook; however, you can discover them if you will spend time carefully researching the habits of the groups in your organization.

Being Productive After reviewing the research in the social sciences on group versus individual productivity, Shaw (1976, 78) concluded: "Groups usually produce more and better solutions to problems than do individuals working alone." Shaw's conclusion is tempered by certain necessary conditions. For example, groups do better than individuals if the problem calls for the creation of ideas or the recalling of information, if the load can be divided among members, and if the group members have an opportunity to identify and correct one another's ideas. Shaw's conclusion (1976, 79) also depends on most members having essentially the same knowledge base.

As you can see, there are a lot of strings attached to the conclusion that groups are better than individuals at solving problems. That is why it often is difficult for a supervisor to decide whether a given task should be assigned to a group or to an individual. For example, if the problem were how to develop architectural drawings for the new plant, it might be better to assign that task to the company's architectural engineer. An executive committee could provide input at the beginning and end of the project, but it would not be helpful to have people unskilled at architectural drawing doing the detail work. However, if a supervisor were in charge of an advertising agency that needed to develop a new ad for a soft drink company, she might conclude that a five-person work group of ad account supervisors would be better than one individual. She might even use the ideational techniques we discussed in Chapter 4.

Most of the real-world decisions that a group faces in assigning work to either a group or an individual are not as clear-cut as the two extreme examples cited above. What usually happens is that a subgroup is formed with broad responsibilities to decide what the division of labor will be—that is, which tasks should be performed by the group and which by an individual. As a work group develops some history, members start to work out this fundamental problem for themselves. There are two basic rules of thumb for resolving this problem: (1) If the group has a member who is much better than the rest, who is committed to the goals of the group, and who can solve some subaspect of the problem, he or she should be assigned the task. (2) Although groups are slower than individuals at completing tasks, there are some problems that the group must solve together. At a general level, the group members have to agree on their goals and their ability to do the work; moreover, they must make sure that the group's work is sufficient and good enough for public scrutiny.

Most groups produce more and better ideas than do individuals and reduce the chance of random error. Yet groups take more time to do their work. A supervisor must constantly weigh the trade-offs of time versus quality and may decide to settle for less quality to get a job done on time. Even when the best way to solve a problem qualitatively is by group effort, a supervisor may still decide that an individual should solve the problem, given the quantity of time the group would have to spend on it.

Maintaining Group Satisfaction Conscientious supervisors are always concerned with the morale of their subordinates. Meetings frequently serve as a focal point for boosting group morale and motivating workers to higher productivity levels. As we indicated in Chapter 2, corporations, particularly their sales divisions, hold CR sessions for their workers. Sometimes outside speakers are brought into the meeting to give inspirational speeches designed to raise the consciousness of the group. First and last meetings for project groups often are CR sessions that induce in individual members the feeling that they are satisfied to be members of the company.

Quarterly meetings in which the profits for the quarter are presented also produce membership satisfaction. It would be sufficient for the supervisor to send out the quarterly productivity figures by way of a memo, but what usually happens is that the work unit is brought together in a meeting, the data are flashed onto a wall, and the group shares in the general satisfaction with a job well done.

The membership satisfaction meeting often is overdone. In fact, we frequently see movies and TV programs with satires on the motivational meeting, in which the supervisor makes one more phony, incompetent plea for more productivity while the overworked group members sit disgruntled in the audience voicing snide remarks. Insincere or overdone motivational meetings are counter-productive; yet when a properly designed membership satisfaction meeting is planned, results for the organization and the individual can be beneficial.

In earlier chapters, we presented ways to help in the development of your group. Implicit in these suggestions is the notion that it is more rewarding for an individual to be praised for good work in the presence of fellow group workers than in private. Holding a group meeting in which rewards are presented may seem corny and group members will always say that they don't need the attention, but if the meeting is well planned and the rewards are meaningful and well chosen, the increase in membership satisfaction can be most dramatic. Group rewards are also important, especially if you can present them in the presence of other groups. The general point to remember here is that meetings often are held in which the major purpose is not productivity, but increased member satisfaction.

Gaining Group Consensus In the business world, people occasionally complain that a meeting was unnecessary because everybody had already agreed to the solution that was proposed at the meeting. However, consensus meetings are important. A group's final face-to-face discussion of a plan of action is important in terms of gleaning commitment from members on the group effort. The group may take an hour kicking the same old reservations about the room and in the end reach the predicted conclusion; however, the ritual of thrashing out all the "ifs" and "buts" is necessary if the members are to feel truly committed to the decision.

Knowing that face-to-face consensus produces commitment has caused some unscrupulous supervisors to call consensus meetings prematurely, thus restricting the time the group has to discuss alternate proposals. Forcing consensus on a group reduces membership satisfaction, and, ultimately, productivity. Consensus is an important group output, but it must flow naturally from the group. An experienced supervisor will delay the calling of a consensus meeting until it can be predicted that consensus is achievable; even then the supervisor will allow ample time for the group members to verbalize all the major issues before they commit themselves to the group decision.

Types of Business Meetings

There are four types of business meetings: Monday morning meetings, monthly meetings, decision-making meetings, and planning meetings. Each of these four fundamental types of meetings in business organizations is distinguished by its own leadership style, discussion format, and agenda system. In addition, each type can encounter unique, potential dangers during the course of routine meetings.

Monday Morning Meetings A routine weekly meeting within a formal organization usually calls for a "tell" leadership style on the part of the supervisor. If it is a Monday morning meeting, the supervisory group may have met the Friday before to hear their boss conduct a "tell" meeting in which information was transmitted down the hierarchical structure. Therefore, on Monday, the supervisor is acting as a communication conduit, transmitting directives from higher up in the organization. Most subordinates appreciate an efficient, task-oriented presentation of this information. You might ask, Why doesn't the supervisor just place this information in a memo or on a bulletin board? The answer is that most organizations have found that these are not reliable channels of information unless the content is reinforced by a face-to-face meeting between superiors and subordinates. Consequently, the Monday morning meeting was created.

City police and fire departments hold Monday morning types of meetings for each shift. The daily meeting is a microcosm of the weekly meeting in that the agenda is a random list of pertinent pieces of information that the work force must comprehend. Television programs frequently dramatize the tone and give-and-take of the typical Monday morning type of meeting, in which humorous one-liners often poke fun at the organization. The supervisor should not misunderstand the meaning of these jokes. The group still wants to receive organizational information firsthand, but it has become traditional in U.S. organizations that the supervisor should bear the brunt of some humor.

The typical hodgepodge agenda of a Monday morning meeting (Figure 10.1) might appear disjointed and incomprehensible to a person who is not a member of the work group.

There are two pitfalls that a supervisor should avoid when conducting Monday morning meetings. The first danger is that the meeting may become a social event in which the work force spends the first hour drinking coffee, eating rolls, and talking about what they did over the weekend. The group members will naturally fall into this conversational pattern and will object, sometimes loudly, when the supervisor drags them away from the social hour to the first point on the agenda. However, the supervisor is responsible for seeing that the meeting starts and ends on time, and

FIGURE 10.1   **Typical Agenda for a Monday-Morning Meeting**

MONDAY MORNING AGENDA

(8:30–8:45 A.M.)

    I. A reminder of OSHA regulations that have been consistently ignored (also posted on bulletin board).

    II. A restatement of production goals and deadlines for unit (10 percent ahead of last year).

    III. Form C needs to be filled out by Wednesday to qualify for additional life insurance coverage.

    IV. Mary delivered her baby last Thursday (8 lbs., 10 oz.). Send cards to City Memorial Hospital, Room 540.

    V. Anyone wishing to bowl in the company bowling league needs to sign up by Friday (nonrefundable $5.00 entry fee required).

both the organization and the work group eventually will hold him or her responsible if the task of the Monday morning meeting is not accomplished. Thus, the supervisor must maintain a "tell" leadership style in running Monday morning types of meetings.

The second danger to the supervisor of Monday morning meetings lies in not strictly regulating participation during the meeting. Almost any point on the agenda can provide sufficient stimulus for an hour-long group discussion. Occupational Safety and Health Administration (OSHA) regulations, production goals, and company social events can easily encourage the more verbal group members into heated discussion. If the supervisor allows these discussions to occur, the planned agenda will not get covered. Over time, the group members will become angry because they were not informed about issues that later proved to be important to them. So despite obstacles and temptations, the leader of a Monday morning meeting must tenaciously stick to the planned agenda and finish it within the brief time allotted.

Monthly Meetings Many organizations bring their work groups together in a formal meeting once a month. Although a monthly meeting has some characteristics in common with a Monday morning meeting, it also has several distinguishing characteristics. Supervisors of monthly meetings tend to adopt a "sell" leadership style. The meeting contains some elements of a CR session. Because the work group meets only twelve times a year, there is a need to spend some time celebrating the reasons for the group's existence and the fact that it is doing a good job.

With this goal in mind, monthly meeting agendas often contain guest speakers. If it is a monthly sales meeting, a vice president might attend to thank the members for the job they have been doing or an outside speaker may give an inspirational speech about the job they do. The agenda may also contain report presentations by several group members. The report presentation tradition is especially prevalent in civic and volunteer groups. Besides conveying information, the presentation of reports by different group members symbolizes the teamwork the group is maintaining.

FIGURE 10.2   **Typical Agenda for a Monthly Meeting**

PTA MONTHLY MEETING
(Thursday, 7:00–9:30 P.M.)

   I. Minutes of last meeting (Secretary)

  II. Reports by officers
     A. President
     B. Treasurer
     C. Historian

 III. Approval of Lincoln School Carnival budget (Marg Weston, Chairperson)

 IV. Principal's moment (Principal Edgar M. Norris)

  V. Presentation of School Board candidates (each allotted fifteen minutes of speaking time)

 VI. Question and answer period

VII. Reception

The leader of monthly meetings adopts a "sell" leadership style because he or she usually feels obliged to explain the group activities of the previous month and to sell the group on what must be done in the next month. Unlike the Monday morning meeting, there often is a period of general discussion on what the group thinks that it can reasonably accomplish over the next thirty days. A typical agenda for a monthly meeting is shown in Figure 10.2.

When a group does not meet on a weekly basis, the danger of a monthly meeting is that it might be used as a vehicle for ventilating the members' complaints. In the course of thirty days, any active group can develop a shopping list of gripes that might lock the group into Stage Two of a CR session, the "they" (i.e., the "enemy") often being the formal leadership of the group and the larger organization to which the group belongs. The designated leader of the monthly meeting must deal with some of the complaints that come from the floor but cannot allow these issues to dominate the meeting. The best way to avoid this problem is for the leader to use one or both of the following methods: agree to meet afterward with group members who have a complaint, or establish a policy that complaints must be brought to the leader a week in advance to become a formal part of the agenda. Such methods will allow the group to discuss major problems formally without becoming immersed in minor and ephemeral gripes.

Decision-Making Meetings Decision-making meetings require considerable leadership skills to run; they also involve distinct risks to the leader. The appointed leader of a group must deliberately decide whether he or she is willing to give up some formal authority and live with the results of a group decision. Group decisions often are better than individually made decisions, and membership satisfaction is increased when everyone participates in making decisions. However, the decision the group reaches may be quite different from the one the leader would make on his or her own. Some leaders try to straddle the fence by adopting a "sell" leadership style for a decision-making meeting. Nothing infuriates a group more than a leader who is trying to "engineer" a group's deliberations to some preordained conclusion.

In a decision-making meeting, the leader needs to adopt a participatory leadership style and be willing to live with the results of the group process. For the group to work effectively, members must receive advance information to discuss the issue effectively, and they must be given sufficient time to reach their conclusion.

The previous history of the group's decision-making experience is an important consideration. If the group is holding its first decision-making meeting, the leader will probably first have to use the nominal group discussion and brainstorming techniques described in Chapter 4 as a means not only for generating ideas and solutions to a problem, but also for increasing the participants' willingness to discuss with one another. On the other hand, if the decision-making group has a history of making decisions, the members have probably adopted their own recognizable pattern for wading through the issues and reaching consensus. The leader would be well advised in these instances to stay with the established procedure. However, most decision-making meetings bring together a group of people who do not fall at either end of the continuum; that is, they are neither a zero-history group nor a well-seasoned, decision-making group. In this middle range, a leader should develop a problem solving agenda as a rough outline for conducting the meeting. An adaptation of the Ross Four-Step Agenda (see Chapter 4) might be used by a decision-making group (Figure 10.3).

Groups hardly ever follow the planned agenda in a decision-making meeting. A leader should expect the group to digress into trivia and to jump around from causes

---

FIGURE 10.3   An Example of the Ross Agenda for a Decision-Making Group

THE ROSS AGENDA FOR A DECISION-MAKING GROUP

  I. Definition of problem
      -15 percent drop in overall production
      -5 percent drop in quality

 II. Analysis of problem
      -possible causes
      1. recent adoption of flextime
      2. increased use of part-time help
      3. antiquated machinery
      4. union contract problems

III. Criteria
      -solution must be attainable within six months
      -solution must meet budget constraints

 IV. Solutions: our primary task is to provide a good solution
      -possible solutions:
      1. ?
      2. ?
      3. ?

to criteria to solutions. Experience will tell a group leader when a group's meandering is excessive and needs to be controlled. Decision-making groups need a guiding hand as they work their way toward a solution. Thus, the planned agenda is a benchmark to measure how far the group has wandered from its major task and should be used as a reminder to the leader to get the group back on track.

If the chronology of the agenda system is rigidly enforced, the group will feel intimidated and the quality of the decision will probably be poor. Also, if a leader forces consensus, many group members may later work against the agreed-upon solution because they did not agree to it at the meeting. It is important that the leader take the time to reach genuine consensus or at least get a commitment from the people holding a minority view that they will work with the majority for the common good.

Planning Meetings Planning committees usually have a great deal of autonomy in structuring their activities and in reaching their final conclusions. The problem with being in charge of a planning committee is that the organization to which the committee belongs will probably react negatively or positively only after the plan has been submitted. This means that a planning committee may have put in hundreds of hours of work and become strongly committed to a plan that might ultimately be rejected by the larger organization. Another problem the leader of a planning committee has is lack of enthusiastic participation on the part of all the members. If a leader is not careful, the workload for planning can easily become a one-person job—his or hers!

Successful planning committees typically go through three phases. The first phase, which sometimes constitutes a whole meeting, calls for the leader to adopt a "tell and sell" leadership style to explain the planning project to the group members and convince them that each of them has an important role to play. A second phase requires the leader to change to a participatory leadership style to gather the information necessary for the group to plan properly. The third phase is the structuring of the activities that the planning committee will perform to reach its final goal. This phase demands that the leader adopt a delegating leadership style because members will be required to work independently on subparts of the plan.

The planning of a company picnic calls for the enactment of all three phases of a planning committee's life cycle. The leader must convince the members that a complaint-free picnic can really be produced if everyone works hard. Next, the leader must join the committee in listing all the important jobs that go into putting on a company picnic. Finally, the committee will need to draw up a modified program evaluation and review technique (PERT) agenda (Figure 10.4) to see that all their efforts are coordinated and that the picnic comes off successfully.

Because a planning committee requires a great deal of planning outside a formal meeting structure, it is necessary for the leader to contact the group members individually to ensure that the reports will be presented on time in meeting the PERT chart schedules. It is also important that influential members of the organization be approached for their reactions to the preliminary thinking of the planning committee. This will ensure that the committee's results do not come as a surprise to the organization and, conversely, that the reaction of the organization to the plan does not come as a surprise to the committee. Sometimes this need for communication between the planning committee and the organization it serves is formalized when an

FIGURE **10.4**   **A Modified PERT Agenda for a Company Picnic**

   I. The goal is the holding of the company picnic.

   II. Events that must occur before picnic can occur:
   -reserving pavilion
   -determining games and programs
   -collecting awards and prizes
   -securing entertainment
   -determining the kinds of food and beverage needed and purchasing them
   -determining who is eligible to come to the picnic
   -assessing company for funds for picnic

   III. Determining the order of events before the picnic is held

   IV. PERT planning chart for picnic

   V. Time needed

   VI. Determine critical path

opinion questionnaire is distributed by the planning committee, seeking information and reaction from the organization. However, most of the time, a planning committee tests its ideas informally in the organization.

□ Principles of Intergroup Communication

The circulatory system of the human body provides a rough analogy for comprehending the importance of information flow in an organization. If information in an organization is not being effectively pumped up from the production groups to the decision-making groups, the effect on the organization is the same as if oxygenated blood is cut off from the brain. If blood does not reach the body's extremities, they soon cease to respond to directions from the brain. Likewise, if information is not accurately transmitted from decision-making groups down to the production groups, work does not get done. Just as the arteries carry the blood to different parts of the body, formal channels such as interdepartmental memos and face-to-face meetings carry information that is the lifeblood of an organization.

Although blood is needed for life, too much of it in one place at one time in the body can produce a hemorrhage. So it is with organizations, in that information overload can occur if too much information gets pumped into a given group. The worst kind of hemorrhage is cerebral. Thus, most organizations attempt to be efficient with respect to the amount of information that their key decision-making committees use. To understand the use of information in a small group, it is necessary to understand how groups fit into the organizational structure of companies.

Ordinarily we think of information as flowing either up and down or laterally in an organization; furthermore, we think of this information as being transmitted in formal and informal channels. One starting point for analyzing information in small groups in organizations is to begin with the first-line supervisor and the work group he or she manages.

The first principle to understand about intergroup communication within an organization is that each group does not communicate all its information to the rest of the organization, nor does the organization communicate all its information upward. Thus, we find that a first-line supervisor does not transmit upward all that he or she knows about his or her group. There are group secrets that never leave the group. For example, in a firefighter group, there may be an older member who can no longer perform the job well; however, the rest of the group protects him or her, and the information remains a group secret. Sometimes a production group in a factory knows the most timesaving way to manufacture a product, but the information is kept secret for fear that production quotas will be raised if the information gets out. When the first-line supervisor goes to meetings with other first-line supervisors, in effect another group is formed. In this group, the first-line supervisors have privileged information that the group does not want to go up or down the organization. Thus, we can see that information is filtered, and there is never one place in an organization where all information is stored.

The second principle is that all managers in an organization are formally members of at least two groups, and thus must keep some information from each of the groups of which they are a member. This principle causes most managers to experience the "between a rock and a hard place" syndrome. The first-line supervisor's work group wants its manager to disclose all his or her information to them; yet if the first-line supervisor does so, the organization will begin to distrust the supervisor, and dismissal will follow. Also, if the first-line supervisor does not disclose any organizational secrets to his or her work group, the workers will not trust their supervisor, and he or she will soon have no information to pass upward. Thus, all managers between the basic production group and the president of the organization must maintain a communication balancing act because of their multigroup membership within the organization. And the more formal groups a supervisor belongs to, the more difficult it is to juggle information so as to maintain the loyalty of the respective group members. For example, if a university professor is chairing an academic department and serving on a university budget committee, that person is a member of three formal organizational groups: the academic department, the college council of department chairs, and the university budget committee. The budget committee has information that it would not want directly communicated to the department—for example, tentative allocations of monies for summer school. The department has information it does not want communicated to the dean's college council of chairs—for example, the frequent classroom absences of an older professor. The college council of chairs has information that it does not want to go down to the department or up to the university budget committee—for example, tentative plans for adoption of flextime for civil service employees in the college. Maintaining loyal membership in each of these three groups is difficult for the professor because all groups in an organization have an insatiable appetite for information. In fact, the *third principle of intergroup communication in organizational settings is that groups constantly crave more information because information is power.* Thus, span of control—that is, the statement of how much horizontal power a manager has—is an important organizational concept. However, because there are limits to the number of groups in which a person can maintain membership and from which he or she can receive reliable information, organizations constantly adjust the number of groups a person is responsible for.

Presumably, the higher up one is in an organization, the more power one has. But this power is in fact information, and information is filtered at each level as it goes up or down. Thus, an organization could be stacked so high that the executives become powerless because they do not have access to enough reliable information. This problem of executive powerlessness is also a problem of the chain of command through which information flows vertically.

Within the formal structure of organizations, information flows both horizontally and vertically, but not effortlessly or accurately. Each group maintains proprietary rights over some information, and each manager has to try to maintain multigroup loyalty through the disclosure or nondisclosure of information. Finally, power in any organization, whether it be through span of control horizontally or chain of command vertically, is tempered by the amount and quality of information that flows from group to group within the organization. The limits of formal intergroup communication within organizations have long been recognized, and informal channels of communication have been developed as a means of supplementing and verifying the information that flows through the formal channels.

Informal Communication Channels Informal communication systems exist in all organizations. In fact, Keith Davis (1978, 116) argues that "informal communication is the other half of a complete communication system, and this is an important part of organizational communication." To relate successfully to one another, groups often depend on the grapevine. The informal channel of communication serves three principles of intergroup communication.

The fourth principle is that the grapevine serves as a supplementary channel of communication. Because everybody recognizes the existence and importance of an organizational grapevine, many managers of groups intentionally send their messages both formally by way of memo and informally through the grapevine. The grapevine is accessible through a number of social settings in which members of different groups interact, such as car pools, morning coffee in the cafeteria, and weekend recreational events. One or two members in an organization occasionally become notorious carriers of grapevine information. In one organization, it might be a switchboard operator; in another, a person who delivers the departmental mail; and in yet another, a social butterfly who moves from department to department giving out and receiving information. These members usually are ridiculed behind their backs; nevertheless, people in the organization rely on them as one source of information.

Several of our graduate students have studied intergroup communication with organizations to understand the grapevine and determine the importance of it to the organization (Sabiani 1979; Sandifer 1976). Their research supports the notion that managers are aware of the grapevine and use it intentionally to ensure that important information gets to all groups. In one study, the researcher found that of five groups reporting to one supervisor, one particular group continually received partial and fragmented information. It was determined that the reason this group was receiving more fragmented information than the others was that its members were housed in a different building and did not eat lunch with the other work groups. This social isolation prevented the grapevine from reaching them (Sandifer 1976).

The fifth principle is that informal communication does serve to check and balance information received in the formal structure. In large organizations that have a long chain of command, the grapevine is used by receivers of downward-flowing information as a check on the accuracy and the intent of the messages. Official organizational communiqués tend to be "machine sounding" and hardly ever give the reasons for organizational policies. The grapevine is used to discover the emotion behind the message and the degree to which the organization is committed to carrying out the policy.

For example, the telephone company in any city in any given year probably sends out a memo to all line crews stating that the company does not want several crews to congregate at the same restaurant for morning coffee. Immediately on receipt of this directive, the line crews ask through the grapevine what happened that caused this memo to be sent and, further, what does it mean? The grapevine may soon contain the information that the memo was prompted by several citizen complaints about six trucks parked at Kelsey's Restaurant. The grapevine message might also indicate that top management is not really mad, but that the line crews had better change to other restaurants and go to them in smaller groups so that the citizens will quit complaining. Similar memos are probably sent each year in police, postal, and all public utility organizations. The point is that all organizations use the grapevine as a means to determine the "real meaning" of official intergroup communication, particularly the information that flows downward in the organization.

The sixth principle is that all groups compete to acquire other groups' "secret" information because information is power. Although, all groups within an organization have information they want kept confidential, some groups—particularly highly cohesive ones existing in highly competitive organizations—systematically gather "secret" information from various groups within the organization so that their group has an advantage over competing ones. In this situation, each member of a group checks out information through his or her own social contacts and shares it later with the others.

Rumors of a pending layoff of personnel usually triggers a work group's efforts to gather another group's secret information about which work groups will be laid off and when. In these crises, work groups are amazingly successful at discovering the best-kept secrets. Hollywood war movies repeatedly dramatized the well-known ability of army platoons to discover where they were being sent to fight, despite the best efforts of command groups to keep the information secret. Sometimes competing organizations do this to one another. In this situation, the small groups of each organization work cooperatively against the groups of another organization. We see this behavior when the news media compete against the executive branch of government, or when executive groups compete against legislature committees. The Watergate scandal is probably the most famous example of this kind of competition. When all work groups are trying to acquire the secrets of other work groups, an organization can rapidly become an unpleasant environment in which to work. As a general rule, work groups should not actively probe for the secret information of fellow work groups unless there is some crisis that makes it necessary. Groups are just like people; they demand and deserve some privacy.

The seventh and overriding principle is that needs exceed resources in an organization, and therefore, groups will compete over scarce resources. The whole process by which work groups are allocated limited resources (the budget process) is a major source of conflict within and among work groups in organizations. Imagine a huge canary cage with 1,000 canaries flying around in it but perches for only 500 canaries. If the canaries are the needs of the organization (equipment, personnel, supplies) and the perches are the money the organization has to spend, we realize the fundamental point about the organizations: The legitimate request of work groups for new personnel, equipment, and supplies always exceeds the resources allocated by the organization for these purposes. Thus, the "Canary Game" is played each year as the new budget for the organization is approved. You can readily see that if a manager has a canary cage with 1,000 canaries and 500 perches, it is tempting for that manager to keep banging the side of the cage so that the canaries keep flying. If the birds settle down, they will realize that there are not perches for everyone, and some will be forced to settle on the newspaper at the bottom of the cage—which is a source of much humiliation and conflict! In an organization, banging on the canary cage is manifested by changes in budgetary forms, delays in processing, and periodic changes in the procedures for distributing resources. Even though it is important for a supervisor to build group morale and be an active team player, it is important, as part of the budgetary process, that he or she reject some funding requests. However, some supervisors don't understand this principle, so they hatch many more canaries than they need and send them to the middle managers in flocks, hoping that some will survive. This tendency produces waste and inefficiency in organizations and, ultimately, affects the productivity of every work group in the organization. Sometimes central management decision-making groups do not follow the advice of first-line work groups and on their own set out to determine the resource needs of the organization. This special form of central management, groupthink, often produces a 200-pound turkey. Central management will wheel in this caged turkey to an unsuspecting first-line work group, and the workers will be forced to pretend it's a canary for fear that they will not receive any more resources. They will paint it yellow and try to teach it to sing, but in the end, it represents a horrible waste of resources.

ASSIMILATION OF GROUPS INTO THE ORGANIZATIONAL CULTURE

The goal of any organization is the same as that of any living species: immortality. Organizations are living entities that have a cultural and symbolic past and a basic impulse to survive. Researchers have found that one of the important ways in which organizations stay alive is by the nourishment and development of "sacred" organizational stories. If a member of a successful organization is asked why the organization grew and became successful, he or she proceeds to tell a story that takes on mythical qualities. If a foreigner asks an American to account for the success of the United States, a similar myth would unfold. Similarly, every organization has a "sacred" story on how the company grew. One company on *Fortune* 500's list told how its humble but talented scientists repeatedly created new products and thus, opened up new markets. The competitive edge of the company was that they always led the field with innovative products, leaving their competitors in a position of playing catch-up. As you might suspect, the most revered part of the company was the research and development division. The high-status work group within the division was the research chemist unit. Placards attesting to the chemists' successes hung on their walls, and pictures of their mythical predecessors were displayed outside the lab. Any chemist who worked for the company knew all the traditional hero stories of the successful group. These kinds of stories form an important part of a company's identification (along with myths, rituals, and corporate sagas), and you can measure a person's involvement in an organization by the number of sacred stories he or she knows (Bormann 1983; Cragan 1971; Pacanowsky and O'Donnell-Trujillo 1983; Sykes 1970).

Sacred stories are the means by which people attain an understanding of and loyalty to their work groups. As the new worker begins to interact with members of other work groups, he or she has to adjust to the other stereotypes created by the sacred stories of competing groups. Finally, the new worker is assimilated into the whole organization by learning corporate stories that are transmitted during companywide social events (Cheney 1983b; Jablin 1984; Putnam and Pacanowsky 1983).

Group Loyalty

The assimilation of a new member into a work group takes place in terms of territory, dress, language, and storytelling. A new member soon learns the territorial boundaries of his or her work group, the unwritten dress code, and the unique idiomatic language of the group. If, say, a man were to go to work as a production electrician in a factory, he would soon discover that all electricians dress similarly, complete to their electrician's pouches, and that their dress is different from that of machinists and painters. Furthermore, the new electrician would soon be immersed in 14 wire versus 12 wire and what size lugs to use on transfers; while he learned where to eat, where to shower, what to wear, and how to sound like an electrician, he would also learn the sacred stories about electricians that would further intensify his recognition of himself as an electrician in the work group.

If the new worker in question had joined the sales force of the company instead of the production electrician work group, the process would have been the same, only he would have learned how to work and talk like a salesperson, and the sacred stories would have related to the success of the sales division. For example, the stories might have explained that the division had the best insurance sales per year, the lowest turnover rate, and the best record of people being promoted to corporate headquarters.

In most companies, the new worker soon identifies with his or her new work group and feels pride in it; however, contact with competing groups within the organization soon tests the loyalty of the group member (Putnam and Stohl 1990).

X, Y, and Z Management Cultures

Organizations are hybrids of X, Y and Z management cultures. These three management styles are discussed in Chapter 7. An X culture has managers who exercise authority and closely supervise subordinates. In an X environment, innovation, quality control, and policy decision making are almost solely the responsibility of management. A Y culture is a humanized analogue of X, in which supervisors are sensitive to the needs of their workers and the workers are allowed input into company decisions. The Z culture is a team-oriented participatory management in which the lines between supervisor and worker are blurred and all members of the organization feel responsibility to one another and to the production of quality products and services.

In U.S. organizations today, wide-ranging discussions and experiments are taking place in an attempt to find the right hybrid management culture that will provide the highest productivity and membership satisfaction for a company. William Ouchi (1981) believes that the Japanese have been successful because they have adopted a Theory Z culture. Peters and Waterman (1982), after studying a number of successful U.S. corporations, concluded that openness in communication and informality in and among work groups were two of the keys to success. Kilmann (1985), in explaining corporate culture, highlighted workers' sense of confinement and restraint in a Theory X culture as a major cause for productivity problems in some U.S. corporations. Cragan, Cuffe, Jackson, and Pairitz (1985) discovered that subordinates who worked in a ZY hybrid management culture were three times more satisfied with their work group than subordinates who were working in an XZ culture.

A worker's ability to be assimilated into an organization in part relates to his or her understanding of the management culture of the organization. Table 10.2 presents twelve salient issues that can be examined to determine the management culture of an organization and describes the way in which each of the three cultures (X, Y and Z) handles each issue.

Intermingling of Groups

The new electrician or salesperson who attends a first meeting in which representatives of other work groups are present discovers that he or she has been stereotyped as a member of a particular work group. The comment might be "Oh, you're the new electrician?" or "So you're our Region Four salesperson!" or "And you're our new accountant!"

At subsequent intergroup contacts, however, the new worker begins to hear some negative stories about his or her work group. For example, at our university, our work group is responsible for teaching the basic communication course to most freshmen. There are numerous sacred stories about the basic course—most of which are good, some of which are bad. One of the bad stories has been around for nearly a decade and refuses to die. The gist of the story is that a nonverbal communication assignment was made that called for the "simulation of a murder" to study the communication reactions of passersby to this kind of incident. Two of the spectators turned out to be carrying real guns while another was the fiancé of the "murdered" student. The experimenters had failed to alert security about the classroom simulation, and the "murdered" student didn't tell his fiancé about the assignment. The simulation created quite a furor both on campus and off, although no one was hurt. The meaning of the story as it is told year after year by competing work groups identifies the course as a "wild and crazy" one and not the "meat and potatoes" curriculum offering it should be. New workers who come into our department are told this story to insulate them from the shock of hearing it from an outside worker. They are

TABLE **10.2**   **Anatomy of Management Cultures: X, Y, and Z**

Organizational Issue	Theory X	Theory Y	Theory Z
Corporate hero	Manager is assertive and task-oriented (has task skills)	Manager is friendly, compassionate, and understanding (has people skills)	Manager is open-minded and committed to participatory management (has group skills)
Corporate villain	Manager is task incompetent; does not know work he or she supervises	Manager is insensitive, aloof, and uncaring; has no concern for workers	Manager is not a team player, does not allow workers to participate in decision making
Innovation	Creation of new ideas is management's responsibility	Workers make some suggestions for new ideas	Managers and workers feel joint responsibility for creating new ideas
Quality control	Management is solely responsible for seeing that work is done correctly	Management encourages workers to take responsibility for quality of their work	The organization is quality control conscious through the use of QCs
Decision making	Decisions are made by those in charge	Managers seek the advice of subordinates before making decisions	Workers participate with managers in group decision making
Personal problems	Personal problems are left at home and not brought to work	Supervisors empathize and counsel workers about personal problems	Organization has formal structures for handling all personal problems of workers: the organization is a "family"
Time management	Workers' time is closely monitored (e.g., time-cards); managers set deadlines for task completion	Worker has some time flexibility to complete task	Time is unstructured; workers are encouraged to set own timetables for completing task
Group meetings	Meetings are held primarily for telling subordinates about management decisions and expectations	Sometimes meetings are held to solicit information from workers for management decision making	Participatory decision-making meetings are held including managers and workers
Trust	Little trust exists between management and workers	Managers are selective in which workers they trust and confide in	Trust is pervasive among managers and workers
Motivation	Major reason for working is to earn income	Employees have developed good working relationships	Employees have strong personal attachment to the organization's goals and identity
Promotion	Hard work gets most people to the top; workers are promoted on the basis of task accomplishments	Hard work, plus knowing the right people, is the way to get promoted	Dedication and persistence to organizational goals are the long-term keys to promotion
Job security	Job security depends on how well a worker does work and how much that work is needed	Job security depends on good relations with management	Company makes lifelong commitment to employees

SOURCE: Derived from Cuffe, M., and Cragan, J. F. "The Corporate Culture Profile." *International Association of Quality Circles Annual Conference Transactions.* Memphis: International Association of Quality Circles, 1983.

also told some good sacred stories so that they can respond to any criticism. This insulating process is done by most work groups so that the new workers' pride will be maintained when they encounter outside competing work groups.

As a new worker gains the trust of a work group, sacred stories that tell "where the bodies are buried" will be told. These are secret group stories and are not to be told to outsiders. One of the important tests of a new member's loyalty is his or her ability to preserve the confidentiality of a work group's secret stories, especially ones that reflect badly on the group.

Socialization into the Whole Organization

Many organizations promote a number of social activities, such as bowling and baseball leagues, and some even have recreational parks for their employees. When a new employee begins joining company-sponsored social and recreational activities, he or she hears corporate-wide stories that all members of the organization know, regardless of the work group they are in. These stories produce an arsenal of material that a new worker can use to explain to outside people why the organization is outstanding and why he or she is proud to be a member of it. Because knowing a number of mythic corporation stories helps in the rapid assimilation of a worker, he or she soon feels like an old-timer. A new worker can look as though he or she has worked for the company for years if he or she can tell a number of organizational stories.

Although organization-sponsored activities help to assimilate a new worker, there are some potential dangers. The first is the problem of never being able to get out of a stereotyped role. Just as people are stereotyped within groups by their race or gender, they are also stereotyped according to their work group. Law enforcement officers frequently get trapped into an organizational "ghetto." There is a tendency in most cities for police officers to work and play together to the exclusion of other people; consequently, they never stop being "cops." Physicians, dentists, and lawyers also fall into the same trap. Fairly soon, members of these groups start to think of themselves exclusively as desk sergeants or urologists and fail to have an existence separate from their jobs. In short, they no longer play the role of desk sergeant or urologist, but the role plays them.

The effect of this organizational lifestyle can be measured in part by high divorce rates. A marriage partner may find it is easy to love John or Mary but not a cop or a dentist. In fact, a psychologist friend of ours recommends that everyone should pound a nail into a tree outside their home, and before they go inside their home at night, they should take off their invisible role and hang it on the tree.

We have long recognized the importance of separating our professional roles from our personal lives; however, many organizational structures create pressures that tend to fuse the two together. When this happens, we usually talk about a person being married to his or her job. When you leave college and join some organization, survey the company-sponsored social activities and select one that appeals to you. Doing so is important because participation in a company organization will expose you to organizational stories; however, remember that you also need to seek outside social contacts so that people will relate to you as a person and not as a member of a work group.

If you want to test the importance of separating role from person, try dropping the stereotyped role you have as college student when you are at home at social gatherings. When college students are home socializing at their neighborhood hangouts, the first few minutes of conversation are filled with asking and answering two questions: What university are you attending? And what is your major? If you want to have a different kind of evening, don't raise these subjects. Instead, simply describe yourself in terms of the role of your summer job; for example, short-order cook, street cleaner, sales clerk, tree trimmer, or lifeguard. You will discover that a lot of people will not talk to you very long. Furthermore, their nonverbal cues will indicate that you haven't much status. But learning to maintain a conversation with another person without "credentialing" yourself through your role description will help you to understand the difference between your professional role and yourself and will permit you to develop more meaningful relationships.

GUIDELINES FOR EFFECTIVE COMMUNICATION AMONG GROUPS WITHIN THE ORGANIZATION

Role of the Chief Executive Officer

Bormann's (1983) research has led him to conclude that a major role of the chief executive officer (CEO) of an organization is to disseminate the organizational saga to as many members of the company as possible. The organizational saga contains the complete professional consciousness of the company. It includes sacred stories that explain what kind of people work at the company, how the company came to be successful, and why the company is immortal. Sometimes these sagas are written in book form and distributed to new employees. For years, new employees at State Farm Insurance Company were given a book, *The Farmer from Merna*, that detailed in dramatic form how this large insurance company had grown from a small farmer-oriented insurance company to nationwide prominence through the retention of certain basic, time-honored principles. Even though a company may have formal documents detailing its saga, the organization is a living entity and is continuing to change, so the CEO must continually retell the old stories and update the saga with new ones.

Role of the House Organ

A new employee should always take time to read the back issues of the organization's regularly published in-house newspaper. Some organizations publish a daily report, but most have a weekly or monthly publication. This publication is rich in group stories and gives a new employee a vivid picture of the successful work groups in the organization. The company newspaper also covers any campaign that the company may have waged in the name of higher productivity. A few of the company's sacred stories occasionally are retold, especially in anniversary issues. If a new employee carefully reads two years' worth of the back issues of the house organ, he or she should be able to communicate with members of other work groups without the worry of making professional blunders. Merely complimenting members of a work group on one of their past successes should provide a healthy basis for communicating with members of that group.

If you are a new supervisor of a work group, you should attempt to get your group some publicity in the company newspaper. The article should contain some mention of the group's productivity if it is to have a beneficial effect. You should also get to know the people in public relations who write the stories and can help you recognize the types of story they are looking for. Sometimes you can get publicity for your group when the members are involved in planning some recreational function for members of the organization. You may think that it is unethical to intentionally seek publicity for your group, but we do not agree. In fact, you have a professional obligation to make visible the positive aspects of your group, not only for the benefit of the group members but also for the health of the organization. The vitality of an organization is in part maintained by various groups' awareness of the positive qualities of other work groups in the organization. The house organ is a major vehicle for facilitating this end.

Role of Interpersonal Communication Channels

The editor of the house organ is the objective third party who reports the stories about your work group. The same communication principle applies to the use of interpersonal communication channels. A supervisor of a work group cannot brag about the accomplishments of his or her work group very often without creating negative reactions from other work groups. The successful way for groups to brag is through a third party. The supervisor of marketing brags to the accounting work group about how good the salespeople are. When the salespeople find out that marketing is bragging about them, they might then feel inspired to brag to the purchasing department about how good a work group the marketing people are. Once this chain reaction gets started, groups will start telling positive stories about other work groups, and the total effect will be beneficial to the organization's productivity and its members' satisfaction.

Negative stories about work groups can spread in an organization in the same way positive stories do—only with terrible consequences. It can be a punishing experience to be part of an organization that is constantly telling bad stories about itself. As a general rule, you should remember that there are no advantages to you or your work group in spreading bad stories about fellow work groups.

Role of Humaneness

Supervisors should attempt to reduce new employees' anxieties on how they will be treated by the company. They can do so most effectively by relating stories in which past new employees have made beginners' mistakes and still were given a chance to improve, or about employees' illnesses and how their jobs were protected while they were away from work. Another way supervisors enhance their humaneness is through the employment of the MBWA (management by walking around) technique. Peters and Austin (1985) stress the importance of this technique in that it allows managers to be close to their workers.

It is also a good idea to spend some time describing the social diversity that exists within the organization so that a new employee's fears of social compatibility will be eased. There is always the question, How will I fit in? Most people have exaggerated fears about how much conformity it will take to be successfully assimilated into a work group.

Work Groups Are Territorial

In Chapter 6, we identified proxemics as being an important nonverbal variable in small group communication. If you want to understand how really important space and territorial rights are in an organization, you should serve on a planning committee that is designing a new building. The majority of the planning committee's time is spent arguing about which work group should occupy which space in the new building. If the presidential and vice-presidential offices are on the top floor, then how high up the building a group is indicates its status in the organization. Who gets the corner offices? Can a work group occupy a whole floor? These kinds of matters are hard for a planning committee to deal with. Some organizations have attempted to minimize the fights over territory and the status attached to space in a building by taking large open rooms and dividing them into modules that form no particular pattern. However, we have heard continual complaints from work groups that this design does not give them a defined territory and they feel frustrated because of it. The work groups feel fragmented and sense a loss of group cohesiveness. Groups seem to need a clear boundary and want to know when someone has entered their work space.

Aside from power and status, the territorial rights of a group also affect formal intergroup meetings. When members of several groups are going to meet, there is always the issue of whose turf they will meet on. Because there is always a "home-team advantage," most major organizations provide neutral meeting rooms. Sometimes the issue of neutrality is solved by agreeing to meet for lunch at some neutral restaurant. However, experienced work groups recognize the importance of competing work groups knowing that they can hold meetings in each other's territory. It is just like visiting someone's house—the first time you visit you feel awkward and uncomfortable; the second time both you and the host or hostess are more at ease. Intergroup meetings share the same principles as a home visit. The host or hostess should provide genuine hospitality and do everything to make the group feel at home.

One of the major reasons organizations try to break down the formal barriers of work groups is that sometimes groups build such psychological barriers that outside groups are afraid to enter their work space. The reduction of intergroup communication usually spawns negative stories about work groups and, in the long run, hurts the productivity of the organization. When territorial walls begin to build up between two work groups, supervisors often schedule a social event for them, such as a softball game or a picnic. The effect of the social gathering is that the two groups feel more comfortable in crossing territorial boundaries at work.

New employees are well advised to form a mental picture of the territorial boundaries that separate work groups in the organization. Without being rude, new employees should cross these boundaries and engage in conversation with members of other work groups. Over time, this type of action on the other part of the new employee will pay dividends as he or she begins to work with outside groups.

Group Goals and Organizational Objectives

Powerful work groups can be so successful in meeting and exceeding their goals that the organization is harmed. Competition among university departments over student majors and general studies requirements of certain basic courses can harm the university—an example that emphasizes the principle that group goals must be consistent with organizational objectives. It is reasonable that an academic department should want to increase its number of majors and ensure that most students are exposed to the basics of its discipline. However, some departments can work so aggressively and successfully that their gains become somebody else's losses. Philosophy and history departments might acquire so few majors that the integrity of their programs is jeopardized. It would certainly be against the goals of the university to allow departments of history and philosophy to be ruined. Most people would argue that students should be exposed to some history and philosophy.

All organizations are similarly limited by the number of people, time, and money available. Work groups within organizations find themselves continually competing for these limited resources. For example, in business organizations, product work groups compete for limited advertising resources. If one product group becomes too successful at monopolizing the advertising department's people, time, and money, the sale of other products may suffer. In governmental agencies, the same problem will occur if one department becomes too effective at acquiring tax money. In other words, work groups in the organization should not succeed at the expense of others. Just as an individuals' goals must be in concert with the purposes of a group, group goals must be in harmony with organizational objectives.

☐ SUMMARY

In this chapter, the communication principles described in the first part of the book are applied to work groups and routine meetings. Each of these two kinds of real-life small group communication events is thoroughly examined. Five basic principles a supervisor should use in determining whether or not to call a meeting are presented. They include mastering time, understanding tradition, being productive, maintaining group satisfaction, and gaining group consensus. Four basic types of business meetings are detailed: the Monday morning meeting, monthly meeting, decision-making meeting, and planning meeting. Such particulars as agenda and supervisory leadership styles are highlighted.

The chapter then focuses on major principles of intergroup communication in organizations. Next, ways in which groups are assimilated into organizational culture are discussed. The chapter closes with the presentation of six guidelines for effective communication among groups within the organization.

Thor Davis—Unit Manager

CASE BACKGROUND

Thor Davis graduated from a midwestern university with a bachelor's degree in applied computer science. He was employed on graduation as a systems analyst with a West Coast insurance firm. He worked there for five years while pursuing an MBA degree. By age thirty-two, Thor had ten years of experience in data-processing departments in the insurance industry. Today Thor is thirty-six. He has been manager of the data-processing department at the corporate headquarters for four years. We would expect Thor Davis to be happy and successful, given his prestigious job. However, Thor is beset by problems that he thinks are related to his ability to manage and participate in work groups. His supervisor has recommended that he develop better communication strategies for handling his problems. In fact, Thor has only eight months to show improvement or he will be terminated.

CASE PROBLEMS

After Thor recovered from the shock of his job appraisal interview, he sat down and systematically outlined what he perceived to be his management problems. He initially classified his communication problems into three general areas:

1. Intergroup conflict among the three data-processing shifts, which included low morale.
2. Communication breakdowns with management units that are served by data processing.
3. Upper management seems suspicious and distrustful of his motives for increasing both software and hardware needs for the data-processing department.

As Thor reflected on the people who report to him, he began to realize that he never really understood the constant bickering that was occurring between the three shifts. The 11 P.M. to 7 A.M. shift continuously left obnoxious memos that indicated that they believed that they were given more production work to do than could be realistically done in eight hours. The same shift occasionally complained that they were being ignored both indi-

vidually and as a group. In contrast, the 7 A.M. to 3 P.M. shift believed that they were under too much scrutiny. They complained that they were not given enough uninterrupted time to get their work done. They also complained about how the graveyard shift must be "goofing off" and "eating pizzas all night." The 3 to 11 P.M. shift was an enigma: they didn't complain, nor did they praise the work Thor was doing. Furthermore, in all honesty, Thor had to admit that all three shifts had lost faith in his ability to "carry the data-processing flag." He had heard through the grapevine that a lot of the programmers thought that he no longer could successfully get new equipment. They no longer believed that Thor was capable of explaining to upper management the needs of the data-processing unit.

Thor's peers (other unit managers) continually chide him about the continual increase in computer costs. They cannot understand why " economies of scale" does not function in the data-processing department. In the past, they supported Thor in the acquisition of a new computer that was more powerful, and all it got them was more cost for computer data and more complaints from their subordinates. The other managers continually received complaints from their workers that they cannot communicate with the system's analysts in the data-processing unit. The systems analysts seemed aloof, busy, and arrogant. Workers from other areas believed that they had to beg to have their work processed. They also thought that the programmers made them intentionally ignorant and helpless in getting their data processed.

Finally, Thor, in his heart of hearts, believes that the other unit managers in the corporation do not regard him as an equal. He thinks that the other managers treat him as a subordinate and not as their peer. He knows that other managers continually air their common problems of management with one another, but he is excluded from the meetings and the social gatherings where such discussions take place. Sometimes Thor feels like screaming, "I have an MBA like the rest of you! I have management problems just like you! Why won't you talk to me?"

Upper management always invites Thor to their key decision-making meetings; however, next to the recording secretary, Thor feels like the lowest peon there. Thor also feels overworked by upper management. Every time management gets in a fight over information, Thor is asked to gather more data. Thor had to admit to himself that he hates to attend upper management meetings because it just means more work. Other managers always think that Thor has the inside track for promotion because he always gets "behind the thick oak doors on the top floor." Yet Thor believes that upper management never seriously considers him upper managerial material and thinks of him only as a lackey who provides data.

CASE QUESTIONS

1. In chronological order (being as specific as possible), list the communication activities that Thor should engage in to solve his three problem areas in the organization. You may want as a group to use the one-time meeting techniques discussed in Chapter 4 (e.g., brainstorming, NGD technique).

2. How do Thor's three problems manifest themselves as three types of group problems? (Thor is a manager of three work groups; Thor is a coacting equal in management meetings; and Thor is a participant in upper management decision-making meetings).

CHAPTER ELEVEN

EVALUATING SMALL GROUP COMMUNICATION

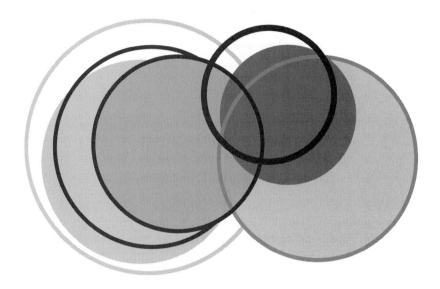

CHAPTER OBJECTIVES

After reading this chapter, you should be able to:
- Use the theory-making machine
- Understand the unified theory of small group communication
- Grasp the small group research issues
- Know how to evaluate small group communication

You are an automatic theory-making machine. Human beings just can't keep from theorizing. We have to theorize or we would not survive. You have already formed many theories about small groups automatically simply because you have been an active member of many discussion groups. Stop and think about the answers you would give to the following questions: What makes for a good work group? Why do groups waste time? What causes conflict among group members? What kind of leadership makes groups work effectively? Why do you get along well in some groups and not so well in others? After reading the first ten chapters, you should be able to formulate answers to these questions because of the small group communication theories that have been presented.

☐ A CONCEPTUAL MODEL OF A
THEORY-MAKING MACHINE

Small group theories are like different camera lenses in that they produce different pictures of group member communication. We are attracted aesthetically to some theories because they conform to our sense of reality about small groups, just as we reject others that do not. It would be possible to take all the small group theories we have and "take a picture" of one small group using all the different theoretical lenses. Afterward we would have many different-looking "pictures" of the group, all of which might be valid explanations of what took place. Initially, we would accept the picture that conformed to our personal idea of reality, but eventually, we might accept the theory that predicted how groups might behave in the future, because in the final analysis, we want production, quality of work, consensus, and member satisfaction.

A number of group theories are described in this book. Recall in Chapter 2 that our model contained important small group theories. Symbolic convergence theory explained team-building, encounter theory explained trust-building, role emergence theory explained the emergence of group roles, and decision-making theory explained how groups solve problems. In fact, we explained that Poole's decision-making theory, Fisher's decision-making theory, and Gouran and Hirokawa's decision-making theory competed with one another. You must decide for yourself which of the three theories best explains problem-solving talk and which best predicts group outcomes. Likewise, we outlined in Chapter 7 seven theories of group leadership. Four explained appointed leadership and three explained emergent leadership. Once again, you must decide which theories you embrace and which you reject. This chapter helps you judge which theories you believe and will use in the future.

Your acceptance of small group theories is predicated on three things:

1. *Aesthetics:* Whether or not you like the metaphor that forms the theory's base, that is, whether or not it is aesthetically pleasing for you to view groups from a given theoretical lens.

2. *Realism:* Whether or not the theory looks at reality in the same way you do. If you tend to look for underlying rules that govern behavior, you will probably like adaptive structuration theory; and if a theory emphasizes the same kinds of communication behaviors of groups that your personal lens sees, you will probably accept the theory as valid.

3. *Utility:* Whether or not you think the theory will be useful to you in future group meetings. Ultimately, you want theories to explain and predict the consequences of behavior. If we can, we will then follow behavior that will produce expected outcomes. In our culture, the usefulness of a theory tends to be the most important measure of its acceptance. Throughout this book, we have presented useful recommendations that various small group theories have suggested. In this chapter, we explain how these theories are formulated and tested.

Once a theory has been "manufactured," we often attempt to model it to explain and describe its important parts. We also might build a physical model to simulate the theory. The conceptual model is probably the most common type of model in small groups. In Table 11.1, we show Hawes's (1975) definition of the key concepts you will need to know to compare and contrast various small group theories. You may want to refer to this table as we discuss these important notions about theorizing.

Figure 11.1 shows a conceptual model of our theory of how theories are produced, so in a sense, it is a model of a theory of theory-making. We hope that you will build conceptual models of your theories that will represent in some different form or substance, or both, your verbal statements and the relations contained in them. We have argued, as we show in the model, that the starting point for a theory is a metaphor. This ignites your brain to form concepts into logical statements that in turn produce a description. Next, or sometimes simultaneously, you begin to test your formulation. You do so first by converting your concepts into variables by way of operational definitions, of which, as the model indicates, there are three types. Afterward you run the appropriate test, followed by an evaluation of the theory according to a threefold criteria system: aesthetics, realism, and utility. Finally, you either accept or reject the theory.

Most organizations are intensely interested in what makes a good group leader. They might, for example, want to know what kind of communication style a leader should adopt to manage an inexperienced small group. In Chapter 7, we provide a number of answers to this question; one answer or theory is that a novice group would need a "telling" style of leadership (Hersey and Blanchard 1977). Hersey and Blanchard believe that when an organization has an immature work group, the

TABLE 11.1   **Basic Parts of a Theory**

Parts	Definitions and Descriptions
Theory	A theory is designed to explain the hows and whys and not just the whats. It describes, and one hopes predicts, but certainly accounts for, the causal relationships among its component parts. Theories are made up of statements consisting of concepts and logical terms, and it is a relationship among these statements that constitutes a theoretical explanation of a phenomenon.
Concepts	Concepts are descriptive terms either for things that we can directly observe, such as people or tables; or for things that are not directly observable, such as emotions and beliefs. Concepts are useful, clear, ambiguous, or well defined, but they are not true or false.
Operational definitions	Well-defined concepts are ones that have been operationally defined; i.e., the procedures that will be done in measuring a concept are clear enough for other scholars to repeat them and get the same measurements. "Communication apprehension" is a concept; it may have the same meaning as "speech anxiety," but a given piece of research would have specified operational definition. While speech anxiety and stage fright may be ambiguous at the semantic level, operational definitions of these concepts could be the same or different.
Variable	A variable is an operationalized concept. Once we have sufficiently defined in operational terms a concept so that we can start to measure it in our research, we call it a variable. Thus a variable is a symbol to which numbers are assigned.
Statements	Theories are made up of statements. Statements contain concepts in some logical form. Statements relate concepts to one another in one of three ways: (1) disjunctive (either A or B); (2) conjunctive (both A and B); or (3) conditional (if A, then B).
Hypothesis	A hypothesis is a statement that is proposed to be true if the statements from which it is derived are true. All the concepts in the hypothesis must have operational definitions. A hypothesis is a statement that specifies the necessary conditions of a prediction. For example, the more orientation statements that occur in a discussion, the greater the likelihood of the group reaching a consensus.
Metaphor	Metaphors create new concepts and help frame our new theories. A metaphor produces an interaction between two ideas that are seemingly unrelated but show certain similarities, thus resulting in new ideas.
Analogy	Metaphors suggest analogies. Analogies demonstrate in detail the correspondence between otherwise dissimilar things. They usually are either structural or functional.
Model	A model represents a theory or part of a theory using new materials. A plastic-tubing-and-Styrofoam splice might be used to represent part of an atomic theory. Models are not theories, but theories are often represented in the form of a model.

SOURCE: Derived primarily from Hawes 1975.

FIGURE 11.1   **Conceptual Model of a Theory of the Theory-making Machine**

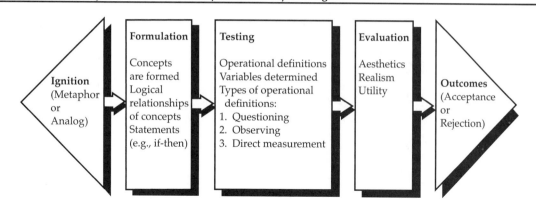

leader needs to adopt a no-nonsense, highly task-oriented leadership style that clearly explains to group members how they should do their work. The ignition metaphor for this theory could well be the pumping up of a flat tire so it will roll smoothly down the road. The leader has an inexperienced work group that needs to be told how to do their job so they may be productive. The important concepts in this theory are a telling-style leader, an immature work group, a task, and the group's productivity. If we put these concepts in logical relation to one another, the research statement we form would read as follows: If the leader tells the group how to do the task, the group will be productive. If communication scholars were to test this theory, they might compare a telling with a delegating style of leadership and directly measure which approach caused an immature group to do more work. On the basis of utility, we would accept or reject the theory.

Throughout this book, we have presented conceptual models of small group communication theories in an attempt to be clear about what a given theory is and how it works. Our judgment about which theory to use has been basically a utilitarian one. Thus, the test of our theory of the theory-making machine is whether or not the model shown in Figure 11.1 makes it easier for you to understand how theories of small groups are created.

☐ THE UNIFIED THEORY OF SMALL GROUP COMMUNICATION

No grand theory of small group communication exists that by itself accounts for all communication and predicts all small group behavior. We have subtitled this book *Theory, Process, and Skills* because we literally have combined, or stitched together, numerous low-level theories of small group communication to provide you with one coherent picture. This picture is representative of the model described in Chapter 2. Figure 11.2 depicts the research version of our bull's-eye model of small group communication We unify the theories of small group communication in much the same way Hawking (1988) did in physics and Sirgy (1988) recommended for the social sciences.

Figure 11.2   Bull's-Eye Model of Unified Theory of Small Group Communication

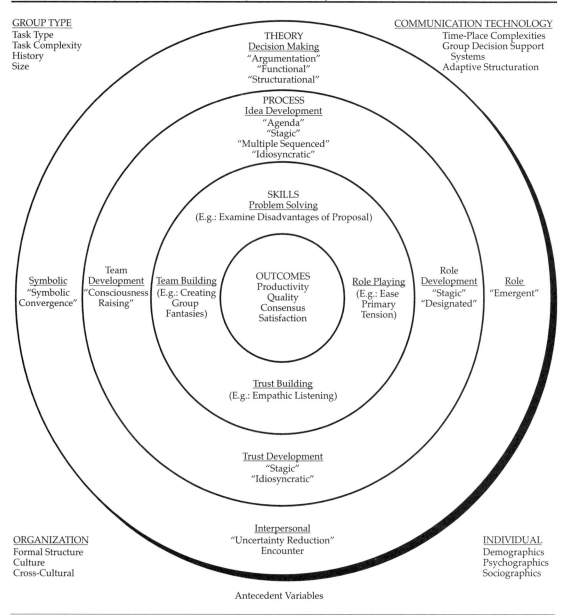

GROUP TYPE
Task Type
Task Complexity
History
Size

COMMUNICATION TECHNOLOGY
Time-Place Complexities
Group Decision Support
Systems
Adaptive Structuration

THEORY
Decision Making
"Argumentation"
"Functional"
"Structurational"

PROCESS
Idea Development
"Agenda"
"Stagic"
"Multiple Sequenced"
"Idiosyncratic"

SKILLS
Problem Solving
(E.g.: Examine Disadvantages of Proposal)

Symbolic
"Symbolic
Convergence"

Team
Development
"Consciousness
Raising"

Team Building
(E.g.: Creating
Group
Fantasies)

OUTCOMES
Productivity
Quality
Consensus
Satisfaction

Role Playing
(E.g.: Ease
Primary
Tension)

Role
Development
"Stagic"
"Designated"

Role
"Emergent"

Trust Building
(E.g.: Empathic Listening)

Trust Development
"Stagic"
"Idiosyncratic"

ORGANIZATION
Formal Structure
Culture
Cross-Cultural

Interpersonal
"Uncertainty Reduction"
Encounter

INDIVIDUAL
Demographics
Psychographics
Sociographics

Antecedent Variables

SOURCE: Derived from Cragan, Shields, and Wright (1996).

The Group Outcomes Bull's-Eye

The starting point for our unified theory is the identification of dependent group outcomes that two or more theories may have in common. Following Sirgy (1988), we sought to integrate two or more theories by searching for their common dependent variables. We noted four dependent outcome variables: *group productivity, quality of group work, membership satisfaction,* and *group consensus.* These outcomes appear repeatedly in the body of research on small group communication. Numerous scholars have linked these group outcome variables to specific group communication skills, processes, and theories. For example, Gouran (1969) identified eight variables, such as *orientation,* that contributed to *consensus building.* Scholars reported a series of studies beginning in the 1980s that linked communication behaviors to the quality of group work (e.g. Hirokawa 1985, 1987, 1988; Hirokawa and Pace 1983; Hirokawa and Scheerhorn 1986). These studies linked the communication behaviors associated with both high and low quality of group work and served as a database for grounding a decision-making theory (Gouran and Hirokawa 1986) that accounts for the quality of group decision-making. Other scholars reported studies linking communicative behaviors to member satisfaction. For example, Wall and Galenes (1986) established some relationships between the interpersonal variables contained in SYMLOG (System for the Multiple Level Observation of Groups) and group satisfaction and quality of group decision (see Chapter 6). Communication scholars have measured group productivity in a variety of ways including the quality of the solutions proposed, uniqueness of the ideas generated, and the number of ideas generated (Jarboe 1988).

The Group Communication Skills Ring

From the vantage point of the unified theory, the current status of small group communication theories allows us to provide a clear and coherent explanation of small group talk in terms of problem-solving talk, role-playing talk, trust-building talk and team-building talk. In terms of impacting the four group outcomes, there appear to be at least one hundred small group communication skills: thirty-five problem-solving, thirty-five role-playing, fifteen trust-building, and fifteen team-building flowing from the research supporting a number of diverse small group theories (see Chapters 2 through 9 for an explanation of these skills). For example, the research on nominal grouping and brainstorming identifies such skills as separating people, ideas, and criticism during the problem-solving process (e.g., Jablin 1981; Jablin, Seibold, and Sorenson 1977).

At present, the series of Minnesota Group Studies, begun in the 1960s and directed by Ernest Bormann, continues to constitute the largest body of research regarding group role talk (Bormann 1975, 1990). This line of research delineates clearly the importance of role emergence and information in groups and instructs the practitioner as to the kinds of communication skills needed to impact group outcomes. As indicated earlier, Hammer and Martin (1992) grounded the linkages among an interpersonal communication theory (uncertainty reduction theory), a team-building communication behavior (self-disclosure), and a group outcome (membership satisfaction).

The Japanese approach to decision-making groups regards building group identity as Job 1 (Ingle 1982; Juran 1976). In the Japanese version of quality circles, the first thing a work team does is name itself, develop a logo, and develop a group slogan (Cragan and Wright 1993). The Japanese also bifurcate the four kinds of group talk. They seek to engage in team-building and trust-building communication before going to the task and role development dimensions (Johansen 1992).

The Group Communication Process Ring

The notion that communication patterns in groups change over time has played a major role in the development of small group communication theories. The explanatory power of the model we present in Chapter 2 is derived in part from temporal process reality. All four types of talk (problem solving, role, trust-building, and team-building) have stages or phases to their communication development (i.e., the talk that occurs at one point in time is different from the talk that occurs at later points in time). Thus, Fisher (1974) found four stages of problem-solving talk; Bormann (1975) found two stages of role talk; Bennis and Shepherd (1956) found two stages of encounter talk; and Chesebro, Cragan, and McCullough (1973) found four stages of CR talk. Attempting to determine the distributional and sequential patterns of communication has been a major line of research for communication scholars.

In terms of team development, Chesebro, Cragan, and McCullough (1973) identified the four stages of consciousness-raising (credentialing, polarization, new identity, and relating to other groups). This progression of stages has been modified by research that says new groups spend a lot of time in Stages 1 and 2, whereas established groups spend most of their time in Stages 3 and 4 (e.g., Bolkum 1981; De Vuono 1982). We postulate that all task groups spend some time engaging in team-building talk.

Bennis and Shepherd (1956) and Phillips (1966) were among the first who reported on the communication process that describes trust development. We now know that if a task group does not have work to do it will make itself the agenda. Mabry (1975) coded nine communication behaviors and described this trust development in three stages: boundary seeking, ambivalence, and actualization. Once again, the vantage point of our unified theory allows us to see that we cannot yet characterize the process by which team, trust, role, and problem-solving development talk occurs as a group goes about its business of doing work. With the exception of studies by Hammer and Martin (1992) and Barker, Melville, and Pacanowsky (1993), we have little research that attempts to ground empirically both team and trust development to outcomes.

Role development is a communication process long associated with group productivity, membership satisfaction, consensus, and quality (Benne and Sheats 1948). Bormann (1975, 1990) has grounded in observational research the relationship between task talk and role talk, in which role development goes through two stages: primary tension and recurring secondary tension. Of course, a considerable body of disciplined-based research is devoted to key roles in groups, especially leadership (e.g., Baird 1977; Barge 1989; Gouran 1969; Schultz 1978).

In 1975, Bormann reported that untrained groups' ideational development is idiosyncratic. In 1970, Fisher, using the Scheidel and Crowell (1964) task communication scales, characterized idea development as going through four stages (orientation, conflict, emergence, and reinforcement). Again using Scheidel and Crowell's communication variables, plus Bales's (1950, 1970) twelve communication acts, Poole (1981, 1983a, 1983b) developed a multiple sequence model of the communication process of decision-making groups. His research indicates that it is possible to code complex sets of data and link it to theory and group outcomes.

The Communication Theory Ring

Functional, structurational, and symbolic convergence theory were developed and grounded in the 1970s and 1980s as partial explanations of small group decision making (Cragan and Wright 1990). When viewed from the vantage point of the unified theory and combined with argumentation theory, developed in the 1950s, role emergence theory, developed in the 1960s, and uncertainty reduction theory, developed in the 1970s, these six group theories cease to compete with each other; indeed, they become the six theories, flowing from three distinct paradigms, that form the basis for grounding our unified theory of small group communication.

Symbolic convergence theory explains how groups come to create a common group identity and develop group pride through the sharing of group symbols, slogans, and traditions. This theory argues that the meaning and emotion contained in symbolic group fact have an impact on the four group outcomes (Bormann 1990). Bormann (1975) developed role emergence theory as another theory to explain task groups in terms of their role formation. This theory explains that decision-making groups will struggle and be low in productivity until the emergent leader role is developed. This struggle takes two primary phases that not all groups successfully complete, thus accounting for differences in group outputs.

Berger and Calabrese (1975) developed an interpersonal communication theory that explains how strangers seek to reduce their anxiety and uncertainty about one another through a series of personal disclosures. This process of reciprocal disclosures allows the group members to make a more predictable interpersonal group environment, in which membership satisfaction and consensus will increase and the group will become more productive (Hammer and Martin 1992).

Toulmin (1958) developed a non-syllogistic approach for laying out logical arguments that moves group thinking from acceptable data through a warrant to a claim. This reasoning process, which looks at arguments of cause, sign, example, analogy and authority assertion, is used to reach group decisions rationally. Ice (1987) used his structurational case study of the Challenger space shuttle disaster to reason that the decision-making process in groups is really the act of overcoming the presumption associated with the specified criteria for judging the adequacy of solutions. Dace and Hirokawa (1987) posited a taxonomy of simple to complex task situations and asserted that the role of argumentation in a group would increase with the difficulty of the task. Later, we discuss argumentativeness as a confounding variable in group research.

In the 1980s, the functional theory was created and grounded (e.g., Hirokawa 1982a, 1982b, 1983a, 1983b, 1985, 1987, 1988; Gouran and Hirokawa 1986; Hirokawa, Ice, and Cook 1988; Hirokawa and Pace 1983; Hirokawa and Scheerhorn 1986). This rationalistic theory flows from a general theory, information processing theory, and argues that communication is central to explaining the outcomes of decision-making groups. To date, the researchers contributing to the program have grounded four functions in terms of their relationship to the quality of group work. These functions are (1) understanding the problem; (2) marshalling a range of alternative solutions; (3) assessing positive consequences of each alternative; and (4) assessing negative consequences of each alternative. The third rational theory to explain the relationship between group process and group outcomes is the structurational theory (e.g.,

McPhee, Poole, and Seibold 1982; Poole, 1983a, 1983b; Poole and Folger 1981; Poole and Roth 1989a, 1989b; Poole, Seibold, and McPhee 1985). This theory explains the process of producing and reproducing the rules and patterns of communication that a group generates in order to reach rational decisions. It does so by assessing group members' initial individual preferences and accounting for change resulting from the communication that occurs in the discussion. (For an interesting discussion of measurement difficulties regarding individual versus group preference through the stagic sequences of problem-solving groups, see Hoffman 1994, Hoffman and Kleinman 1994, and McPhee 1994.) This theory has been adapted to explain how decision-making groups use group support systems and reinvent themselves as they integrate computer-based communication technology (Poole and Jackson 1993).

The six theories just listed explain the communication process of small decision-making groups. Each of these theories is homegrown—that is, developed indigenously by the contributions of scholars within the communication discipline. We would be remiss not to say that we expect other communication theories to be developed and grounded that will also explain small group communication. Other outcomes, skills, processes, and confounding variables will likely surface as well. We would predict that any such new phenomena will be capable of explanation within the parameters of our unified theory of small group communication.

The Antecedent Variables Ring

The bull's-eye model of our unified meta-metatheory (above-metatheory) also provides a representation of four classes of antecedent variables: communication technology, group type, individual, and organization. We call these areas antecedent variables because they precede group interaction and theories represented by our communication theories at the present time do not typically account for the impact of these variables; yet research is beginning to show that when such variables intervene they would appear to effect group outcomes.

Regarding communication technology, studies by Brashers, Adkins, and Meyers (1994) and Meyers, Seibold, and Brashers (1991) identified the impact of group support systems (GSS) on argumentation in groups. They indicated that computer software will alter our argumentation theories of small group decision-making. Also, cyborg groups, which are part human and part machine, are a form of group we are trying to account for with our theories (e.g., Arnold 1994). Adaptive structuration theory (AST), developed by Poole and others (see, for example, Poole and DeSanctis 1992), accounts for group outputs, but we have yet to develop theoretical explanations of communication technology's impact on group decision making in terms of role playing, trust building and team building.

Group type also appears to impact the outcomes of small group decision making. We use the team group type expansively to include such differences as task type, task complexity, group history, and group size. For example, McGrath (1984) argues that small group tasks can be divided into four different task circumplexes (generate, choose, negotiate, and execute) with each type potentially producing different decision-making processes. Dace and Hirokawa (1987), positing a taxonomy of simple to complex task situations, asserted that the role of argumentation would increase with the difficulty of the task facing the group. Studies conducted by Cragan and Wright (1993) and Arnold (1994) established that changing types of tasks may alter our small group communication theories as we attempt to account for small group outputs. Focus groups (e.g., Bormann, Bormann, and Harty 1995; Cragan and Shields 1995; Shields 1981), a special type of information generating group used extensively in the discipline as part of our communal research tool kit, would appear to be another antecedent of task groups.

Differences in the characteristics of individuals are also a class of variables that complicate a unified communication-based theoretical explanation of group output (Gouran and Fisher 1984). Here, we again define the term *individual* rather expansively to include any demographic (e.g., gender, age, race), psychographic (e.g., belief, attitude, ego involvement), or sociographic (e.g., student, Mason, argumentative) factor that may impact group outcome. For example, the tendency to make argument (e.g., Schultz 1982) or avoid argument (e.g., Scheerhorn 1987) is sometimes viewed as an individual trait (sociographic) that affects the outcomes of decision making. As well, communication apprehension (e.g., Comadena 1984; Jablin, Seibold, and Sorenson 1977), and gender (e.g., Alderton and Jurma 1980; Bunyi and Andrews 1985; Spillman, Spillman, and Reinking 1981; and Owen 1986) have made our explanation of communication process and our ability to account for group outputs more complex. Schutz's FIRO theory (1966) and Bales's SYMLOG (e.g., Bales and Cohen 1979; Cegala, Wall, and Rippey 1987; Lustig 1987; and Wall and Galanes 1986) indicate that interpersonal needs and individual personalities have potentially significant effects on communication processes, the communication skills that are performed, and their concomitant effects on group outcomes. Zimmermann (e.g., 1994) has been adapting Delia's (Delia, O'Keefe, and O'Keefe 1982; O'Keefe 1984; Sypher and Zorn 1986) discipline-indigenous constructivist explanation and measures of an individual's cognitive complexity to the study of naturalistic hospice work teams' effectiveness in message production and member satisfaction.

Putnam and Stohl (1990) have argued for an understanding of organizational variables and their impact on small group processes. However, few studies of small decision-making groups have been conducted in an organizational or cross-cultural setting (Cragan and Wright, 1990). Berteotti and Seibold (1994), in their case study of health care teams, provided some evidence that Stohl and Putnam are correct. Furthermore, Schall (1983) and Stohl (1987) have shown the importance of studying organizational influences on groups. Hirokawa, Gouran, and Martz (1988) examined the faulty decision-making processes of those associated with the Challenger disaster, and Putnam (1988) identified three variables (connectivity, hierarchical structure, and multiple-group membership) that appear to impact on small group interaction. Bantz (1993) used Hofstede's (1984) Uncertainty Avoidance Index, an instrument that measures one's lack of tolerance for uncertainty by nation-state culture, to help analyze the effect of cultural background on the group dynamics (leadership, norms, conflict, and roles) of a ten-member international research team. Bantz concluded that intercultural work teams must gather information; adapt to differing situations, issues, and needs; build social as well as task cohesion; and identify mutual long-term goals. Booth-Butterfield and Jordan (1989) found that the distinct cultural differences evident in the communication of same-race women's groups disappeared from the communication patterns of racially heterogeneous women's groups. Hess (1993) suggested the use of symbolic convergence theory—sharing fantasies to create common symbolic ground—to increase cohesion between a newcomer and the orga-nization. Helmer (1993) noted that SCT's fantasy chaining process explains how some organizational group members "distance and distinguish" themselves from other members of the organization (p. 41).

☐ Studying Small Group Communication

By now you are probably ready to get started on your own research project. How to ignite your ignition metaphor is always a puzzling first question. In the end, no scholar is ever quite certain of the exact origin of his or her research idea. Usually you can remember where you were sitting when you got the idea but not how the notion came into your head. Yet you can't think of something by thinking of nothing. You need to look at some "stuff." We suggest three reservoirs that may stimulate your creativity. They are the unified theory, previous research in groups, and your own experience as a group member.

Getting Started

The most common starting point is to read research on small group communication, on the assumption that something will attract you and lead you to create a new re-search idea. There are basically two strategies you can take in conducting this review of the literature. The first is to read secondary sources that summarize research find-ings for you, and the second is to read the original research reports that are con-tained in scholarly journals.

Two representative reviews of small group research outside the communication discipline are McGrath's *Groups: Interaction and Performance* (1984) and Shaw's *Group Dynamics: The Psychology of Small Group Behavior* (1981). McGrath organizes his re-view of social-psychological group research by classifying task groups into four cat-egories in terms of their interaction patterns and the types of work they do. One type is a planning or creativity group, which specializes in generating new ideas; a sec-ond type is a problem-solving or decision-making group, such as a jury, which fo-cuses on getting the right answer; the third type includes groups that deal with con-flict resolution, in which there is a great deal of bargaining and negotiation; and the fourth type contains groups that are performing to meet a standard of excellence or competing with groups in a contest or battle, such as competitive team sports. Using a "laws" analog, Shaw reviews psychological and social-psychological group litera-ture in an attempt to generate plausible hypotheses about group behavior. His major topics include personal characteristics of members, composition and structure of groups, how groups form and develop, the physical environment of groups, leader-ship of groups, and how groups perform tasks, especially as they relate to individual performance.

Within the communication discipline, two representative reviews of the literature are Gouran and Fisher's "The Functions of Human Communication in the Formation, Maintenance, and Performance of Small Groups" (1984) and Cragan and Wright's *Theory and Research in Small Group Communication* (1996). Gouran and Fisher use a mechanistic analog to describe communication research in small groups. They sum-marize the research on categories of variables such as characteristics of members and groups, group environment, communicative relations occurring in groups, types of performance characteristics (e.g., problem solving and creativity), and other responses such as consensus and member satisfaction. Cragan and Wright summarize research of the 1970s and 1980s under six lines of research, three continuing and three new. The three continuing lines of research are studies on discussion, leadership, and the teaching of small groups. The three new lines of research are communication variables that affect group outcomes, process of communication in groups, and communication variables studied in small group settings. When you read these reviews, you should look for a topic that might attract your attention. For example, is it harder for a woman than a man to emerge as a leader? Does brainstorming increase the quality of the ideas a group can generate? What effect does trust-disrupting communication behavior have on membership satisfaction? If you find a topic area that interests you, you can then look up the original studies (primary sources) that are cited in the review so that you can see how these studies were conducted.

All professionals have scholarly journals in which they report their research. In the field of communication, the two professional organizations that sponsor journals are the Speech Communication Association and the International Communication Association. Three representative journals in which you will find original small group communication research reported are *Communication Monographs, Human Communication Research*, and *Communication Studies*.

A final source of stimulation for a research idea is your personal experience in groups. If you think back to some of the questions you thought would be answered by taking a course in small group communication, you might find that one of those questions remains unanswered and that you are going to answer it conducting your own original research. Typical questions that students ask us are these:

- What makes a good leader?
- How do I become a leader?
- What communication skills will make me more successful in groups?
- How do you make groups more productive?
- How do you resolve conflict in groups?
- How do you handle members who won't work?
- How do you build group identity and pride?
- How do gender, race, and age of group members affect group outcomes?

Remember that you are a natural-born theory-making machine. You should not shy away from systematically seeking your own answers to small group communication questions.

Research Design Considerations

In the late 1960s and early 1970s, a number of communication scholars became concerned with the nature of research that was being done in small group communication. Some believed that too much of our knowledge was derived from laboratory studies in which concocted groups were put together for a short period of time to manipulate a couple of communication variables and that too little attention was being given to communication theories that explained small group behavior (Bormann 1970a; Fisher 1971; Mortensen 1970). Since that time, efforts have been made to study groups in more natural settings and to see that communication variables are central to the study and properly operationalized. It is impossible to construct the perfect study. There are always trade-offs. Ideally, your research should try to maximize three things: (1) the generalizability of the group or groups that you study to the whole population of groups; (2) the precision of control you have over your variables (i.e., how well they are operationalized); and (3) the realism of your research context (McGrath 1984). If you conduct a field study of natural decision-making groups in an organization, you will have great realism, but your control over the group and the concepts you are studying may be weak and your ability to generalize will be low. On the other hand, if you create groups in the laboratory, you may have much precision but lack realism. In other words, no matter what kind of research design you develop, it will always have some methodological weakness in it. Your decision on what type of study to conduct should, therefore, depend on the type of research question you want to pose, not on any a priori notions of design or data manipulation procedures. Once you've settled on a research question, there usually are about ten major concerns or checkpoints you need to consider in designing your research. Table 11.2 outlines these issues and lists sample questions you need to ask about each one.

Size of Group   Some researchers in social psychology regard dyads (two persons) as a group (Shaw 1981). We do not. As indicated in Chapter 1, we regard three as the minimum number of members for a group to exist. A more difficult question is to determine the outer limits of a group for your study. Certainly any number over nine would be risky, unless you are studying the formation of cliques into groups. Most researchers who concoct groups for laboratory studies choose sizes ranging from four to seven, with the most common group size being five members. In laboratory studies, most researchers try to control the variable of size by having each group have the same number of members. However, in field studies (conducted in natural settings), you often cannot control group size. It is important to remember that your study will always have to defend your choice of group size as falling within the definition of a "small group."

Unit of Group Communication   Communication scholars have a keen interest in how communication is treated in a small group study. Trying to figure out your operational definition of communication is deceptively difficult. Conceptions of the unit of communication range from single thoughts, individual statements, interacts, themes, and even whole-length discussions (Cragan and Wright 1980, 204). For example, Bales set forth the idea that there were twelve communication "acts" that needed to be observed and counted to understand the development of a decision-making group. We provide Bales's (1950) operational definition in the form of his Interaction Process Analysis (IPA) instrument later in the chapter, in Table 11.4. McCroskey and Wright (1971) believe that it is important to study not only the communication act, but also the reaction to that act, so they created a different operational definition of communication interaction groups. Gouran (1969) concluded, after a lengthy review of communication literature, that eight communication acts appeared to affect group outcomes; they are clarity, opinionatedness, interest, amount of information, provocativeness, orientation, objectivity, and length. In Chapter 2, we explain the communication stages that Fisher found in task groups, Mabry found in encounter groups, and Chesebro, Cragan, and McCullough found in

TABLE 11.2   **Small Group Communication Research Considerations**

Issue	Questions
Size of group	Same size? Minimum size? Maximum number of members?
Unit of group communication	Communication act? Group interaction? Selected segments? Entire discussion?
Duration of discussion	Thirty-minute discussion? Sixty-minute discussion? Daylong discussion? Yearlong discussion?
Characteristics of group members	Gender? Race? Age? Trained?
Setting	Concocted (laboratory)? Natural (field study)? Historical-fictional?
Group goal or task	Information sharing? Problem solving? Idea generation? Consensus achieving?
Operational definitions	Self-report? Trained observers? Direct measurement?
Researcher intervention	Little control? Tightly controlled? Use confederates?
Data analysis	Descriptive? Critical-analytical? Content analysis? Numerical manipulation of data?
Size of research sample	One group? Six groups? Thirty groups? 1,000 members of groups surveyed?

CR groups. Table 11.3 lists the communication acts that were measured in these studies. We present these examples of operational definitions of communication to underscore that an operational definition of the unit of group communication is essential in explaining the communication you studied and why that communication is important in answering your research question.

TABLE 11.3   **Communication Acts Present in Three Small Group Studies**

Author	Fisher (1970)	Chesebro, Cragan, and McCullough (1973)	Mabry (1975)
Unit of Communication	Verbal Interaction	Themes (rhetorical characteristics)	Behavior Scores System
Communication variables	Assertive Seeking Interpretation Substantiation Clarification Modification Summary Agreement Favorable toward proposal Unfavorable toward proposal Ambiguous toward proposal	"I - you - us - we - they" Noncombative vs. combative Climate: somber, warm, hostile Temporal aspects: present, past, future Fantasy	Neutral system Neutral assertions Dominant assertions Antagonism Withdrawal supportive acts Assertive-supportive acts Group laughter Group tension Task-determining acts Group-maintaining acts Tension displays

Duration of Discussion   Group scholars refer to *zero-history groups,* a term that usually means a group concocted for purposes of research (i.e., the members had never worked together before). Ongoing groups occasionally are used for field experiments in which they are given a new topic to discuss for purposes of research, but the members have worked together in the past. The reason this issue is important relates to the argument over how long it takes for a group to develop its "groupness" (group cohesion). For example, if five college freshmen are brought together for the first time to discuss an issue of common concern for fifteen minutes, would we think of them as really being a group? Is thirty minutes enough time? What about an hour? As you can see, this is a difficult issue to resolve but as we said earlier in this section, there are trade-offs in each research design. A zero-history group talking for thirty minutes might give you great control over your variables, but you would sacrifice much in the way of contextual realism. Again, the type of research question you are asking would determine whether a thirty-minute discussion would be adequate.

Characteristics of Group Members   Group composition is another sticky issue. In Chapter 6, we indicated that a number of group member characteristics may affect group development and outcomes. These included demographics such as age, race, and gender. These characteristics will be treated differently by you, depending on your research question. If you are wondering what effect these characteristics would have on the group, then you would manipulate a given characteristic or characteristics to see what would happen. On the other hand, you may have a research question that might be difficult to answer unless you make sure membership characteristics don't affect it. In historical-fictional studies and field studies, an after-the-fact analysis may be done in which group composition is used to explain what happened in the group. For example, in our case study at the end of Chapter 7, we asked you to assess the group's failure in light of the gender issue. All small group communication studies can be analyzed to see if membership characteristics can explain what is happening in the group.

Setting What would be the ideal group for providing the best answer to your research question? When you attempt to answer this question, there are three general types of groups you can use. You can use a natural setting in which you would have a preexisting work group that would exist whether you conducted research or not. This might be a strategic type of planning group for a corporation, a jury, or a paramedic team. You also can create a group in the laboratory, and because you are the creator, you can concoct any type of group you want. Finally, you can study the historical record of past small groups or examine fictitious groups created by novelists, screenwriters, and playwrights.

Group Goal or Task A group goal or task is controlled or uncontrolled, and it may be important or unimportant to answering your research question, but certainly you have to be aware of what it is. Many times the dependent variable of small group communication is the outcome of the group task. For example, studies that attempt to determine how many ideas are generated by brainstorming or nominal groups would regard the task as central to their study. This would also be true if a researcher were trying to assess what group communication variables affect consensus. On the other hand, if you are studying the communication stages of a problem-solving group, you might only want to ensure that the group has a good problem to work on and not really care what the actual conclusion is for each group in the study. For example, if the group is discussing the parking problem on campus, you might be concerned only with the interaction the group has and not with the actual solution. In field studies, you often cannot control the topic but still may be interested in the task outcomes. For example, a survey of quality circles (QCs) might want to report the impact or quality of the solutions developed and implemented by QCs. In this case, the researcher might want to analyze the process of the QC and make inferences about its impact on group outcome, even though the research had no control over the task topic. Sometimes laboratory studies use group tasks that maximize precision of control but lack real-world context. Once again, the nature of your research question will determine how important the group goal or task is to your study.

Operational Definitions Operational definitions are procedures you follow in assessing each concept in your study that are clear enough so that other scholars could repeat your procedures and get the same results (Cragan and Wright 1993). Operational definitions often are referred to as instruments, and we discuss their reliability and validity. In other words, does the test measure what it is supposed to measure, and does it measure it the same time after time? For example, if you were trying to determine whether there was an inverse relationship between communication apprehension and leadership emergence, you would need an operational definition for leadership and apprehension. One strategy for a beginning researcher might be to search small group communication literature for a communication anxiety instrument that had already been found to be reliable and valid by previous researchers and, likewise, an instrument to measure leadership. The three general classes of operational definitions that we include in our theory-making machine are self-report (questioning), observing, and direct measurement. Self-reports usually are paper-and-pencil tests that operationalize important concepts, but sometimes they are simple open-ended questions like, Who do you think is the leader of this group? Bale's IPA is probably the most frequently used instrument in which trained observers record communication acts as they see them occurring in small group discussions. Direct measurement can include biofeedback, content analysis of group transcripts or minutes, and examination of group outputs such as productivity. Some researchers prefer to operationalize the same concept by all three means to ensure that they really have what they think they have.

Researcher Intervention If you are analyzing the decision-making process of President Nixon's Committee to Re-elect the President in an attempt to see whether the committee was beset by groupthink, you are not intervening in the group process. On the other hand, if you are trying to determine what effect trust-disrupting communication has on a group, you might actually "plant" a confederate in your laboratory group and have that person operationalize your trust-destroying behavior. In this case, you, the researcher, are exerting significant control over the communication process that is occurring in the group. The amount of direct manipulation of group processes needed to answer your research question should be tempered by the trade-off between your desire for precision and your need for realism.

Data Analysis By the time you have resolved the eight concerns in research design, it should be apparent to you what kind of data analysis is appropriate for answering your research question. Many times a qualitative analysis of your data is most appropriate. If you are doing a descriptive analysis of a historical group, you may simply want to analyze and reason critically from the small group communication evidence you have assembled. Other times your research question may require that you count and sum up different types of group communication and outputs. For example, how many procedural leadership behaviors do appointed leaders use in routine business meetings? This count might then be correlated to the number of topics covered in a forty-minute period. Here we would not only count and sum things up; we would also correlate them with other things we had counted. Thus, correlation statistics often are used in communication studies. If your research question requires complex statistical manipulation, you usually can look these statistical procedures up in standard textbooks. The advent of high-speed computers and home computers (PCs) have popularized the development of statistical packages that have taken much of the drudgery out of quantification. One package to start with is the Statistical Package for the Social Sciences (SPSS-X), which is available at every university computer center as well as for PCs. It is important that you understand the strengths and weaknesses of each statistical procedure in light of the research question you are asking; the best way to learn these statistics is on a need-to-know basis. If you need to know how to run a chi-square to answer your research problem, you will learn chi-square much more thoroughly and intimately than if you just study chi-square in the abstract. So your in-depth knowledge of statistical procedures will accumulate in direct relation to the number of research studies you undertake.

Size of Research Sample Should you study one group? Six groups? Thirty groups? Or should you survey 1,000 members of different groups? Once again, our trade-off problem raises its head. An in-depth case analysis of a small group in a field setting might produce rich data that maximize our realism goal. The 1,000-member survey might maximize our goal of generalizability to the population, but lack precision and realism. If you are conducting a laboratory study, how many groups should you have? We don't have a good answer for you. If we went by custom, lots of small group studies report sample sizes from six to thirty. On the other hand, many of these thirty-groups studies only had thirty-minute discussions. Rest assured that no matter how many groups form the basis of your study, you will have some discomfort in answering the question, Is my sample size large enough?

The preceding ten issues are not necessarily all the issues you might consider when conducting a small group communication study, but they are the essential ones. We hope that this book stimulates you to go forth and conduct your own research in group communication. Chances are, most of you have other plans! In any event, the preceding ten issues, combined with the eight analogs, can provide you with criteria for evaluating small group communication research. They will allow you to formulate your own judgments about the research you read and, as a consequence, the small group communication theories you accept.

☐ ASSESSING SMALL GROUP COMMUNICATION

Research instruments are essentially operational definitions of some theoretical concept. It is quite natural and, in fact, necessary that the communication literature contains numerous articles in which some instrument was used to systematically study small group communication. As you begin reading these studies, you'll discover that the same small group concept may be operationalized through the use of a number of instruments. When you use an instrument that measures leadership, for example, the items contained in the instrument are, by definition, the key components that the researcher thinks constitute leadership. Thus, scholarly debates frequently occur over which instrument is the most valid measure of a given concept. Even apparently clear-cut and simple concepts like group consensus meant that all group members had agreed to a specific policy, whereas in others, consensus was operationalized in the form of an instrument that measured how close a group was to reaching consensus (Cragan and Wright 1980). As indicated in Chapter 9 in our discussion of risky shift, the operationalization of the same concept using different instruments can produce different findings. When the choice dilemma questionnaire was used to operationalize the concept of risk taking, a risky shift was found to occur; however, when group risk taking was operationalized differently, the group effect was not found (Cartwright 1973). It is important that you carefully assess the items that make up an operational definition of a key concept because if you don't accept these items as being a valid measure of a concept, then, by definition, you would have to reject the findings of the study.

In this section, we do not attempt to produce a compendium of all the instruments that have been used to study and evaluate small group discussions. Instead, we present several examples to demonstrate how you can systematically assess group communication. Research instruments fall under the three-part category system of self-report, observation, and direct measurement described earlier in the chapter.

Self-Report

When you ask group members to report information, you can have them describe or evaluate themselves, other group members, or themselves and other group members. You can ask for information from a group member before, during, and after a discussion. Prediscussion items of information often are demographic items that constitute an operational definition of a group member. Sometimes the prediscussion instruments measure some psychological concept or the discussant's predisposition toward a group communication concept or discussion topic. It is difficult for group members to do lengthy self-report instruments during their actual discussion, so sometimes research designs require that the group members stop their discussion, fill out a paper-and-pencil test, and then resume talking. Probably the most common type of self-report is the postmeasure. Another common type of instrument is one that calls for group members to evaluate the discussion in terms of some important group concept, such as membership satisfaction or group effectiveness. Figures 11.3 and 11.4 are examples of these instruments.

FIGURE 11.3   **The Wright Group Satisfaction Index**

Directions: At the conclusion of your group's discussion, please mark each scale according to *how you think* the group *feels* about itself. None of the scales are necessarily "good" or "bad," "high" or "low." Please mark the space on each scale which you think identifies how the group *feels*. Answer all of the scales.
   Thank you.

Group Number_____
Group Name_____
Group Size_____

1. Relaxed	:___:___:___:___:___:___:	Pressured
2. Tension inducing	:___:___:___:___:___:___:	Tension releasing
3. Conformity	:___:___:___:___:___:___:	Nonconformity
4. Dissimilar	:___:___:___:___:___:___:	Similar
5. Unsatisfied	:___:___:___:___:___:___:	Satisfied
6. Constrained feeling	:___:___:___:___:___:___:	Casual feeling
7. Coordinating	:___:___:___:___:___:___:	Noncoordinating
8. Incompatible	:___:___:___:___:___:___:	Compatible
9. Gratifying	:___:___:___:___:___:___:	Nongratifying
10. Withdrawing	:___:___:___:___:___:___:	Contributing
11. Accord	:___:___:___:___:___:___:	Discord
12. Contention	:___:___:___:___:___:___:	Harmony

The Wright Group Satisfaction Index shown in Figure 11.3 lists twelve components that Wright believes constitute a measure of the concept of group satisfaction. As you look at these twelve items, you need to ask several questions: Are there important attributes of group satisfaction that are *not* contained in this instrument? Are there unimportant items that don't appear to be attributes of group satisfaction? If the answer is yes to either one of these questions, you might want to argue that this instrument is not a valid operationalization of group satisfaction. Another question you need to ask is how this instrument was created. Did Wright just jot down these twelve items off the top of his head, or on the basis of observing groups, did he conclude that these were the right items? If the latter were the case, this instrument would have what we call face validity; that is, just looking at the instrument, one would conclude that it seems to contain the important components of group satisfaction. Some instruments used in research have only face validity; that is to say, experts in group communication say that, based on their knowledge of group satisfaction, these twelve items are a good operationalization of it. However, scholars frequently go to a lot more trouble to see if their instruments are valid. Sometimes they compare their instruments with other instruments that are known to be valid. Other times, as is the case with the Wright Group Satisfaction Index, a factor-analysis procedure is

FIGURE 11.4 Group Evaluation Form

Directions: Check the evaluative term which best describes the group's performance on each of the following aspects of the symposium or the panel discussion. Turn in this form to your instructor at the conclusion of the group presentation.

Group Identification

Symposium	Excellent	Good	Average	Fair	Poor
Definition of problem					
Limitation of problem					
Analysis of problem					
Information sharing in question and answer period					

Panel Discussion	Excellent	Good	Average	Fair	Poor
Summary of definition and analysis of problem					
Establishment of criteria					
Evaluation of solution					
Group productivity					
Group cohesion					
Group leadership					

Directions: Circle the evaluative term which best describes the group's effectiveness on the symposium or the panel discussion.

Excellent   Good   Average   Fair   Poor used to "boil out" key discrete items from a much larger list of potential factors. The Wright Group Satisfaction Index was derived from a list of more than 100 items. Other instruments we have referred to in this book that have been created in a similar manner are Bales's IPA, McCroskey and Wright's IBM, Leather's Feedback Rating Instrument, and McCroskey's Personal Report of Communication Anxiety.

An instrument like the Wright Group Satisfaction Index might be used in a study in which you are trying to determine if highly productive groups tend to be more satisfied than unproductive groups. Or you might use it in a study in which you are manipulating group membership characteristics and then assessing whether all-female groups are happier than mixed-gender groups. Yet you may simply want to use this instrument as a way to systematically assess your group's satisfaction.

Figure 11.4 contains a rather typical example of a group evaluation form. It asks the group members to rate the group's performance on items that most group discussion scholars would say are important for producing an effective symposium or panel discussion. The assumption is that if the group was "excellent" on these items, an effective discussion should have occurred. If you were going to do a research project using the panel discussion items as a measure of group effectiveness, you might want to include other measures of group effectiveness to ensure that you are studying what you thought you were studying. For example, you might examine the audience's reaction to the discussion to see if they thought it was excellent. You might ask observers to rate the effectiveness of the discussion. In each case, you might use a different operationalization of group effectiveness. If this triangular strategy produced results in which the audience, observers, and discussants rated the discussion "excellent," you would have confidence in your conclusion. The two group evaluation measures (for the symposium and the panel discussion) contained in Figure 11.4 ask the group member to make a rather global evaluation on a number of items. These sorts of instruments frequently are used as an in-class teaching aid in small group communication classes. If they were used in a research project, you might want to ask whether all group members are likely to have the same understanding of what is meant by group leadership or group cohesion. You might ask if there are other group concepts that should have been included to have a more "complete" evaluation form. Finally, you would probably want to provide operational definitions for such concepts as leadership and productivity to check the reliability of the members' rating ability.

Observation

You can't see cohesion. You can't see membership satisfaction. In fact, most of the communication concepts you would systematically want to observe in small groups you can't see. What you can look at are communication behaviors, and you can assign meaning to them. The first step, then, to systematically observing small group communication involves two procedures. One is to train observers to recognize different types of interaction. For example, in Figure 11.5, we list a leadership behavior called "clarifying." What is "clarifying" communication, and how is it different from "summarizing"? To reduce this ambiguity, observers are trained by showing them behavior that the researcher thinks is "clarifying" behavior and distinguishing it from "summarizing" behavior. The second procedure is to allow observers to prac-

FIGURE 11.5   **Group Leadership Observation Form**

Communication Behaviors	Group member A	Group member B	Group member C	Group member D	Group member E
Task Leadership:					
Contributing ideas					
Seeking ideas					
Evaluating ideas					
Seeking idea evaluation					
Visualizing abstract ideas					
Generalizing from specific ideas					
Procedural Leadership:					
Goal setting					
Agenda making					
Clarifying					
Summarizing					
Verbalizing consensus					
Interpersonal Leadership:					
Regulating participation					
Climate making					
Instigating group self-analysis					
Resolving conflict					
Instigating conflict					

tice coding behavior to become skilled at observing the communication behavior you want them to see or to become adept at using the observational instrument.

The second step is creating intercoder reliability. Assume that you chose to conduct a study, and part of your research design called for trained observers to determine which group members most frequently played which group roles. Or you might want observers to code leadership behavior as operationalized in Figure 11.5. In this situation, you might want to develop a frequency count of which group member performed the largest number of procedural leadership behaviors. A typical strategy in social-science research is to train three observers and have them simultaneously observe the same group discussion. If all three observers essentially saw the same thing, you have a strong case that the event actually happened. In the case of observing leadership communication, some simple correlation statistics could be computed to see how much alike the three coders' observations were of the same discussion. If they agreed 75 percent of the time or better, you would believe that they were accurately recording what you wanted them to record.

If the sixteen leadership communication behaviors contained in Figure 11.5 are viewed as an operational definition of leadership, we raise a question of validity just as we did in our discussion of self-reporting instruments. Just because you can train three persons to see and accurately record what you trained them to see, does not mean that you have necessarily found what you were trying to observe. To put it another way, instruments used by observers are operational definitions of concepts and you may disagree that the operational definition really captures the essence of the concept. If you were conducting a leadership study and were trying to determine who the task leader was in a discussion, you might use the instrument in Figure 11.5 and, with the help of trained observers, assess which group member engaged in the largest number of procedural leadership behaviors. Additionally, you might use a self-report instrument and ask the group members who they thought the group leader was. This strategy would give you an additional argument for concluding that you had identified the task leader. In using observational instruments, you need to make certain that your observers can see the behavior they are supposed to observe and that they have had the opportunity to practice to become skilled in using the instrument. But remember that even when you achieve intercoder reliability, you must still ask, Is the instrument a valid operational definition of the small group communication report you are studying?

Bales's IPA is the most frequently used observation instrument studying small group behavior. After years of using the instrument on various groups, Bales was able to sum up the normative distribution of twelve communication acts in a decision-making group. Table 11.4 displays Bales's findings.

Direct Measurement

The advent of QCs in U.S. industry has created a lot of natural field settings in which the quality and quantity of a group's productivity can be directly measured. Heavy industry has, for a long time, had some rather exacting standards that had to be met or a part would be thrown off the assembly line. These direct measurements became easy dependent measures for assessing what types of groups produce better results. Also, groups' logos, memos, and communication patterns are things that can be directly observed and counted. In designing a small group communication study, including some direct measurement in a design usually is a good idea.

A rather typical laboratory study in which direct measurement instrumentation would be used is one in which nominal grouping, brainstorming, and unstructured discussion techniques are pitted against one another to see which technique produces more and better ideas. If the groups in the study were asked to suggest ways to improve parking on campus, some rather simple direct measurement should be used. First of all, the researcher could count the number of ideas generated by each group. Second, a committee of parking experts could rate the quality of each idea. Although counting the ideas is clearly a direct measurement, rating the quality of ideas brings us back to our same old question: What is the operational definition of quality the judges use, and is it valid? In the case of quality control of manufactured parts, there are exacting standards that have to be met. In the case of our parking experts, ambiguity is more obvious.

Our point here is that regardless of whether you use self-report, observation, or direct measurements, the reliability and validity of your instrumentation are constant. Whether you are creating your own instruments or using someone else's, recognize that it takes a great deal of thought and effort to systematically study small group communication.

TABLE 11.4   **Adaptation of Bales's Interaction Process Analysis**

Major Categories	Subcategories	Percentage of Communication Acts
SOCIAL Positive reactions	*Shows solidarity,* raises others' status, gives help, rewards. *Shows tension release,* jokes, laughs, shows satisfaction. *Shows agreement,* shows passive acceptance, understands, concurs, complies.	25
Negative reactions	*Disagrees,* shows passive rejection, formality, withholds help. *Shows tension,* asks for help, withdraws out of field. *Shows antagonism,* deflates others' status, defends or asserts self.	12
TASK Answers	*Gives suggestion,* direction, implying autonomy for other. *Gives opinion,* evaluation, analysis, expresses feeling, wish. *Gives information,* orientation, repeats, clarifies, confirms.	56
Questions	*Asks for information,* orientation, repetition, confirmation. *Asks for opinion,* evaluation, analysis, expression of feeling. *Asks for suggestion,* direction, possible ways of action.	7

SOURCE: Reprinted from *Interaction Process Analysis* by R. F. Bales, by permission of The University of Chicago Press. © 1976 by The University of Chicago. Reprinted also by permission of author.

☐ SUMMARY

This chapter introduces you to some fundamental ideas for evaluating small group communication. The chapter begins by identifying each person as an automatic theory-making machine. Moving from a person's natural curiosity to engage in theory-making, we present a conceptual model of a theory-making machine. Key distinctions among concepts, operational definitions, and variables are highlighted as they relate to statements and predictions we make about group communication.

We then present a unification and description of theory and research in our unified theory of small group communication. This bull's-eye theory is isomorphic to the more pragmatic model we presented in Chapter 2. It goes from the four outcomes at the center of the bull's-eye, to the four types of skills, to the four kinds of group processes, to the theory ring.

Next, we look at ways of systematically studying small group communication. You can begin doing small group research by being stimulated by the unified theory, by doing literature review, or by personal experiences you have had in groups. When doing research or, for that matter, reading the published results of previous research, one finds that there are numerous design considerations that must be taken into account. What is the size of the group? What is the unit of group communication? What about data analysis? These questions are discussed along with seven other research design considerations. The chapter closes by looking at three specific ways (self-report, observation, and direct measurement) that are used to systematically assess small group communication. The reliability and validity of your instrumentation are most important when systematically studying groups.

REFERENCES

Alderton, S. M., and Frey, L. R. "Effects of Reactions to Arguments on Group Outcome: The Case of Group Polarization." *Central States Speech Journal* 34 (1983): 88–95.

Alderton, S. M., and Jurma, W. E. "Genderless, Gender-Related Task Leader Communication and Group Satisfaction: A Test of Two Hypotheses." *Southern Speech Communication Journal* 46 (1980): 48–60.

Andrews, P. H. "Sex and Gender Differences in Group Communication: Impact on the Facilitation Process." *Small Group Research* 23 (1992): 74–94.

Arnold, M. S. "Communication Apprehension, Computer Anxiety, and Satisfaction in Group Decision Support Systems." Unpublished master's thesis, Illinois State University, 1994.

Bailey, K. "A Descriptive Analysis of the Group Communication Interaction of Television News Teams." Unpublished master's thesis, Illinois State University, 1985.

Baird, J. E., Jr. "Sex Differences in Group Communication: A Review of Relevant Research." *Quarterly Journal of Speech* 62 (1976): 179–192.

———. "Some Nonverbal Elements of Leadership Emergence." *Southern Speech Communication Journal* 40 (1977): 352–361.

———. *Quality Circles: Leader's Manual.* Prospect Heights, Ill.: Waveland Press, 1982.

Bales, R. F. *Interaction Process Analysis.* Reading, Mass.: Addison-Wesley, 1950.

———. *Personality and Interpersonal Behavior.* New York: Holt, Rinehart & Winston, 1970.

Bales, R. F., and Cohen, S. P. *SYMLOG: A System for the Multiple Level Observation of Groups.* New York: Free Press, 1979.

Bantz, C. "Cultural Diversity and Group Cross-Cultural Team Research." *Journal of Applied Communication Research* 21 (1993): 1–20.

Barge, J. K. (1989). "Leadership as Medium: A Leaderless Group Discussion Model." *Communication Quarterly* 37 (1989): 237–247.

Barker, J. R., Melville, C. W., and Pacanowsky, M. E. "Self-Directed Teams at XEL: Changes in Communication Practices during a Program of Cultural Transformation." *Journal of Applied Communication Research* 21 (1993): 297–312.

Barnlund, D. C. "Experiments in Leadership Training for Decision-Making Groups." *Speech Monographs* 22 (March 1955): 1–14.

Barnlund, D. C., and Haiman, S. *The Dynamics of Discussion.* Boston: Houghton Mifflin, 1960.

Bell, M. A. "A Research Note: The Relationship of Conflict and Language Diversity in Small Groups." *Central States Speech Journal* 34 (1983): 128–133.

Benne, K. D., and Sheats, P. "Functional Roles of Group Members." *Journal of Social Issues* 4 (1948): 41–49.

Bennis, W., and Nanus, B. *Leaders: The Strategies for Taking Charge.* New York: Harper & Row, 1985.

Bennis, W. G., and Shepherd, H. A. "A Theory of Group Development." *Human Relations* 9 (1956): 415–437.

Berger, C. R. "The Covering Law Perspective as a Theoretical Basis for the Study of Human Communication." *Communication Quarterly* 25 (1977): 7–18.

Berger, C. R., and Calabrese, R. J. (1975). "Some Explorations in Initial Interaction." *Human Communication Research,* 1, 99–112.

Berteotti, C. R., and Seibold, D. R. (1994). "Coordination and Role-Definition Problems in Health-Care Teams: A Hospice Case Study." In L. R. Frey (Ed.), *Group Communication in Context: Studies of Natural Groups* (pp. 107–131). Hillsdale, N.J.: Erlbaum.

Billingsley, J. "An Evolution of the Functional Perspective in Small Group Communication," *Communication Yearbook* 16 (1993): 615–622.

Blake, R., and Mouton, J. *The Managerial Grid.* Houston: Gulf Publishing Co., 1964.

Bochner, A. P., and Bochner, B. "A Multivariate Investigation of Machiavellianism and Task Structure in Four-Man Groups." *Speech Monographs* 39 (1972): 277–285.

Bolkum, A. T. "A Descriptive Analysis of Communication Behavior Occurring in Consciousness Creating Groups." Unpublished master's thesis, Illinois State University, 1981.

Booth-Butterfield, M., and Jordan, F. "Communication Adaptation Among Racially Homogeneous and Heterogeneous Groups." *Southern Communication Journal* 44 (1989): 253–272.

Bormann, E. G. "The Paradox and Promise of Small Group Research." *Speech Monographs* 37 (1970a): 211–217.

———. "Pedagogic Space: A Strategy for Teaching Discussion." *The Speech Teacher* 19 (1970b): 272–277.

———. *Discussion and Group Methods.* 2nd ed. New York: Harper & Row, 1975.

———. *Communication Theory.* New York: Holt, Rinehart & Winston, 1980.

———. "Symbolic Convergence Theory of Communication Application and Implications for Teachers and Consultants." *Journal of Applied Communication Research* 10 (1982): 50–61.

———. "Symbolic Convergence: Organizational Communication and Culture." In L. L. Putnam and M. E. Pacanowsky (Eds.), *Communication and Organizations: An Interpretive Approach.* Beverly Hills, Calif.: Sage, 1983.

———. "Symbolic Convergence Theory: A Communication Formulation." *Journal of Communication* 35 (1985): 128–138.

———. *Small Group Communication: Theory and Practice.* 3rd ed. New York: Harper & Row, 1990.

Bormann, E. G., and Bormann, N. C. *Effective Small Group Communication.* 2nd ed. Edina, Minn.: Burgess, 1976.

Bormann, E. G., and Bormann, N. C. *Effective Small Group Communication.* 4th ed. Edina, Minn.: Burgess, 1988.

Bormann, E. G., Bormann, E., and Harty, K. C. "Using Symbolic Convergence Theory and Focus Group Interviews to Develop Communication Designed to Stop Teenage Usage of Tobacco." In L. R. Frey (Ed.), *Innovations in Group Facilitation* (pp. 200–232). Cresskill, N.J.: Hampton Press and the Speech Communication Association, 1995.

Bormann, E. G., Pratt, J., and Putnam, L. "Power, Authority and Sex: Male Response to Female Leadership." *Communication Monographs* 45 (1978): 119–155.

Boster, F. J., Fryrear, J. E., Mongeau, P. A., and Hunter, J. E. "An Unequal Speaking Linear Discrepancy Model: Implications for Polarity Shift." *Communication Yearbook* 6 (1982): 395–418.

Boster, F. J., Mayer, M. E., Hunter, J. E., and Hale, G. E. "Expanding the Persuasive Arguments Explanation of the Polarity Shift: A Linear Discrepancy Model." *Communication Yearbook* 4 (1980): 165–176.

Bostrom, R. P., Watson, R. T., and Kinney, S. T. (Eds.). *Computer Augmented Teamwork: A Guided Tour.* New York: Van Nostrand Reinhold, 1992.

Botan, C. H., and Frey, L. R. "Do Workers Trust Labor Unions and Their Messages?" *Communication Monographs* 50 (1983): 233–244.

Bradley, P. H. "Sex, Competence, and Opinion Deviation: An Expectation States Approach." *Communication Monographs* 47 (1980): 101–110.

———. "The Folk-Linguistics of Women's Speech: An Empirical Examination." *Communication Monographs* 48 (1981): 73–90.

Brashers, D. E., Adkins, M., and Meyers, R. A. "Argumentation and Computer-Mediated Group Decision-Making." In L. R. Frey (Ed.), *Group Communication in Context: Studies of Natural Groups.* Hillsdale, N.J.: Erlbaum, 1994.

Brilhart, J. K. *Effective Group Discussion.* 2nd ed. Dubuque, Ia.: Wm. C. Brown Co., 1974.

Brilhart, J. K., and Jochem, L. M. "Effects of Different Patterns on Outcomes of Problem-Solving Discussion." *Journal of Applied Psychology* 48 (1964): 175–179.

Brock, B. L., Chesebro, J. W., Cragan, J. F., and Klumpp, J. P. *Public Policy Decision-Making: Systems Analysis and Comparative Advantages Debate.* New York: Harper & Row, 1973.

Brockriede, W., and Ehninger, D. "Toulmin on Argument: An Interpretation and Application." *Quarterly Journal of Speech* 46 (1960): 44–53.

Bunyi, J. M., and Andrews, P. H. "Gender and Leadership Emergence: An Experimental Study." *Southern Speech Communication Journal* 50 (1985): 246–260.

Burgoon, J. K. "Unwillingness to Communicate as a Predictor of Small Group Discussion Behavior and Evaluations." *Central States Speech Journal* 28 (1977): 122–133.

Burgoon, M. "Amount of Conflicting Information in a Group Discussion and Tolerance for Ambiguity as Predictors of Task Attractiveness." *Speech Monographs* 38 (1971): 121–124.

Burleson, B. R., Levine, B., and Samter, W. "Decision-Making Procedure and Decision Quality." *Human Communication Research* 10 (1984): 557–574.

Cartwright, D. "Determinants of Scientific Progress: The Case of Research on the Risky Shift." *American Psychologist* (March 1973): 222–231.

———. "Risk Taking by Individuals and Groups: An Assessment of Research Employing Choice Dilemmas."

Journal of Personality and Social Psychology 20 (1970): 361–378.

Canary, D. J., Brossman, B. G., and Seibold, D. "Argument Structures in Decision-Making Groups." *Southern Speech Communication Journal* 53 (1987): 18–37.

Cegala, D. J., Wall, V. D., and Rippey, G. "An Investigation of Interaction Involvement and the Dimensions of SYMLOG: Perceived Communication Behaviors of Persons in Task-Oriented Groups." *Central States Speech Journal* 38 (1987): 81–93.

Chen, Z., Lawson, R. B., Gordon, L. R., and McIntosh, B. "Groupthink: Deciding with the Leader and the Devil." *Psychological Record* 46 (1996): 581–590.

Cheney, G. "On the Various and Changing Meanings of Organizational Membership: A Field Study of Organizational Identification." *Communication Monographs* 50 (1983a): 342–362.

———. "The Rhetoric of Identification and the Study of Organizational Communication." *Quarterly Journal of Speech* 69 (1983b): 143–158.

Chesebro, J. W., Cragan, J. F., and McCullough, P. "The Small Group Technique of the Radical Revolutionary: A Synthetic Study of Consciousness-Raising." *Speech Monographs* 40 (1973): 136–146.

Cline, R. "Detaching Groupthink: Methods for Observing the Illusion of Unanimity." *Communication Quarterly* 38 (1990): 112–126.

Cline, R., and Cline, T. R. "A Structural Analysis of Risky-Shift Discussions: The Diffusion of Responsibility Theory." *Communication Quarterly* 28 (1980): 26–36.

Collins, B., and Guetzkow, H. *A Social Psychology of Group Processes for Decision-Making.* New York: John Wiley & Sons, 1964.

Comadena, M. E. "Brainstorming Groups: Ambiguity Tolerance, Communication Apprehension, Task Attraction, and Individual Productivity." *Small Group Behavior* 15 (1984): 251–254.

Conrad, D. *Strategic Organizational Communication: Cultures, Situations, and Adaptation.* New York: Holt, Rinehart & Winston, 1985.

Courtright, J. A. "A Laboratory Investigation of Groupthink." *Communication Monographs* 45 (1978): 229–246.

Cragan, J. F. "Organizational Myths: A Possible Methodology." Unpublished paper, University of Minnesota, 1971.

Cragan, J. F., Cuffe, M., Jackson, L. H., and Pairitz, L. "What Management Style Suits You?" *Fire Chief* 29 (1985): 25–30.

Cragan, J. F., and Shields, D. C. *Applied Communication Research: A Dramatistic Approach.* Prospect Heights, Ill.: Waveland, 1981.

———. "The Use of Symbolic Convergence Theory in Corporate Strategic Planning: A Case Study." *Journal of Applied Communication Research* 20 (1992): 199–218.

———. "Using SCT-Based Focus Group Interviews to Do Applied Communication Research." In L. Frey (Ed.), *Innovations in Group Facilitation: Applications in Natural Settings* (pp. 233–256). Cresskill, N.J.: Hampton Press and the Speech Communication Association, 1995.

Cragan, J. F., Shields, D. C., and Wright, D. W. "A Unified Theory of Small Group Communication." In J. F. Cragan and D. W. Wright (Eds.), *Theory and Research in Small Group Communication.* Edina, MN: Burgess, 1996.

Cragan, J. F., and Wright, D. W. "Small Group Communication Research of the 1970s: A Synthesis and Critique." *Central States Speech Journal* 31 (1980): 197.

———. "Small Group Communication Research of the 1980s: A Synthesis and Critique." *Communication Studies* 41 (1990): 212–236.

———. "The Functional Theory of Small Group Decision-Making: A Replication." *Journal of Social Behavior and Personality* 8 (1993): 165–174.

———. *Theory and Research in Small Group Communication.* Edina, Minn.: Burgess, 1996.

Cuffe, M., and Cragan, J. F. "The Corporate Culture Profile." In *International Association of Quality Circles Annual Conference Transactions.* Memphis: International Association of Quality Circles, 1983.

Cushman, D. P. "The Rules Perspective as a Theoretical Basis for the Study of Human Communication." *Communication Quarterly* 25 (1977): 30–45.

Cushman, D. P., and Pearce, W. B. "Generality and Necessity in Three Types of Human Communication Theory: Special Attention to Rules Theory." In B. D. Ruben (Ed.), *Communication Yearbook I* (pp. 173–182). New Brunswick, N.J.: Transaction Books, 1977.

Dace, K., and Hirokawa, R. Y. "The Role of Argumentation in Group Decision-Making Efficacy." In J. W. Wenzel (Ed.), *Argument and Critical Practices: Proceedings of the Fifth SCA/AFA Conference on Argumentation* (pp. 405–409). Annandale, Va.: The Speech Communication Association, 1987.

Dalkey, N. D. *Delphi.* Chicago: Rand Corp., 1967.

Daniels, T. D., and Spiker, B. K. *Perspectives on Organizational Communication.* Dubuque, Ia.: Wm. C. Brown, 1987.

Danowski, J. A. "Group Attitude Uniformity and Connectivity of Organizational Communication Networks for Production, Innovation, and Maintenance Content." *Human Communication Research* 6 (1980): 299–308.

Davis, K. "Methods for Studying Informal Communication." *Journal of Communication* 28 (1978): 112–116.

Delbecq, A. L., Van de Ven, A. H., and Gustafson, D. H. *Group Techniques for Program Planning: A Guide to Nominal Group and Delphi Processes.* Glenview, Ill.: Scott, Foresman & Co., 1975.

Delia, J. G., O'Keefe, B., and O'Keefe, D. "The Constructivist Approach to Communication." In F. Dance (Ed.), *Human Communication Theory* (pp. 147–191). New York: Harper & Row, 1982.

DeSanctis, G. L., Dickson, G. W., Jackson, B. M., and Poole, M. S. "Using Computing in the Face-to-Face Meeting: Some Initial Observations from the Texaco-Minnesota Project." Paper presented at the 51st Annual Meeting of the Academy of Management, Miami Beach, FL (August, 1991).

DeVito, J. A. *The Interpersonal Communication Book.* 6th ed. New York: Harper Collins, 1992.

DeVuono, J. "A Descriptive Analysis of Consciousness-Raising Occurring in Everyday Task Groups." Unpublished master's thesis, Illinois State University, 1982.

Dewey, J. *How We Think.* Boston: D. Heath, 1910.

Donohue, W. A., Cushman, D. P., and Mabee, T. "Testing a Structural-Functional Model of Group Decision-Making Using Markow Analysis." *Human Communication Research* 7 (1981): 133–146.

Donohue, W. A.; Cushman, D. P.; and Nofsinger, R. E., Jr. "Creating and Confronting Social Order: A Comparison of Rules Perspectives." *Western Journal of Speech Communication* 44 (1980): 5–19.

Douglas, A. *Industrial Pacemaking.* New York: Columbia University Press, 1962.

Downs, C. W., and Pickett, T. "An Analysis of the Effect of Nine Leadership Group Compatibility Contingencies upon Productivity and Member Satisfaction." *Communication Monographs* 44 (1977): 220–230.

Edelmayer, K. "The Space Shuttle Disaster: A Groupthink Phenomenon." Unpublished paper, Central Michigan University, 1987.

Edwards, C. A. "Leadership in Groups of School-Age Girls." *Developmental Psychology* 30 (1994): 920–927.

Ellis, D. G., and McCallister, L. "Relational Control Sequences in Sex-Typed and Androgenous Groups." *Western Journal of Speech Communication* 44 (1980): 35–49.

Fiedler, F. E. *A Theory of Leadership Effectiveness.* New York: McGraw-Hill, 1967.

Fiedler, F. E. "Research on Leadership Selection and Training: One View of the Future." *Administrative Science Quarterly* 41 (1996): 241–250.

Fisher, B. A. "Decision Emergence: Phases in Group Decision-Making." *Speech Monographs* 37 (1970): 53–66.

———. "Communication Research and the Task-Oriented Group." *Journal of Communication* 21 (1971): 136–149.

———. *Small Group Decision Making: Communication and the Group Process.* New York: McGraw-Hill, 1974.

Fisher, B. A., and Hawes, L. C. "An Interact System Model: Generating a Grounded Theory of Small Groups." *Quarterly Journal of Speech* 57 (1971): 444–453.

Foley, T. M. "Family of Challenger Pilot Files $15-Million Claim Against NASA." *Aviation Week and Space Technology* (July 21, 1986): 29–30.

Forston, R. "The Decision-Making Process in the American Civil Jury: A Comparative Methodological Investigation." Ph.D. diss., University of Minnesota, 1968.

French, J. R. F., and Raven, B. "The Bases of Social Power." In D. Cartwright and A. Zander (Eds.), *Group Dynamics: Research and Theory* (pp. 259–269). 3rd ed. New York: Harper & Row, 1968.

Geist, P., and Chandler, T. "Account Analysis of Influence in Group Decision-Making." *Communication Monographs* 51 (1984): 67–78.

Gibb, J. R. "Defensive Communication." *Journal of Communication* 11 (1961): 141–148.

Goldberg, A. A., and Larson, C. E. *Group Communication: Discussion Processes and Applications.* Englewood Cliffs, N.J.: Prentice-Hall, 1975.

Goldhaber, G. M. *Organizational Communication.* 6th ed. Dubuque, Ia.: Wm. C. Brown, 1993.

Gouran, D. S. "Variables Related to Consensus in Group Discussions of Questions of Policy." *Speech Monographs* 36 (1969): 387–391.

———. *Making Decisions in Groups: Choices and Consequences.* Glenview, Ill.: Scott, Foresman & Co., 1982.

———. "Group Decision Making: An Approach to Integrative Research." In C. H. Tardy (Ed.), *A Handbook for the Study of Human Communication.* Norwood, N.J.: Ablex, 1988.

Gouran, D. S., and Baird, J. E., Jr. "An Analysis of Distributional and Sequential Structure in Problem-Solving and Informal Group Discussion." *Speech Monographs* 39 (1972): 16–22.

Gouran, D. S., and Fisher, B. A. "The Functions of Human Communication in the Formation, Maintenance, and Performance of Small Groups." In C. C. Arnold and J. W. Bowers (Eds.), *Handbook of Rhetorical and Communication Theory*. Boston: Allyn & Bacon, 1984.

Gouran, D. S., and Hirokawa, R. Y. "Counteractive Functions of Communication in Effective Group Decision-Making." In R. Y. Hirokawa and M. S. Poole (Eds.), *Communication and Group Decision-Making*. Beverly Hills: Sage (1986): 81–90.

Gouran, D. S., and Hirokawa, R. Y. "The Role of Communications in Decision-Making Groups: A Functional Perspective." In M. S. Mander (Ed.), *Communication in Transitions: Issues and Debates in Current Research*. New York: Praeger, 1983, 168–185.

Gouran, D. S., Hirokawa, R., McGee, M., and Miller, L. "Communication in Groups: Research Trends and Theoretical Perspectives." In Fred Casmir (Ed.), *Building Communication Theories*. Hillsdale, N.J.: Lawrence Erhbaum Associates, 1993.

Greenbaum, T. L. *The Practical Handbook and Guide to Focus Group Research*. Lexington, Mass.: D. C. Heath, 1988.

Gulley, H. E. *Discussion, Conference, and Group Process*. 2nd ed. New York: Holt, Rinehart & Winston, 1968.

Gulley, H. E., and Leathers, D. G. *Communication and Group Process*. 3rd ed. New York: Holt, Rinehart & Winston, 1977.

Haag, L. L. "The Dramatistic-based Focus Group Interview: A Comparative Analysis." Paper presented at Annual Convention, Speech Communication Association, New Orleans, November 1988.

Haiman, F. S. *Group Leadership and Democratic Action*. Boston: Houghton Mifflin, 1951.

Hall, R. L. "Social Influence on the Role Behavior of a Designated Leader: A Study of Aircraft Commanders and Bomber Crews." *Dissertation Abstract* 13 (1953): 1285.

Hamilton, P. R. "The Effect of Risk-Proneness on Small Group Interaction, Communication Apprehension, and Self-Disclosure." Unpublished master's thesis. Illinois State University, 1972.

Hammer, M. R., and Martin, J. N. "The Effects of Cross-Cultural Training on American Managers in a Japanese-American Joint Venture." *Journal of Applied Communication Research* 20 (1992): 162–182.

Harper, N. L., and Asking, L. R. "Group Communication and Quality of Task Solution in a Media Production Organization." *Communication Monographs* 47 (1980): 77–100.

Harris, T. *I'm OK, You're OK*. New York: Harper & Row, 1967.

Hawes, L. C. *Pragmatics of Analoguing: Theory and Model Construction in Communication*. Reading, Mass.: Addison-Wesley, 1975.

Hawking, S. W. *A Brief History of Time: From the Big Bang to Black Holes*. New York: Bantam Books, 1988.

Hawkins, K. and Powell, C. "Effects of Communication Apprehension on Perceptions of Leadership and Intragroup Attraction in Small Task-Oriented Groups." *Southern Communication Journal* 53 (1991): 279–292.

Hayakawa, S. I. *Language in Thought and Action*. 2nd ed. New York: Harcourt, Brace & World, 1964.

Helmer, J. "Storytelling in the Creation and Maintenance of Organizational Tension and Stratification." *Southern Communication Journal* 59 (1993): 34–44.

Hersey, P., and Blanchard, K. H. *Management of Organizational Behavior*. 3rd ed. Englewood Cliffs, N.J.: Prentice-Hall, 1977.

Hess, J. A. "Assimilating Newcomers into an Organization: A Cultural Perspective." *Journal of Applied Communication Research* 21 (1993): 189–210.

Hewes, D. E. "Sysmatic Biases in Coded Social Interaction Data." *Human Communication Research* 11 (1985): 554–574.

———. "A Socio-Egocentric Model of Group Decision-Making." In R. Y. Hirokawa and M. S. Poole (Eds.), *Communication and Group Decision-Making* (pp. 265–291). Beverly Hills, Calif.: Sage, 1986.

Hewes, D. E., Planalp, S. K., Streibel, M. "Analyzing Social Interaction: Some Excruciating Models and Exhilarating Results." *Communication Yearbook* 4 (1980): 123–141.

Higham, J. (Ed.). *Ethnic Leadership in America*. Baltimore: Johns Hopkins University Press, 1978.

Hill, T. "An Experimental Study of the Relationship Between Opinionated Leadership and Small Group Consensus." *Communication Monographs* 43 (1976): 246–254.

Hiltz, S. R., Johnson, K., and Turoff, M. "Experiments in Group Decision-Making: Communication Process and Outcome in Face-to-Face Versus Computerized Conferences." *Human Communication Research* 13 (1986): 225–252.

Hirokawa, R. Y. "Consensus Group Decision-Making, Quality of Decision and Group Satisfaction: An Attempt to Sort 'Fact' from 'Fiction.' " *Central States Speech Journal* 33 (1982a): 407–415.

Hirokawa, R. Y. "Group Communication and Problem-Solving Effectiveness I: A Critical Review of Inconsistent Findings." *Communication Quarterly* 30 (1982b): 134–141.

———. "Group Communication and Problem-Solving Effectiveness: An Investigation of Group Phases." *Human Communication Research* 9 (1983a): 291–305.

Hirokawa, R. Y. "Group Communication and Problem-Solving Effectiveness II: An Exploratory Investigation of Procedural Function." *Western Journal of Speech Communication* 47 (1983b): 59–74.

———. "Discussion Procedures and Decision-Making Performance: A Test of a Functional Perspective." *Human Communication Research* 12 (1985): 203–224.

———. "Group Communication and Decision-Making Performance: A Continued Test of the Functional Perspective." *Human Communication Research* 14 (1988): 487–515.

Hirokawa, R. Y. "Why Informed Groups Make Faulty Decisions: An Investigation of Possible Interaction-Based Explanations." *Small Group Behavior* 18 (1987): 3–29.

Hirokawa, R. Y., Ice, R., and Cook, J. "Preference for Procedural Order, Discussion Structure, and Group Decision Performance." *Communication Quarterly* 36 (1988): 217–226.

Hirokawa, R. Y., Mickey, J., and Miura, S. "Effects of Request Legitimacy on the Compliance-Gaining Tactics of Males and Female Managers." *Communication Monographs* 58 (1991): 88–101.

Hirokawa, R. Y., and Pace, R. "A Descriptive Investigation of the Possible Communication-Based Reasons for Effective and Ineffective Decision-Making." *Communication Monographs* 50 (1983): 363–379.

Hirokawa, R. Y., and Poole, M. S. (Eds.). *Communication and Group Decision-Making.* Beverly Hills, Calif.: Sage, 1986.

Hirokawa, R. Y., and Scheerhorn, D. R. "Communication in Faulty Group Decision-Making." In R. Y. Hirokawa and M. S. Poole (Eds.), *Communication and Group Decision-Making* (pp. 63–80). Beverly Hills, Calif.: Sage, 1986.

Hoffman, L. R. Reply to McPhee. *Human Communication Research* 21 (1994): 64–66.

Hoffman, L. R. and Kleinman, G. B. "Individual and Group in Group Problem Solving: The Valence Model Redressed." *Human Communication Research* 21 (1994): 36–59.

Hofstede, G. *Culture's Consequences: International Differences in Work-Related Values.* Abridged ed. Beverly Hills, Calif.: Sage, 1984.

Homans, G. C. *The Human Group.* New York: Harcourt, Brace & World, 1950.

Hong, L. K. "Risky Shift and Cautious Shift: Some Direct Evidence on the Culture-Value Theory." *Social Psychology* 41 (1978): 342–346.

Huseman, R. C. "The Role of the Nominal Group in Small Group Communication." In R. C. Huseman, C. M. Logue, and D. L. Freshley (Eds.), *Readings in Interpersonal and Organizational Communication* (pp. 493–507). 3rd ed. Boston: Holbrook Press, 1977.

Ice, R. "Presumption as Problematic in Group Decision-Making: The Case of the Space Shuttle. In J. W. Wenzel (Ed.), *Argument and Critical Practice: Proceedings of the Fifth SCA/AFA Conference on Argumentation* (pp. 411–417). Annandale, Va.: The Speech Communication Association, 1987.

Ingle, S. *Quality Circles Master Guide: Increasing Productivity with People Power.* Englewood Cliffs, N.J.: Prentice-Hall, Spectrum, 1982.

Jablin, F. M. "Cultivating Imagination: Factors That Enhance and Inhibit Creativity in Brainstorming Groups." *Human Communication Research* 7 (1981): 245–258.

———. "Assimilating New Members into an Organization." In R. N. Bostrom (Ed.), *Communication Yearbook 8* (pp. 594–626). Beverly Hills, Calif.: Sage, 1984.

Jablin, F. M., Putnam, L. L., Roberts, K. H., and Porter, L. W. (Eds.). *Handbook of Organizational Communication: An Interdisciplinary Perspective.* Newbury Park, Calif.: Sage, 1987.

Jablin, F. M., Seibold, D. R., and Sorenson, R. L. "Potential Inhibitory Effects of Group Participation on Brainstorming Performance." *Central States Speech Journal* 28 (1977): 113–121.

Janis, I. L. *Groupthink: Psychological Studies of Policy Decisions and Fiascos.* 2nd ed. Boston: Houghton Mifflin, 1972, 1983.

Jarboe, S. "A Comparison of Input-Output, and Input-Process-Output Models of Small Group Problem-Solving Effectiveness." *Communication Monographs* 55 (1988): 121–142.

Jessup, L. M., and Valacich, J. S. *Group Support Systems: New Perspectives.* New York: Macmillan, 1993.

Johansen, R. "An Introduction to Computer-Augmented Teamwork." In R. P. Bostrom, R. T. Watson, and S. T. Kinney (Eds.), *Computer-Augmented Teamwork: A Guided Tour* (pp. 5–15). New York: Van Nostrand Reinhold, 1992.

Jourard, S. M. *The Transparent Self.* 2nd ed. New York: D. Van Nostrand Co., 1971.

Juran, J. M. "The QC Circle Phenomenon." In D. M. Amsden and R. T. Amsden (Ed.), *QC Circles: Application, Tools, and Theory.* Milwaukee: ASQC, 1976.

Jurma, W. E. and Wright, B. C. "Follower Reactions to Male and Female Leaders Who Maintain or Lose Reward Power." *Small Group Research* 21 (1990): 97–112.

Khan, A. A., Rahim, M. A., and Uddin, S. J. "Leader Power and Subordinates' Organizational Commitment and Effectiveness: Test of a Theory in a Developing Country." *The International Executive* 36 (1994): 327–341.

Kilmann, R. H. "Corporate Culture." *Psychology Today* 19 (1985): 62–68.

Kilmann, R., and Thomas, K. "Interpersonal Conflict-Handling Behavior as Reflections of Jungian Personality Dimensions." *Psychological Reports* 37 (1975): 971–980.

Kirchmeyer, C., and Cohen, A. "Multicultural Groups: Their Performance and Reactions with Constructive Conflict." *Group and Organization Management* 17 (1992): 153–170.

Kline, J. A., "Orientation and Group Consensus." *Central States Speech Journal* 23 (1972): 44–47.

Knapp, M. L. *Nonverbal Communication in Human Interaction.* 2nd ed. New York: Holt, Rinehart & Winston, 1978.

Knutson, T. J., "An Experimental Study of the Effects of Orientation Behavior on Small Group Consensus," *Speech Monographs* 39 (1972): 159–165.

Kogan, N., and Wallach, M. *Risk-Taking: Study in Cognition and Personality.* New York: Holt, Rinehart & Winston, 1964.

Krager, K. J., and Fiechtner, S. B. "Measuring Group Maturity: The Development of a Process Oriented Variable for Small Group Research." *Southern Speech Communication Journal* 50 (1984): 78–92.

Krueger, R. A. *Focus Groups: A Practical Guide for Applied Research.* Beverly Hills, Calif.: Sage, 1988.

Larson, C. E. "Forms of Analysis and Small Group Problem-Solving." *Speech Monographs* 36 (1969): 452–455.

Larson, C. U. "The Verbal Response of Groups to the Absence or Presence of Leadership." *Speech Monographs* 38 (1971): 177–181.

Lawler, E. E., and Mohrman, S. A. "Quality Circles After the Fad." *Harvard Business Review* 63 (1985): 65–71.

Leathers, D. G. "The Process Effects of Trust-Destroying Behavior in the Small Group." *Speech Monographs* 37 (1970): 180–187.

———. "Quality of Group Communication as a Determinant of Group Product." *Speech Monographs* 39 (1972): 166–173.

———. "The Informational Potential of the Nonverbal and Verbal Components of Feedback Responses." *Southern Speech Communication Journal* 44 (1979): 331–354.

Lederman, L. C. "Assessing Educational Effectiveness: The Focus Group Interview as a Technique for Data Collection." *Communication Education* 38 (1990): 118–127.

Lewin, K. *Field Theory in Social Science*. New York: Harper & Bros., 1951.

Lieberman, M. A., Yalom, J. D., and Miles, M. B. *Encounter Groups: First Facts*. New York: Basic Books, 1973.

Luthar, H. K. "Gender Differences in Evaluation of Performance and Leadership Ability: Autocratic vs Democratic Managers." *Sex Roles* 35 (1996): 337–359.

Lustig, M. W. "Bales's Interpersonal Rating Forms: Reliability and Dimensionality." *Small Group Behavior* 18 (1987): 99–107.

Mabry, E. A. "Sequential Structure of Interaction in Encounter Groups." *Human Communication Research* 1 (1975): 302–307.

Mann, R. D. "A Review of the Relationships between Personality and Performance in Small Groups." *Psychological Bulletin* 56 (1959): 241–270.

Marr, T. J. "Conciliation and Verbal Responses as Functions of Orientation and Threat in Group Interaction." *Speech Monographs* 41 (1974): 6–18.

Marston, W. M. *Emotions of Normal People*. New York: Harcourt, Brace & Co., 1928.

Mayer, M. E. "Explaining Choice Shift: An Effects Coded Model." *Communication Monographs* 52 (1985): 92–101.

McBurney, J. H., and Hance, K. G. *The Principles and Methods of Discussion*. New York: Harper & Bros., 1939.

McCroskey, J. C. "Measures of Communication-Bound Anxiety." *Speech Monographs* 37 (1970): 269–277.

———. "Oral Communication Apprehension: A Summary of Recent Theory and Research." *Human Communication Research* 4 (1977): 79–96.

McCroskey, J. C., and Wright, D. W. "The Development of an Instrument for Measuring Interaction Behavior in Small Group Communication." *Speech Monographs* 38 (1971): 335–340.

McGrath, J. E. *Groups: Interaction and Performance*. Englewood Cliffs, N.J.: Prentice-Hall, 1984.

McGrath, J. E., and Altman, J. *Small Group Research: A Synthesis and Critique of the Field*. New York: Holt, Rinehart & Winston, 1966.

McGregor, D. *The Human Side of Enterprise*. New York: McGraw-Hill, 1960.

McPhee, R. D. "Response to Hoffman and Kleinman." *Human Communication Research* 21 (1994): 60–63.

McPhee, R. D., Poole, M. S., and Seibold, D. R. "The Valence Model Unveiled: A Critique and Reformulation." In M. Burgoon (Ed.), *Communication Yearbook 5* (pp. 259–278). New Brunswick, N.J.: ICA-Transaction Press, 1982.

Meyers, R. A., Seibold, D. R. and Brashers, D. "Argument in Initial Group Decision-Making Discussions: Refinement of a Coding Scheme and a Descriptive Quantitative Analysis." *Western Journal of Speech Communication* 55 (1991): 47–68.

Miller, G. R. "Taking Stock of a Discipline." *Journal of Communication* 33 (1983): 31–41.

Monge, P. R. "The Systems Perspective as a Theoretical Basis for the Study of Human Communication." *Communication Quarterly* 25 (1977): 19–29.

Moorhead, G., Ferrence, R., and Neck, C. "Group Decision Fiascos Continue: Space Shuttle Challenger and a Revised Groupthink Framework." *Human Relations* 44 (1991): 539–550.

Moreno, J. L. *Who Shall Survive? A New Approach to the Problem of Human Interrelations*. Washington, D.C.: Nervous and Mental Disease Publishing Co., 1934.

Morgan, R. *Sisterhood Is Powerful*. New York: Random House, 1970.

Mortensen, C. D. "The Status of Small Group Research." *Quarterly Journal of Speech* 56 (1970): 304–309.

Mosvick, R. K., and Nelson, R. B. *We've Got to Start Meeting Like This: A Guide to Successful Business Meeting Management*. Glenview, Ill.: Scott, Foresman and Company, 1987.

Naisbett, J., and Aburdene, P. *Megatrends 2000*. New York: William Morrow, 1990.

Neck, C., and Moorhead, G. "Jury Deliberations in the Trial of U.S. v. John DeLorean: A Case Analysis of Groupthink Avoidance and an Enhanced Framework." *Human Relations* 45 (1992): 1077–1091.

Norton, R. "Manifestations of Ambiguity: Tolerance through Verbal Behavior in Small Groups." *Communication Monographs* 43 (1976): 35–43.

Ogden, C. K., and Richards, I. A. *The Meaning of Meaning*. New York: Harcourt, Brace & World, 1923.

O'Keefe, B. "The Evolution of Impressions in Small Working Groups: Effects of Construct Differentiation." In H. Sypher and J. Applegate (Eds.), *Communication by Children and Adults: Social Cognitive and Strategic Processes* (pp. 262–291). Beverly Hills, CA: Sage, 1984.

Olmsted, M. S., and Hare, A. P. *The Small Group*. 2nd ed. New York: Random House, 1978.

Osborn, A. F. *Applied Imagination*. New York: Charles Scribner's Sons, 1959.

Osgood, C. E. *An Alternative to War or Surrender*. Urbana, Ill.: University of Illinois Press, 1962.

Ouchi, W. G. *Theory Z*. Reading, Mass.: Addison-Wesley, 1981.

Owen, W. F. "Rhetorical Themes of Emergent Female Leaders." *Small Group Behavior* 17 (1986): 475–486.

Pacanowsky, M. E., and O'Donnell-Trujillo, N. "Organizational Communication as Cultural Performance." *Communication Monographs* 50 (1983): 126–147.

Peters, T. J., and Austin, N. *A Passion for Excellence: The Leadership Difference*. New York: Random House, 1985.

Peters, T. J., and Waterman, R. H., Jr. *In Search of Excellence*. New York: Harper & Row, 1982; reprinted by Warner Books, 1984.

Pfeiffer, J. W., and Jones, J. E. *A Handbook of Structured Experiences for Human Relations Training*. Vol. 2. LaJolla, Calif.: University Associates, 1974.

Phillips, G. M. *Communication and the Small Group*. Indianapolis: Bobbs-Merrill, 1966.

Phillips, G. M., and Santoro, G. M. "Teaching Group Discussion via Computer-Mediated Communication." *Communication Education* 38 (1989): 151–161.

Phillips, J. D. "Report on Discussion 66." *Adult Education Journal* 7 (1948): 181–182.

Poole, M. S. "Decision Development in Small Groups. I. A Comparison of Two Models." *Communication Monographs* 48 (1981): 1–24.

———. "Decision Development in Small Groups. II. A Study of Multiple Sequences in Decision-Making." *Communication Monographs* 50 (1983a): 206–232.

———. "Decision Development in Small Groups. III. A Multiple Sequence Model of Group Decision Development." *Communication Monographs* 50 (1983b): 321–341.

Poole, M. S., and DeSanctis, G. "Microlevel Structuration in Computer-Supported Group Decision-Making." *Human Communication Research* 19 (1992): 5–49.

Poole, M. S., and Folger, J. P. "A Method for Establishing the Representational Validity of Interaction Coding Systems: Do We See What They See?" *Human Communication Research* 8 (1981): 26–42.

Poole, M. S., and Jackson, M. H. "Communication Theory and Group Support Systems." In L. M. Jessup and J. C. Valacich (Eds.), *Group Support Systems* (pp. 281–293). New York: Macmillan, 1993.

Poole, M. S., and Roth, J. "Decision Development in Small Groups. IV. A Typology of Group Decision Paths." *Human Communication Research* 15 (1989a): 323–356.

———. "Decision Development in Small Groups. V. Test of a Contingency Model." *Human Communication Research* 15 (1989b): 549–589.

Poole, M. S., Seibold, D. R., and McPhee, R. D. "Group Decision-Making as a Structural Process." *Quarterly Journal of Speech* 71 (1985): 74–102.

Polley, R. B., Hare, A. P., and Stone, P. J. (Eds.). *The SYMLOG Practitioner: Applications of Small Group Research.* New York: Praeger, 1988.

Putnam, L. "Preference for Procedural Order in Task-Oriented Small Groups." *Communication Monographs* 46 (1979): 193–218.

Putnam, L., and Holmes, M. "Framing, Reframing, and Issue Development." In L. L. Putnam and M. Roloff (Eds.), *Communication and Negotiation* (pp. 128–155). Newbury Park, Calif.: Sage, 1992.

Putnam, L. L., and Jones, T. S. "The Role of Communication in Bargaining." *Human Communication Research* 8 (1982): 262–280.

Putnam, L. L., and Pacanowsky, M. E. *Communication and Organizations: An Interpretive Approach.* Beverly Hills, Calif.: Sage, 1983.

Putnam, L. L., and Roloff, M. (Eds.). *Communication and Negotiation.* Newbury Park, Calif.: Sage, 1992.

Putnam, L. L., and Stohl, C. "Bona Fide Groups: A Reconceptualization of Groups in Context." *Communication Studies* 41 (1990): 248–265.

Roberts, H. *Roberts' Rules of Order, Newly Revised.* Glenview, Ill.: Scott, Foresman, 1970.

Rogers, C. R. *Carl Rogers on Encounter Groups.* New York: Harper & Row, 1970.

Rosenfeld, L. B., and Fowler, G. D. "Personality, Sex and Leadership Style." *Communication Monographs* 43 (1976): 320–324.

Rosenfeld, L. B., and Jessen, P. A. "Compatibility and Interaction in the Small Group: Validation of Schutz's FIRO-B Using a Modified Version of Lashbrook's PROANA 5." *Western Speech* 36 (1972): 31–40.

Rosenfeld, L. B., and Plax, T. G. "Personality Determination of Autocratic and Democratic Leadership." *Speech Monographs* 42 (1975): 203–208.

Ross, R. S. "Leadership in Small Groups." Lecture No. 5 in the Illinois State University Speech Communication Audio Cassette Library, Normal, Ill., 1974a.

———. *Speech Communication: Fundamentals and Practice.* 3rd ed. New York: McGraw-Hill, 1974b.

———. *Small Groups in Organizational Settings.* Englewood Cliffs, N.J.: Prentice-Hall, 1989.

Rothwell, J. D. "Risk-Taking and Polarization in Small Group Communication." *Communication Education* 35 (1986): 182–185.

Sabiani, D. D. "An ECCO Analysis of the Informal Communication Patterns at the Illinois State University Union-Auditorium." Master's thesis, Illinois State University, 1979.

Sandifer, N. G. "Communication Patterns in a System: A Field Study." Master's thesis, Illinois State University, 1976.

Sargent, J. F., and Miller, G. R. "Some Differences in Certain Communication Behaviors of Autocratic and Democratic Leaders." *Journal of Communication* 21 (1971): 233–252.

Sattler, W. M., and Miller, N. (Eds.). *Discussion and Conference.* 2nd ed. Englewood Cliffs, N. J.: Prentice-Hall, 1968.

Schall, M. S. "A Communication-Rules Approach to Organizational Culture." *Administrative Science Quarterly* 28 (1983): 557–581.

Scheidel, T. M., and Crowell, L. "Idea Development in Small Discussion Groups." *Quarterly Journal of Speech* 50 (1964): 140–145.

———. *Discussing and Deciding: A Desk Book for Group Leaders and Members.* New York: Macmillan, 1979.

Schultz, B. "Predicting Emergent Leaders: An Exploratory Study of the Salience of Communicative Functions." *Small Group Behavior* 9 (1978): 9–14.

Schultz, B. "Argumentativeness: Its Effect in Group Decision-Making and Its Role in Leadership Perception." *Communication Quarterly* 30 (1982): 368–375.

Schutz, W. C. *The Interpersonal Underworld.* 2nd ed. Palo Alto, Calif.: Science & Behavior Books, 1966.

Scheerhorn, D. R. "Perceived Causes of Argument Avoidance in Group Decision-Making." In J. W. Wenzel (Ed.), *Argument and Critical Practices: Proceedings of the Fifth SCA/AFA Conference on Argumentation.* Annandale, Va.: The Speech Communication Association, 1987.

Semlak, W. D. *Conflict Resolving Communication: A Skill Development Approach.* Prospect Heights, Ill.: Waveland, 1982.

Semlak, W. D., and Jackson, T. R. *Conflict Resolving Communication.* Dubuque, Ia.: Kendall/Hunt, 1975.

Shaw, M. E. *Group Dynamics: The Psychology of Small Group Behavior.* 2nd ed. New York: McGraw-Hill, 1976.

———. *Group Dynamics: The Psychology of Small Group Behavior.* 3rd ed. New York: McGraw-Hill, 1981.

Shepherd, C. R. *Small Groups: Some Sociological Perspectives.* Scranton, Pa.: Chandler, 1964.

Shields, D. C. "Dramatistic Communication Based Focus Group Interviews." In J. F. Cragan and D. C. Shields (Eds.), *Applied Communication Research: A Dramatistic Approach.* Prospect Heights, Ill.: Waveland, 1981.

Shields, D. C., and Kidd, V. "Teaching Through Popular Film: A Small Group Analysis of the Poseidon Adventure." *The Speech Teacher* 22 (1973): 201–207.

Sirgy, M. J. "Strategies for Developing General Systems Theories." *Behavioral Science* 33 (1988): 25–26.

Smith, C. M., and Powell, L. "The Use of Disparaging Humor by Group Leaders." *Southern Speech Communication Journal* 53 (1988): 279–292.

Smith, H. W. "Generalizing the Scope of Group Problem-Solving Models." *Central States Speech Journal* 32 (1981): 126–131.

Smitter, R. "The Case Study Method in the Speech Communication Classroom." *Journal of the Illinois Speech and Threatre Association* 60 (1989): 55–63.

Sorensen, G., and McCroskey, J. C. "The Prediction of Interaction Behavior in Small Groups: Zero History Versus Intact Groups." *Communication Monographs* 44 (1977): 73–80.

Spillman, B., Spillman, R., and Reinking, K. "Leadership Emergence: Dynamic Analysis of the Effects of Sex and Androgyny." *Small Group Behavior* 12 (1981): 139–157.

Spitzberg, B. H. "Interpersonal Competence in Groups." In R. S. Cathcart and L. A. Samovar (Eds.), *Small Group Communication: A Reader* (pp. 424–432). 6th ed. Dubuque, Ia.: Wm. C. Brown, 1992.

Spitzberg, B. H., and Cupach, W. R. *Interpersonal Communication Competence.* Beverly Hills, Calif.: Sage, 1984.

Steeves, H. L. "Developing Coorientation Measures for Small Groups." *Communication Monographs* 51 (1984): 185–192.

Steiner, I. D. *Group Process and Productivity.* New York: Academic Press, 1972.

Steinfatt, T. M., Seibold, D. R., and Frye, J. K. "Communication in Game Simulated Conflicts: Two Experiments." *Speech Monographs* 41 (1974): 24–25.

Stogdill, R. M. *Handbook of Leadership: A Survey of Theory and Research.* New York: The Free Press, 1974.

Stohl, C. "Quality Circles and Changing Patterns of Communication." *Communication Yearbook* 9 (1986): 511–531.

———. "Bridging the Parallel Organization: A Study of Quality Circle Effectiveness." *Communication Yearbook* 10 (1987): 416–430.

Stohl, C., and Coombs, T. "Cooperation of Cooption: An Analysis of Quality Circle Training Manuals." *Management Communication Quarterly* 2 (1988): 63–89.

Stohl, C., and Jennings, K. "Volunteerism and Voice in Quality Circles." *Western Journal of Speech Communication* 52 (1988): 238–251.

Stohl, C., and Schell, S. E. "A Communication-Based Model of a Small-Group Dysfunction." *Management Communication Quarterly* 5 (1991): 90–110.

Stoner, J. A. F. "A Comparison of Individual and Group Decisions Involving Risk." Unpublished master's thesis, Massachusetts Institute of Technology, 1961. (Cited in Cartwright 1973.)

Sturgis, A. *Sturgis Standard Code of Parliamentary Procedure.* 2nd ed. New York: McGraw-Hill, 1966.

Sykes, A. J. "Myth in Communication." *Journal of Communication* 20 (1970): 17–31.

Sypher, B., and Zorn, T. "Communication-Related Abilities and Upward Mobility: A Longitudinal Investigation." *Human Communication Research* 12 (1986): 420–431.

Tetlock, P., Peterson, R., McGuire, C., Chang, S., and Feld, P. "Assessing Political Group Dynamics: A Test of the Groupthink Model." *Journal of Personality and Social Psychology* 63 (1992): 403–425.

Tompkins, P. K. "The Functions of Human Communication in Organization." In C. C. Arnold and J. W. Bowers (Eds.), *Handbook of Rhetorical and Communication Theory* (pp. 659–719). Boston: Allyn & Bacon, 1984.

Toulmin, S. *The Uses of Argument.* London: Cambridge University Press, 1958.

Trujillo, N. "Organizational Communication as Organizational Performance: Some Managerial Considerations." *Southern Speech Communication Journal* 50 (1985): 201–224.

Vasquez, G. "Group Role Type Indicator." Unpublished paper, Illinois State University, 1991.

Veiga, J. F. "The Frequency of Self-Limiting Behaviors in Groups: A Measure and Explanation." *Human Relations* 44 (1991): 877–895.

Wall, V. D., Jr., and Galanes, G. J. "The SYMLOG Dimensions and Small Group Conflict." *Central States Speech Journal* 37 (1986): 61–78.

Wallach, M. A., Kogan, N., and Bem, D. J. "Diffusion of Responsibility and Level of Risk-Taking in Groups." *Journal of Abnormal and Social Psychology* 68 (1964): 263–274.

White, R. K., and Lippett, R. "Leader Behavior and Member Reaction in Three Social Climates." In D. Cartwright and A. Zander (Eds.), *Group Dynamics: Research and Theory* (pp. 318–335). 3rd ed. New York: Harper & Row, 1968.

Whyte, W. J., Jr. *The Organization Man.* Garden City, N.Y.: Doubleday Anchor, 1957.

Wischmeier, R. R. "Group and Leader-Centered Leadership: An Experimental Study." *Speech Monographs* 22 (1955): 43–48.

Wood, J. T. "Leading in Purposive Discussion: A Study of Adaptive Behavior." *Communication Monographs* 44 (1977): 152–165.

Wood, J. T., Phillips, J. M., and Pedersen, O. J. *Group Discussion: A Practical Guide to Participation and Leadership.* 2nd ed. New York: Harper & Row, 1986.

Wright, D. W. *Small Group Communication: An Introduction.* Dubuque, Ia.: Kendall/Hunt, 1975.

Yerby, J. "Attitude, Task, and Sex Composition as Variables Affecting Female Leadership in Small Problem-Solving Groups." *Speech Monographs* 42 (1975): 160–168.

Zimmermann, S. "Social Cognition and Evaluations of Health Care Team Communication." *Western Journal of Communication* 58 (1994): 116–141.

NAME INDEX

Aburdene, P., 6
Alderton, S. M., 146, 273
Altman, I., 141, 145, 191
Andrews, P. H., 146, 273
Arnold, M., 272, 273
Austin, N., 258

Baird, J. E., Jr., 19, 158, 270
Bales, R. F., 30, 41, 44, 49, 57, 134, 138–140, 154, 179, 270, 273, 276, 287
Bantz, C., 147, 273
Barge, J. K., 270
Barker, J. R., 270
Barnlund, D. C., 175–176
Bem, D. J., 213
Benne, K. D., 190
Bennis, W .G., 37–39, 270
Berger, C. R., 271
Blake, R., 170
Blanchard, K. H., 170–72, 265
Bolkum, A., 44, 270
Booth-Butterfield, M., 273
Bormann, E. G., 9, 29, 38, 41, 44, 49, 50, 61, 146, 154, 174–175, 228, 230, 253, 269–271, 273
Bormann, N. C., 61, 175, 273
Boster, F. J., 215
Bostrom, R. P., 6, 20
Bradley, P. H., 146
Brilhart, J., 101
Brockriede, W., 121
Bunyi, J. M., 273

Calabrese, R. J., 271
Cartwright, D., 167, 214, 217, 281
Cegala, D., 273
Chen, Z., 219
Cheney, G., 253
Chesebro, J. W., 47, 270
Cohen, A., 147, 273
Cohen, S. P., 134, 138–140
Collins, B., 217, 263
Comadena, M. E., 133, 167, 273
Cook, J., 219, 271
Courtright, J., 210, 263
Cragan, J. F., 6, 29, 42, 47, 102, 228, 253–255, 268–279
Crowell, L., 57, 270
Cuffe, M., 254–255
Cupach, W., 14, 134

Dace, K., 271–272
Dalkey, N. D., 87
Davis, K., 250
Delbecq, A. L., 85, 87
Delia, J., 273
Deming, E., 19
DeSanctis, G., 21, 102, 272
DeVito, J. A., 150
DeVouno, J., 46, 270
Dewey, J., 28, 30, 97–98
Dickson, G. W., 102
Douglas, A., 224

Edelmayer, K., 219
Edwards, C. A., 178
Ehninger, D., 121

Ferrence, R., 219
Fiedler, F. E., 173, 176
Fisher, B. A., 31, 47, 52, 139, 263, 266, 269, 270, 272
Foley, T. M., 219
Folger, J. P., 272
Forston, R., 193
French, J., 167–168
Frye, J. K., 220
Fryrear, J. E., 215

Galanes, G. J., 269
Geier, J., 161
Gibb, J. R., 159
Gordan, L., 219
Gouran, D.S., 9, 57, 65, 102, 146, 182, 231, 269–271, 273–274
Greenbaum, T. L., 94
Guetskow, H. A., 217, 263
Gustafson, D. H., 85, 87

Haiman, F. S., 175–176
Hale, G. E., 215
Hall, R. L., 13
Hamilton, P. R., 215
Hammer, M. R., 147, 269–271
Hance, K. G., 30, 97
Hare, A.P ., 138, 215
Harris, T., 142
Harty, K. C., 273
Hawes, L., 265
Hawking, S. W., 267
Hawkins, K., 167
Hayakawa, S. I., 150

Helmer, J., 274
Hersey, P., 170–171, 265
Hess, J., 273
Hewes, D. E., 7
Hiltz, S. R., 88
Hirokawa, R. Y., 9, 35, 62, 102, 146, 219, 231, 269, 271–273
Hoffman, L. R., 272
Hofstede, G., 273
Holmes, M., 232
Hong, L. K., 215–216
Hunter, J. E., 215

Ice, R., 219, 271
Ingle, S., 19, 20

Jablin, F., 90, 253, 269, 273
Jackson, M., 6, 23, 102, 272
Janis, I. L., 214, 217–219
Jarboe, S., 269
Jesser, P. A., 137
Jessup, L. M., 6, 161
Johansen, R., 20, 269
Johnson, K. A., 88
Jordan, F., 273
Juran, J. M., 19
Jurma, W. E., 146, 168, 273

Kahn, A. A., 168
Kilmann, R. H., 225–226
Kinney, S. T., 6, 20
Kirchmeyer, C., 147
Kleinmann, G., 272
Kline, J. A., 57
Knapp, M. L., 156
Knutson, T. J., 57
Kogan, N., 213, 216
Krueger, R. A., 94

Larson, C. E., 91, 92
Lawler, E. E., 19
Lawson, R., 219
Leathers, D. G., 40
Lederman, L. C., 94
Lewin, K., 9, 30
Lieberman, M. A., 36
Lippett, R., 169
Lustig, M., 273
Luthar, H. K., 169

Mabry, E. A., 38, 270, 278

297

SUBJECT INDEX

Date Due
